WONDERLAND

ALSO BY BRETT WESTWOOD
& STEPHEN MOSS

Tweet of the Day

Natural Histories

WONDERLAND

A YEAR OF BRITAIN'S WILDLIFE, DAY BY DAY

BRETT WESTWOOD & STEPHEN MOSS

*

JOHN MURRAY

First published in Great Britain in 2017 by John Murray (Publishers)
An Hachette UK company

2

Copyright © Brett Westwood and Stephen Moss 2017
Illustrations © Josie Shenoy 2017

The right of Brett Westwood and Stephen Moss to be identified
as the Authors of the Work has been asserted by them in accordance
with the Copyright, Designs and Patents Act 1988.

Internal design by Georgie Widdrington
Map drawn by Rodney Paull

A CIP catalogue record for this title is available from the British Library

ISBN 978-1-473-60924-2
Ebook ISBN 978-1-473-60925-9

Typeset in ScalaOT by Palimpsest Book Production Ltd, Falkirk, Stirlingshire

Printed and bound in Great Britain by Clays Ltd, St Ives plc

John Murray policy is to use papers that are natural, renewable and
recyclable products and made from wood grown in sustainable forests.
The logging and manufacturing processes are expected to conform to the
environmental regulations of the country of origin.

John Murray (Publishers)
Carmelite House
50 Victoria Embankment
London EC4Y 0DZ

www.johnmurray.co.uk

TO HARRY GREEN, WORCESTERSHIRE NATURALIST,
CONSERVATIONIST AND FRIEND, WHOSE COMPANIONSHIP
AND KNOWLEDGE IN THE FIELD HAVE INSPIRED
MANY OF THE ENTRIES IN THIS BOOK (B.W.)

*

TO CHARLIE, GEORGE AND DAISY,
WITH THANKS FOR SHARING SOME OF MY
MOST MAGICAL MOMENTS IN NATURE (S.M.)

CONTENTS

INTRODUCTION

This afternoon, a short stroll in the garden reveals the sharp call of redwings piercing the canopy of yellow birch leaves, connecting the neighbourhood to Iceland. It's already Hallowe'en, but three species of shield-bugs are basking in a shaft of late sunlight. Below them in the grass is a huddle of turquoise-capped verdigris agaric toadstools. Droneflies and wasps are crawling woozily over late ivy blossom. Only a fleeting survey, five minutes at the most, but a small cornucopia, just a few paces from the back door.

There's a common misapprehension that wildlife only turns up where naturalists live. 'We don't get those round here' or 'I've never seen that before' are frequent complaints. There's a suspicion that, assuming they're not making it all up, naturalists have special powers of vision, hearing or insight that allow them to detect the presence of plants and animals. That's not true: anyone can be a naturalist, but it does help if you know where, when and how to look.

Wildlife is everywhere, not just in the remotest rural spots or nature reserves. All we need to do is step outside – or, sometimes, stay indoors – and simply look and listen in a different way. It is, as someone once said, a wonderful world.

Wonder can feel a somewhat old-fashioned emotion today. But wonder can be both an aesthetic experience – the awe we feel at the frosted geometry of a spider's web or the synchronised swirling of 100,000 starlings over their reed-bed roost – as well as a fascination with the unexplained or seemingly impossible: the swallows that return to the same barn each year after wintering in South Africa; trees that are virtually immortal but dependent on the fungi that simultaneously rot their heartwood and yet sustain them through their smallest rootlets. Like Lewis Carroll's Alice, the twenty-first-century naturalist can still be spellbound by the surprises that the natural world can spring: it's those surprises that we want to reveal to you in this book.

Wonderland is our day-by-day account of a wildlife year in the United Kingdom. It would take a superhuman effort to see all the animals and plants we describe in a single year: the 366 daily entries in this book have been cherry-picked from our trips throughout Britain over the last forty years or more. Many of them are based on our own home ranges, Brett's through the woods and farmland of the West Midlands and Stephen's among the grazing marshes and reed-beds of the Somerset Levels. But although a few are local specialities, most of the plants and animals that we write about are much more widespread.

This is not a field guide. Instead we've tried to convey the wonder of experiencing plants and animals in the field. There's room for familiar creatures such as foxes, badgers and buzzards of course, but we've also found it impossible to leave out our own favourites which is why the strange and rarely noticed snow flea and *Wolffia* duckweed (our smallest flowering plant) also pop up in these pages. British wildlife may be the most intensively studied of any region, but there's always something new or obscure to look for and we hope that you'll be inspired to find your own lemon slugs or wild boar.

Go for a walk – almost anywhere in Britain from a city-centre park to a remote offshore island – and the chances are that you will come across a naturalist (or, as they may prefer, birder, botaniser, wildlife-watcher, or nature-addict . . .).

What are the giveaway signs? They might be carrying a pair of binoculars, and gazing either up into the sky or down towards the ground. Every now and then they may pause and cock their head, to listen to some distant sound; or crouch down to pick up an object to take a closer look.

If you stop, and ask them what they have seen (perhaps using the classic birder's greeting of 'Anything about?'), they are likely to be friendly, eager to discuss their latest sighting with another enthusiast. Having shared your mutual enjoyment of the natural world, you will both continue on your way.

When we were growing up, such encounters were less frequent and usually less friendly. Most people out and about in the countryside were birdwatchers (to use the old term), and it often seemed as if they had chosen their hobby to allow them to escape from the rest of humanity and indulge their mildly sociopathic tendencies. Just occasionally, you would meet a kindred spirit: willing to share their sightings and to enthuse about yours in equal measure. But meetings like this were few and far between.

Fortunately, during the last thirty or forty years, things have improved. Most naturalists are only too eager to offer help and advice. The former dominance of the older male birder has given way to a far more mixed bag, with old and young, men and women, families and groups of friends all out enjoying the natural world.

This is a very British phenomenon: no other nation has embraced the natural world quite as strongly as we have. But how did this come about? How did the British learn to fall in love with nature? And what does this story tell us about the very varied ways in which we interact with the natural world today?

For most of humankind's existence, the notion that we would enjoy nature – 'consume' it, if you like, as we do art, music, sport and so on – would simply not have existed in anyone's mind.

Nature was present, certainly; indeed playing a much larger part in our ancestors' lives than in ours. But it was not there to be enjoyed, but to be exploited: as Genesis, the opening book of the Bible explains, we were given dominion over the beasts of the field and the birds of the air. Wild animals and plants were primarily there to be killed or picked and eaten, to sustain human life. Any consumption was purely visceral, not intellectual.

Fairly early on, though, our ancestors began to view the wildlife around them in subtly new ways. Ancient cave paintings hint at a growing appreciation of nature: the cavern at Lascaux in France, dating back at least 17,000 years, is decorated with some 600 painted and drawn animals (and only one human figure). Numerous horses and red deer, bison and big cats run across the walls. The detail is impressive – the animals are well observed. Archaeologists believe these depictions were used as totems to ensure enough animals would be there to hunt and to ward against natural predators.

With the shift from their earlier nomadic, hunter-gatherer existence into farming, which began about 10,000 years ago, our ancestors' relationship with nature changed and deepened again. The crops that they farmed and their dogs, sheep and cattle were all domesticated versions of the nature around them. Now fixed in one place, they relied on watching the comings and goings of seasonal visitors such as migrating birds, and noting other time-sensitive markers including the emergence of insects or the blooming of wild flowers, in order to plan when to grow and harvest their crops and how best to husband their livestock.

Birds in particular attracted plenty of folklore (some still around today) regarding their supposed human characteristics – based on their observed behaviours, crows (the clever eaters of carrion) were seen as evil, while colourful robins were friendly, and so on – whereas many plants were enlisted as cures and medicines, some of which worked, and some did not. One example from medieval times is birthwort, a continental plant whose uterus-shaped flowers seemed, by the principles of the Doctrine of Signatures, to have been signposted by God as a remedy for problems in childbirth or to bring on abortions. This 'cure' was based more on devotional belief than its medical efficacy, but didn't stop it being grown in convent gardens.

But none of these uses really touches on the way we regard the natural world today: as a source of pleasure and interest, fuelled by a spirit of curious enquiry. The first seeds of this were sown in ancient Greece and Rome, by careful observers and thinkers such as Aristotle and Pliny. After going into abeyance for many centuries, this way of looking at nature was resurrected first during the Renaissance and later by the Enlightenment, two movements that created what we know today as 'science'.

It was between roughly 1500 and 1800 that a major shift happened in the way the natural world was regarded, particularly in Britain: a change Dr Rob Lambert of Nottingham University calls the progress from 'Use to Delight'; from exploiting nature without any concern for its well-being, to enjoying it for its own sake. Historian Keith Thomas also traces this major shift in attitudes in his masterful book *Man and the Natural World*.

This period saw the rise of men (and a few women), who first called themselves 'naturalists'. Perhaps the first self-acknowledged British amateur naturalist – and a hero of ours – is Gilbert White (1720–93). White was a curate who wrote the bestselling *Natural History and Antiquities of Selborne*, the Hampshire village where he was born and where, after moving to Oxford, he finally settled in 1755. Here he meticulously noted the comings and goings of local wildlife. In his words: 'Men that undertake only one district are much more likely to advance natural knowledge than those that grasp at more than they can possibly be acquainted with.' White was what we'd call today a supreme 'patch-worker' – someone who becomes intimately associated with the wildlife of his own neighbourhood. But he was far from parochial: the questions that White asked about wildlife had a wider relevance and he was always willing to challenge the observations of respected naturalists. He was right, for example, to query the claim of seventeenth-century zoologist Francis Willughby that cuckoos laid their eggs in chaffinch and ring-dove (woodpigeon) nests.

Gilbert White was also making discoveries of his own: he was first to distinguish the songs of the chiffchaff, willow warbler and wood warbler and he found and named the harvest mouse as a new British mammal. Impressive enough, but he also seasoned his scientific observations and communications with other naturalists with a poetic flair for describing his finds. A harvest mouse nest is 'a wonderful procreant cradle, an elegant instance of the efforts of instinct'. It's small wonder that his natural history is still in print today and as eagerly read as it was following publication in 1789.

Women naturalists were fewer, though they famously included Eleanor Glanville, who lived during the second half of the seventeenth century and who posthumously gave her name to the Glanville fritillary, one of our rarest butterflies. Her will was famously set aside on the grounds that beating bushes to obtain caterpillars and going 'in pursuit of butter-flies' was regarded as evidence of an unsound mind. But eccentric or not, one trait that linked the growing band of naturalists is that they went out into the world to see for themselves how nature worked. Some leaned towards science; for others pleasure was the primary motivator. Yet just like modern naturalists, they sought to understand the wild world around them.

The growing movement towards cataloguing and categorising the natural world was not, of course, exclusively British; indeed the godfather of natural history, Carl Linnaeus (1707–78), lived and worked in his native

Sweden. But it was the British who recognised how important his work was and Joseph Banks (Darwin's great friend and an early director of the Royal Botanic Gardens at Kew) brought Linnaeus's library and manuscripts to London where they remain to this day. Charles Darwin (1809–82) was a true giant among naturalists, as intrigued by earthworms as he was by apes, spending time when not travelling southern oceans observing orang-utans at London Zoo in Regent's Park. He is most celebrated for his revelations on evolution by natural selection, studying, among many other subjects, barnacles and the intimate relations between some orchids and their pollinating insects. On seeing a Madagascan orchid with an enormously long 'throat', he predicted correctly that a moth would eventually be found with a proboscis long enough to reach its nectar.

During the late eighteenth and early nineteenth centuries, the rise of the naturalist was more marked in Britain than elsewhere, for one simple reason. This period saw the greatest population movements in our history, as the onset of the Industrial Revolution impelled millions of rural people to move into towns and cities.

You might imagine that this would have had a negative impact on their passion for nature; but in fact it had the very opposite effect. Nostalgic for the countryside they or their parents and grandparents remembered so fondly, they sought to return. But not, this time, to work the fields, but to enjoy their new-found 'leisure time' in the pursuit of nature.

The Victorian era saw this passion for all things wild multiply apace. Helped by the arrival of the railways, hordes of botanisers, birdwatchers, ramblers and entomologists flocked to the wilder parts of Britain. Some of this, of course, was accomplished down the barrel of a gun, in an era when a lack of good quality optical aids meant that anything unusual had to be shot to be properly identified. But many people – especially a growing cohort of independent women of means – enjoyed nature in more benevolent ways. The novelist George Eliot was inspired to write her first novel by spending a summer observing the life that went on in a rockpool. London-born Beatrix Potter dedicated her enormous wealth to preserving the Lake District as a National Park.

As railways, canals and roads spread across Britain and the population snowballed, the late nineteenth and early twentieth centuries saw the formation of many of the great conservation organisations we know today, including the RSPB, the National Trusts and the Wildlife Trusts. This was partly driven by a concern for animal welfare and partly a new worry, that Britain's countryside was under threat. Being a naturalist was now something you could do with other like-minded souls, and a host of smaller clubs and local societies – many still going today – were founded around this time.

There was also a boom in cheap, popular books on natural history, many of which were aimed at children. Titles such as *The Boy's Own Nature Book*, by W. Percival Westell, encouraged young people to engage in hobbies such as finding birds' nests and catching butterflies. These two pastimes were later discouraged because of their potentially destructive consequences, but they schooled whole generations in the details of natural history.

In the years between the two world wars various nature-related hobbies, especially birdwatching, gained increasing traction, with the founding of organisations such as the British Trust for Ornithology. From the early 1930s onwards, pioneering birdwatcher-ornithologists such as Phil Hollom and Max Nicholson enrolled so-called 'amateur naturalists' (mostly experts in their own right) to take part in nationwide surveys, which still contribute a huge amount to our collective knowledge of Britain's wildlife and its changes in status.

About this time, an interest in natural history also began to filter down the social classes. During those earlier eras, pursuing birds was mostly the preserve of the upper echelons of society, as only aristocrats and the landed gentry had the means to afford guns and the land on which they could shoot. Working-class naturalists mostly gravitated towards entomology, which required less money and could be done around their local area.

But all this changed once decent binoculars and affordable motor transport arrived in the middle years of the twentieth century. The Second World War both interrupted and encouraged nature study – many naturalists were confined to the area around their home, while others were sent to far-flung places abroad – but as soon as the war ended there was a real thirst for a greater understanding and appreciation of nature.

The post-war years saw a surge in wildlife-watching, helped from the mid-1950s onwards by the early television programmes from influential conservationist Peter Scott. On radio, James Fisher and Julian Huxley became household names through programmes such as 'Nature Parliament', part of *Children's Hour*, which like its TV counterparts influenced new generations of naturalists, many still active today.

Nature writing, too, continued to be popular: books such as the pre-war classic *Tarka the Otter*, by Henry Williamson, and Gavin Maxwell's *Ring of Bright Water* (also featuring otters), became bestsellers.

Meanwhile the first proper field guides – to start with mainly on birds, but soon including all forms of wildlife – began to appear. New publishing ventures such as the Wayside and Woodland series and the Observer's Books sold millions of copies, allowing amateur naturalists to identify what they found far more quickly and easily than before.

For those of us who wanted more than field guides, the advent of what's come to be known as the 'new nature writing', focusing on our relationship with the natural world, was a revelation. The publication in 1973 of Richard Mabey's *The Unofficial Countryside* was an affirmation that wildlife didn't only thrive in the remotest, most cosseted reserves, but was busy insinuating itself into our towns and cities. Among its pages was vindication for our childhood obsessions with tracking down plump elephant hawkmoth caterpillars among willowherb thickets and for mild trespass in the overgrown factory yards and canalsides now known as edgelands. It gave burgeoning naturalists like us permission to wonder at the adaptability of our wildlife. For Brett, living in the urban West Midlands, Bunny Teagle's report on urban wildlife in the Birmingham/Black Country conurbation, entitled *The Endless Village*, was a spellbinding discovery. Stephen was likewise influenced by the writings of the campaigning journalist and broadcaster Kenneth Allsop. Not only did these post-war naturalists take notice of city wildlife – they appreciated its value too, even of one of Britain's largest spiders that had made its home under the concrete supports of Spaghetti Junction. A car journey over what was then a new section of motorway was doubly exciting, knowing that fanged monsters lurked beneath the serpentine coils of the carriageway.

Since then, thanks to modern pioneers such as Chris Baines, urban wildlife has become a mainstream interest and appears regularly in this book. Our streets, gardens and parks are natural laboratories, often the best places to see the latest arrivals and for us to monitor the changes in status and distribution of plants and animals, whether native or introduced.

From the mid-1960s onwards, conservation organisations such as the RSPB and the Wildlife Trusts saw a huge rise in membership, the RSPB growing from just 20,000 members at the start of the 1960s to over 1.2 million today. Other, smaller organisations also proliferated, covering everything from bugs to butterflies and mammals to plants, so that nowadays virtually every group of organisms has its own charity or society, where enthusiasts can gather and share their knowledge and sightings.

Radio and TV helped spread both knowledge and a passion for the natural world much further. Much of the credit for this must go to the people who present these programmes. Bill Oddie and Kate Humble, Ellie Harrison and Chris Packham, and of course the great Sir David Attenborough, have become household names, and in doing so have helped to make natural history mainstream again. A key recent turning point in transforming Britain into a nation of self-taught naturalists was a long-running BBC series we've both been involved with – *Springwatch*. What was so refreshing about it was its focus on intimate portraits of common creatures rather than the more exotic and far flung. The ongoing drama of the nature going on all around us was far more gripping than any soap opera.

The Internet has also allowed the immediate sharing of knowledge, observations, photos and videos. So if you should find some unknown insect lurking in your flowerbed or local wood, you can immediately get an accurate identification simply by sharing images online. This in turn has fuelled a new fascination with hitherto obscure groups such as caddis flies (a favourite with Brett) and slugs (another one). Those of us who struggle to identify much beyond birds and butterflies can only watch in awe.

Perhaps even more importantly for the future of natural history in Britain, social media has also enabled a new generation of young naturalists to connect with their peers, publish their own observations and opinions via blogs, and provide a much needed injection of energy and enthusiasm. Ten years ago, articles appeared that glumly predicted the 'death of the naturalist'. But these now look both overly pessimistic and premature, as organisations such as A Focus on Nature and Next Generation Birders help hundreds of young people discover and share the joys and pleasures of wildlife-watching.

*   *   *

Whether you spend all your holidays searching for rare orchids, or have devoted your life to the study of a single species of beetle, or simply enjoy watching the blue tits on the bird-table, you are a naturalist. There's no set definition, but it helps to have an inquisitive mind and to enjoy asking questions and discovering answers. You don't need much equipment, though for birds a pair of binoculars is more or less essential. Clear glass or plastic tubes and a sweep net will considerably improve an entomological trip and allow you to search for and examine all invertebrates more easily. Bat detectors, fishing nets and hand lenses are also important accoutrements at different times. A camera or mobile phone is now a must for the modern naturalist if only to act as a visual diary. If you're feeling flush, a microscope, either portable or back at home, will be invaluable for identifying smaller specimens.

There's an abundance of field guides, either in book form or on online, which make it much easier to identify your chosen groups of animals or plants. The Internet offers a phenomenal amount of information on nearly everything you're likely to find. But please don't spend all your time hunched over a book – even this one – or staring at a screen. Instead, get out and meet other inspirational naturalists. You can do this by joining a national organisation such as the British Trust for Ornithology, the RSPB or the National Trust, to name but three of the most important: there are many more that focus on different interest groups. Most counties have their local Wildlife Trusts which are excellent for meeting fellow enthusiasts and finding out more about the wildlife in your area: there's no better way to learn than being shown by other helpful and experienced people, and we have both benefited enormously from the expertise of friends and colleagues.

One last tip: keep a notebook. While Mae West's claim 'always keep a diary and one day it will keep you' might not apply strictly to naturalists, your diary will remind you of the extraordinary (and more ordinary) days out, help you to fix identifications in your memory and, as information builds, allow you to follow changes in the status of different species whether on your local patch, in the garden or across much larger areas. We've found our notes invaluable in compiling our own wildlife year.

As we've already mentioned, this is as much a book for urbanites as well as country dwellers. For many of us a brush with natural history occurs as we go about our daily business: commuting to work, walking the dog, or taking the kids to school. Often by default, our towns and cities are becoming important habitats for many species from hedgehogs and buzzards to dragonflies and frogs. But wherever you live in Britain, within a couple of hours' drive there is a variety of different habitats all of which have their own signature species: here's a whistle-stop tour of a few of our most typical, starting, as we all do, on the doorstep.

TOWNS AND CITIES

The urban scene is a crucible of change, the place where colonising plants and animals, brought in by us deliberately or otherwise, make their first footholds. Many London parks now echo with the screeches of rose-ringed parakeets while city waterways throughout the British Isles are lush with exotics such as giant hogweed and Himalayan balsam. Not all city life is introduced: the black redstarts that sing scratchily from old buildings gained a foothold here after the bombing raids of the Second World War. The latest new birds on the block are herring and lesser black-backed gulls which nest high above shoppers on inner-city rooftops and trading estates, and peregrine falcons which pursue street pigeons – and in London, parakeets – through canyons of concrete and glass.

GARDENS

Our gardens can be complex habitats in themselves, a mixture of meadow (the lawn), scrub (shrubs), rocks (patios and paths) and woodland edge (older trees). Individually this might not seem a great deal, but on a landscape scale it adds up to a vast mosaic of micro-habitats which flying creatures are particularly good at exploiting. Some insects, such as bumblebees, seem to be faring better in urban areas than they are in less flowery, agricultural landscapes. Birds, too, know no boundaries and take what they need from our neighbourhoods: an old tree with a nest-hole, shrubberies in which they can roost, and, of course, a smorgasbord of delicacies laid out on the array of backyard bird-tables: each of our gardens and parks adds up to a greater whole. With garden wildlife, the secret is providing a varied structure for feeding and breeding, so if you can squeeze in a pond, a log-pile and spare a few spots from the strimmer, you'll reap the wildlife rewards, and so will your neighbours.

FARMLAND

The richest farmland for wildlife includes wetlands, old hedgerows, meadows and woodland around which most of its plants and animals concentrate. The open fields themselves are home to skylarks and brown hares, but, increasingly, agricultural intensification has reduced the typical farmland species to a fraction of their former abundance. Birds such as yellowhammers, tree sparrows, corn buntings, lapwings and grey partridges are now scarce in many places, but always good to find. Similarly, cornfield plants such as cornflowers and corn marigold have declined sharply because of herbicide use, though poppies can still put on a dramatic display on well-drained soils. In winter, find a weedy field and you may see twittering flocks of finches and buntings. In some agricultural landscapes, wintering lapwings and golden plovers find a home and gaggles of pink-footed geese fly in from Iceland to grub for beet and potatoes under wide-open skies.

GRASSLANDS

Older grasslands including downs, commons and hay meadows are often superb places to study bees, beetles and butterflies. A handful of the best locations are home to specialist insects such as the rare wart-biter cricket and the Duke of Burgundy butterfly. Limestone grassland, grazed moderately by livestock or rabbits, can be rich in wild flowers, including orchids.

Old hay-meadows, untreated by herbicides, are scarce finds today. In northern England and Scotland they will be sulphur with buttercups, interspersed with white cow parsley and purple wood cranesbill. In other places green-winged orchids and hay rattle put on a fabulous show in May and June and may be buzzing with grasshoppers later in the summer. If you're lucky you may stumble on a breeding pair of lapwings.

Some of our favourite grasslands are the rolling commons of the Welsh borders, when autumnal bracken turns russet and the turf is studded with brilliant yellow and red waxcap fungi: in a few select spots, delicate autumn crocuses join them in pushing through the sward.

HEATHLAND

There are several types of heathland and for simplicity we've divided them into two broad groups: upland and lowland heath

A high-quality lowland heath crackles and buzzes with wildlife from the pebbly calls of stonechats and the grinding song of Dartford warblers to the hum of bee-wolves attending their burrows in the loose sand. Usually dominated by heather and gorse, the best surviving heaths are on well-drained sandy or gravelly soils that are poor in nutrients. The largest are in south and south-east England in places such as the Thames and Poole basins and in the New Forest. Some are home to sun-loving reptiles such as sand lizards and smooth snakes and are especially rich in solitary bees and wasps. Boggy patches on acid heaths often contain insectivorous plants such as butterwort and in summer glisten with the leaves of sundew and wings of dragonflies. Visit on summer nights and listen for the eerie song of nightjars.

Upland heath is known generally as moorland, the habitat of red grouse and in places intensively managed for this bird. A wildlife-rich moor will have a mixture of other plants including rushes, sedges and bilberries among the grass. In boggy places on northern moors, snipe, golden plover and dunlin nest, but the classic moorland sound in spring is the bubbling of displaying curlew.

DECIDUOUS WOODLAND

A beech wood in May, light filtering through a million leaves on to pools of bluebells is probably as good as it gets. Most woods, apart from the dullest plantations, have this in common: the interplay of light and leaf, the illusory feeling of isolation and the sense of being personally re-wilded, however close to home you are. The more woods you visit, the more of a connoisseur you will become. No two woodlands are the same and their wildlife varies according to their age, their structure, their location and their constituent species: beech woods and oak often have very different floras and faunas. Ancient deciduous woodland, that is woodland on land continuously forested for 500 years or more, is often very rich in wildlife, especially if it has a strong understorey of shrubs, open glades and rides and pools or streams.

There are too many woodland delights to list here, but most of the joy that comes from visiting a wood derives not from any one species, but the sense of being in what can seem like primeval or undisturbed habitat. Few experiences beat walking through autumn woods echoing with the groans of rutting fallow deer. In a few places, such as the Forest of Dean in Gloucestershire, wild boar are taking re-wilding to a new level. They've released themselves from captivity relatively recently, but even so it's thrilling and slightly unnerving to stumble on their muddy wallows and realise that they're among us again, as sharp-tusked and bristling as they once were in our medieval forests.

CONIFER WOODS

Most conifer woods in the British Isles are plantations, the first of these established during the years after the First World War in a bid to restore our depleted timber reserves. The conifers grown then were often quick-sprouting non-natives such as Douglas fir, larches and Norway spruce which thrived on damp moorland and heaths. Their dense foliage and thick planting shut out light and acidified the ground, making the new plantations unfriendly to most wildlife. But as the conifers matured and were thinned or felled, they attracted birds such as crossbills, goshawk and long-eared owls; clear-felled areas in the south are now popular with nightjars and woodlarks. Mature plantations such as those in Kielder Forest in Northumberland have been colonised by red squirrels and in Scotland pine martens have moved in from the native Scots pine woods.

There are native conifer woods too. The most extensive of these are the Caledonian pine forests in central and west Scotland. A visit is essential and one excellent site is Abernethy Forest near Aviemore, where turkey-sized capercaillies display among the bilberries and red squirrels and crested tits scold from the huge old pines. There are pine martens here as well and a wonderful range of rare fungi.

HILL COUNTRY

The high tops of the Cairngorms are probably the closest we come in the British Isles to having an Arctic flora and fauna. Here, where scouring winds have reached a UK record of 194 mph and snow lies all year round in sheltered corries, only the hardiest wildlife survives: ptarmigan, dotterel and snow buntings all breed here and there's even a free-ranging herd of reindeer. One August, while watching ptarmigan among the scree, I was amazed to see a mother reindeer plodding below me along the contour of the hill, new-born calf in tow. These and other Scottish mountains also have a scattering of golden eagles which patrol the slopes for mountain hares.

On lesser, but still impressive hills, look for ring ouzels and wheatears in spring and summer. Walk the high ridges in winter, though, and all you'll have for company are ravens.

WETLANDS

There is a vast diversity of habitats, from bogs and mires to rivers, lakes and floodplains, which are lumped together as wetlands and at any time of year they are wildlife magnets. In autumn and winter our lakes and marshes are a refuge for millions of waders and wildfowl that breed in northern climes and come to our milder waters to feed and roost. These range from the Icelandic whooper swans, among the world's heaviest flying birds, to the mallards that dabble for bread on the park lake: not all are as local as you might think.

For all its rain, much of the British Isles is comparatively dry, though this has been balanced in places by the creation of conservation wetlands and water supply reservoirs. Chains of pits remain after mineral extraction and these in such places as the Cotswold Water Park can be locally important for birds. Reed-beds are being planted to attract flagship species such as bitterns and bearded tits and in the Somerset Levels are luring in great white egrets and even little bitterns. On winter evenings, the starling murmurations above their reed-bed roosts are mesmerising.

Slow or fast-flowing, many rivers are gradually recovering from pollution and otters have returned to most parts of the UK. Although fish, invisible to most of us, are the forgotten members of our fauna, they can put on impressive displays: the leaping salmon that power upstream on many swift-flowing rivers are an important part of many a naturalist's calendar each autumn. In late 2016 Scotland officially recognised the beaver as a native mammal once again after extermination centuries ago for its fur. Now reintroduced animals are swimming in a few select spots.

Even your garden pond is a small wetland and will be colonised as if by magic soon after you create it. Within a day of filling it, a frog can be lounging in the shallows and a southern hawker dragonfly laying its eggs.

THE COAST: MUD AND SAND

Muddy shores, shifting with the tides, are jam-packed with food and are magnets for wintering birds. The Wash alone draws in up to 400,000 birds including oystercatchers, knot, dunlin and grey plovers, to feed on molluscs and crustaceans hiding in the nutritious mud. Brent geese and wigeon graze on eelgrass on exposed muddy shores around our coast. Brave the winter blasts and you might see harriers and short-eared owls fanning over saltmarshes, hoping to flush roosting birds.

In summer the mud has rich pickings for us too as we forage for succulent samphire or dig for cockles in the sand. On sandy beaches, ringed plovers feign broken wings to lead people away from their nests and terns defend their chicks with ear-splitting shrieks

THE COAST: ROCKS

Rocky shores are rare in the south-east of England, but frequent elsewhere. Our finest spots support seabird colonies and a visit in June is a must not only for the sights but also for the sounds. Braying guillemots, wailing kittiwakes and belching shags are all testament to the richness of our surrounding seas. Smells too – a gannet colony in the breeding season is one of our most pungent and yet most beautiful sights: from a distance the snow-globe swirl of arriving and departing birds is breathtaking.

What could be better on a summer holiday than a rockpooling expedition? During the Victorian aquarium craze of the 1850s and 1860s, some rockpools were regularly plundered, their inhabitants doomed to die in suburban parlours. Now though, armed with a field guide or an app, we can identify and photograph crabs, anemones, prawns and blennies, or simply watch them through clear-bottomed buckets.

*   *   *

During our lifetimes, we have witnessed unprecedented changes in the way we watch, enjoy and learn about Britain's wildlife. Fifty years ago, no one could have predicted the way wildlife-watching would go from a niche hobby (memorably described by one sneering journalist as 'organic trainspotting') to a mainstream activity enjoyed by tens of millions of people.

There is, however, a looming cloud on the horizon. During the past seventy years or so (from roughly 1945 to the present day), much of Britain's wildlife has gone into what may prove to be a terminal decline. Modern industrial farming, habitat loss and fragmentation, and the biggest issue of all, global climate change, have all combined to make life increasingly difficult for many of our best-loved species. Even thirty years ago, the notion that hedgehogs and house sparrows would suffer major falls in numbers, and disappear from large swathes of our urban and rural landscapes, would have been simply inconceivable.

Our natural history is undergoing huge changes in a relatively short space of time. Many of these changes begin close to home: the arrival of the harlequin ladybird, the ivy bee and the tree bumblebee have happened since 2000 and their presence is most obvious in town. From the west native polecats and ravens have returned in force and in the south-east introduced parakeets and Egyptian geese are part of the urban scene in many places. We live in changing times and while some species are arriving, others are becoming hard to find, often as a result of human influence. Everything in the garden is far from lovely, but the news isn't all bad and so we've tried our best to reflect the varying views of twenty-first-century naturalists.

Despite the challenges, we do tend towards optimism. There has never been a better time to be a naturalist.

The irony is that there is less to see in terms of abundance. Once familiar birds such as the cuckoo, turtle dove and willow tit are now hard to find in many places. The garden tiger is one of a host of large moths that are fast disappearing. The times when swarms of insects would flutter in our headlight beams or splatter against our cars on long journeys are gone.

Once these losses would have been unthinkable, but it's depressing that, as a nation, most people accept the decline of these creatures as necessary sacrifices to progress in the form of cheaper food and faster road and rail services. Collectively, we are slow to recognise the potential effects of neonicotinoids on our insect life, still insist on drenching most of our arable land with herbicides and pesticides, and we continue to import trees and their associated fungal pests.

It's not all bad, though. The creation of large-scale reserves, especially wetlands such as those in the Somerset Levels and East Anglia, is attracting new birds to breed and providing home for many insects and plants. Introductions of common cranes and white-tailed eagles have been remarkably successful. Even beavers and wild boar have defied the nay-sayers by re-establishing themselves.

We live in exciting times and as naturalists it's up to us all to keep wildlife in focus, to do our bit as volunteers, as recorders, as local nature defenders or as society members to remind those who don't notice wildlife that it is worth saving, for its own sake but also because of what it does for us. We hope that *Wonderland* spurs you to explore the area around your own home, and further afield, and that you end up getting as much delight from Britain's wildlife as we continue to do.

> There is a pleasure in the pathless woods,
> There is a rapture on the lonely shore,
> There is society where none intrudes,
> By the deep sea, and music in its roar;
> I love not Man the less, but Nature more.
>
> Byron, from *Childe Harold's Pilgrimage*

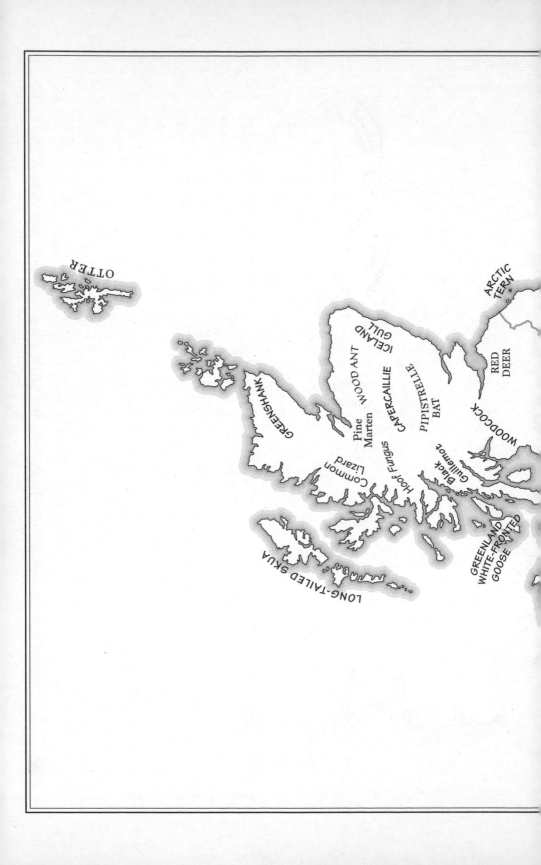

Our map can only hint at the richness of British natural history and, although we've been inspired by seeing these species in the locations shown here, many occur much more widely.

JANUARY

A NEW YEAR, and the slate wiped clean.

Why the shift from one year to the next makes such a difference is hard to fathom. Why do we look at birds on New Year's Day that we ignored on New Year's Eve, just because we are on day 1 rather than day 365?

Competition, albeit against oneself, is one reason: most birders I know keep a 'year list', of the various different species they see during the next twelve months, and today's the day to get it off to a flying start. We do so partly because we like the order of lists; and partly to remind us, many years hence, of what we saw in the past. But as I get older, I wonder if there's another, more deep-rooted reason for this sense of urgency. Maybe it's because, mixed with the thrill and anticipation of the seasons to come, we are unconsciously counting down the years to the point at which either we won't be here, or nature won't be.

We live in a changing – some would say terrifyingly changing – world. Climate change, habitat loss and a host of other problems are affecting the wildlife we love and cherish, and at times it seems as if there is nothing we can do about it. But then I step outdoors before dawn on 1 January, and within seconds I encounter my first birds of the year: a robin singing unseen in the nearby shrubbery, followed by a ragged jackdaw flying overhead in the lightening gloom.

That sound, that sight – that sensation of being there at a new beginning – banishes all thoughts of mortality. In the next hour, as more and more birds appear, I see each one anew; and appreciate them all the more for that.

What I see, in and around my home on the Somerset Levels, depends on two factors: the weather – cold and icy or mild and wet – and how long I am able to stay out. Later in the month I may venture further afield – January is a great month for seeing bird spectacles: the ducks, geese, swans and waders that spend the winter here in vast numbers on our coasts and estuaries.

But today, even if I only spend an hour or so engaging with nature on the morning of New Year's Day, I feel refreshed, renewed and ready for anything the year can throw at me. I think ahead to the first swallow of spring, the (hopefully) long hot days of summer, and the fading beauty of autumn, and I feel what can only be described as a mixture of expectation and joy.

S.M.

THE CHALLENGE OF struggling out of bed on a grey dawn, with an hour's drive in front of me, has set the pattern for 1 January over the last fifteen years or so. Four of us, all naturalist friends, tour the south of Worcestershire, pulling in at gateways to count winter thrushes, poking in ivied hedges for hardy insects and spiders and scanning floodwater for rafts of wildfowl.

Our wanderings have settled into a pilgrimage of sorts, seeking affirmation that the natural world, locally at least, is still on track. The markers are simple: the first crocuses and snowdrops blooming precociously in an Avon valley churchyard; a lesser celandine like a sunburst gleaming among fallen leaves and, if we're lucky, blackcaps guzzling mistletoe berries in windswept lime trees.

We don't ask for sensation and we rarely get it. What we're searching for is a renewal of shared interests and companionship. Swapping local wildlife anecdotes, or whingeing about unsympathetic land management, are an essential part of our New Year ritual. Underlying it all is the hope that spring can't be far off.

It is of course. Those snowdrops and celandines are false prophets. January can be unpredictable and sometimes harsh. As a gateway to the natural year, it offers more ends than beginnings: in icy weather, it's a hungry season for many birds and in mild winters sleeping butterflies and bees are lulled by mould and other infections into everlasting slumber. If insects are your thing – and increasingly they're mine – January is a month to weather with fortitude. There's little to see, so with the New Year in its infancy, I'm hungry for signs of spring: the skirl of mistle thrushes from the high tree-tops or the faint ripples of frogs in the garden pond. On wet days, I riffle through diaries and notebooks, planning trips and imagining splendours to come. Not all will materialise, but naturalists love to dream.

B.W.

BLACK REDSTART

1 January

A parents vs kids football match on a wide, windswept beach – the perfect way to blow away the cobwebs on New Year's Day. Above the shouts of excitement, the cries of herring gulls echo away across the receding tide, while the deep croak of a raven fills the air, as this huge black bird sails over the clifftops above.

Out of the corner of my eye I notice a brief movement on the huge granite rocks at the top of the beach. A robin perhaps, or maybe a stone-chat, flicking its wings as it lands on the top of a raggedy bramble?

At first, as I scan from side to side, I see nothing. Then a bird pops up, perching on top of a rock as if it owns it, which for the moment it does. Neither a robin nor a stonechat, but a far more enticing prize: a black redstart, a scarce species on the edge of its range here in Britain, and one that I rarely encounter. A splendid male, whose sooty black plumage is set off with a rust-coloured tail and, when he opens his wings, contrasting flashes of white. Like other members of the chat family, he has a brisk, jaunty air – each movement both deliberate and graceful.

Black redstarts are curious birds. Not for them the woodlands of their migrant relative, the redstart. They prefer bleak industrial sites in the urban jungle, where their metallic song, like that of a robin performed on a synthesiser, fits rather well with the stark, concrete landscape.

In autumn they head south and west, most leaving our shores. But a few – including the bird sitting right in front of me – choose to spend the winter on our rocky coasts, where the milder climate produces plenty of tiny insects for them to feed on, such as shore flies. This one certainly appears to be settled in for the duration.

The name 'redstart' often puzzles people. Like so many of our bird names, it comes from Old English, and simply means 'red tail'. Other of its European names, especially in languages related to English, such as German and Scandinavian, follow the same pattern. But my favourite of all is the Italian: *codirosso spazzacamino*, which translates as 'red-tailed chimney-sweep', the perfect rendering of this perky little bird.

HOOF FUNGUS
2 January

The boundaries between living and non-living are blurred, especially in early January, when the countryside is stripped bare. On a stroll through local birch woods today, I spot an anthracite excrescence on one of the dead trees. It's the size and shape of a shire-horse's hoof and seems more mineral than vegetable, layered with tough accretions like sedimentary rock. It looks older by some magnitude than the host whose life it has sapped.

But this odd growth is alive: a hoof fungus. It's a kind of bracket fungus, named for its shelf-like fruiting bodies which project from the bark of trees and which can last for many years. These are simply the visible signs of a much larger organism, most of which lies underground.

Although hoof fungus is widespread and locally common in northern England and Scotland, until very recently it has been rare in my neighbourhood. Now, though, it seems to be increasing in this corner of the West Midlands. It's hard to associate with the usual suspect, global warming, as its southward spread seems counter-intuitive, but the comings and goings of fungal life are mysterious affairs, to me at least.

For the few victimised trees, it's a fatal attraction because hoof fungus rots their timber and kills them. That's good news for the local wildlife. As the birches succumb, sunlight can reach the woodland floor and create a gap for young trees to sprout. Soft birch timber is food for a host of insects and furnishes perfect nest-holes for woodpeckers, tits and redstarts, whose song will fill these airy birch woods when April comes.

Hoof fungus has been useful to us too. Its woody brackets burn very slowly and make good kindling. When the body of Otzi the Iceman was found in 1991 – preserved after 5,000 years of cold storage in an Alpine glacier – among the fungi he carried were slivers of hoof fungus, presumably as fire-lighting aids whose benefits he was never to enjoy.

SMEW

3 January

Crisp frost encrusts the leafless hedgerows, and as a January dawn begins to break, a tight flock of even frostier-looking birds floats serenely on the still, grey waters. They are smew – one of the scarcest and most attractive of all our ducks.

Smew breed on remote lakes in Scandinavia and Siberia, and in autumn head south to the Dutch polders. But when these glaze over in hard weather, and the ducks can't find the food they need, they flee south and west in search of ice-free waterbodies. One favourite destination is an unlikely spot for such a wary bird: the gravel-pits squeezed between the arterial roads and perimeter of Heathrow Airport, which stud the Ordnance Survey map of west London like scattered pearls. This is where I grew up, and where, back in the 1970s, I first encountered these rare and charismatic birds.

They still gather here each winter in tight, compact flotillas, easily spooked by the dog-walkers, joggers and fishermen who share their winter home. When not keeping an eye out for danger, each bird dives, disappearing beneath the surface for a minute or more before bobbing up again, often with a tiny fish held in its stubby, serrated bill.

Shy and suspicious, smew are easily flushed, and over the years I have learned the hard way to approach the flock with great care, so as not to scare them. I tread slowly, using the line of trees along the edge of the water to conceal myself. Peering through the foliage, I can see that most of the birds are females or immatures. They are known as redheads from their dark, rusty crowns, which set off their snowy throats and pearl-grey bodies. Another folk name is weasel duck, also from the russet coloration of their heads.

Attractive though the females are, they are easily outshone by their mates. A male smew is white with a black mask, and has a cheeky black tail sticking out behind like a boat's rudder. Subtle grey scribblings known as vermiculations (after the Latin for 'worm') wriggle across its flanks. Its cowl-like head pattern gives the bird another of its many folk names – white nun – while fine black fault-lines craze across the pure white body like clumsily mended porcelain.

Smew don't call very often, even if they could be heard above the constant rumbling of passing aircraft, but it's their soft, whistling sound that earned them their curious name.

When one bird, warier than the rest, finally spots the intruder, the show is abruptly over: the flock whirrs skyward in a blur of wingbeats. Given that they are so panicky about people, why they choose to spend the winter here beneath the Heathrow flightpath is a mystery. Yet they do, and one fine day in early March they will eventually depart, heading north and east to Scandinavian lakes to breed.

WINTER HELIOTROPE

4 January

In south Devon, visiting family, I notice several clumps of winter heliotrope in bloom by a Plymouth roadside. The washed-out lilac flowers and broad, green, kidney-shaped leaves, spattered with mud from passing cars, are not exceptional; this relative of coltsfoot and butterbur flowers from December onwards, even in cold winters. It's the memories that they've evoked that are so powerful.

Although the plant's name refers to its supposed sun-seeking habit, it thrives in the dullest weather, though it doesn't always flower, spreading instead by rhizomes. These thick root-mats often preclude other competition, and allow the heliotrope to commandeer extensive patches of road verge.

We should be surprised that it survives here at all, because this unremarkable plant is native to the Mediterranean basin and was introduced to the British Isles by horticulturalists eager for winter cheer. Whether its pale mauve tassels supply this depends on your taste, but for me it's a Proustian plant that recalls New Year holidays spent on the south Devon coast and a particular series of books that I treasured as a young boy – and still do.

The Ladybird 'What to Look For' series described the natural world in spring, summer, autumn and winter in lucid text accompanied by masterful illustrations by Charles Tunnicliffe. Among the many paintings in the *Winter* book is a Siamese cat eyeing blue tits in overhead branches surrounded by flowering winter heliotrope. Each of these intimate scenes is a miracle of compression, unquestionably authentic and, as a result, enduring.

Revisiting them, I'm whisked back to a time when a jam jar full of tadpoles or sticklebacks was my main wildlife experience. When I did eventually see winter heliotrope, it was already an old friend. And now each time I see the plant I'm transported back to my first experience of this marvellous quartet of books.

BROWN RAT

5 January

On this fine, clear morning, through a windowpane framed in frost, I watch the birds flocking around the garden feeders, jostling one another to get to the energy-rich seeds within. Below them, trailing its long tail in the frozen husks of spilled seeds, a sleek, furry creature scavenges the fallen food, while always keeping a beady black eye out for danger.

Brown rats first arrived in Britain in the early eighteenth century, probably via trading ships from Russia. In the 300 years or so since, they have completely displaced an earlier invader: the black (or ship) rat, widely thought to have carried the fleas that spread the deadly bubonic plague, and which is now almost extinct here, with the last few individuals clinging on in the remote Shiant Islands off the north-west coast of Scotland.

The oft-quoted 'fact' that you are never more than fifteen feet from a rat (the actual distance appears to vary depending on the teller) is an urban myth. Nevertheless rats do live right beside us, with plenty of opportunities for our paths to cross. When they do, if you watch them for a while, and set aside your prejudices, you will begin to appreciate why they have become so successful.

Brown rats are omnivores, a double-edged sword when it comes to survival. Being able to eat virtually anything means they are unlikely to starve; on the other hand it also makes them very vulnerable to eating the wrong thing, and being poisoned.

As a result, rats have a highly developed fear of anything new or unusual – a trait known as neophobia – which stands them in good stead in a world where humans make every effort to kill them. So once a rat has discovered a new source of food, it will usually sample small amounts for the first few days, to ensure that it is safe.

There are no such worries for the rat squatting beneath my bird table on a cold winter's day. It knows that if the food is okay for the birds to eat, then it will be fine for it too; and so enjoys a free meal at my expense.

UNSEASONAL HOGWEED

6 January

There are hints of summer on the road verges even in the depths of winter. Take hogweed for instance, a bristly member of the carrot family known to children as a winter source of hollow peashooter sticks. Every January, I can guarantee hogweed flowers in bloom on local road verges. These freaks are anaemic versions of the robust panicles produced in June and July, their umbrellas of creamy blossom held high on bristly stems, irresistible to insects.

But the winter flowers mock us with hollow promises of sunny days to come. Dripping with mist under a lowering January sky, they look lost and unfulfilled. It's hard to imagine any biological advantage to blooming this early. Maybe there isn't one and these are simply sports like the famous Glastonbury thorn, a variety of hawthorn that flowers at the end of the year and again in spring.

When the sun shines, though, even these unseasonal hogweed flowers have visitors. Fuzzy yellow dung-flies forsake the warmth of cowpats for this serendipitous nectar source and may even perform a pollination service if the weather remains mild enough for them to travel between the umbels. Here, at winter's heart, we have a pale imitation of summer, but no less welcome for all that.

FIELD VOLE

7 January

Just because an animal is common, doesn't mean you see it very often. Although there are more field voles than people in Britain – about 75 million at the last estimate – I can tally on the fingers of one hand how many I have seen in the past few years. And when I do spot one, it is usually a brief, unsatisfying glimpse of a small, brown rodent dashing away as fast as it can across my garden lawn.

The field vole – also known as the short-tailed vole, because of its rather stumpy tail – is elusive for a very good reason. During its brief but eventful life it has just three main aims: to eat, reproduce and avoid being eaten.

There are certainly enough predators queuing up to have a go: kestrels and barn owls from the air, and foxes, stoats and weasels on the ground, all make short work of catching and despatching this endearing little rodent. Indeed some species – notably kestrels and barn owls – mostly depend on voles to feed their young.

When voles have a good year, so do these birds. Vole populations go up and down in roughly four-year cycles, and owl and kestrel numbers tend to rise and fall likewise, depending on how many voles are around.

So even though I may hardly ever see them, I know when field vole numbers are booming, as there are barn owls quartering the fields behind my Somerset home, and kestrels hovering motionless in the winter skies above. In bad vole years, both are much harder to find.

The best way to see the voles themselves is to put a sheet of corrugated iron in some long grass. Voles often take refuge under these, so if you lift one quickly you may be treated to a momentary sight of the animal as it scuttles away to safety.

I did once enjoy a longer, closer view of a field vole, when a neighbour popped over with her mammal traps. We set the devices overnight, baited with a morsel of food, and the next morning checked to see if a curious vole had fallen for the oldest trick in the book.

It had. Close up, this wriggling little ball of fur was quite distinctive. Voles have a more rounded snout, smaller eyes and furrier ears than mice; and the field vole also has that distinctive short, stubby tail. They are greyer than the more reddish-brown bank vole, and have smaller ears.

Given that field voles don't usually start breeding until March or April, you might not expect them to be active as early as January. But when it snows, they seize the opportunity to breed beneath a thick, protective layer of white, which keeps their young warm and safe from predators. So as soon as the snow begins to settle, voles start digging tunnels through the snow with all the enthusiasm and effort of the inmates of Colditz.

After such a good start, a female field vole can have six or seven litters of up to six young in a single year. She needs to, for very few voles live longer than a few months, and the vast majority will die or be killed long before then.

YEW TREES AND HAWFINCHES
8 January

A red sandstone church on the forest edge is encircled by sombre yews, beaded with red berries, which attract thrushes. Today there are redwings balancing precariously on the trailing twigs and a rattling mistle thrush trying to see them off.

Yews are staple trees of churchyards. They were sacred to our pagan ancestors, and it's likely that some churches, built on ancient sites of pre-Christian worship, inherited their yews from these sites. Others suggest that they were planted when churches were founded following the Norman Conquest. The sombre evergreen yew needles may carry intimations of a dark afterlife; or given the great age to which a yew tree can live – 2,000 years is not unusual – life eternal. Yews may also have been deliberately planted in churchyards to discourage livestock from venturing in, as their leaves, bark and seeds are poisonous.

Today, there are so many discarded yew stones that they crunch underfoot like vegetable shingle. The tiny kernels inside these stones are sought by a very special bird: on cue a hawfinch flies up from the path and is lost in the cascades of leathery foliage. Later it perches, blunt-tailed and big-headed, at the very top of a lime tree, broadcasting its ticking alarm call.

The hawfinch's massive bill, used to crack open fruit stones and seeds with a force of 180 pounds per square inch, is feared by bird-ringers keen to unravel the mysteries that shroud one of our most secretive birds.

Where, for example, has this bird come from? Is it one of the dwindling local breeders or an immigrant from the Continent? The ringing of hawfinches in west Wales reveals movements between continental

Europe and other sites in the British Isles. With such a mobile population, low numbers and secretive habits, hawfinches are hard to find,
but you could do worse than check out winter churchyards and their
ancient yews.

WILD BOAR
9 January

A winter's walk through an ancient woodland can be a dull affair, enlivened only by the distant sounds of a flock of small birds as they forage
in the leafless canopy. But look down, and you may find evidence of a
recent addition to our fauna: patches of freshly turned soil that indicate
the presence of wild boar.

Hunted to extinction by the fourteenth century, wild boars remained
absent from Britain for hundreds of years. Then, some time during the
1990s, reports began to surface of these mighty animals in the Forest
of Dean, Dorset and Sussex. The wild boar was back.

But how? Birds and insects can colonise Britain from continental
Europe simply by flying across the Channel, but mammals have no such
option. However, having been responsible for their extinction, we were
also vital to their reappearance: it was soon discovered that pig farmers
had imported wild boars from mainland Europe to make sausages and
other meat products. Some animals had inevitably managed to escape
and, finding our woodlands an ideal place to live, had begun to reproduce.

For anyone who lives alongside wild boars, their presence can be
rather terrifying. At over a metre tall and weighing up to 175 kilos (more
than twice the weight of the average human being) the wild boar comes
second only to the red deer as our largest terrestrial mammal.

Yet for such a huge beast they are both shy and elusive, staying deep
in the forest where they forage for (mostly vegetable) food such as acorns,
bulbs and berries. As with many mammals, you're more likely to see
the signs of wild boars than the creature itself. Look out for areas of turf
that have been rolled back as the animals dig for food; or smooth areas
on trees where they have rubbed away the bark with their bulky bodies.

These new arrivals have been the subject of some hostility, especially
when they venture out of their woodland home. When they do our

attitudes towards them can be contradictory: witness the sheer panic when one was seen in a school playground, or the anger when they dug up a football pitch; yet not very far away, people are queuing up to feed them in a forest car park.

For conservationists, the boar's unexpected return presents a dilemma. Some argue for eradicating the animals, especially as many of them may not be pure-bred wild boars at all, having been crossed with domestic pigs when in captivity. They also claim that because the boar's natural predators – including bears and wolves – are now lost to Britain, the population is likely to explode over the next few decades.

But most welcome this animal's accidental comeback. After all, we are not exactly over-endowed with large, charismatic mammals, and the presence of such a huge and fearsome-looking beast reminds us that even a routine walk in the woods may provide us with an unexpected thrill. In accepting the boar we are, in some small but crucial way, rewilding ourselves.

WINTER MOTHS

10 January

Translucent petals trapped in a cobweb slung between the roots of a hedgerow oak tell a poignant tale on a freezing January day. On closer inspection, they turn out to be the severed forewings of winter moths, one of our few species of moth that flies in January. You'll see these insects on damp nights, fluttering weakly in the car headlights, scraps of living tissue that look utterly vulnerable and ill-equipped for such a harsh season. Visually, they are not much to write home about: a drab greyish brown, with a few markings that guide the proficient moth expert in identifying them.

Examining the web more closely, I find another insect trapped in its mesh. Leggy and desiccated, it sprouts the greyish remnants of wings, small tattered triangles that are clearly useless for flying. It is a female winter moth and unwittingly, by falling into this trap, she has lured several potential mates to their deaths.

The female winter moth doesn't have wings. After emerging from her pupa in the soil, she climbs a tree-trunk or fence-post and broadcasts a cloud of invisible scent particles – pheromones – into the winter night. This olfactory summons is picked up by the males' sensitive antennae. Tuning in on a windless evening, they spiral towards her. Normally this ends in mating. This time, though, she has fallen into a spider's web and her mating signal has become a siren song, luring her hapless suitors to their doom.

WINTER REEDS

11 January

Walking along a path fringed with tall stands of reeds is always a strange experience, especially at dusk on a dull winter's day. The tall stems wave in the bitter wind, their dark, feathery plumes filtering the late afternoon light and scattering it in shards through the chill air. As the wind strengthens, so a whispering sound reaches my ear: the muffled conversation of tens of thousands of swaying reeds.

Phragmites australis – the common reed – is actually a giant grass. They grow far taller than us, dwarfing other vegetation and soon crowding out any but the most determined competitors. Reeds are also opportunists, quickly colonising any damp patch of ground or newly dug lake or pond, growing like the proverbial Topsy, and forming dense stands known as reed-beds.

Reed-beds are an unusual and very specialised habitat for wildlife: not many creatures can live there, as they need to adapt to what is essentially a vertical way of life. When spring comes to my local patch reed warblers, just back from Africa, weave their neat, cup-shaped nests between these upright stems, while harvest mice clamber around using their prehensile tails to avoid falling into the water below.

Marsh harriers and bitterns breed here too, each making their nest on a platform of reeds to prevent their eggs and chicks getting water-logged. Smaller inhabitants include the plum-reed aphid, a tiny insect that starts life on plum and damson trees and then migrates to reed-beds in midsummer, providing much needed food for the reed and sedge warblers, as they prepare for their long journey south.

But now, in the depths of winter, the only bird in view is a solitary, morose-looking reed bunting perched near the top of a reed stem. Small, brown and streaky, its feathers are hunched up against the cold like an old man wearing a coat several sizes too big for him.

Reed-beds may look permanent, but they are essentially temporary: a starter home for wetland wildlife. Any colonisers have to be quick: fast-forward twenty years or so, and this reed-bed may no longer exist. If left to its own devices it will soon be taken over by encroaching alder and willow scrub, eventually turning into wet woodland.

So conservationists here regularly cut the reeds, allowing the beds to regenerate and provide a home for a suite of wetland creatures, those whose lives are closely interwoven with these vistas of whispering grass.

STONECHAT

12 January

Winds have dropped, skies have cleared and for several nights there's been a sharp frost. On a distant, ice-furred fence-post, a robin, backlit by brilliant sunshine, is scanning the ground for any sign of prey. But what brings a robin out here in the fields, far from cover?

Closer views reveal that this is a male stonechat, perky and robin-sized. Stonechats are scarce here in midwinter, but it's always worth a scan along fence-lines or in brambly corners where the hedge-cutters have spared a few dry thistle stalks. They don't breed nearby – they're birds of gorsy heaths and commons – but wander in autumn and winter from other parts of the British Isles and even continental Europe.

Ornithologist Jim Flegg says that having a stonechat around 'adds something extra to the place' and I agree. Stonechats are sentinels, animated dots in the landscape, always perching in the open. Although spring males are dazzling in their black hoods and orange breasts, in his winter plumage this one has a muted charm, breast feathers the colour of old beech leaves and with a hint of a pale collar.

He's a lone chat – often they travel in pairs even outside the breeding season – and allows a closer approach than stonechats usually do. Cold winters, especially when snow lies for long periods, are devastating for insect-eaters like him and mortality can be high. So he expends as little energy as possible, a trade-off between hunger and the need to escape from a potential enemy.

Now, just a few paces from him, I scuff the grass with my boots and retreat. After a nervous, tail-flicking appraisal, he flies down to the ground, seizes an invisible insect disturbed by my actions and returns briskly to his perch. We repeat this teamwork several times and I'm struck by the similarity to garden robins, which follow me around as I weed, much as they would have tracked the snufflings of wild boar in ancient woods. Perhaps stonechats once did this too.

I'm cheered by our brief partnership on this cold winter's day, but aware that his companionship has only been brought by the extreme weather. There's a month or more to go before he returns to defend his gorsy territory with flint-knapping calls, and his survival is far from certain.

BLACK SQUIRRELS

13 January

A churchyard in the middle of a Home Counties market town is not, perhaps, where I would expect to see one of Britain's most unusual mammals. But if I sit and wait a while, one does appear: a perky little squirrel, with bright eyes and a tufty tail just like the grey squirrels we see in our towns and cities every day. There's only one difference: this creature is not grey, but jet-black.

Colour apart, the black squirrel behaves just like its commoner cousin. It bounds along between the gravestones, occasionally halting to look warily around; though I don't imagine there are many predators lurking here in this suburban setting. Like all squirrels in winter it must feed throughout the short hours of daylight, in order to survive the cold weather and scarcity of food at this time of year.

Black squirrels are a strange phenomenon, for they share virtually all their genes with the familiar grey squirrels; all bar the crucial strand of DNA that produces lighter pigment in the animal's fur. As a result they are as black as ebony.

The first black squirrel ever seen in this country was not far from here, near Letchworth Garden City in Hertfordshire, in the early years of the twentieth century. It was almost certainly the descendant of escapees from the collection at Woburn Abbey, just down the road. Since then they have spread, though not any great distance: their range has only expanded by about half a mile a year since that very first sighting.

Back in their native North America, black squirrels are scarce but fairly widespread, especially in the colder, more northerly regions, where having black fur – which retains heat – gives them a marginal evolutionary advantage over the greys. Whether this brings them any benefit in our more benevolent winter climate is unlikely; yet the black squirrel continues to thrive, despite frequently interbreeding with the greys.

As I watch it scamper up a tree and out of sight, I reflect on the one, admittedly important, difference: our attitude towards these curious creatures. Whereas many people hate, or at best tolerate, the pesky greys, these black squirrels have become a source of local pride.

WINTER GULLS

14 January

Ornithologists, birders and twitchers are usually lumped together by non-naturalists, but among their ranks are subtle subdivisions. Some have hankerings for hawks; some are never happier than when ringing waterfowl or extracting tiny migrants from the mesh of mist-nets. Others dangle from sea-cliffs counting gannets and guillemots.

But it's in midwinter that the hardiest extremists emerge. Visit an urban reservoir on a raw January afternoon and you will see them, hunched over their telescopes, which rock slightly in the blast that scours the concrete banks and whips the steely water into wavelets. What can possibly have caused them to abandon a cosy fireside for this Siberian setting? Follow the sight-line of lenses out across the water and you have your answer: these birders are larophiles: gull-worshippers.

Laridae is the technical name for the gull family and, for some birders, they provide the ultimate challenge. Gulls, especially the larger ones, have a bewildering array of plumages, from mottled brown youngsters to familiar grey and white adults. In winter, after scavenging on rubbish-tips, they roost in vast flocks on reservoirs and gravel-pits, so are there in quantity on our doorsteps. But then so are blue tits or robins. What makes gulls so attractive (to some) is that they offer limitless possibilities for speculation.

About forty years ago, when I first began birding, the pearly-grey and white bird that stole your seaside chips was a herring gull. Since then, those in the know have decreed that there are three species of 'herring gull' visiting our shores, their identity based on small differences in structure, leg colour, wingtip patterns and other features. These new species were once thought to be races or subspecies, since larger gulls are prone to variations within populations.

So now the herring gull has been 'split'. One new species is the yellow-legged gull from the Mediterranean, which had been lurking regularly in the British Isles, but had not been elevated to specific status. More recently, the Caspian gull, which breeds in eastern Europe and looks like a slightly longer-legged, pot-bellied herring gull, has also been deemed a true species. Each of these has a variety of different plumages as the birds age. And herring gulls are just the beginning: there are also several races of the lesser black-backed gull, a charcoal and white bird with yellow legs, jostling for specific promotion.

These new species can be bewildering to separate in the field guides, let alone among the blizzard of birds arriving to roost on a monochrome winter afternoon. As they ride the leaden skies, they are undeniably impressive, but gull spotting is rarely about aesthetics. Rather, it's an exercise in puzzle-solving, a journey to the furthest frontiers of scientific classification and a test for the latest optical equipment.

With more new species in the offing, the connoisseurs will be out there, scanning the rafts of roosting birds for that elusive first Baltic or Armenian gull or whatever, among the hordes. It's not for everyone, and few of us can be absolutely sure where one gull species ends and another begins. But it is a brilliant illustration of the shifting sands of modern natural history. And if you've got the stamina and the attitude, it's only a stone's-throw away.

HOODED CROW

15 January

If most people were asked to pick out one bird that sums up Scotland, they would probably choose the golden eagle. But for me, the hooded crow has a far better claim. For as soon as I cross the Great Glen at

Inverness, and enter the wilder northern half of the Highlands, then hoodies – as they are affectionately known – begin to appear.

That name is an apt one: unlike our familiar carrion crow, an unremittingly black creature, hooded crows are piebald; with a pale, dirty-grey body, nape and back contrasting with the jet-black head, throat and wings. Plumage apart, though, hoodies behave much like other crows. They are in turns sociable and quarrelsome, often gathering in large flocks with rooks and jackdaws to feed in stubble fields or along the seashore, where they happily scavenge any flotsam and jetsam washed up by the incoming tide.

Although I think of hooded crows as quintessentially Scottish, even on these islands they are found elsewhere. They more or less replace their all-black cousin in Ireland, and I once came across one on Anglesey in north-west Wales. This was presumably a pioneering bird that had flown the short distance across the Irish Sea to see what life was like on the other side. Migrants from Scandinavia are even occasionally seen in eastern England during the winter: one now obsolete name, Royston crow, was earned because the birds used to turn up regularly on the heath outside this unremarkable Hertfordshire town.

Sadly in Scotland hoodies are now being forced back by an invader from the south, their own cousin the carrion crow. Their numbers and range have declined in the past twenty years or so, and the 'hybrid zone' – the area in which these two closely related species interbreed – is shifting further north and west all the time. It is ironic that having only been recognised as a full species relatively recently, the hoodie may now be on its way out.

Strangely for a bird so associated with the far north, the hooded crow is the default species of crow in south-eastern Europe and the Middle East. I have encountered flocks of them in the Po Valley in Italy and the Negev Desert in Israel. When I do it always takes me back to the Highlands, and memories of watching these birds squabbling with one another against a backdrop of snow-covered mountains.

SNOW FLEAS

16 January

The wind rattles the branches of the oaks, like the clash of rutting stags. Below, on the forest floor, conditions are calmer among the cushions of velvet moss. We are looking, my companions and I, for snow fleas.

There's no snow, but it is four degrees Celsius and few creatures are stirring, though as we brush the moss lightly with our palms, tiny insects known as springtails do an excellent imitation of a flea as they somersault away. The real snow flea remains stubbornly elusive.

Snow fleas aren't fleas at all, but flies, closely related to the scorpion flies that you often see on low vegetation in summer. Scorpion flies have speckled wings and the males sport reddish genitalia held curved over the end of the abdomen rather like the sting of a scorpion: fearsome-looking, but completely harmless.

Snow fleas can't fly. Only the male has the remains of wings, two curved vestigial spurs with which he holds down the female in the mating ceremony, conducted among moss in heathy woodlands or on moorland. Adult snow fleas are around from November to March when they feed on dead and dying insects. Often they will venture on to snow to explore its surface for hapless casualties, which they probe with long beaks. This is your best chance of finding one, though at just four millimetres long they are easy to miss.

At last we strike lucky, finding one and then another, near a rotten stump furred with grey lichen. They are leggier than I'd imagined and have a brassy sheen, which catches the weak winter sunlight. On their sides is a yellow band and even without a hand lens I can see the long probing beak: closer focus allows me to see the larger female's sword-like ovipositor which she uses to lay her eggs in moss-clumps.

Get too close and they leap into the air, though without the athletic aptitude of a true flea. Unsung and overlooked, these tiny, hopping, flightless flies that flourish in midwinter and scavenge carrion deserve more attention. They are curiously fussy about where they live and tend to be more common in older, relatively undisturbed places in the north and west of Britain. They could be entomological barometers of the quality of our countryside, but today we're not asking big questions, merely savouring the discovery of this strange inhabitant of our local woods.

CHINESE WATER DEER

17 January

I stare across the flat east Norfolk landscape, scanning from left to right against a backdrop of reeds. A marsh harrier effortlessly floats on the January air while, as dusk begins to fall, a single barn owl quarters up and down across the marsh like a beacon in the gathering darkness. But I'm searching not for a bird, but for one of Britain's most bizarre mammals. And time is running out.

Then, on the umpteenth scan, I see one: a pale greyish-brown creature that appears to have emerged from the reeds in the very spot I was staring at just a minute or two earlier. A Chinese water deer: of all the alien creatures now at large in our countryside, surely one of the oddest.

It doesn't take a geography degree to work out that this small, stocky deer originally came from China. Like so many other non-native creatures at large in Britain, it was brought over to adorn stately homes and gardens: in this case, Woburn Abbey and Whipsnade Zoo in the early years of the last century.

Inevitably some escaped, but in the intervening hundred years or so they haven't travelled very far: Chinese water deer are found mainly in East Anglia and the area north of London where they were originally released. They love the Norfolk Broads – where I am now – and spend much of their time up to their knees in the damp, marshy fens. The best chance of encountering these curious mammals is to visit at dawn or dusk, when they are feeding more actively and so more likely to show themselves.

The animal I am watching doesn't seem all that bothered by my presence, so I slowly move forward, keeping a careful eye to make sure I am not frightening him. I say 'him', but it may be a 'her': this is the only British deer species, whether native or introduced, that doesn't sport antlers.

What both sexes do have is a fine pair of tusks, which as I get closer I can now just make out in the gloom. The deer use these to ward off rivals during the winter rut, though this one doesn't look as if it will be needing them today.

This is just one of about 4,000 Chinese water deer at large in Britain. Compared with 50,000 or so muntjacs, that doesn't seem all that many; yet it now represents a significant proportion of the entire world population. Given the plummeting numbers in its native China, where the species has been all but wiped out through hunting and habitat loss, Britain may soon be the world stronghold of this shy and retiring mammal.

LICHENS

18 January

A mild January day, the hedgerows in local farmland golden in the afternoon sun. An idyllic rural scene perhaps, but things are not as they might seem.

On closer inspection, each hawthorn and elder twig is barnacled with yellow lichen, related to the species whose paintball splashes enliven old tiled roofs and add thousands to the value of country cottages. These are *Xanthorias*, and in common with all lichens are a symbiotic partnership between a fungus and an alga: the alga makes food from sunlight for the fungus, which provides the alga with a stable substrate. *Xanthoria* lichens are one of the crustose lichens, so called because they form bright yellow or orange crusts on flat surfaces or encase the twigs of well-lit trees and shrubs.

Lichens are well known as pollution watchdogs. Many species are sensitive to sulphur dioxide in the atmosphere and so are scarce around heavy industry and in city centres. In recent years, cleaner air has brought many species back into town. One is the confusingly named oak moss *Evernia prunastri*: not a moss at all, but a lichen, which festoons twigs with tiny grey-green antlers. It's especially common on deciduous trees and has returned to my nearest town park on the edge of the Black Country in the last decade or so: not bad for a place that spawned the Industrial Revolution.

But the picture is more complex than this narrative suggests. The yellow hedgerows bristling with lichen in the local countryside might seem to be a sign of improved air, but are not. *Xanthoria* lichens are very tolerant of high levels of nitrogen dioxide, which derives partly from nitrates used in agricultural fertilisers.

Many of our more specialised wild plants prefer poorer soils, and can't compete with the taller species such as nettles and goose grass, which thrive on nitrogen-enrichment. Run-off from farmland where nitrates are applied encourages algal growth such as blanket weed in pools, choking out sunlight and other plants. While those effects might not be immediately obvious, as we drive past the hedges, the glut of *Xanthoria* lichen is there for us to see – a jaundiced view of an over-fertilised landscape.

ROOKS

19 January

The sign says 'Rooksbridge', though the signwriter was clearly not an expert ornithologist, as the bird portrayed is not a rook, but a crow.

The birds don't seem to mind, though: right above the main road, a loose gathering of rooks is perched in the tops of the bare-branched trees, like scattered fragments of bin liner against the grey January sky. Spring seems an awfully long way away.

But not if you are a rook. It may be the middle of winter, but they have already started spring-cleaning their homes: making minor repairs to the structure, and adding a twig here, and another there, to spruce up their nest. It's almost as if they want to impress the neighbours; an impression echoed by the constant chorus of caws as they chat to one another, and also to me as I gaze up from below. From here, I can easily see the dark nests against the winter sky; but in a couple of months they will be hidden by leaves.

Rooks are one of those birds that, like the stock dove (which gets mixed up with the woodpigeon), are often overlooked in favour of their more assertive cousin, the carrion crow. The two are often confused, yet while the carrion crow is all black, the rook has a pale greyish bill and face, contrasting with the rest of its dark plumage.

There are over 1 million breeding pairs of rooks in Britain, and where I live on the Somerset Levels they are the commoner of the two species. For many places, the presence of a rookery in a clump of tall trees – often next to the church, where their sound competes with the chacking of the jackdaws – is an important part of the village identity; especially here in Rooksbridge, where the bird features in the village's name.

When we first moved here, a decade ago now, we had a rookery at the bottom of our garden in the tall ash trees on our neighbour's adjacent plot. But soon after we arrived, our local farmer popped round to inform us that he was off to shoot the rooks, as they wreak havoc with his newborn lambs. Sadly, a few years later, the rooks disappeared, and now I only occasionally see them flying overhead on their way elsewhere, raggedy wings etched against the sky.

I miss their noisy neighbourliness on a cold winter's day, a timely reminder that spring will eventually be here.

FUSSY FERNS

20 January

Swallowed any rare ferns lately? You probably have, as their minute spores are swirling around us all the time. It's a question that struck me years ago, while visiting a Worcester pub with a well in the lounge bar. Glass-topped for safety, the well was originally outside, but now formed the centrepiece of a new extension.

Peering into its depths, I saw sprays of leaves sprouting tropically far below. Somehow ferns had settled here and were flourishing in the warmth, moisture and artificial light. There were leathery strap-like leaves of hart's-tongue ferns, and the delicate lacy fronds of maidenhair fern.

Maidenhair ferns had surprised me decades before on school trips to the limestone caves of Cheddar Gorge, when I saw them clustering around the lights that illuminated the show caverns. This impossible greenery in the Stygian blackness was as odd and unexplained as the stalagmites and stalactites that we'd paid to see. Where had these plants come from and how did they survive?

Ferns are flowerless and produce not seeds, but spores, minute specks of primeval dust, which surround us wherever we are. We inhale them constantly, and the vast majority perish. But where they reach damp surfaces, they can germinate and produce a tiny green mat called a gametophyte or prothallus.

This isn't a fully-fledged fern, but has on its underside male and female reproductive organs. The male organs, called antheridia, contain sperm cells, which need to travel in order to fertilise the egg cells in the separate female archegonia. To do this they need a film of water. Once fertilisation is complete and the fern has its full complement of chromosomes, it can grow into a spore-bearing plant or sporophyte.

That's why most ferns crave moist places. The British maidenhair fern needs a bit more. It's a Mediterranean plant that prefers mild frost-free conditions and just survives in south-west England, often near the coast. Its spores travel far and wide and some even penetrate caves such as those at Cheddar or the insides of wells. Add a light source for photo-synthesis and the ferns can grow even in the depths of winter in sheltered spots.

Not all these ferns are the native maidenhair. In central London, perceptive – some might say nosy – botanists stare down into secluded basements in search of alien ferns, which have escaped from hanging baskets or local nurseries. One of these is the delta maidenhair, a common houseplant native to South America. In the 'heat island' of the capital where temperatures can be three or four degrees Celsius above those in the surrounding countryside, such exotic ferns are able to ride out the English winter and gain a fragile toehold.

TURNING OF THE TIDES

21 January

A blowy January day at a place where three rivers meet, and eventually, via the Bristol Channel, end up in the sea. I have arrived at the very moment when high tide reaches its peak, and the waters spill over on to the adjacent foreshore in an ominous reminder that they still have the power to inundate the land.

Not today, though. Today the grassy shoreline, as flat as a cricket pitch but rather muddier, is spared the surge of saltwater. My wellingtons, which have sprung a small leak, squelch deep into the ooze as I fruitlessly tramp downriver, hoping to flush a jack snipe (I never have, though I do displace its larger cousin the common snipe, which towers high into the air, uttering a short, fart-like sound).

There are meadow pipits: lots of them, bouncing up from the green sward as if pulled by a long strand of elastic, uttering their distinctive 'sip sip' call. I have seen rock pipits here too: larger and darker birds, with a stronger and more metallic call than their relatives.

A more mellifluous, multi-faceted burst of sound is issued by a bulky bird rising just in front of my feet: a skylark. Not yet quite ready to sing its full song, despite the mild weather, it instead opts for a gentle warble, as if someone has sampled a bar or two and repeated it over and over again.

No sooner has the skylark appeared than my eyes are drawn to the tideline, where a flock of a thousand or more small waders – dunlins and knots – has risen into the air as one. They swirl around like a single organism, before landing again out of sight, beneath the bank on the water's edge. A moment of magic, granted to me and the occasional dog-walker – the only people bold enough to enter this ephemeral world at the turning of the tides.

GREAT GREY SHRIKE

22 January

There are times when intuition tells you that the stage is set for a particular bird, that the landscape around you would be incomplete without it. This is no guarantee that the bird will appear, of course, but every now and then a gut feeling pays off.

Some birds lend themselves more than others to these flights of fancy. I'm forever populating dusky river meadows with the ghosts of quartering barn owls or spotting imaginary ring ouzels bounding across the steep sheep-nibbled pasture on my local patch. You can dismiss this as wishful thinking maybe, but sometimes the prickle of premonition is so strong that it raises the hairs on your nape (wonderfully, zoologists call this horripilation).

It happened to me recently, in Mortimer Forest, near Ludlow in Shropshire. On a grey midwinter morning, we'd left the Forestry Commission car park to clamber and backslide our way up a near-vertical hillside on to the high ridge known as Climbing Jack Common. Emerging in an icy cloud of our own exhalations out of the dark tunnel of spruce and hemlock, we found the light. Around us, crossbills chip-chipped and a buzzard complained from a dead branch.

At the summit, a vast clearing had been gouged out of the conifers. Now it was a tangle of regrowth: fallen branches and iron-grey tree-stumps, dotted with groves of birch saplings. It looked – and I said this out loud to my bemused friends – just the place for a great grey shrike. And, to my astonishment, perched like a snowball in a haze of burgundy birch twigs, there was the shrike itself, scanning its surroundings for prey.

If you find a great grey, you're allowed to be a little smug. Fewer than a hundred winter each year in the British Isles, and these are usually solitary birds, which can roam over large territories on heaths or where conifers have been clear-felled. Our wintering shrikes probably come from Scandinavia, where they breed in open forest clearings.

Few birds are as mesmerically watchable: the great artist and orni-thologist Donald Watson described them as one of the birds that made his 'fingers itch for pencil and paper'. Poised on the topmost bough of a sapling, great grey shrikes are winter sentinels, as grey as the January sky, as white as hoar frost with black Lone Ranger masks. When they fly in great looping bounds, their long tails act as a counterbalance.

The fiercely hooked bill can tear the flesh of small mammals and birds, which the shrike pounces on from its vantage point. Sometimes they will hunt more actively: I once saw one in grim pursuit of a chaf-finch, ten metres above the ground. Shrikes famously impale their prey on thorn bushes in 'larders' to which they return regularly and because of this habit were once known as butcher birds. Regular perches are often surrounded by prey remains, the wings of an early bumblebee or the violet shards of a dor beetle's carapace winking brilliantly in the winter sun.

Great grey shrikes tend to return to the same winter quarters each year. Certain places are favourite haunts: the New Forest and Thames basin heaths, Cannock Chase in Staffordshire and clear-felled areas in conifers in Scotland and Wales. But nowadays it can be easier than ever to pinpoint your shrike. Birding websites are not everyone's cup of tea, especially if you prefer to avoid the crowds, but for finding birds as scarce and faithful to territory as this, they can be very useful. Nothing, though, can beat the shiver of excitement when you stumble across your own: it won't happen often, but you will always remember the day you cross paths with a great grey.

FAIRY SHRIMPS
23 January

Searching for fairies in a January pond sounds like a fool's errand. At a time when pond-dipping is often hampered by a crust of ice, you'd think there's little comfort in trawling the depths for anything, let alone a British rarity with very exacting requirements.

But it can be done. Pick a mildish day, in the right location, and you may be surprised at what turns up wriggling in the bottom of your net. A remarkable amount of wildlife is active throughout winter: for example, water snails, leeches, newtlets, caddis larvae in their silk-bound cases and the backswimmers whose hypodermic mouthparts can give a nasty nip to the unwary handler.

In a few select pools, other creatures swim upside down – fairy shrimps. These delicate crustaceans, which hatch around Christmas time, propel themselves by pulsating several pairs of blade-like limbs called phyllopodia and look like animated feathers wafting slowly through the shallow water in which they thrive. Large eyes and forked red 'tails' contrast with their translucent bodies as they filter minute organic fragments from the water.

With no shortage of small ponds and an undemanding diet, why should they be so scarce? These are highly specialised shrimps and if we hark back to our schooldays we can find the answer.

Those of us of a certain age remember the advertisements in the back of comics. Among other alluring offers of red-face soap and seebacko-scopes, were irresistible adverts for 'sea monkeys'. When you ordered them, you received a sachet containing a mixture of salt and shrimp eggs which, when added to water and fed supplements, hatched into a shoal of living sea monkeys. Disappointingly, they looked nothing like the crude drawings of micro-simians depicted in the *Dandy* or *Beano* and, worse, only lasted a week or so.

For many of us youngsters, this was an early life-lesson in the power of advertising. But for budding naturalists, these are fascinating creatures:

not tiny primates, but brine shrimps or *Artemia*, desert-living crustaceans whose eggs could survive desiccation when their pools dried out. This process, called cryptobiosis, literally means hidden life, and as the eggs blow around like seeds in the desert winds, they seem as lifeless as the sand grains in which they settle.

But when rains fall, the shrimps emerge to begin their brief life cycle in temporary predator-free pools. In Britain we have our own 'sea monkey', the closely related fairy shrimp, which needs similar conditions: freshwater pools that dry out in summer and re-fill in autumn rains.

In our modern efficiently drained, agriculturalised landscape, these habitats are dwindling, so now fairy shrimps are almost confined to wet heaths and old commons, clay pits and places with regular puddling; the tank tracks across military ranges on Salisbury Plain are a famous site for them. One January day, I stopped with Jeremy Biggs, founder of the charity Pond Conservation (now the Freshwater Habitats Trust), by a small roadside pool on a New Forest heath and we watched the shrimps cruising slowly just below the surface as traffic thundered past.

This was a good year, but Jeremy explained that climate change is not on their side. Dry autumns can prevent the eggs from hatching if ponds don't fill, while if they become permanently full in wet summers, the shrimps risk attack from colonising predators. Add pollution from agriculture and road run-off to the mix and you have a combination of threats that have conspired to restrict the shrimps to a handful of suitable sites. New places have been found, though, so if you're lucky enough to find a fairy in a winter pond do let the Freshwater Habitats Trust or your local wildlife trust know.

TREECREEPER

24 January

Cold weather may be bad for birds, but it can be very good for birders. When finding enough food to survive is the only aim in life, birds don't exactly turn tame, but they tend to ignore us, having more important things on their minds.

So, on a chilly January morning I head to my local patch, where the mist is beginning to lift to reveal a clear, crisp winter's day. The lake is full of birds: wigeon and shovelers from Siberia rubbing shoulders with the resident gadwall and coots. The usual tit flock passes along the wooded drove, each bird calling out to its peers to ensure they stay together in their constant search for food. And in the reed-bed, the water rails squeal and bearded tits ping, filling the air with sound.

And then I notice it. A brief movement, which is somehow different from the long-tailed tits; more deliberate, jerky and intense. A treecreeper appears from around the side of a thick oak tree, clinging to the vertical trunk with its sharp claws as it searches for food. Every second or two this tiny, mouse-like bird pauses momentarily, probing into the bark with its thin, curved bill, and extracting an insect so small I have no chance of seeing it.

Once it has exhausted the possibilities of one tree, it flits a few yards to the next, loosely following the tit flock without ever actually joining forces with them. And, unlike the tits, it is silent; focusing solely on finding food, it has no time for social niceties.

Moments after I first saw it, the treecreeper has gone, leaving me with a sense of privilege at having shared its world for a brief moment. Feet now frozen, I trudge back to the warmth of home, leaving the birds to their fate.

ISLAY GEESE

25 January

As dusk falls, they begin to arrive, the skeins etched across the sunset-drenched sky as in a children's painting. Flocks of geese – some 100 strong – heading towards their winter roost on the island of Islay.

Islay may be better known for malt whisky than for geese, but for the dedicated anserophile, this is the place to come. From November through to March, the island's fields are thronged with geese. Two species make up the vast majority of the birds here: the black and white barnacle geese, which have travelled south all the way from the eastern side of Greenland; and the Greenland white-fronted geese, which as the name suggests also breed on that vast northern island.

They come here in autumn for the same reason swallows and swifts head south to Africa: to find a regular and reliable supply of food. During the winter months they feed almost constantly during the short hours of daylight, thronging the farmers' fields and consuming vast amounts of grain.

For decades this caused conflicts between conservationists and hard-pressed farmers. But in recent years the two sides have come to a sensible compromise, in which payments are made to the farmers for loss of income, and the geese are left undisturbed.

The feeding flocks are pretty impressive, but they are nothing compared with the evening spectacle as the birds come in to roost on a sea-loch in a sheltered bay. As they approach, individuals break off from the flock and fold their wings, plummeting down to earth like an out-of-control child on a runaway bicycle. The rest then do the same, as if galvanised by that first brave and reckless individual.

It may look chaotic, but this is a clever ruse. By making their descent so crazily unpredictable, the geese confuse any potential predators. Just before they reach the ground they brake, as if opening a parachute, and glide serenely down to rest.

EGRETS

26 January

As a child, I knew there were just two species of the heron family in Britain: the familiar grey heron and the elusive bittern, an almost myth-ically rare creature that was virtually impossible to come across.

Yet today I can see five species of heron within spitting distance of my home. Bitterns have colonised the West Country in force, and can easily be spotted as they fly low over the vast reed-beds of the Avalon Marshes. Little egrets are ubiquitous, as they are now across most of southern Britain. These Persil-white herons are the epitome of elegance as they hunt for tiny fish in the shallow lagoons, their crisp white plumage shining like a beacon on a dull winter's afternoon.

In the past few years, they have been joined by their much larger relative. The great white egret does what it says on the tin: it is big, white and even more elegant than its smaller cousin. Second only to the crane as Europe's tallest bird, these long-necked waterbirds arrived here a few years ago from France, and soon began to breed, with several pairs now nesting in the reed-beds here on the Somerset Levels.

They should by now have been joined by a fifth species of heron, the cattle egret. About a decade ago, flocks of cattle egrets turned up in south-west England one autumn, and two pairs stayed on to breed the following spring. But the expected colonisation by this highly successful species then stalled, and the cattle egret is now only an occasional visitor, a smaller bird among the flocks of little egrets, with a short yellow bill and, during the breeding season, orange patches on its head, breast and wings.

Cattle egrets, as their name suggests, are often seen feeding in fields of cows, whose hooves trample the earth and make insects and inverte-brates easier to find. One theory as to why they failed to colonise suggests that the local custom of bringing cattle indoors during the winter months meant that there simply wasn't enough food for them to eat, forcing them back across the Channel.

BUTCHER'S BROOM

27 January

Consider the lilies and you may think of exotic trumpet-shaped blossoms and glossy foliage, tender slug-fodder to be cosseted in the herbaceous border. Or you might reflect on the purity of white Madonna lilies which symbolise peace, and which accompany many of us on life's final journey. But you probably won't think of a shady shrubbery in midwinter.

Here lurks an enigmatic plant, a lily that lacks the glamour of most of its tribe. It is tough and uncompromising, and if we do allow it into our gardens, it's usually by default, because of its ability to grow in dry shade where few other plants can thrive. This is the butcher's broom.

As a native plant, butcher's broom is confined to the south and west of the British Isles, but has been widely municipalised by planting in parks and churchyards, the grounds of hospitals and crematoria where its spiky sheaves persist under sombre hollies and laurels and may be as old as the sheltering trees.

The stiff sprays of sharply pointed leaves were supposedly used for sweeping floors, though Geoffrey Grigson in *The Englishman's Flora* finds scant evidence for this, quoting a reference from 1657 by William Coles to butchers 'who make cleane their stalls . . . therewith'. Other uses for it included keeping mice off butcher's slabs and decorating cuts of meat. Being evergreen, it has always been a flower-arranger's favourite; at Christmas its sea-green spikes are enlivened by spraying them gold or silver.

Although it seems dull and unexceptional, it is a remarkable plant. Look at the leaves closely and at their centre are tiny pale stars, in bloom in midwinter. These are the flowers, though which insects pollinate them is a mystery (to me at least). When successfully pollinated, they become scarlet berries, apparently defying gravity on the leaf's surface.

But butcher's broom leaves are not leaves at all: they are flattened stems called cladodes. This might remind you of asparagus, which is a close relative and also a lily: indeed the soft young shoots were once reputedly eaten like asparagus spears. When the plants are in berry, they look rather like diminutive holly bushes; an old name for the plant is knee-holly, remarkably apt, as you'll find out if you stumble into a patch.

DADDY-LONG-LEGS SPIDER

28 January

This evening there's carnage on the living room carpet. In the glow of the fire, a dark clot among the fibres resolves, on closer inspection, into a struggle for life and death.

This one's over already, in a sixteen-legged tangle, only half of those limbs moving. A huge and hairy house spider has been swaddled in silk and its vital juices are being drained. The vampire responsible is another arachnid, a daddy-long-legs spider *Pholcus phalangioides*, impossibly frail and with thread-like legs five times the length of its body. It's David versus Goliath right here on the hearth, but how can something so feeble and fragile overcome one of our largest spiders?

First, a little history. Daddy-long-legs spiders are on the march. They can't survive our winters outdoors, but are well adapted to cosying up to us, living in outhouses, sheds and especially public lavatories where they find a ready supply of flies and moths attracted by the strip-lights.

Our heated houses are irresistible too, and they've colonised them by hiding in furniture and travelling around in removal vans. They're increasing, maybe because of climate change or perhaps because property booms mean that more of us are on the move.

It's a far cry from the 1930s and 1940s, when they were much scarcer and surveying them in other people's homes was a tricky business. Pointing them out in a friend's parlour could imply domestic negligence. The arachnologist Bill Bristowe, author of the New Naturalist volume on spiders, got round this delicate social problem by affecting an interest in hotels and B&Bs, zigzagging his way across southern England using his room inspections to look for the spiders, but then failing to book the room.

Since Bristowe's surveys, *Pholcus* has spread its wings, so to speak, and is now fairly common in the southern half of the UK and heading north. Lurking behind radiators, bookcases, fish-tanks and microwaves by day, the spiders emerge at night to trail their cobwebs incontinently across every surface: it's hard to be house-proud when *Pholcus* is your guest. They often hang in their silken hammocks in the corners of rooms and if you approach with a feather duster or suction nozzle, they vibrate rapidly to become a grey blur, a trick that rarely works against the Dyson, but presumably confuses non-mechanical predators.

Both sexes have long thin bodies, but the females swell as they produce their large eggs, which they carry in their jaws like clusters of pinkish-brown grapes. On hatching, the spiderlings are like living cobwebs themselves, so flimsy as to be almost invisible.

As they mature and look for prey, their ridiculously long legs reveal their purpose. They allow the daddy-long-legs spider to fling strands of sticky silk from afar and that's how they can immobilise much larger prey such as house spiders. Once their victim is bound and gagged, *Pholcus* moves in to suck out its yellow blood or, to be technical, haemolymph. A meal like this can last them for months, which is why however clean you think your house may be, there's always room for an extra guest – or 100.

INVADING SLUGS

29 January

Silvery trails have appeared across the living room carpet. This particular January has been positively tropical, with temperatures three or four degrees above average, and the sight of night-going slugs abroad on the streets has been commonplace. Only when I came downstairs one dark morning in bare feet and felt something wet between my toes did I manage to spot one of the culprits.

Revulsion is my first reaction to a domestic slug invasion. This particular specimen had the colour and texture of phlegm, a mottled bilious-looking creature that exuded copious slime. I quickly sent it packing into the garden, but it had been a pioneer; more appeared within days, one even emerging in the best Hammer Horror traditions from the kitchen sink overflow. Clearly something odd was happening in this mildest winter for decades.

These speckled olive molluscs were green cellar slugs, *Limacus maculatus*, a species from the Caucasus and Black Sea coast that has found a home in western Europe. In Russia it lives in woods, but in the UK and elsewhere it has become synanthropic, living side by side with us.

That cosy relationship doesn't end in the garden. As its name suggests, this slug likes to come indoors, living in damp cellars and even our living space where it rasps on old wallpaper and munches cat food from pet dishes. Apparently it is on the increase, so further encounters are likely.

But the green cellar slug has a doppelgänger called the yellow cellar slug, which has similar habits and markings. The safest way to separate them, I'm told, is to tease out their innards and inspect the glistening coils like a classical soothsayer, which takes revulsion to a new level. I'm happy to remain in ignorance, but left marvelling at the dedication of natural historians.

STARLINGS

30 January

On a late January evening, as the light lingers beyond five o'clock in the afternoon for the first time since early November, I take a walk around my local patch. As I expect, things are fairly quiet: just the odd robin trying out its spring song, answered by the porcine squeals of water rails, hidden deep in the reeds.

I hope to flush a woodcock in the damp, wooded south-west corner, but no luck this time. As I turn for home, only the soft calls of long-tailed tits and the louder chacking of distant jackdaws break the companionable silence.

And then, whoosh . . . and another . . . and yet another . . . as several thousand starlings pass low over my head, almost skimming the tops of the reeds. I realise it is later than I thought – past sunset – and the starling roost must have shifted west from its normal site, so that they are now coming down very close to where I stand.

I usually share this astonishing spectacle with dozens of other people, for the starling roost here on the Somerset Levels has become nationally famous, thanks to repeated showings on wildlife TV shows such as *Springwatch*.

But tonight I am alone. And as the birds pass overhead, something truly extraordinary happens. The flock is silent – at least the birds do not call – but every bird's wings make a tiny whisper as they displace the air with each wingbeat. Individually this is beyond my ability to hear; but when a flock of tens of thousands flies overhead, the collective 'whoosh' is clearly audible. No wonder a flock of starlings is known as a murmuration.

As well as sight and sound, the starlings also engage our sense of smell. One time I was walking back along the path after the birds had roosted, when for some reason they were disturbed and took off again. In the rapidly failing light the flock – perhaps a quarter of a million strong – flew right over our heads. As they did so, pearls of liquid fell out of the sky, spattering us with the birds' droppings. My children were unaccountably delighted by this, though other observers seemed less happy with the acrid smell clinging to their clothes.

No such drama tonight, though I am treated to my very own private display: not, perhaps, as large or spectacular as some I have seen in the past, but just as rewarding. Nature is a wonderful thing when shared; but sometimes – and this was one of those moments – I want it all to myself.

WINTER GOLDFINCHES

31 January

There's hardly a day now when I don't step outside and hear splinters of sound from goldfinches flying over the garden. It wasn't always so;

once they were hard to find, especially in winter when many of our resident birds migrated south to avoid starvation.

That's no longer a problem now that niger seeds and sunflower hearts are widely available. These small morsels fit the bill quite literally for the goldfinch, whose small tweezer-like beaks have evolved to deal with the fine seeds of plants such as thistles, teasels and groundsel. With the exception of teasels perhaps, these are not plants we usually welcome as garden guests, and so in winter goldfinches, faced with an old-fashioned diet of peanuts and bread on garden bird-tables, usually went hungry.

Niger (or nyjer) is an Asian relative of the sunflower and its small black seeds are so popular with goldfinches that numbers have soared in our gardens. According to the British Trust for Ornithology's Garden Birdwatch scheme, which involves thousands of volunteers, the amount of garden-watchers reporting goldfinches has risen by over 70 per cent in the last twenty years. It looks very much as if a wider menu is helping them to survive the winter.

I'm particularly interested in the seeds goldfinches are eating that I haven't provided. On this grey January afternoon, for instance, I'm watching a small flock just outside the office window, silhouetted against the lowering sky in the top of a lilac bush. They are breaking into the seed-capsules of lilac and gorging on the seeds – something that I've noticed several times in recent years.

I've also seen them perching on the dead spires of mullein or Aaron's rod, again breaking into the seed capsules and extracting seeds as fine as sand grains. Does this sustain them in the cold of winter, or is it a *bonne-bouche* before they get down to the serious banquet on the neighbours' bird-tables?

FEBRUARY

I SPEND THE least time out of doors in February. Its short days and grey weather collude with what feels like obstinacy in the natural world. Buds remain stubbornly tight, most birds lie low: insects are grounded or hidden.

Out on my local patch where north Worcestershire and south Staffordshire intertwine, the weed-free farmland is green with winter cereals, the hedges trimmed as neatly as in town. Finding wildlife here can be a challenge, though when I do look some birds are more obvious. Ravens are cronking over their favourite pine wood and may already be sitting on eggs. In sunny spells buzzards mew and dive over the valley, contesting invisible aerial boundaries.

If I want spectacle, I must travel south. High water in the Severn and Avon valleys pushes the swollen rivers across the fields and conjures flocks of wildfowl seemingly from nowhere. Choose your time and in late afternoons short-eared owls glide like wraiths over the tussocky hams, flood-meadows where, within some naturalists' living memory, corncrakes rasped in summer. Owls have become a February preoccupation for me, the time when annual hopes of calling long-eared owls resurface and once again I vow to track down their breathless hoots in chilly plantations.

As February matures and spring drops hints, there may even be sunshine. Queen bumblebees struggle from their nests of moss and plunder the early crocuses. In the garden, the annual amphibian orgy begins in the pond, a pulsing rumble that is spring's drumroll. After a winter of insect starvation, I'm desperate for anything new, even a pair of strange flies skirmishing on their holly-leaf arena.

Spring is at the door though and I relish every sign that confirms it: the laser-sharp chants of great tits, the green goblets of stinking hellebore flowers and the stellar blooms of whitlow-grass grouting the cracks of the town-centre pavements.

B.W.

IN SOME FEBRUARYS, it seems as if winter will never end, with snow and ice making life difficult for us, and potentially fatal for wild creatures.

In others, winter doesn't seem to have come at all: snowdrops and daffodils line roadside verges, song thrushes and chaffinches sing from dawn to dusk, and even the odd butterfly or bumblebee ventures out from its winter hiding-place to sample the unseasonably warm air and, if it is lucky, some early spring nectar.

When I was a lad (cue Monty Python Four Yorkshiremen sketch), we had proper winters. Even in the soft suburban setting where I grew up, on the outskirts of London in the mild and balmy Thames Valley, we always had snow – sometimes lots of it. Mornings dawned with a shiver, and only the gradual onset of lighter evenings, which we noticed because we walked home from school at the same time every day, told us that spring would – eventually – arrive.

Nowadays, here in rural Somerset, I rarely need to scrape the ice from my car windscreen – even in February, traditionally the coldest month in the calendar. I sit and write serenaded by a chorus of birdsong: not just the usual robins and wrens, but dunnocks, great tits and even the occasional mewing from a buzzard soaring high overhead.

Sceptics will tell you that this is not due to climate change, but simply an example of the natural variability of the (notoriously fickle) British weather. But those of us old enough to recall the winters of the past know that something odd is happening; something that is likely to have incalculable consequences for our habitats and wildlife.

In the meantime, I long for the Februarys of my childhood: cold, bleak and yet – with those lighter evenings – hinting at a change to come.

S.M.

RAVEN

1 February

A chill winter's day, with a glowering, grey sky. Hardly the time, I reflect, that any creature's thoughts will be turning to courtship and raising a family.

But when two jet-black birds pass overhead, each uttering a deep, throaty call that resonates in the very depths of my body, I know that even now, in the dead of winter, the breeding season has begun.

Ravens are one of the first birds to start to breed, soon after the turn of the year. They can do so because they mainly feed on carrion; and in cold weather there are always enough dead creatures to provide food for their growing youngsters.

When I see a raven flying, it's the bird's sheer size that really strikes me. Ravens are the Big Daddy of the passerines, or perching birds – the tribe that encompasses more than half of the world's bird species. Weighing in at well over a kilo – more than 250 times as much as our smallest bird, the goldcrest – they are not easily intimidated, even by our resident buzzard, who utters a plaintive mew whenever their dark shadows appear.

Try saying the raven's name in a suitably deep voice and its origin becomes clear: it is onomatopoeic in origin, deriving from that croaking call. A group of ravens has some unusual collective names, including 'a conspiracy' and 'an unkindness', which hint at the many superstitions connected with the bird.

The raven is the very first bird mentioned in the Bible, in the Book of Genesis, when Noah sends forth a raven, 'which went forth to and fro, until the waters were dried up from off the earth'. They feature frequently in the literary canon, too: I recall them in Shakespeare (greeting Duncan on his fateful entrance to Macbeth's castle), Tolkien and Stephen King, and they are also a continual presence as messengers in George R.R. Martin's epic saga *Game of Thrones*. But my favourite literary raven appears in Edgar Allan Poe's eponymous poem, with its memorable refrain 'Quoth the raven, "Nevermore!"'

These all-black birds have usually been seen as a sign of the dark side of nature; confirmed by the way scavenging ravens would flock to battlefields to feed on the newly dead corpses, plucking out their eyes before tearing at their open wounds.

Ravens have long been regarded as a scarce bird in Britain, confined to the rocky crags of the uplands. But things are changing – and rapidly, thanks to a virtual end to the persecution and random killing of this mighty bird.

As a child I had to travel all the way to Snowdonia to see ravens; ten years ago, when I first moved to the West Country, I still rarely heard their call. Yet almost every day now I hear that deep, guttural sound echoing across the Somerset skies, bringing a touch of the wild to these tame lowland landscapes.

SNOWDROP

2 February

In a quiet corner of our village churchyard, something is stirring. Tiny green shoots, each with a specially toughened tip, are poking up through the stone-hard soil, in infinitesimal stages. Not for nothing is the snow-drop known in France as the *perce-neige*, or 'snow-piercer'.

For me, snowdrops are the first small but significant sign that winter may finally be reaching an end. I'm far from alone. Their early appearance – long before primroses, crocuses, or daffodils have deigned to show themselves – has endeared them to us for generations; only the bluebell rivals the snowdrop as Britain's favourite wild flower. Their faithful followers are known as galanthophiles after the plant's scientific name, *Galanthus nivalis*, which roughly translates as 'snowy milk-flower'.

So it may come as a shock to learn that these white, waxy blooms, hanging demurely in shady corners behind the gravestones in my local churchyard, may not be British at all. Though they were once considered native, botanists now believe they were brought here from continental Europe to adorn Elizabethan gardens.

The first definite record in the wild dates from the 1770s, when they were discovered in Gloucestershire and Worcestershire. If these showy flowers were truly native before then, it is hard to imagine them being overlooked.

They are now widespread, especially on the grassy banks of streams and rivers, whose floodwaters carry their bulbs downstream and re-plant them in fertile silt. In the west of England and the Welsh Marches, snow-drops crowd dingles and carpet winter woods, often near old dwellings.

So it's not surprising that we have taken them to our hearts, bestowing on them a fine selection of alternative names, including dewdrops, early white, Eve's tears and – my favourite – fair maids of February.

Tradition demands that, as symbols of purity, snowdrops first appear on 2 February to coincide with Candlemas, the Christian Feast of the Purification. But of course their timing is mainly governed by the prevailing weather at the time, especially soil temperatures. So the flowers can bloom at any time from December to early March.

The appearance of the first snowdrops has generally been a cause for celebration. Yet their white shade has a darker aspect: in many parts of Britain bringing snowdrops into a house was supposed to lead to the death of one of the inhabitants. So however tempting it may be to pick a bunch of these delicate little flowers, you might be best advised to leave them well alone.

RED ADMIRAL

3 February

For a moment, I do a double-take. It is as if the seasons have collided, and summer has somehow squeezed through a wormhole in the wardrobe and ended up, Narnia-like, in the very depths of winter.

Yet my eyes are not deceiving me: that really is a red admiral, the classic butterfly of summer. Its appearance is a signal that the world is changing, and the familiar cycles of nature are definitely being disrupted.

I usually see my first red admirals in April or May, and the last in October, when they flutter drunkenly around my garden, feasting on fermented juices from the last decaying apples of the Indian summer. These striking butterflies appear and disappear at roughly the same time as our swallows, which is hardly surprising, as they too are migrants to Britain.

In spring, red admirals travel here all the way from Spain or North Africa, the already pregnant females ready to lay their eggs and produce the new generation of butterflies we see later in the summer.

But this gaudy individual, its flashes of orange bringing colour to the otherwise monochrome winter season, has not travelled anything like as far. Having hatched from its pupa last autumn, when the weather turned chilly it must have sought shelter in one of our many sheds and outbuildings, and settled down to hibernate.

Now, on an unexpectedly sunny day in February, it has emerged, to find a very different world; a world where nectar is as scarce as water in the desert. Sadly, this colourful creature will almost certainly not survive.

But in a decade or more's time, it may have a better chance. For the winter survival of red admirals is a sure sign that climate change is no longer something we can ignore.

A warming world presents both opportunities and threats. It gives insects such as the red admiral the chance to get a head start in early spring. But as the seasons become more and more unpredictable, this may upset their complex life cycles, with equally unpredictable consequences. Meanwhile this vivid butterfly basks in the weak winter sun, its world temporarily turned upside down.

FLIES AND FRIENDS
4 February

It takes a striking fly to grab my attention in winter, but I couldn't fail to notice a stand-off between two spectacular orange flies semaphoring with their wings at each other on a garden holly leaf. It seemed odd behaviour, especially in February, and so I took photographs of them. Their wings were inked with dark blotches and they had curved, paint-brush clusters of bristles guarding their mouthparts, almost like the tusks of a wild boar. I'd never seen anything like them.

Once I would have given up trying to find out, but now, thanks to the Internet and the generosity of experts and colleagues, wildlife that we'd once have brushed aside as unidentifiable is now within our reach, and even fly ingénues like me have a new confidence. With a few hunches and a bit of detective work, from my computer desk only a few metres from the jousting flies themselves, I was able to nail my species as the gloriously named *Chetostoma curvinerve*. Of the 7,000 species of flies in the British Isles – and that number is growing annually – this is one of the least recorded in spite of its size and appearance.

It got better. With the help of some entomologist friends who directed me to the wonderful *Dipterists Digest*, a publication for fly-fanciers, I was delighted to discover that *C. curvinerve* is a very local insect in Britain, with only one previous record for Worcestershire. So far no one seems to know what it feeds on, but the observations that I read suggest that the adult flies probably overwinter in evergreen foliage such as holly or ivy and emerge on sunny days to display on the leaves.

All this from a casual sighting in the garden on a February day. It's a jungle out there, but, when it comes to identification and communication, modern naturalists have never had it so good, and there's no need even to leave the garden.

CHIFFCHAFF

5 February

A wetland in the coldest month of the year, when temperatures often fall well below freezing – and stay there. Ice grips land and water, leaving a small, unfrozen patch where a gaggle of ducks has gathered to feed. Summer is but a distant memory.

Perhaps not all that distant. I notice a movement at the base of the reeds, and seconds later a tiny bird emerges briefly, before vanishing back between the palisade of stems. Dull olive-brown above, paler below, with a short, slender bill: it's a chiffchaff, one of our smallest warblers. As I stand and watch over the next half-hour or so, it appears every few minutes, forages busily for food, and then squeezes back into the safe haven of the reeds. As it does so, it pumps its tail up and down, a behaviour often displayed by chiffchaffs.

Whenever I see this quintessential bird of spring at this chilly time of year it catches me by surprise. Warblers feed on insects, so the vast majority have by now migrated south, to warmer and more hospitable climes in Africa. Many chiffchaffs migrate too, but don't fly all that far, usually stopping in Spain or Portugal, where there are plenty of small insects to satisfy their appetite.

A few, though, stay put – like this creature foraging in a southern English reed-bed. It may seem like madness, but this apparent folly is a carefully calculated gamble. Do the benefits of staying put outweigh the risks, and how does that balance against the unknown dangers of a long, and potentially hazardous, journey south? The bird isn't making these calculations itself, of course: its migratory instinct is passed on in its genes and, if its parents were sedentary, the chances are that it will be as well.

One reason chiffchaffs can survive the winter here is that they are so small: ten centimetres long and weighing just nine grams, about the same as a £1 coin. This means they can survive by feeding on the tiniest of insects, such as midges and aphids, which can still be found among these thick clumps of reeds, even on the coldest day.

In the past couple of decades, the balance has tipped slightly in favour of the chiffchaffs that choose to stay put, especially those in the milder south-west. Climate change is bringing less severe winters; and this is good news for these little birds.

But survival is never certain, and there's always the risk of weather extremes, including the occasional really cold spell, with prolonged ice and snow. So the chiffchaff spends the short February days perpetually searching for food, to give it the energy it needs to survive until the spring.

GIRDLED SNAILS

6 February

Clinging to the window as I write is a snail. Among the climbing hydrangea twigs around the windows are more of them, small and nut brown. It's a mild February, but even so, a Mediterranean mollusc is not a creature I expect to see active in winter. But the girdled snail is very much at home here – and increasing in numbers.

Girdled snails are named for the pale band that encircles the largest whorl of their shells. This sleek go-faster stripe aligns with a sharp keel, which you can feel with your fingertips: these two features along with its small size, just a centimetre in diameter, make identification relatively simple.

It's native to various Mediterranean countries including Italy and France, but was first seen in the British Isles in Devon in 1945, and since the 1970s it has spread rapidly through England and Wales and has now travelled as far as Scotland. About ten years ago it turned up in my own garden in Stourbridge, brought in, I suspect, with nursery plants from local garden centres. That probably explains the rapid progress of a slow-moving mollusc, which is being shuttled around by unwitting gardeners.

Until recently I'd have said that it does little damage. Lately though, I have found several of them tucked up inside the tattered bells of fritillaries and in summer among rose blossoms, so they're not entirely blameless. But it's hard to begrudge such an attractive snail a meal or two.

NEWTS AT NIGHT

7 February

Something is stirring at the bottom of my garden. Unseen and unnoticed, an invasion is under way. On damp, mild, late winter nights, smooth newts are on the move.

For the past few months they have been in a state of hibernation: hiding beneath the stones in a nearby rockery, or in a pile of logs left behind the previous autumn. Here they are safe from predators, and can remain in a state of torpor while their little world is covered with snow or ice, and insect food is hard to find.

But now, as the mercury rises, a few invertebrates have been lured out on to the lawns and flowerbeds, and the newts are taking advantage of this sudden and unexpected source of food.

If the mild weather continues, these newts may even be tempted to begin breeding. They seek out water – a garden pond or a water-filled ditch, preferably free of fish, which will lay their eggs – and begin courtship.

Before they get down to business, male smooth newts undergo a dramatic change in their appearance. When on land during the autumn and winter, their unremarkable shape and colour mean they can easily be mistaken for lizards. But as soon as they reach water they transform into tiny dragons, growing a jagged crest along the length of their body and tail, blushing orange on their belly. Indeed they become so colourful that they are often mistaken for their larger and more glamorous relative, the great crested newt.

As if fired up by his smart new appearance, the male smooth newt then performs a courtship display that would put many birds to shame. He vibrates his tail, slapping it from side to side against his body. If the watching female is suitably impressed, she allows him to deposit a packet of his sperm, which she then absorbs into her body – a sexually loaded game of pass-the-parcel.

Mating can happen at any time of the day or night, and if the conditions are right a visit to a suitable pond will reveal dozens of mating newts, and in a week or two, females laying several hundred eggs, each of which will be carefully concealed in the fold of a leaf.

They hatch between ten and twenty days later, and the tadpoles (known as efts) stay in their birth pond until they finally turn into adults later in the summer. At least, that's what happens to the lucky ones; most get eaten.

OFFICE SPIDER
8 February

Returning to the computer this evening, I have an audience: a plump, honey-coloured spider suspended in its silken hammock below the BT junction box. At first I suspect it's a stowaway, brought in with the tender garden plants I've saved from the cold, but this one looks a little different.

I catch it in a glass tube for closer inspection of its back – many spiders hang upside down in their webs, so you can only see the undersides. Its abdomen has a lapidary gleam, as shiny as tiger agate and attractively dimpled. After consulting books and websites, I am reasonably happy that it's *Steatoda bipunctata*, a close relative of the false widow spider *Steatoda grossa*, which has garnered so much unwarranted press hysteria. Some *Steatoda* spiders can pierce human skin, though they are very unlikely to, and only a small minority of people have a bad reaction.

Steatoda bipunctata is happy in houses and I'm happy to have it aboard. I return it to the overhang and it hauls itself rapidly along a thread into the shadow beneath the junction box. Within an hour, though, it is back in view, slung under its sheet-web, a silent monitor of my late-night efforts.

SONG THRUSH
9 February

The sound, when it comes, is so familiar I feel as if I am being greeted by an old friend. It's been more than half a year since I last heard him, but the song thrush singing outside my bedroom window is, it seems, in a talkative mood. I listen as he pours out phrase after measured phrase, as if engaged in conversation with someone else, just out of my earshot.

Few birds – apart, perhaps, from the nightingale and skylark – are quite so defined by their sound as the song thrush. Perhaps this is because his diction is so human in tone: whereas the blackbird and robin are musical, the song thrush is chatty and loquacious, almost as if he is having a good gossip.

He utters each phrase, then repeats it – usually modified a little – and then sings the original phrase again in a slightly different tone. For some listeners, this reiteration can seem rather tedious, while others regard it as one of the most beautiful of all our birdsongs. I am in the smaller (and, I like to think, more select) group who far prefer it to that of the more popular, but to my mind rather predictable, blackbird. The blackbird may be Mozart, but with his almost mathematical patterns, the song thrush is surely Johann Sebastian Bach.

But whatever you think of the thrush's song, you cannot help but admire his sheer persistence. Having begun to sing in the middle of winter, he will carry on all the way through the breeding season until finally falling silent in late June or early July. By then my garden and the surrounding landscape will have been transformed – and hopefully there will be another brood of four newly fledged song thrushes in the neighbourhood.

WHITLOW-GRASS

10 February

When I walk into town, I either have to cross the ring road through the underpass or brave three busy traffic lanes. Today, dithering on the kerb as I wait to cross, I'm distracted by a strip of tiny white stars where the gap between pavement and kerbstone is crammed with flowers of annual whitlow-grass.

Each bloom is two or three millimetres wide, its four petals split almost in half – you could fit half a dozen plants on a penny. This is whitlow-grass, also known as shadflower and nailwort. Here on this grimy verge, it's a heart-warming herald of spring.

There's a delicacy and economy to the whitlow-grass's appearance that rivals any cosseted greenhouse Alpine. Instead of rocky Swiss crags, whitlow-grass has chosen concrete: a constellation of over a hundred diminutive plants has burst into bloom on the bulwarks of a multi-storey car park. For this plant, anywhere that can supply moisture and scrape together a few grains of soil can provide a home but show it a well-nourished flowerbed and it turns up its nose. When it comes to nutrients, whitlow-grass is parsimonious.

It is a member of the cress family, and its strategy is to germinate in autumn, ride out winter as a rosette of leaves and burst into bloom with the first sunshine of spring. This winter has been so mild that I found plants in bloom in early January, but late February and March are the best times to see it en masse.

By flowering early and scattering its seeds in May, the whitlow-grass avoids desiccation when its miniature rock gardens dry out, and over-shading by bigger plants. This habit also avoids the over-zealous weed control that accompanies the municipal efforts for Britain in Bloom. The gaudy petunias and jazzy fuchsias of midsummer may appeal to the judges, but for me the real show, unnoticed by most, is already over.

WILLOWS

11 February

I live in a watery world – the Somerset Levels – where reflections are a constant feature of the winter scene. The best time to appreciate them is just before dusk, when the setting sun illuminates the whole width of the view with a dazzling golden light.

And of all the reflections I see on this winter's afternoon, the willow trees are those most connected to this unique landscape. The twigs reach out into the water from their gnarled, twisted branches, as if they were trying to grasp something hidden in the shallows below.

Willows are not only beautiful, in their own quiet way, they are useful, too. Since human beings first settled on these islands we have turned them into baskets and furniture, cricket bats and even coffins.

As our ancestors knew, the bitter-tasting bark of the willow tree was a cure against the 'ague', or malaria. Scientists eventually discovered that the active ingredient was acetylsalicylic acid, better known as aspirin.

But today, these ghostly reflections take me back to my early childhood. I lift my head to see the pussy willow catkins, which we used to give to my nan on her birthday every 11 February. For me, these strange, furry objects always seemed to hold the promise of spring.

Then a gust of wind rustles through the bare twigs, rippling the water below, and my distant memories dissolve in the vanishing reflection.

FERAL GOATS
12 February

The Somerset town of Cheddar is famous for two things: its eponymous cheese and the geological marvel of Cheddar Gorge.

Standing in the narrow gap between the gorge's tall, towering cliffs and looking up towards the sky, I find it hard to imagine that any animal would choose to live in these bleak, uncompromising surroundings, especially on this icy February day.

But almost at the very top of the steep, grassy hillside, clambering over the slippery grey limestone rocks, is a small herd of animals. From this distance they remind me of a flock of feral pigeons, sporting their usual motley array of shades from dirty white, through greys and browns, to black. But then one of them raises its head to reveal a pair of horns and I realise that I am looking at the feral goats of Cheddar.

Not just Cheddar, of course. Feral goats – animals originally domesticated that have since 'gone wild' – can be found in rocky places all over Britain, including Snowdonia and the Scottish Highlands. I first came across them on the Devon island of Lundy, where I watched them clinging on to the edges of steep sea-cliffs with an insouciance bordering on the insane. Both males and females sport horns, but the males are slightly larger than the females, and are more prone to fighting among themselves.

The oldest feral population, in Northumberland's Cheviot Hills, is thought to descend from animals brought here from south-eastern Europe by our Neolithic ancestors. But these Cheddar goats are a much more recent arrival, introduced to stop the proliferation of scrub on the walls of the gorge, which was leading to dangerous rock falls. Today they look as if they have been here for centuries.

FROZEN RHYNES

13 February

By the middle of February, the globe has shifted just enough to make cycle rides before breakfast possible again. But today I must be more careful than usual, for a thin film of ice covers the surface of the country lanes behind my home – a lethal mixture of water and mud, which could easily unseat the unwary rider.

I am travelling more slowly than usual as I turn the corner by a bridge over a rhyne. Just as the Eskimos were always supposed to have fifty different words for snow, and the Scots have several hundred terms for different kinds of rain, so we in Somerset have an extensive vocabulary to describe the various types of ditches dug to drain this watery land, and keep homes and fields from flooding. A rhyne (pronounced 'reen', not 'rine') is a medium-sized ditch whose bankside vegetation must be cut every year to allow the water to run through.

But there's no water running today: the surface of the rhyne is mostly covered with ice. Further down, though, a small pool of water remains ice-free, next to which I can see a small, slender bird. A grey wagtail – the name is a misnomer, as its most prominent feature is a bright flash of yellow under the tail – is searching for whatever tiny invertebrates may be hiding in the mud.

It sees me, but doesn't seem all that bothered. On a day such as this, survival is the only thing on its mind. Sadly the chances are, if this cold spell continues, that it will be dead within days.

POLECAT

14 February

At a glance, it looked like a fur stole stretched out on the tarmac. It wasn't the first I'd noticed on this busy stretch of road leading south over the sandy farmland outside Stourbridge, on the fringes of the industrial Black Country. Had it been flung from a vintage Bentley by champagne-fuelled revellers returning late from a country ball, in a scene reminiscent of F. Scott Fitzgerald? Not a frequent sight in Stourbridge, but then again, neither was this rarest of mammals.

What I'd seen was the flattened remains of a polecat, foiled by traffic in its quest for a mate. The polecat's return is one of British wildlife's greatest success stories. These sleek, brown mustelids with pale masks are related to stoats and pine martens, and were once widespread throughout large areas of the British Isles. But their penchant for poultry and wild game – the name polecat derives from the French *poule-chat* – invited heavy persecution, so by the mid-eighteenth century they had been forced to retrench to the hills of mid-Wales, where gamekeepers were thinner on the ground.

Gamekeepers themselves were thinned out during the two world wars and in their absence, under cover of night, the polecats came back. So secretive are they that it was some time before the full extent of their spread was appreciated.

There were other reasons for the confusion over their return. The domesticated form of the polecat is known as the ferret, and although it occurs in several colours including albino, it has been back-crossed by breeders with wild polecats to produce 'polecat-ferrets'. These can look very much like the wild polecat and escaped animals have certainly accounted for some of the road casualties that have turned up. I also once saw a hybrid loping along a pavement in broad daylight near my home.

But in the south and west of Worcestershire, mammalogist Dr Johnny Birks has investigated traffic victims and noted their vital statistics, in particular crucial skull measurements. In an operation best conducted with a clothes-peg on the nose – polecats were once known as foumarts (foul martens) because of the ripe muskiness that cloaks their bodies – he was able to prove that the real, wild polecat had arrived in force and was spreading eastwards.

By trapping wild polecats and fitting them with radio collars, Dr Birks discovered that they fed and bred regularly around farms and houses. Some even raised their young, known as kits, in dens under suburban decking in Droitwich and Kidderminster. He also found that they slept by day in rabbit burrows, ranged over one or two square kilometres and led mainly solitary lives outside the breeding season. In late winter and early spring, males range in search of mates, crossing roads on which they often come to grief.

Only once have I seen a live animal locally. Early one morning by a sedge-bed where I waited for a glimpse of a water rail, I noticed a sudden movement in the tussocks and there was a polecat, the first genuinely wild specimen I'd ever seen alive, its pale mask framed by chocolate fur, grizzled with beads of dew. Then, just as suddenly, it was gone, precious evidence that in the right circumstances even the rarest creatures can return.

ROE DEER

15 February

They always appear when I least expect it. I'm taking a quiet stroll along a reed-lined drove, untroubled by anything more active than the odd wren trilling out of sight, when out of nowhere an animal leaps across my path, followed immediately by a second.

I recover my composure just in time to watch two roe deer as they run away – well, not exactly run, but jump away on spring-loaded legs, like antelopes on the African savannah. This strange habit is known as stotting, from a Scots term meaning 'walk with a bounce'. As they depart, the white patches on their backsides shine like beacons in the dim light of this dull winter's afternoon.

Sometimes I have less intimate but perhaps more satisfying encounters with roe deer. It may be when I am taking a winter's walk through a wood, or cycling along a country lane. In the distance a head pops up, followed by another: a pair of roe deer is staring straight back at me.

This is one of only two native species of deer in Britain, the other being the much larger red deer. Actually, even that statement is contentious: roe deer were hunted to extinction in England and Wales by the early eighteenth century, and those we see today are probably the descendants of animals introduced here from mainland Europe.

They are certainly doing very well across much of rural Britain, though the boom in numbers does mean they are causing problems on some nature reserves, as their browsing can damage the woodland understorey.

This raises a tricky question: when does a native mammal become a pest? Roe deer have no natural enemies, now that lynxes, wolves and bears no longer roam our countryside, and shooting has also declined across much of their range. So will we eventually need to cull these attractive creatures for their own good?

In the meantime, though, I can still enjoy the sight of a pair of roe deer dashing away from me on this chilly day, their breath hanging like smoke in the winter's air.

FEBRUARY BLUES

16 February

There are very few days when I go out without seeing something interesting, but in February I often have to make a special effort. Today, torn between staying warm and the need for exercise, I shrug off the hibernal gloom and trudge the rectangle of green lanes that encircle a patch of local farmland. The mist-laden air softens the sound of main-road traffic. A lone crow complains from a hedgetop and I'm reminded of the saying of her father's often quoted by Miriam Rothschild, that if we carry on simplifying our countryside, the only survivors will be 'crows and bluebottles'.

Today, it's too chilly for bluebottles and the hedges have been cut by the farmer's contractors who've punished them with mechanical trimmers, leaving a floss of frayed twig-ends, as low as waist height. In places the hawthorns are reduced to a few stunted, squared-off remnants; you could drive a couple of combine harvesters through the gaps between them.

At what point does a hedge cease to be a hedge? This pitiful remnant has no function any more and yet someone still takes the trouble to flail it mercilessly for no apparent economic gain. It reeks of vindictiveness, and the pessimism that sometimes assails me in late winter begins to assert itself.

Naturalists have too often been portrayed, or have portrayed themselves, as joyous optimists. To some extent that is true, but they are also keepers of the national conscience as far as wildlife is concerned. I suspect that I'm one of the few people who notice how the wildlife of this place has changed.

On this monochrome day, with the cold air seeping through my clothes, I'm haunted by the ghosts of corn buntings that used to jingle from these hedgerow oaks, the wailing of lapwings and the creaking of grey partridges, all of which now seem part of another world. They disappeared in the 1980s and early 1990s, in line with national trends, which intensified farming, changed sowing and reaping timetables and increased herbicide and insecticide use. They could return if we cared enough, but they won't, because we don't. As a nation our demands for food production way outstrip our concern for what is lost. And so it is that the remorseless decline of many species continues.

Such reveries don't improve my spirits on this bleak afternoon. But then the mood changes. A dark arrow hurtles across the field, shadowing the lowest contours with ease, jinking in and out of view. It pitches on to the top of a flailed hedge and I know even before I raise my binoculars that it's a merlin. Only one or two of these diminutive falcons turn up locally in most years, so this is cause for celebration, a visitor from Scotland or maybe Iceland, finding refuge in these empty fields. The bare landscape is made liveable again by this mercurial bird, whose fleeting visit has banished the gloom, for a while at least.

IVORY GULL AND PORPOISE
17 February

February can be an unrewarding month and that leads to hankerings for more exotic fare. At this time of year, a rare bird can provide relief, but it needs to be a very special one. So it was that in 2002 I drove west along winding roads through the Welsh hills to see a dead porpoise and a tracker of polar bears.

We arrived at Black Rock beach in Porthmadog to find a large crowd of people gathered around the cetacean's corpse, which was clearly old and had split open like a ripe melon. It was surprisingly small, just four feet long, but was the centre of attention because it had attracted a very special vagrant – an adult ivory gull. Within minutes, we saw the bird approaching distantly along the tideline, spectrally white and more like a dove than a gull. Showing no fear, it flew towards us, settled near the porpoise just a few metres from its watchers (cue breathless gasps) and waddled on short black legs to its buffet, from which it tore small strips of meat and blubber.

Ivory gulls breed on pack ice in the High Arctic and are the world's most northerly breeding birds. They are very rare in the British Isles, and when one does appear, about once a year on average, it is usually a black-spotted youngster with the trademark dirty face, created by sooty plumage around its bill. Our dazzling white bird at Porthmadog was special because it was the first adult to turn up since 1954.

Pure in colour they may be, but ivory gulls are ghoulish feeders, specialising in dead seals and cetaceans. This one may well have been scavenging at polar bear kills a few weeks before. Quite how it found a small porpoise on the Welsh coast is hard to tell: perhaps it followed the drifting corpse south.

Whatever its provenance it was popular with photographers and ridiculously tame, presumably because it had met very few humans in its Arctic homeland. Twitching usually leaves me disappointed, but this act of crowd participation was different, a joint celebration of an extraordinary bird which drew in dog-walkers, families out for a Sunday stroll on the beach and other local residents. As often happens when an accessible rarity turns up, there was a sense of shared local pride in this stranger, which had singled out a Porthmadog beach for its short stay.

LIVERWORTS

18 February

One winter day a few years ago, I found myself in a market-garden among a straggle of twitchers scanning the remnants of wilting runner beans for an Arctic redpoll, a rare northern finch that has only appeared a handful of times in Worcestershire.

When I arrived, about thirty people had gathered in a corner of a damp field and were scanning the flocks of lesser redpolls among the crop, hopeful of finding something greyer and frostier-looking. After a frustrating hour, my attention began to wander and hopes of the rarity showing up foundered. In the event though, a rarity did turn up – one that we had all been trampling over as we patrolled the field edges.

Glancing down, I noticed gobbets of tiny bubbles, like emerald cuckoo-spit almost underfoot on the wet ground between the strawberry plants. They were less than a centimetre across, but something reminded me of photographs I'd seen taken in a nearby rhubarb field. Could this be the elusive Texas balloonwort?

Balloonworts are a type of liverwort: a simple plant that thrives in damp places like moss. Those liverworts that you find on arable land or on garden paths usually form a leafy plate or have lobes growing close to the ground.

One of the commonest is *Marchantia*, which often coats the soil in damp plant pots or on compacted soil in greenhouses. Female plants sprout spore-bearing structures that look like small cocktail umbrellas and are easy to identify. Other liverworts creep on marshy ground, their leaves ruched into frills like terrestrial seaweed, or drape their translucent leaves over wet logs and stones.

Balloonwort is different. It's an annual liverwort, which is most conspicuous in winter. It grows on arable land that isn't over-disturbed and which hasn't been exposed to herbicide. For this reason, it's now quite rare and mainly found in places such as market-gardens or the bulb-fields of Cornwall and the Isles of Scilly. The ones I found were the third county records and the landowner, a market-gardener, was pleased to see them.

Each tiny plant was made up of hundreds of minute inflated pods, which protect the male and female liverwort's sex organs. They're a connoisseur's plant, rare and short-lived; and though scarcely more common locally than an Arctic redpoll, failed to impress the birders. In a few weeks, the plants' tiny balloons would dry out and release their spores, unseen and largely unappreciated.

LONG-EARED OWL

19 February

Tonight I'm planning a trip. Nowhere far-flung – just a few miles down the road – but into the unknown. It's an outing that will almost certainly be unsuccessful, but has to be done. When you've watched a local patch for four decades, there aren't many surprises left, but one bird remains a nagging uncertainty.

In March 1976 a birding classmate and I set off to explore a small copse near my house which was off the public paths and rarely visited for fear of gamekeepers. Both of us were relatively inexperienced, so when two long-winged shapes lifted silently from the trees and floated off across the surrounding fields, we were perplexed and naively suspected they might be woodcock. But what we didn't know then was that woodcock never rise silently; what we had seen were our first long-eared owls as they departed in silent soft-winged flight.

Later we found out that the winter of 1975–6 was a record year for these rare owls in the West Midlands, when the very few residents were boosted by continental visitors. Long-ears are among our most elusive breeding birds, mysterious night-hunters, rarely seen by day. They are commoner in northern and eastern England and Scotland. In Ireland, where the bigger and stronger tawny owl is absent, they are more widespread.

Here in Worcestershire, they are very special finds and notoriously elusive, though whispers reach me occasionally. I was once shown a recuperating bird in an aviary, which had been picked up as a traffic casualty from a local lane in June; surely a sign that birds may be breeding.

This evening, a friend told me that he'd heard one hooting in a belt of dark pines just three miles from my house. I went to investigate. There are no rights of way through this forbidding plantation of Corsican pines, one of my least favourite trees, whose dull green brushes of long needles sprout from tall, featureless trunks. In February and March male long-eared owls proclaim their territories with a low hoot, often described as the sound made by blowing across a bottle-top. After making a slightly illegal manoeuvre, I found myself shivering beneath the huge pines as the wind soughed through a million needles.

I was hoping it, or my chattering teeth, wouldn't mask the sound I'd come to hear. Perhaps it did because there was nothing, not even the quavering hoot of a tawny owl.

And so the mystery persists but there's a certain romance in ignorance. Each time I drive past the dark woods, I imagine that somewhere in their depths, fierce black and orange eyes are scanning the forest floor and a pair of ear-tufts is silhouetted like satanic horns against the rising moon. And perhaps that is enough.

LESSER CELANDINE

20 February

A winter's walk through a woodland can sometimes be a rather dismal affair; apart from a clump of snowdrops and bunches of hazel catkins, I can detect few if any signs of floral life.

Yet just as I am giving up hope that spring will ever arrive, the sun emerges from behind a cloud, and tiny, yellow, star-shaped flowers miraculously begin to open all around me. The lesser celandine is in bloom.

Apart perhaps from the snowdrop and primrose, no other plant is so closely linked with the onset of spring as the lesser celandine. Its shiny leaves appear first in early December, a welcome touch of greenery in a drab winter's landscape. Then, at last, the flowers emerge too, tiny globules of yellow scattered across a backdrop of green.

The name 'celandine' is thought to derive from the Latin meaning 'swallow', suggesting that the flower appears at the same time as these birds' welcome return from Africa. However, this is more likely to refer to the greater celandine, a similar-looking (but unrelated) species that appears from April onwards.

I don't see any swallows today – indeed it will be a month or more before they twitter under English skies. But I am seeing celandines: aptly so, as I am in the Hampshire village of Selborne, home of eighteenth-century curate and naturalist Gilbert White and today – 21 February – was the usual date when White first saw lesser celandines in the woods above his home.

But this was more than 200 years ago, when winters were far longer and harder than they are nowadays. Looking at the carpets of yellow around me, I suspect that these particular flowers emerged at least a week ago, perhaps even longer. This is confirmed by the observations of countless 'spring-watchers' up and down the country; the average date for the celandine's emergence has shifted earlier by about a fortnight.

This attractive little flower also inspired other writers, including D.H. Lawrence, J.R.R. Tolkien and C.S. Lewis. Wordsworth dedicated three whole poems to it, and when he died it was proposed that a celandine be carved on his grave at Grasmere in the Lake District. Unfortunately, though, the stonemason was no botanist, and depicted the greater celandine by mistake.

HOODED MERGANSER

21 February

Many people visit Corsham in Wiltshire for its lichened stone buildings, including the imposing Corsham Court, whose parkland was designed by Lancelot 'Capability' Brown. Today, though, we are in search of a very rare bird. Or possibly not.

Of all the species to trouble the British Birds Rarities Committee, the 'ten rare men' who pronounce on the identification and provenance of rare birds, the hooded merganser is one of the most controversial. Its identification is rarely a problem: this is a dapper little duck, the drake crisply black, white and chestnut with a wonderful coiffure of feathers which he fans when displaying to the brown female. Both sexes have narrow bills armed with tiny serrations, which help them to grasp their fishy prey. They're native to North America, where they live on wooded lakes and pools.

Most of the North American hooded mergansers migrate south in autumn and very rarely, disorientated vagrants perhaps blown off-course by hurricanes, cross the Atlantic and turn up in places such as Iceland or the Azores. Here they are eagerly sought after by twitchers. But hooded mergansers can also occasionally be found at large in the British Isles, and that's where the headaches begin.

These attractive birds are widely kept in wildfowl collections where they breed well. Inevitably, some escape and unless their captive origins can be proven, by rings or clipped wings, the escapees cloud the pattern of genuine vagrancy; so much so that between 1831 and 2001 there were no accepted records of genuine wild North American hooded mergansers having reached the British Isles. After this astonishing 170-year wait the British Ornithologists' Union, which presides over the British List, grudgingly relented, announcing that a female or immature bird that had arrived on the Outer Hebrides in October 2000 was, on the balance of probabilities, a wild bird.

Their reasoning: the North American population had increased and the merganser had turned up after westerly storms, which also delivered a selection of other North American ducks. But in the absence of a ring fitted in the US, or DNA evidence, balance of probability is as good as it gets. Since 2001 another half-dozen or so hooded mergansers have been added to the UK tally, none of them proven beyond reasonable doubt.

But that doesn't stop birders dreaming. Which is why, as we approached Corsham Lake, we had no delusions that we were about to see a wild hooded merganser. This female had been reported two days earlier and was entertaining a huddle of hopeful birders, bobbing jauntily in the wake of two goosanders, close relatives: a good start. I asked a couple of birders why they had travelled sixty miles to see a likely escapee and they cautiously replied that they were in the area anyway. Others were clearly there for 'insurance purposes', hoping to add it to their lists later, if in future the bird is accepted by the rarity assessors as a genuine vagrant. That began to look increasingly unlikely as the small, ginger-maned duck approached the shore, intent on committing the ultimate betrayal.

'Coming to bread' is damning evidence that a bird has been tamed by captivity and this one was happy to linger with a pack of crust-munching mallards, approaching within a few metres of its watchers. Cue drooping of shoulders, as the last vestiges of hope faded, and the birders trudged back to their cars. It wasn't over yet though. Since then, online twitchers have tied themselves in knots, trying to justify its wildness: the bird was unringed and fully winged, flying across the lake at one point, they maintained, and may have consorted with mallards for fish they had stirred up.

It's a dilemma that faces some hardened twitchers, but is incomprehensible to many people. Escapees or not, hooded mergansers are extremely beautiful birds, and our day was enriched by seeing it. It shouldn't cause the ten rare men much problem. Then again, three days after we saw it, like Lewis Carroll's Snark, it 'softly and suddenly vanished away'. I wonder . . .

TREE BUMBLEBEE

22 February

Today something small and furry is moving through the garden crocuses, but this is no traditional harbinger. Time was, I'd expect the buff-tailed bumblebee to be the first bumblebee of spring, but for the last few years things have been different.

Naturalists are by and large an accommodating bunch, though not all arrivals are welcomed unreservedly. This particular addition, however, has been greeted with open arms. In 2001 the first tree bumblebee – native to continental Europe – was found on a Hampshire bramble patch, and its arrival preceded an extraordinary colonisation.

My first Worcestershire sighting of the tree bumblebee was in 2009: a rather tatty worker, which I photographed with great excitement in a flowery meadow. Little did I know that in two years' time they'd be knocking on my office window, the commonest bumblebees in my urban garden, and that by 2013 this welcome invader would have reached most corners of England and Wales and crossed the Scottish border. In 2014 one was seen in Ireland.

When tree bumblebees first appear in late February or early March, the queens, which have overwintered in sheltered places, are on the hunt for nectar, eager to build their energy for the business of founding a new colony. They are handsome creatures with a unique colour combination among British bumblebees. On their thorax is a thick pile of ginger hairs, which contrast with the black abdomen and white tail.

They are what bee specialists call polylectic, which means that they take nectar and pollen from a wide range of flowers. It's this ability to forage almost anywhere that has helped to fuel their rapid spread and they seem to be as happy in gardens as in the wider countryside – which makes them the perfect insect to look out for in late February.

Unlike other British bumblebees, which nest in the ground, tree bumblebees build their colonies in holes in trees, in disused bird-boxes or under roof-spaces – and with an early start in spring can have two generations each year. The queens we see in late winter will produce female workers in spring, males by late May and further queens which will repeat the cycle in high summer.

Being productive and not too choosy in your nesting and feeding habits is a recipe for rapid expansion, so as a result the tree bumblebee is bucking the trend of decline in our native bees. As it bustles among the early spring flowers, it is an insect to celebrate.

GOOSANDER

23 February

The Severn is in spate at Bewdley, its tumbling waters carrying a cargo of woody debris as it roars around the pillars of Thomas Telford's stone bridge in the town centre. Mallards and mute swans keep to the water's edge and the anglers have stayed indoors, but there are three fishers out in the main current, luminously pale goosanders, riding the turbulence with ease.

To someone who began his birding here in the 1970s, this is still a remarkable sight. Back then goosanders were very rare in this northern corner of Worcestershire found only locally across most of the West Midlands. Now, not only are there more birds but they even breed on the Severn here: broods of russet and white ducklings have appeared just north of Bewdley in the last two years. During the same period, a small flock has appeared on my local park lake, where they cruise magisterially among the mallards, apparently oblivious to dog-walkers.

Drake goosanders are spectacularly beautiful, their torpedo-shaped bodies white with a hint of peach, their diamond-shaped heads glossed bottle-green. Females and youngsters are greyish with white necks and reddish heads. But their standout feature is the bill, long and thin with a hooked tip and rimmed with tooth-like serrations.

Goosanders belong to the group of ducks known as sawbills, a strong clue to their fishy diet. They dive for these in the main current, when touch must be more useful to them than sight. Where the silt-laden floodwaters are the colour and consistency of melted chocolate, goosanders nose under overhanging banks for sheltering fish. On Windermere, I have even seen them jostling with mallards for bread.

Just why they've increased as breeding birds over the last forty years isn't clear. Cleaner rivers and warmer winters may have helped, but whatever the reason, they are sensational birds to watch, whether in flotillas on a calm lake or surfing the rapids of a swollen river.

COLD-WEATHER MOVEMENTS
24 February

Britain's weather is notoriously changeable, so it's no surprise when I wake up on a winter's day to find frost covers every available surface, an icy Arctic wind whips across the countryside, and the weather forecasters are predicting heavy falls of snow.

But every cloud has a silver lining, and I wonder if this may provide an opportunity to see one of the greatest winter spectacles in nature: the cold-weather movement of birds as they flee the freezing weather, and head south and west in search of a reliable, ice-free supply of food.

So with the mercury well below freezing, I wrap up, head outdoors and simply look up. My timing is perfect: there are flocks of winter thrushes, skylarks and waders, all heading in the same direction – away from the oncoming weather.

In this bright, clear winter sky, their shapes are etched against the vivid blue: loose, loping flocks of fieldfares, accompanied by groups of smaller, more compact redwings, their brick-red wing-patches flashing like warning lights as they pass low overhead. Purposeful squadrons of starlings are accompanied by flocks of larger birds – lapwings, winking black and white, and sharp-winged golden plovers – all fleeing as fast as they can from the bad weather to come.

Having seen these birds, I can be sure that within twenty-four hours – maybe much sooner – the landscape will be covered in a thick eiderdown of snow; and that those birds that have chosen to remain here will be struggling to find food.

What happens next depends partly on how long the cold spell lasts. Sometimes the weather switches back as rapidly as it came, bringing Atlantic depressions, milder air and showery rain. If so the travellers will soon return to the homes they left only a short time before.

But if the high-pressure system gets stuck, and bitter winds, ice and snow persist, they will be gone for the rest of the winter. Fields and hedgerows that were packed with noisy, quarrelsome flocks will remain silent until late March or April.

BUFF-TAILED BUMBLEBEE

25 February

We're on the woodland edge near a sunlit churchyard. A buff-tailed bumblebee, huge and furry with yellow bands on her thorax and abdomen, is nosing the leaf litter around a tree-stump. She's a founding queen, the only survivor of last year's colony and has spent winter snug below ground in a mossy hole, protected from frosts, mould and marauding mammals. It is she who will begin the new colony and so, carrying her cargo of stored sperm from last summer's nuptial fling, she is looking for a nest-site.

She crawls into each crevice with the discernment of the pickiest house-hunter, rejecting one potential des res after another. What she's looking for is a dry, sheltered hideaway below ground where wind, rain and predators can't reach her brood. These are early days, though, and before the real business of nest founding begins, she has to build up energy. A patch of winter-flowering heather near the church is an ideal fuel-stop where she joins other buff-tails and honeybees greedily sucking the nectar from the tubular white flowers. Soon they will begin to build their empires, and their offspring will go on to pollinate spring and summer blooms.

WINTER REDPOLLS

26 February

An alder wood alongside a river or stream is a good place to search for insects, especially for a flock of hungry birds wondering where their next meal is going to come from. It is a late winter's afternoon when I head out to look for them.

As always, the first thing I notice is the usual feeding flock of great, blue and long-tailed tits, frantically calling to keep in touch with one another as they move purposefully from tree to tree.

But if I lean back and look up, in the topmost branches there is another, tight little group of birds, feeding methodically on the alder cones. Some are siskins: tiny, green and yellow finches, their plumage lined with black like a child wearing face-paint. But others are a plainer brown, with a finer, streakier plumage. As they hang upside down from the twigs, I can just about make out the small but prominent crimson patch on their forehead that gives these birds their name: redpolls.

Redpolls are a group of small finches found right across the northern latitudes of Europe, Asia and North America, some living way beyond the Arctic Circle.

The ones we see most commonly in Britain are smaller and darker than their cousins, and are known as lesser redpolls. But in winter it's always worth taking a close look at any redpoll flock, for there may be other kinds of redpoll present too.

One snowy winter's day back in the early 1990s, by the River Wensum on the outskirts of Norwich, I remember seeing larger, paler birds from continental Europe, known as mealy redpolls, and two even paler, bulkier and much rarer individuals, looking as if someone had shaken icing

sugar over them. These were Arctic redpolls, tough little birds that originate far to the north of Britain.

Since then, redpoll taxonomy has become even more confusing, with
potentially six different races of the three species to consider – enough
to confuse even the keenest birder. But sometimes trying to identify a
bird can get in the way of simply enjoying it. So I decide to chill out,
and simply enjoy the sound and sight of these charismatic little birds
as they feed on a cold winter's day, without worrying about their exact
name.

MARSH HARRIER

27 February

On a bitterly cold February evening, as I watch a procession of marsh
harriers flying low over a Norfolk reed-bed towards their night-time roost,
I feel I have something to celebrate. For along with many other British
raptors, the marsh harrier has bounced back in style.

In the early 1970s I remember seeing the only confirmed breeding
pair of marsh harriers in Britain, at Minsmere in the neighbouring
county of Suffolk. I say 'pair', but actually there was one male and two
females: for marsh harriers are notoriously polygamous, with each male
having a harem of several females.

Marsh harriers have, in the past few years, headed north and west
from their East Anglian stronghold to colonise new parts of the country.
I now regularly see the bulky, chocolate-brown females, with their distinctive pale yellow cap and shoulder-flashes; and, less frequently, the smaller,
skewbald males, skimming across the sky on their long, narrow wings.

The marsh harrier's comeback is partly the result of an end to
poisoning with agricultural pesticides, and a reduction in shooting, but
also because wetlands are enjoying something of a renaissance.

With this population boom have come two important changes in
behaviour. In East Anglia, where numbers are now reaching saturation
levels, I have seen marsh harriers nesting in arable crops rather than
the more traditional reed-beds. And most no longer head south to Africa
in the autumn, as they once did, preferring to stay put, so that I and
others can enjoy this spectacular winter roost.

WILD GARLIC
28 February

If I recall anything from O-level geography, more than forty years ago now, it is that the further south and west you go, the milder the winter climate becomes. This explains why the growing season starts several weeks earlier in Devon and Cornwall than it does in the north and east.

Even so, I am surprised, on a blustery wet February day, to find the early shoots of spring flowers bursting into life in a wooded valley on the edge of Dartmoor. As I scramble up the bank above the fast-flowing stream, I am greeted by the unmistakable pea-green leaves of wild garlic, together with some smaller, but just as recognisable, bluebell shoots.

I stop, glad of the chance to catch my breath, and pick one of the garlic leaves. Crushing it between my fingers, I release the distinctive aroma into the damp air; then take a tentative nibble, feeling the slightly burning sensation on my tongue. Because the plants have only just emerged from the dark red earth, the fragrance is not yet overpowering; but if I return here in a month or two, I'll be able to smell that garlicky scent well before I see the carpets of white-flowered plants – also known, curiously, as ramsons.

Wild garlic leaves make a fine addition to salads or scrambled eggs. True to his eccentric nature, woodland ecologist Oliver Rackham apparently used to enjoy them mixed with peanut butter in sandwiches. If you wish to try them for yourself, you can find them in almost any damp lowland wood or forest from late February through to June.

GREAT SPOTTED WOODPECKERS
29 February

The annual bouts of head-banging have begun in the lime trees at the top of the road.

Great spotted woodpeckers are setting up territories by bashing their bills against tree-trunks to create the familiar bursts of drumming. It is now well known that they are able to do this because the blows are cushioned by their skulls, honeycombed like an Aero bar with countless tiny cells, separated by bony struts. But it was once widely believed that the birds produced their sound vocally and it wasn't until 1943 that a sound-recordist, Norman Pullen, proved the case beyond doubt by placing a microphone inside a drumming tree and watched the woodpecker synchronising its bill contact with the sound.

The birds are sonic connoisseurs, which test the percussive qualities of different trees and will extemporise freely if the right materials are to hand. Some enhance their machismo by banging on metal plates attached to telegraph poles, others improvise on garage doors.

A friend once told me that he'd never seen a woodpecker. He didn't seem especially regretful, but I found his admission hard to credit. They are, after all, loud and brightly coloured birds, fairly common and widespread.

Indeed, great spotted woodpeckers are doing well, their numbers up fourfold since the late 1960s. Regular visitors to bird-tables, they arrive in a flurry of red, black and white to attack peanuts and fat-balls with business-like bills; these garden service stations could be driving their increase. Also, the numbers of hole-nesting starlings in our woods have declined and so there is much less competition for the woodpeckers in the breeding season.

How then, is it possible to miss them? Well, many species are easy to ignore until you know the little signs that betray them. I first latched on to the great spotted woodpecker's penetrating 'chik' call, and soon began finding them everywhere, in the local park, flying between woods, or even over the garden. If I followed my ears, the sight of a dumpy starling-sized bird bounding away or perched at the very top of a tree confirmed the find. It's a technique that works for many birds and with each new trick we learn, the natural world becomes a larger and more enticing place.

MARCH

FOR ME, MARCH is a month of tantalising promise, a good deal of frustration and the occasional pleasant surprise. Each morning I venture out into my garden, straining my ears for a single snatch of birdsong. Day after day I am disappointed: the syncopated great tits can momentarily fool me, but after two or three notes I know I am mistaken.

Then, almost when I have given up hope, I hear it: the simple, repetitive song of the chiffchaff. Although this small, olive-coloured bird may have spent the winter no further away than the reed-beds down the road, it might also have flown here from Morocco or Spain. Yet this doesn't matter: the chiffchaff is still such a classic sign of spring that my heart soars when I hear it.

The chiffchaff's arrival spurs me to venture further afield. Down on the coast flocks of waders are starting to pass through on their way north; while on my local patch I hear another migrant, the blackcap, singing its tuneful and melodic song.

If I am really lucky – and this has only happened in March once or twice since I moved to Somerset ten years ago – as I drive back through my village there will be a long, slender bird perched on the wires, taking a well-earned rest after flying thousands of miles back from southern Africa.

One swallow may not, indeed, a summer make; but it is enough for me to know that the winter is, finally, over.

S.M.

MARCH CAN MAKE me impatient, fractious even, especially if winter's grip is slow to loosen. Like Stephen I wait for the chiffchaff's seesaw song, often in the second week of the month, as a marker that spring is on its way.

But chiffchaffs can be silenced. In late March 2012 blizzards turned my local fields into folds of white laundry. Instead of singing high in a blackthorn bush, my first chiffchaff of the year skulked at ground level in grass tussocks by the local canal, desperately searching for insects in temperatures barely above freezing.

A sunny day instantly banishes the winter blues and has me scurrying towards the local sallow bushes that, miraculously, are suddenly humming with insects. The golden catkins provide a banquet for newly emerged queen bumblebees, butterflies such as commas and peacocks and a host of hover-flies and solitary bees. In the garden, flower-bees, which have become my March 'must-see', patrol the early flowers for nectar. This entomological exuberance is the best affirmation of spring that I know, a curtain raiser for the season to come.

Then suddenly, March is dropping hints of spring everywhere. Coaxed from the earth by sunshine, adders coil on cushions of dry bracken, common lizards sprawl on sunny logs and by night toads plod towards their breeding ponds and their annual orgy.

It seems that towards the month end, every day brings something new. Constellations of wood anemones and violets bloom in woodland clearings. The spring fever is contagious. As March gathers momentum, the word spreads among naturalists. A first sand martin or swallow fresh in from Africa, or maybe reports of a precocious cuckoo, not in a letter to *The Times* as tradition demands, but via a myriad of apps and websites. There's a lot to be seen: new species to find – a chance to test those field guides you were given for Christmas – and re-acquaintances to be made. Unstoppable and incomparable, spring has arrived.

B.W.

URBAN BUZZARDS
1 March

As I stand watching three buzzards spiralling overhead, locked in a silent, circular battle for territory, I feel as though I could be in the wild Welsh hills or on a Devonian moor, though I am in fact standing in my back garden in the urban West Midlands.

On sunny days in spring this is now the norm, but as someone who began birdwatching in the 1970s when buzzards were at a nadir locally – and across most of southern and eastern England – it's a sight that I still find hard to credit. Since the 1980s the buzzard's recovery from persecution has been phenomenal, one of the most spectacular changes in the population and distribution of any British bird. As a birding novice, I had to rely on family trips to Wales or the West Country to see soaring buzzards, but now all I have to do is step out of the office door and look up.

Buzzards now sit scanning for prey on the lampposts along busy and very built-up roads. For me, no train trip into the heart of Birmingham is complete without seeing a pair wheeling over the factories and breakers' yards of the Black Country. But are they merely passing through, birds of the rural fringe that have wandered into town? Not at all; they are making a living here.

Last March a friend in a neighbouring street told me about a 'huge bird of prey' that he'd flushed from his garden. Other people had seen it apparently and it had caused a lot of interest, tinged with alarm. I had my suspicions, but wasn't sure until one day I surprised a buzzard that had been sitting on the fence just above the table-top pond in my narrow garden.

It was a far cry from a Devon combe and in this cramped setting the buzzard did look incongruous as it flapped off and landed in a neighbour's conifer-top, reluctant to leave. Checking the spot where it had been sitting, I found out why it was in no hurry to go. Drying along the fence in the spring sunshine were clusters of black gelatinous beads, spawn torn from the oviducts of a frog. These bold and resourceful birds of prey are finding a life in town, adapting their survival techniques to their new surroundings as they soar back into our lives.

PRIMROSES
2 March

As I drive down the narrow, twisting Devon lanes it almost feels as if my car needs to go on a diet: on both sides the high earth banks – each topped with a thick blackthorn hedge – seem to get closer and closer. And then I notice a clump of lemon-yellow flowers with custard-yellow centres blooming on the roadside bank: our native primrose.

Primrose comes from the Latin *prima rosa*, meaning 'first flower', and here in the damp, deep-red West Country earth they are indeed one of the earliest to bloom. Here in the south-west, with such a benevolent winter climate, primroses usually appear in February or March, though they can sometimes be seen before Christmas in very mild winters. It's appropriate, then, that they are the county flower of Devon.

In my favourite book on botany, *The Englishman's Flora*, Geoffrey Grigson complains that the primrose was picked more often than any other wild flower apart from the bluebell. This made it hard to find around London and other British cities. Today, now that we are more reticent about picking wild flowers, the problem is not over-picking, but the dilution of our native wild primrose by a host of gaudy garden varieties. Recently the Highways Agency planted thousands of polyanthus plants along a main road near Cirencester in Gloucestershire – which bloomed into red, rather than yellow, flowers.

But the wild variety does live on, especially along railway cuttings and roadside verges that have escaped being mown or sprayed with chemicals.

If you feel adventurous, you can eat both the flowers and the leaves of the wild primrose. They are said to have a taste that is bitter but palatable, though I haven't yet dared to try them. You can, if you wish, also make tea from the leaves, and wine from the flowers – making the primrose not just pretty, but useful too.

GOSHAWK
3 March

You don't see it to begin with: the first sign of its presence is a distant nervousness as clouds of woodpigeons lift from a far-off copse. Ahead of them more birds rise in successive waves over the trees until the sky is full of tattered flocks.

Two things usually bring on this response: an air balloon or a raptor. There are no balloons on this grey, breezy afternoon and so we scan the hundreds of panicking birds. Below the main melee, something larger and more purposeful is cruising, an aerial shark among mackerel. They are safe; the goshawk isn't hunting, merely gliding between blocks of woodland. Our group on this bird-walk is ecstatic – for some, this is their first 'gos'.

Field guides will tell you about the niceties of identifying goshawks, in particular how to separate them from sparrowhawks. They mention the goshawk's larger size, its shorter tail, broader hips and protruding head, all very useful if the bird shows itself well. However, so many views of goshawks are glimpses, a blunt crucifix above a tracery of branches, a dark speck so far off that field characteristics become redundant.

Field guides are about feather maps, leg and bill colours, sizes, seasons and behaviour. What they can't do is convey the other dimension to seeing the bird: the way it makes you feel and how important that feeling is in naming it. With a little experience, you know intuitively when you've seen a goshawk by the initial frisson followed usually by a gasp of admiration.

The goshawk may not be the rarity that it once was, but it still has a mystique that few British birds can match. Exterminated as a native breeding bird by the late 1800s, its return, fuelled by falconers' escapees and some unofficial reintroductions, has gathered momentum since the 1960s. Now goshawks are locally common in parts of Wales, Scotland and northern England and scattered elsewhere in sizeable blocks of woodland, especially in mature conifer plantations.

The best time to look for goshawks is on sunny mornings in late winter and early spring, when they display over their nesting territories. Males and the much larger females perform dramatic slow-flapping displays, high over their breeding woods; by demonstrating their power to fly with exaggeratedly slow wingbeats, they are flagging up both their presence and their fitness.

They puff out their white undertail coverts as a signal to rivals and as the display ramps up, they hurtle down from a great height towards the treetops, pulling up abruptly, then rising and falling again in a roller-coaster spectacle that writes their presence across the skies. It's one of the most dramatic aerial displays of any British bird and is now probably more frequently visible than it has been for a couple of centuries. Goshawks are still illegally persecuted, though, and those in the know remain tight-lipped as to their whereabouts, but there are watchpoints in places such as New Fancy View in Gloucestershire's Forest of Dean that will rarely disappoint on a clear March day.

MOLE

4 March

On a foggy late winter's day, the mist finally lifts to reveal a group of herons, hunched up against the cold, standing by the edge of the flood-waters near my home on the Somerset Levels. They're not waiting for fish or frogs, but for moles, which have been forced to flee their underground homes by the floods.

The mole is a paradox among mammals. It's thought that there are about 30 million of them in Britain, making it one of the commonest of all our wild creatures. And yet the closest most of us ever get to actually seeing a mole is when we awake to find our lawn covered with heaps of earth thrown up by nocturnal burrowing: the dreaded molehills.

The mole is proverbially secretive, living virtually the whole of its short but active life underground, where it constructs a vast network of tunnels. These don't just provide a handy home for the mole; they are also a home delivery service, acting as a 'pitfall trap' for earthworms, insects and other invertebrates on which the mole can then feed.

There's no doubt that moles are unpopular, because a determined digger can do a lot of damage to a suburban lawn. But they are also a valuable pest controller, feeding as they do on garden pests, and so surely don't deserve the ignominy of death by poisoning.

So perhaps we should give moles a little more respect. After all, they did play a small but significant part in English history when in 1702 King William III of England (William of Orange) died following a fall from his horse, which had stumbled into a mole's burrow and thrown the monarch out of his saddle. His rivals, the Jacobites (supporters of the restoration of the deposed Catholic monarch James II and his heirs), reportedly toasted 'the little gentleman in the black velvet waistcoat' for causing the king's death. For centuries afterwards mole catchers would make velvet waistcoats out of the fur of the moles they had trapped and killed. My great-grandfather was the proud owner of one, which has sadly long since disappeared.

DANISH SCURVY-GRASS

5 March

It may only be March, but already the central reservation of the M5 motorway is green. Next month, it will be whitened by a frosty coating that spreading salt will not melt away. All along our arterial roads, the same story is being played out as one of the fastest-spreading plants moves inland.

Danish scurvy-grass is an annual member of the cress family and grows around the British coast. Like many coastal flowers it has fleshy, shiny leaves that retain water and are resistant to salt, allowing it to grow in places where many plants would become desiccated and perish. It's an annual, germinating in autumn and can thrive in very little soil. It also hates competition from other plants and so bare ground on the edge of roads is the perfect habitat. Add the salt that we use to keep ice at bay, and the stage is clear for this rather demanding plant to invade our road verges.

The succulent leaves of the several species of scurvy-grass are rich in vitamin C and were once eaten by sailors to alleviate the effects of scurvy. Presumably they preferred the larger and juicier species to the diminutive Danish scurvy-grass, which is rarely more than a few centimetres high.

In bloom, though, it makes an impact: en masse the pale lilac flowers look white and in their tens of thousands along the central reservation of a motorway resemble a sharp frost or a fresh snowfall.

They first began to spread inland in the early 1980s and since then have travelled rapidly along our highways. Flowering is over by early May after which the plants dry out, scattering millions of tiny seeds into the slipstream of fast-moving vehicles. Here, inverting the message of the biblical parable, *only* the ones that fall on stony ground will thrive; those lost on the grassy verges, where the competition is too great, will not germinate.

But in late autumn you can see the successful seedlings even at 70 mph, a lush green veneer coating the film of salt, grime and oily particulates that accrues along the road verges. In this inhospitable saline mulch they are safe from marauding slugs and are now spreading to smaller roads where they huddle in sheltered spots under lamp standards or lurk in the lee of kerbstones. But to see them at their best, drive along a motorway in March and when that boy racer in a BMW (possibly my co-author) tears past, don't get annoyed; instead, think of him as potential sower of scurvy-grass.

LADY AMHERST'S PHEASANT

6 March

It took me several long and fruitless attempts before I finally caught up with Lady Amherst's pheasant. During the late 1980s I would head out of London and spend hours walking round the Bedfordshire countryside in search of this beautiful but – as I discovered to my cost – surprisingly elusive bird. Then, on one particular trip, just as I was giving up hope, I returned to my car and noticed no fewer than four splendid males feeding unobtrusively along the edge of a stubble-field, next to a wood.

Some might wonder why I bothered. After all, like the Canada goose and ruddy duck, the Lady Amherst's pheasant – which was named, incidentally, in honour of an English aristocrat who first brought the pheasant to Britain – is not a native British species. Instead, like its equally colourful cousin the golden pheasant, it was brought here from its native Asia to adorn the gardens of stately homes, including nearby Woburn Abbey.

But on sheer looks alone, this exotic game bird is well worth seeing. The males are a stunning combination of green, blue and white, with a black and silver cowl across the back of the head, and a long tail, also alternately striped in black and silver.

Fortunately, unlike the more controversial non-native species already mentioned, Lady Amherst's pheasant proved to be a relatively benign presence in the Home Counties countryside. Indeed it was so low-key – despite its striking appearance – we didn't even notice that it was starting to disappear. At the time I finally saw them, there were probably fewer than 100 individuals left. With problems caused by inbreeding, numbers continued to fall.

Today the Lady Amherst's pheasant is down to just a solitary male bird. It will soon inevitably become the first non-native species on the official British List to subsequently go extinct here – though not before crowds of twitchers, desperate to get the bird on to their own British List, try to see it.

FEATHER-FOOTED FLOWER BEE

7 March

There are so many ways to measure the advent of spring. The first primroses and celandines really appear in winter, swallows are unoriginal (but still thrilling) and cuckoos increasingly unreliable as their numbers plummet.

So a few friends and I have adopted a garden insect as our vernal icon and we even hold a good-natured competition each year to record the first sighting. In the first week of March I place my binoculars next to the computer keyboard, and keep an eye on the window, watching for a small dark shape zooming along the flowerbeds: the feather-footed flower bee.

I don't know how long I'd been noticing these bees probing the purple tubes of lungwort and crocuses before I realised that they weren't bumble-bees. There was something about the way they darted about and hovered in front of flowers that seemed too energetic for a drowsy dumbledore.

More puzzling was that there seemed to be two species, one tawny and dark brown, the other black with yellow pollen baskets. Browsing later through a field guide, the penny dropped: I realised that they were the males and females of a solitary bee called *Anthophora plumipes*. That epithet *plumipes* means 'feather-footed' because of the long hairs on its legs. The thickset males emerge first in early spring, and the furry black females a week or so later. Both sexes have long tongues for probing tubular flowers and lungwort (*Pulmonaria*) is a firm favourite. Males patrol territories in search of mates, chasing off rivals in dazzling pursuits low over the ground.

After mating, the female lays her eggs in cells in old walls, chimney-stacks or sandy quarries and leaves each egg with a pollen cake on which the young bee-grub will feed. Once sated, it forms a pupa in summer and waits in its chamber for spring to arrive. The adult bees live for a few weeks between late February and mid-May.

Our competition results from Worcestershire have produced an earliest sighting on 2 March. Most males first appear in the first ten days of March, though in the very late spring of 2013 they didn't show up until early April. Once you've noticed these charismatic insects, you'll wonder how you ever missed them and they'll become a sign of spring for you too.

FERAL PIGEONS

8 March

The sluice stands, proud and strong, a tribute to those skilled wartime engineers who built it to control the water flow from the River Huntspill back in 1942. Its vast concrete structure provides a home to a colony of refugees from the urban world: a colony of feral pigeons. Out of place in this rural, coastal setting, they stay close to their comforting fortress, rarely taking flight.

Two miles or so to the north, another structure over the River Brue also houses a colony of feral pigeons. The clyce (a Somerset word for a sluice so obscure it isn't even in the *Oxford English Dictionary*) is so constructed that as the pigeons call, their sound echoes spookily off the walls as if in an echo chamber. Their sound is a strange accompaniment to a walk across these windswept coastal marshes.

Feral pigeons are, of course, far more common in our towns and cities – indeed it is hard to imagine urban life without their ubiquitous pres-ence. Like so many familiar birds, we often ignore them – yet by doing so, we may miss out on observing some fascinating behaviour.

Just sit quietly in a city square and watch as – especially at this time of year – the male pigeons court their mates, strutting around after the female as she feigns apparent indifference to his efforts, before she finally gives in to his charms.

GREEN HELLEBORE

9 March

Many natural historians are sublimated hunters, who like nothing better than the challenge of tracking down their chosen quarry. We revel in the obscure and the elusive, animals and plants that dance on the edge of possibility, and so spend winter days plotting routes and planning trips for the coming season, burrowing into reference books and mouse-clicking our way through the tangle of websites. Few things are as exciting as seeing in the field what we've been anticipating from our winter armchairs.

In March 2014 my goal was a plant with all the right attributes: a striking flower with a propensity for lurking in ancient places, the lure of genuine scarcity and a whiff of ambivalence about its origins.

The green hellebore has the largest wholly green flowers of any British plant. They are like giant buttercups, the colour of a Granny Smith apple, and appear in late February and March among the long-fingered fan-shaped leaves that reminded herbalists of ursine claws: this plant and the related stinking hellebore were once known as bear's-foot.

During the eighteenth century an annual consignment of hellebore roots was delivered to Guy's Hospital in London where it was used to kill infestations of worms in children, but the naturalist parson Gilbert White was wary of its powers: 'Where it killed not the patient it would certainly kill the worms, but the worst of it is, it will sometimes kill both.' Plants were often gathered from the wild and grown in physic gardens. Sometimes they would re-wild themselves and so, centuries on, it can be hard to distinguish native hellebores from escapees.

This mystique surrounds the green hellebore in many places, clouding its origins and confounding its pursuers. Preparing my own search in the Midlands, I scanned county floras for potential locations, but the plant was as elusive as a will-o'-the-wisp. So it was that I ended up flailing around a deep Worcestershire dingle, clutching at tree-roots and searching for footholds on vertiginous slopes of glutinous red marl, without success of course. Even the clusters of snowdrops spilling from the churchyard on the dingle's lip were poor consolation. It was an undignified start.

But then I recalled how, thirty-odd years before, I'd been told of a handful of plants in a copse just off the M5 motorway, a place I'd passed at 70 mph umpteen times since. Enlisting the help of friends from the Worcestershire Wildlife Trust, I set off on a last-ditch hellebore hunt.

Three decades on, the landscape had changed dramatically. The fragment of woodland was now encircled by a vast new housing development and even though prescient planning had saved the trees and some old hedgerows, our chances looked poor. Celandines and wood anemones starred the ground, but there was no sign of hellebores. After about twenty minutes of searching, we headed back to the car along an old boundary ditch, once used to keep out livestock and there they were, four clumps of palm-like leaves, sheltering the shy, apple-green flowers, all within a few paces of the footpath. Incredibly, this haunter of ancient places had survived anonymous among the brambles on the woodland floor. For us it was a heartening encounter and testimony to the contradictory resilience of some of our scarcest plants.

OTTER

10 March

The sighting was so brief I almost thought I had imagined it. A big dog otter emerged from the reeds a few yards in front of me, did a double-take at my unexpected human presence, and was gone, melting back into the reeds so quickly I didn't even have time to raise my binoculars. The image left on my retinas was that of a sleek, muscular creature, greased like a Channel swimmer, with splendid whiskers and beady black eyes.

As otter sightings go, this one was pretty typical. I have had half a dozen such encounters during my time in Somerset: each one totally unexpected, incredibly fleeting and very, very exciting. The brevity of my meetings with this elusive animal only adds to the thrill I feel when they occur, for this is the most charismatic of Britain's mammals. Perhaps because they are equally at home in water or on land.

Otters have also made a comeback from the very edge of extinction, in one of the greatest conservation success stories of the past few decades. They have moved back across Britain from their refuges in the north and west; a few years ago they reached the very last English county from which they had been absent: Kent. They are still tricky to see – you can't just go out assuming you will come across one – but we know that they are there, which is good enough for me.

Only on one occasion have I seen the same otter more than once. It was a late August afternoon, looking out over a waterlogged scene filled with ducks, geese and other waterbirds, when an otter popped up in the distance. Struggling to put up my telescope, I let my son George, who was not yet four years old, take a look.

A few moments later the otter resurfaced, then dived again, and George announced that he had seen it. Wanting to make sure that he really had, I asked him what it was doing. His answer – 'it went plop' – elicited a murmur of assent from those around us. As a description of a diving otter, it's pretty hard to beat.

SALLOW INSECTS

11 March

A switch has been flicked. After days of lowering cloud, wind and squally showers, temperatures have risen. There's a definitive day each March when spring finally breaks through and warmer weather coincides with clear skies. Now is the time to scrutinise the local sallows.

Sallows are better known as pussy willows from the appearance of their furry catkins, which botanists describe as 'sericeous', meaning 'silkily hairy'. At least the male catkins are. Sallows produce their catkins on separate male and female bushes. The female catkins are inelegant and greenish, like spiky caterpillars on the upright twigs. Male catkins are much showier cat's-paws erupting from chestnut bud-scales, which when the sun hits them erupt in a fuzz of stamens and pollen-coated anthers. The catkins can be so abundant that each sallow twig is haloed with light in spring sunshine, a botanical St Elmo's Fire.

These early flowering catkins are a lifeline for newly emerged insects searching for nectar, so a sallow bush on a March day bustles with life.

Queen bumblebees of several species drone amid the golden catkins. Among them you might see a smaller leggier 'bee', which looks a little different. This is the bee-mimicking hoverfly *Criorhina ranunculi*, a hairy, blackish insect with either a red or a white tail: these two forms mimic different bees. Its similarity to bumblebees may well deter birds from taking an investigatory peck.

Through binoculars you may see many droneflies, hoverflies that mimic honeybees and of course plenty of honeybees too. The most numerous insects are clouds of tiny willow-catkin flies of the genus *Egle*, which drift around the bushes, not looking for nectar, but a place to lay their eggs: their small grubs will feed on the developing willow seed which falls to the ground. These smaller flies are a lure to olive-brown chiffchaffs, which sing their monotonous but welcome spring song as they flit among the twigs.

As you track the chiffchaff through the haze of twigs a splash of bright colour reveals an overwintering butterfly. Peacocks, commas and small tortoiseshells, wings held wide open to catch the sun's rays, love sallow nectar, sipping it greedily with their long probosces. For me, this free-for-all is the essence of early spring and all the better for being on our doorsteps. Sallows grow in woods and in marshes, but they are also excellent colonisers of waste ground in towns and cities, where they provide a superb banquet to kick-start another entomological year. If you have room in your garden for one, you won't be disappointed.

GOLDCREST

12 March

A quick Sunday morning bike ride to the local shop, to pick up news-papers and milk, is enlivened by a familiar sound coming from the local churchyard. The song of a goldcrest: a jaunty little ditty, unfurling on the early spring air with equal volume and joy.

As it is hidden inside the dark-green depths of an ancient yew, I have no chance of seeing this tiny bird; yet I know it is there. But one day, maybe quite soon, I won't be able to hear this song.

Goldcrests sing at the very top of the register, still within the hearing range of younger people. But those of us approaching late middle age sometimes struggle to hear it, while many birders over the age of seventy can no longer pick out the sound at all.

Richard Porter, one of the post-war generation of pioneering birders now in his seventies, has suggested that, as most people who carry out bird surveys are from the older generation, we may be seriously under-recording species that, like the goldcrest and treecreeper, have very high-pitched sounds. I'm not sure what the solution might be – hearing dogs for birders, perhaps?

PEACOCK BUTTERFLY

13 March

A dark shape flutters outside the office window and powers off over the house. Peacocks are up and about after a winter rest.

I was eight or so when I caught my first peacock butterfly. Until then, I'd contented myself with meadow browns, sundry whites and skippers, which I grabbed with my hands on the local waste ground and kept imprisoned in jars that soon became greasy with their wing-scales. In my hazy hierarchy of butterflies, these were the underlings, all subservient to the ultimate lordly prize.

Peacocks were high-fliers, hard to catch without a net, either out of reach in buddleia bushes, or basking on bare ground where their four huge eyes seemed to watch your every move. Back then I was drawn hypnotically to the magic eyespots on their wings and suspected that the peacock somehow used them to give me the slip.

Then, one August day on a Welsh coastal path, I caught a peacock as it was engrossed in feeding on hemp agrimony flowers. As I ran full-tilt back to the holiday cottage, I could feel its powerful wings beating against my cupped hands, matching the flutters of my heart. My parents' friends kindly found a Kilner jar in their holiday cottage – humble jam jars were too cramped for such aristocracy – and I gazed in awe at my prize: its fabulous colours, the pelt of foxy fur on the body, the tigerish bars bordering its forewings, and the mauve teardrops falling from those huge all-seeing eyes.

There's a shocking vulgarity about those art deco eyespots, but then that is the point. Aesthetics aside, the peacock is a scare-merchant, flashing its 'eyes' to frighten predators away. These are mainly birds and large insects, which can see in the ultraviolet spectrum, so those vibrant colours must be dazzling to a potential attacker. The hindwing spots, either side of the dark abdomen, look like the eyes and beak of a mournful owl.

Then, just as suddenly, the eyes vanish, as the butterfly clamps its wings together to show the blackish undersides, pencilled with wavy lines like charred timber. It's a wonderful disappearing trick, but works less well in the dingy places where the butterflies spend the winter. Here the peacock has another defence. By grinding its forewings together, it produces a hissing sound, which suggests something large and sinister lurking in the gloom. This doesn't always work. Mice can wreak havoc in butterfly dormitories during winter, gnawing off the wings and eating the softer bodies.

Fortunately, unlike many of our butterflies, peacocks are still common and widespread. They don't need the cachet of rarity to enhance them; their reappearance in spring is a fresh opportunity to wonder at their unexpected brilliance.

WOODCOCK

14 March

Some birds just have an air of mystery about them. Their presence here is defined, as it were, by their elusiveness. Numbers mean nothing – they may be widespread and reasonably common, but their shy and retiring habits elevate their status to almost mythical rarity.

One such is the woodcock. This is a wader that doesn't wade, but spends its life hiding among the leaf litter it so closely resembles. Even here, you can walk right past a woodcock and it will stay hunched to the ground, perfectly camouflaged and completely out of sight, as you pass by.

When I was growing up, this was a near-legendary species. I knew that it was found in the Surrey woods near my home – it said so in John Gooders's *Where to Watch Birds*, the birder's equivalent of the Bible.

Knowing it was there was one thing, actually seeing it quite another. As a teenager I remember cycling down to Nower Wood, near Leatherhead, with my birding companion Daniel. Stupidly, we hadn't realised that woodcocks are much more likely to be seen at dawn or dusk; we had decided to visit in the middle of the day. So it was hardly surprising that we failed to see them. Indeed it wasn't until I reached my early twenties that I finally caught up with this mysterious creature – at Wicken Fen in Cambridgeshire.

A few years later, though, I had a classically intimate encounter with a woodcock. I was driving at a snail's pace around the 'Wolferton Triangle' in north-west Norfolk. As dusk fell, I was hoping to see the gleaming yellow headdress of a golden pheasant. That was not to be. But I then noticed a small lump on the road in front of me. As I approached, the lump turned into a bird with an impossibly long, straight bill, staring back at me with one black, beady eye.

It sat, crouched as if hidden, but in full view. I stopped, turned off my headlights and gingerly opened the car door. As I did so, the wood-cock exploded into flight, disappearing into the shadows in an instant. The meeting may have been brief, but even thirty years later it's one I shall never forget.

FIRST BUTTERFLIES

15 March

Like many naturalists, I keep regular lists and diaries. This may seem the height of pedantry – after all, who cares when you saw your first swallow of the year, or last dragonfly? Yet over time, personal records such as this allow us to spot patterns and changes. Only when climate change became a reality around the turn of the millennium did we realise just how important these personal records are: going back through time enabled scientists to chart the way springs are earlier than they used to be.

Looking back over the ten years or so since I moved to Somerset, I'm struck by how variable the date of our first garden butterfly can be. Back in 2007, our first spring here, a small tortoiseshell and brimstone appeared on 6 March – a date not equalled until 2015, when I saw a peacock fluttering over the lawn on the same day.

In the years between, the first butterfly has appeared any time between

8 March and as late as 5 April. By the end of March, the most species I have seen is four – the quartet of small tortoiseshell, brimstone, peacock and comma, all of which overwinter as adults here.

Elsewhere, though, I have seen a butterfly even earlier: on one unseasonably warm January day a few years ago, as I watched my son Charlie playing football, a comma emerged and basked on a sunlit wall.

GORSE AND HONEYBEES

16 March

When gorse is out of bloom, kissing is out of fashion, goes the old saying. However dark the winter days, its prickly hummocks of foliage are sprinkled with golden flowers, an important spring nectar source for early insects. A few local landowners tolerate gorse, which grows vigorously on the sandy soil, and so each spring I check it for bees.

Among the masses of thorns are scattered glints. These are reflections of sunlight from the shiny carapaces of basking gorse shield-bugs. The bugs winter among the prickly thickets and are the colour of unopened gorse flowers, rich olive green with an eye-catching yellow border to their plump bodies. Brighter still are scarlet seven-spot ladybirds, which have also spent the cold months in the gorse clumps; and all around are honeybees.

I've long been interested in the honeybees here. Their nest is a few hundred metres away in the valley, not in a carefully tended hive, but low in a deep cleft in the trunk of an old crack willow that forms part of an ancient fence-line. Willow used to make fence-posts stays 'quick' (alive) for some time and will often sprout in wet ground, which I suspect is what happened several decades ago.

Now its hollowed trunk is home to a colony of 'wild' honeybees, one of several in the area, which have become established in old trees and crumbling buildings and almost certainly originate from honeybees introduced by apiarists.

The ancestors of nearly all the modern honeybees in the British Isles were probably imported from continental Europe, but there's a lot of interest among hymenopterists – people who study ants, bees and wasps – in the 'black bee', a darker and hairier form of the honeybee that some consider native to our islands. Its pigmentation and hairiness are considered to be adaptations to our cooler climate, helping the insects to conserve heat.

Untangling the honeybee's complicated British heritage and genetics is a challenge. Some of these valley bees are very dark, though, and each year I wonder as I watch them squeezing into the gorse blossoms whether they have links to ancient populations that may be hanging on in this sheltered valley.

ADDER
17 March

Yesterday, a herpetological consultant friend told me about the last adder in Oxfordshire. What was once a healthy population of the snakes has dwindled to a solitary female.

Oxfordshire isn't alone. Adders have also gone from Nottinghamshire and Warwickshire and are on the very brink in Buckinghamshire, Hertfordshire and Greater London. In my own county of Worcestershire, they are disappearing so fast that even in their remaining hotspot they are in grave danger. It is one of the most serious wildlife losses in the modern British countryside and it is worsening. But why should we care so much about conserving our only venomous snake?

From the age of fourteen, I've been entranced by the adder. It all began on family holidays near the Isle of Purbeck in Dorset. While the rest of the family lounged on the beach, I would catch the ferry across the narrow mouth of Poole Harbour to find adders coiled like ammonites among the dunes of Studland Bay. Once, with the ignorance of youth, I brought one home where it allowed me to handle it, until the day I was bitten (and serve me right). A dose of antivenin and a couple of weeks with my green and purple arm in a sling and all was well for me at least: not so the adder, which was despatched by my father.

Since then, with a sense of wonder laced with guilt, I've watched adders from a distance, straining to pick out their tessellated coils among the dried bracken fronds that line their spring basking spots. Male adders emerge from hibernation in late February to soak up the sun's rays and mature their sperm in preparation for mating in April and May. I've even seen them basking while snow was falling: their ability to harness the warmth of the sun is so well developed that they are the only European snake to live within the Arctic Circle.

In March and April, the males slough their old skins by rubbing themselves against bark or stones: in some cases the entire translucent skin peels off like a debutante's evening glove, complete with the watch-glass that protects the snake's eyes. The males are at their finest now, either golden brown with a darker dorsal zigzag or silvery grey with a blackish zigzag stripe. They look obvious when in the open, but on a couch of dead bracken they are easy to miss.

Even after several months of hibernation, they are in no hurry to feed, but in the presence of the larger females they will vie with rivals by performing a ritual wrestling match known as the dance of the adders. During this vigorous activity, they seem unaware of observers and I've had them dash across my boots on more than one occasion.

They are magnificent animals and one of the genuine sadnesses of recent times is that they have gone for ever from some sites where I've known them for many years. For ever is an ominous phrase, but in the case of adders it is almost certainly true. Human persecution is part of the problem, as is simplification of habitat: too much shading can force the snakes into less suitable areas and, because they hibernate commu-nally, a forestry bulldozer can easily wipe out large elements of the population. In the case of mature females this can be disastrous.

Adders breed slowly and may have a brood of youngsters only once every two or three years. The real threat in addition to habitat loss comes from the tens of millions of pheasants released annually for shooting. Pheasants will peck instinctively at snakes and can wipe out smaller populations. It's a tragedy being repeated in many areas. Depleted numbers are further at risk from burgeoning buzzards, though we shouldn't blame the birds for losses we've already inflicted. Add in the fact that the snakes will not cross open land to recolonise other sites, giving rise to inbreeding, and you have a perfect recipe for the extinction of isolated populations. Reintroduction is probably pointless while pheasant-rearing remains at its current level and that situation is hardly likely to improve.

One irony of its rare status is that in places even the adder's fans are doing it no favours. Photographers keen to take shots of them in spring can unwittingly disturb basking areas and frighten off the snakes, while some thoughtless individuals tweet where to find them, an unhelpful act at a time when we should all be giving adders some peace and quiet.

SAND MARTIN

18 March

On a breezy March day, when the wind whips across the land with a chill that suggests that warm weather is still a while away yet, the loose flock of birds skimming the surface of the reservoir look as if they wish they were anywhere but here.

Given that they have spent the last few months sunning themselves under cloudless African skies, they may have a point. And yet these sand martins – the first I have seen this year – have not come back early by accident. They are the first of the aerial insect-eaters to return: it will be another week or two before I see my first swallow or house martin, and a month before the first parties of swifts are screaming overhead.

I have already caught up with some other migrants: a wheatear bounding along the beach, and a blackcap singing in my garden. But these are sturdier birds, weighing considerably more than the delicate sand martins, which tip the scale at barely half an ounce.

So for the birds fluttering across the water in front of me, getting back as early as this is a real gamble. March sometimes brings fine weather, so that when the birds return there is plenty of insect food around, and they can get down to breeding ahead of their rivals. But in other years, winter persists well beyond the spring equinox, and returning sand martins find themselves struggling to find food.

That's why at this time of year I usually see them congregating over our local reservoir, where the tiny aerial plankton on which they feed gather in swarms over the choppy water. Only when April arrives, and with it a spell of fine weather, will they head away from here to their breeding colony by the banks of a local river (the sand martin's scientific name, *Riparia riparia*, appropriately means 'of the riverbank').

Back in the late 1960s, and again in the early 1980s, far fewer sand martins returned from Africa than usual, having suffered population crashes due to a drought in their wintering grounds. Since then, this little bird has bounced back, and though numbers have fallen in the south of Britain they are offset by a steady increase in the north.

Why that should be is a bit of a puzzle; but one thing is certain. We are now seeing more and more sand martins even earlier in the year – sometimes in February – long before the main cohort gets back.

BEE-FLY
19 March

Flies have few friends even among naturalists, but one that rarely fails to attract attention first appears in early March, a tiny furry blimp hovering in front of spring flowers. It's the dark-bordered bee-fly which, with its thick pelt of ginger hairs and fondness for nectar, does indeed resemble a small bee. Hovering motionless at the mouth of a primrose, the fly inserts a long proboscis to delve for nectar and, when sated, lands on the flower's lip, displaying its two delta-shaped wings (bees have four wings). It's a handsome harbinger of spring, which is a treat to see in our gardens; last year I saw four together patrolling a patch of forget-me-nots.

Watch one for a while, along a hedge bank or woodland ride where there are patches of bare earth, and you will see it dip repeatedly towards the ground. This odd behaviour is accompanied by a flicking motion, almost too fast for the human eye.

The bee-fly's behaviour can seem puzzling until you discover more about its life cycle. The clue is in the name: it emerges in mid to late March to capitalise on the large numbers of solitary bees around at this time, which, unlike honeybees, have no caste system. The female solitary bees emerge after winter to mate with smaller males, and many lay their eggs in small chambers in burrows, which they furnish with pollen for their growing grubs. Sunny banks or sandy quarries are popular sites for solitary bees, so the bee-fly seeks these out. Its own larva will snuggle up to the growing bee-grub, sit on its skin and suck out its bodily fluids, with fatal results.

The challenge for the bee-fly is how to get its eggs into the bee's burrow without being detected by its owner. To do this, it bombards the burrow-mouth with a fusillade of eggs, many of which fall wide of the mark, but a few hit their target. When the tiny bee-fly grub hatches it crawls into the burrow to find its prey.

But aiming eggs successfully in mid-hover is a tricky business and so the bee-fly has refined its technique. When you see one dipping towards the soil, it is picking up tiny particles of earth in a special chamber on the end of its abdomen. As its eggs emerge, they are dusted with earth to disguise them, and to provide more ballast for a better aim. It's a technique that clearly works well, because bee-flies are successful insects. But spotting them in the garden shouldn't be cause for alarm: they have little effect on solitary bee populations, and their presence is a sign that your local solitary bees are flourishing.

MARCH BLACKBIRD
20 March

Cold March winds have ceased and warm Atlantic air has reached us, bringing a soft mizzle to my street. This evening, the smell of spring is suddenly all around, an indefinable cocktail of mown grass, early flower scents and the ichor of damp earth, a compound released by soil bacteria.

A blackbird is singing from the roof: soft, mellow phrases that match the weather's mood. Although it's been eight months since I last heard him perform, he's recognisable from certain unique passages in his repertoire: a flourish here, a fluty gargle there and an impeccable sense of timing, pausing briefly to let you savour each phrase. Cars roll over the wet road with a sound of unpeeling sticking plaster but his song rises above it, proclaiming his ownership to other blackbirds nearby. Tonight, there are three of them, each parcelling out the neighbourhood into invisible bubbles, which they will defend during spring and summer.

Their chorus represents a change of habits. Blackbirds were once shy haunters of woodland; you can still see hints of this behaviour as they dash low over roads between gardens, much as they would cross a wood-land ride to avoid a hawk. Here in town they are just as much at home and are one of the most successful urban birds.

They are resourceful and can colonise most habitats: I remember especially one bird singing from a pinnacle of rock at Lizard Point in a natural amphitheatre while waves washed against the cliffs far below.

The male, Shakespeare's 'ousel cock so black of hue, with orange-tawny bill' is instantly recognisable. Not so the dark-brown female, who's more self-effacing. Invisible on her nest in a hedge or outbuilding, she incubates her clutch of sea-green, brown-freckled eggs, while her mate warbles from a nearby rooftop. On this damp, mild March evening, I am just happy to listen in.

NORTHERN WHEATEAR
21 March

It's a blustery March morning and I'm greedy for more signs of the rapidly approaching spring. On a ploughed field, a small flash of white betrays one: the first wheatear. Its scientific name is, wonderfully, *Oenanthe oenanthe*, Greek for the 'vine-flower', because it arrives from Africa as the grapevines begin blooming. This sprightly migrant has been welcomed for centuries.

Wheatears are crispness personified, natty dressers without a feather out of place. Soft grey, buff and peach tints contrast with dark wings and glaring white rumps, from which they get their English name: wheatear is a garbled version of a much older name meaning 'white arse'.

On long legs, they sprint after flies and bound on to eminences, flicking their tails sideways like a shuffling card-sharp. Every movement is neat and precise; wheatears don't fidget and dawdle like dunnocks or pipits. They make even blackbirds look like slouches.

This sense of pent-up energy and economy of movement suggests a restlessness in these spring migrants. Although our paths cross theirs on downs, clifftops, fields and even sports pitches, for most of us it's a brief encounter. Wheatears breed on mountains and moorlands in the British Isles, but the majority of birds we see stopping off to refuel have their sights set further north and westwards. Some are bound for Scandinavia, others as far away as Greenland and even Canada, making them one of the smallest long-distance migrants in the world.

Birds breeding in those northern climes leave their wintering grounds south of the Sahara, cross the desert and head through Europe to the British Isles before flying out across the North Atlantic via Iceland to Greenland and beyond. On the way back in September, fattened by Arctic insects and with a following wind, they can migrate from Greenland across the ocean to south-west Europe in a thirty-hour non-stop journey of 2,400 miles.

Writing in 1766, the naturalist Thomas Pennant remarked on the wheatear's delicate flesh and reported that more than 20,000 were caught in one autumn alone on the downs near Eastbourne, sold for sixpence a dozen and apparently made good eating. It's hard to imagine those quantities now, but today I'm happy with just the one bird, dipping out of sight between furrows and re-surfacing jauntily on the ridges in between.

BROWN HARE

22 March

As a child I remember reading *Alice's Adventures in Wonderland*, and being particularly struck by her singular description of what for me was then a very unfamiliar animal: 'The March Hare will be much the most interesting, and perhaps as this is May it won't be raving mad – at least not so mad as it was in March.'

Since then I have got to know hares rather better and have also learned that Lewis Carroll's bold claim about the madness of hares is utterly and completely wrong. For at this time of year hares aren't going mad – they're just getting frisky.

The common misconception about 'mad March hares' comes from the brown hare's unusual habit of 'boxing' at the start of the breeding season. For a long time it was assumed that these were rival males fighting it out for the chance to mate with the watching females. But as we now know, what we are seeing is actually a female fighting off the amorous intentions of a sexually charged male. This is always a great sight to see, as she breaks stride and confronts him, up on her hind legs with forepaws flailing, as he desperately tries to fend her off.

Hares, however, are really rather magical. Few British animals have such a huge body of folklore attached – including the widespread notion that they can disappear into thin air, because of their ability to crouch low to the ground and thus seeming to vanish. This is ironic, given that hares are not truly native. They were brought to Britain some time during the Iron Age (or perhaps even earlier, during the Bronze Age), when farmers crossed over from mainland Europe. But like many of our arable weeds, including the corn poppy and the cornflower, the hare has been here so long it is now part of the furniture.

So at this time of year I try to make the effort to get up early, and watch a group of hares chasing and boxing one another on a crisp and sunlit March morning. When I do, I feel privileged to witness one of the finest spectacles of the season.

URBAN SYCAMORES

23 March

Remember the slogan 'Plant a tree in 73'? Back then tree planting took off in spite of the waggish riposte 'Buy a saw in 74' and we recognised the need to re-forest our land. Now, so inured are we to the idea of planting trees that it's easy to forget that many of our trees are perfectly capable of planting themselves. Next time you travel by train, look at the young woodland crowding the edge of the tracks. Most of these trees are self-sown and many are sycamores.

Trees with light seeds, which blow in the breeze, are regular denizens of the urban forest. Birch, for example, has papery seeds that find a lodging almost anywhere.

But for sheer aerial prowess, sycamore wins hands down. Its large winged seeds are known technically as 'samaras', but as children we called them helicopters because they spin like rotor blades in the wind and allow the sycamore seeds to waft far from the parent tree on to waste ground, riverbanks, railway cuttings and into back gardens. That's where I'm aware of it in late March because at the top of my narrow plot is a large sycamore.

There are more in my neighbours' gardens and now their pink-flushed buds are bulging with tightly pleated leaves. Some have already burst open and fat yellow flower-clusters are hanging at the ends of the stout twigs. A stroll around the wider neighbourhood reveals a host of syca- mores and I'll bet that none of them has been planted deliberately.

Sycamore is a member of the maple family and was probably intro- duced to Britain from the Continent before the sixteenth century. Introduction or not, this resourceful tree is found the length and breadth

of the British Isles. Visit an upland farm and you'll see sheltering sycamores, often the only large tree around. But in older woods, sycamores
are not always welcome because their large leaves create dense shade
and they are faster growing than native trees such as oaks.

In town their size and speed of growth can make them unpopular
too. But sycamores are a boon to wildlife. Lichens love their bark, bluebells prosper beneath them and they're a magnet for birds in spring
– especially in late March and April.

As the leaves unfurl, the eggs of the sycamore aphid, which have
overwintered near the bud-clusters, hatch in their thousands as the young
bugs emerge to suck the sap of the new foliage. In my garden, chaffinches, goldfinches, tits and blackcaps flock to the sycamores to take
advantage of this springtime bounty.

Sitting at my desk, binoculars in hand, I've seen bramblings en route
to Scandinavia fatten up on aphids at the same time as a willow warbler
fresh in from sub-Saharan Africa. All this wildlife and you don't even
need to do any planting.

GARDEN THROWOUTS

24 March

When I say that I have a favourite lay-by, I realise it's a statement that
could be open to misinterpretation. Every few days, I park in a lane on
the extreme south-western tip of the Black Country conurbation, a lane
that passes through three counties: West Midlands, Staffordshire and
Worcestershire. It's my customary starting point for a stroll around the
local patch, which in late March presents me with a botanical dilemma:
which plants to record and which to walk past.

Urban fringe botany is a marginal affair. Local rat-runs are dumping
grounds for gardeners who jettison their unruliest plants near the most
convenient parking place and as a result some of these lanes are far
richer in species than many of our rural roadsides. Plants such as green
alkanet and white comfrey romp away in their new homes. Spanish
bluebells travel more slowly along hedgerows, where they thrust sheaves
of fleshy foliage through damp, discarded pizza boxes. In this lane they
have forged alliances with native bluebells and their sturdy hybrid

offspring are proliferating. Although purists may frown on this botanical motley, they are all worth noting, because they are clearly on the move and their history will inform future recorders.

But other curios loitering in my chosen lay-by are slower off the mark. Every March, I promise to identify the cluster of pallid mauve crocuses that has persisted stubbornly for over two decades on the edge of the bridleway. I can never quite summon up the enthusiasm, partly because crocuses and their cultivars can be tricky to name and their flowers are short-lived, but also because their relevance to the local flora is tenuous. The same principle applies to the stray daffodils along the verges. The naturalist in me tells me I should try to pin them down simply because they are there, but sometimes life is too short.

This is not botanical snobbery: in the urban fringe, you're glad of all the variety you can get. Over half the plants growing wild in the British Isles are introductions or garden escapes, so we should rejoice in their diversity and profusion. That's why next March I promise to check out those crocuses once and for all.

EGYPTIAN GEESE

25 March

A stiff breeze in Hyde Park was whipping up the waters today, forcing joggers to dodge the breakers as they slopped over the margins of the Round Pond. There were no picnickers on the grass in this weather, but eighty or so Egyptian geese were cropping the turf in small family groups, some resting, others watchful. One mother goose sheltered her brood of six goslings under her wings when a speculative gull passed too close.

Egyptian geese are odd-looking birds, not to everyone's taste, with their smudged-mascara eye patches, sugar-pink legs and enormous white wing-lozenges, invisible at rest, but dazzling in flight.

Here in the heart of London, grazing the municipal turf, these birds – which often share African waterholes with hippopotami – have found an ecological niche. There's water for swimming and roosting, grass and titbits thrown by Londoners and old trees in which to nest: to see one perching on the lip of a hollow sweet chestnut trunk in Hyde Park is a slightly dislocating experience for older British naturalists.

Bar the odd fox, life here is predator-free and the geese are doing well. Their nasal honks mingle with the screeches of ring-necked parakeets, new facets of our multicultural capital.

Egyptian geese were brought here from Africa in the seventeenth century, and escaped or deliberately released birds have been breeding in the wild for over 200 years. Until thirty years ago they were mainly concentrated in Norfolk and south-east England, but recently they have begun a dramatic spread; and although still rare in the west of England, Scotland and Wales, they could turn up anywhere.

This rapid increase after a slow start suggests that Egyptian geese are now firmly entrenched in our fauna and that it's probably too late to do anything about them, even if we wanted to. So, while we can admire them for their ability to flourish in a foreign land, we should also watch them carefully to make sure they don't cause problems by ousting native hole-nesting birds such as owls and kestrels.

As an occasional visitor to London, I'm secretly pleased to see them around the Hyde Park waterholes where, instead of sidestepping African elephants and antelopes, they move aside for the joggers and dog-walkers.

BUZZARD

26 March

Even though winter never seems to be coming to an end, one March morning things are different. I wake up, and the skies are cloudless, the air is warm, and spring is well and truly here. Above my garden, this momentous day is marked by the plaintive mew of buzzards, as they soar high overhead in a shimmering blue sky.

That's because – for the first time this year – the air is warm enough to create thermals: rising columns of warm air that allow the birds to gain height without using precious energy. All they have to do is to hold out their broad, fingered wings, flap a couple of times, and then rely on physics to get them airborne.

Sometimes, if I am lucky, they may decide that the time is right to indulge in the first courtship display of the year. The smaller male approaches the female and, when she indicates that she is receptive, the two of them begin to tumble through the air like acrobats, to cement the crucial pair bond between them.

This is a sight that many people now take for granted, even in the south and east of Britain. Yet just twenty years ago the mewing calls of spring buzzards were missing from huge swathes of the countryside, as this bulky raptor struggled to recover from decades of persecution by farmers and gamekeepers. It had also declined because of the terrible effects of agricultural pesticides, which poisoned the birds or thinned their eggs so that the chicks inside failed to hatch.

Today, buzzards are not just our commonest, but also one of our most familiar, birds of prey – a reminder that not everything is getting worse for Britain's wildlife. And yet not everyone welcomes their return: there have been calls for the licensed killing of buzzards where they take pheasant chicks; even though, as conservationists point out, the buzzards are a native species, while the pheasants are artificially bred and released for shooting.

This brings into question the way we view birds of prey. Are there, as the detractors claim, 'too many' of them, or should we celebrate the fact that a healthy population of predators suggests that the environment itself may at last be getting better? I know which side of the argument I'm on.

ORANGE UNDERWING MOTH
27 March

The removal of conifers in my local woodlands has encouraged a growth of silver birch coppice, which is now twice my height. In late March fat catkins are lolling at the ends of drooping twigs, before the leaves emerge. These young trees, about seven or eight years old, show only a hint of the black and white bark that characterises them later in life.

En masse, silver birches have a special beauty. The purple haze of their young twigs is silvered by March spring rains, a brilliant gauze against the backcloth of dark spruce. As the weather warms, sunshine is the cue for the mating flight of the orange underwing moth. Usually a binoculars-only moth, occasionally an orange underwing will flutter to the ground and allow closer inspection. At rest its hindwings are hidden beneath the russet forewings, which are clouded with white, but as it flutters it reveals the fiery underskirts that give the insect its name.

Few day-flying moths are about this early in the year, and so the males are relatively easy to identify as they gyrate around the birch-tops, following invisible scent-trails to the females, sitting on the high twigs. Here they will lay their eggs and the caterpillars will munch on the unfurling leaves. 'Copulating pairs', says my field guide, 'may be knocked out of trees', which seems a little harsh.

It is a stunning creature, which is all the more appealing for being transient and nearly always out of reach. Now that biologists have split it into two species, which look very similar, the true orange underwing has become that bit more elusive, but its dancing flights among the birch-tops are one of the many fleeting pleasures of early spring.

POND LIFE

28 March

As a child, I remember going 'down the watersplash': to a shallow ford across the River Ash near my suburban home on the outskirts of west London. We were, I suppose, 'pond-dipping', but for us this was just a few hours spent mooching around, trying to catch whatever we could find in the crystal-clear waters.

Among the sticklebacks and minnows we most prized was the smaller stuff: those tiny aquatic insects that skim across – or hang below – the taut surface of the water, such as pond skaters, backswimmers and water boatmen.

It may be hard for us lumbering heavyweights to grasp, but to an insect the surface of a pond is basically solid – though also flexible, rather like us walking on a bouncy castle. The surface tension creates a tangible border between the air above and the water below, enabling pond creatures to either walk across the surface, or hang below it.

That small, slender insect whose six long legs are spread out to support it is a pond skater: a water bug, specially adapted to live in this precarious halfway house. Of its three pairs of legs, the middle ones act as oars, enabling it to skim rapidly across the surface to search for food or to escape from predators. The tips of the other legs are able to detect tiny vibrations, allowing it to catch even tinier insect prey.

Nearby, a larger, stockier creature appears to be lying upside down – which indeed it is. The backswimmer is shaped like a tiny boat, and like the pond skater propels itself across the water's surface with its powerful legs. It has a powerful bite, injecting its hapless victim with toxic saliva – if you happen to get bitten, it can be very painful!

The final member of this pond-dwelling trio is the water boatman, of which there are almost forty different kinds on Britain's ponds and waterways. These superficially resemble their cousins the backswimmers, but unlike them they travel the right way up, using their long hind legs to swim beneath the surface.

Unlike backswimmers, which are predators of smaller aquatic invertebrates, water boatmen are vegetarians. They also, like crickets and grasshoppers, communicate with one another by stridulating: rubbing their feet – or in some cases, their genitalia – against the sides of their head.

Even now, almost fifty years after I first encountered these creatures, I can still watch them for hours as they go about their business on an early spring day; a reminder that the smallest creatures can sometimes be the most fascinating.

BARN OWL
29 March

A couple of days after British Summer Time begins, and my body clock still hasn't quite adjusted to the clocks springing forward by an hour. So I forgo the usual early morning visit to my local patch, and instead take a leisurely stroll around after supper, secure in the knowledge that the sun won't now set until almost half past seven.

I love this time of day: the wind has dropped, the rain stopped and the wildlife seems relaxed, too: a roe deer standing on the path 100 feet ahead of me would normally turn and flee. But this one stands stock-still, staring right back at me, as if it plans to take root. Not for long, though: as I gingerly edge forward, it finally does its classic magic trick of vanishing into the reeds.

A sighting like this makes any visit worthwhile; but there is more to come. As I reach the point where I turn for home, a white shape momentarily appears in the corner of my vision, and then does its own vanishing trick.

An egret? A gull? And then it reappears, a vision of ochre and white: a barn owl, taking advantage of the lull in the rain to search for voles and mice in the long grass alongside the watery drain that runs along the south end of the reserve.

I crouch, lift my binoculars, and watch as it floats right past me, so focused on searching for food that it remains unaware of my presence. Barn owls are consummate hunters, moving low over the land while listening intently for tiny rustles from mice or voles hidden in the long grass below. Even their wing-feathers are especially soft, to avoid making any noise that might mean the owl was unable to hear its prey.

The owl reaches a gate by the water, and turns, flying back towards me. This time it comes so close I can barely focus on its spangled upperwings, then it finally becomes aware of my presence and hurriedly veers away.

ELM

30 March

In some ways, the elm is the Peter Pan of trees: the one that never grew up. But while J.M. Barrie's boy hero got to remain a child, these days the elm is not so fortunate: at the very moment it is about to reach adulthood, it weakens, fades and dies.

That death – along with millions of others – leaves a big hole in the British, and especially the English, lowland landscape. It leaves a gap in our culture, too: one of the best known of all English paintings, Constable's *The Hay Wain*, features mature elms, tall and slender trees with distinctively heart-shaped leaves. For me too, this is a very personal loss – as a child we had a row of elms along the back fence of our garden, and they were the very first tree I ever got to know, even before the horse chestnut with its tantalising conkers.

The reason for the English elm's disappearance is that, since the 1970s, it has suffered from Dutch elm disease. This is actually a fungus transmitted by a tiny beetle, which kills off the trees as soon as their bark becomes thick enough for the larvae to live beneath.

So the elm, once rivalled only by the oak and ash for its ubiquity, vanished from most of our rural landscape for ever. Only in a few isolated locations where the disease was prevented from spreading, such as

Brighton and Hove in East Sussex, can you still see mature elms in all their glory.

Yet each March, young elms – each a genetic clone from a long-dead ancestral tree – continue to grow and bud in the hedgerow alongside my home. They straggle towards the sky, rising several metres until, still wearing the bloom of youth, they are struck down with the dreaded disease.

Their continued presence is, however, a lifeline for one very specialised butterfly, the white-letter hairstreak, whose tiny caterpillars can still feed on their unfurling leaves. But for the rest of us, majestic, mature elms remain but a distant memory.

MARCH NIGHTINGALE

31 March

One fine March morning, some time in the early nineteenth century, the poet John Clare observed a boy listening to what he assumes is the song of the nightingale. But as Clare knew – and so do we – that species is rarely heard before mid-April, a full month or more from now.

What the 'wondering boy' was actually hearing was a blackcap – dubbed by Clare 'the March Nightingale', because of its perceived resemblance to the sound of this famous songster. To be honest, the songs are not that similar – to my ears, the blackcap always sounds like a speeded-up blackbird, or a robin in a good mood – but they are close enough for some people to briefly confuse the two. If you do catch a glimpse of the blackcap, they are easy to identify, though only the males have that distinctive black crown, which in the females is chestnut brown.

Blackcaps do now spend the whole winter in Britain, but these are German birds, which sometime at the start of March head back east to breed. There follows a short blackcap-free gap, until 'our' birds return from their winter home in Spain or North Africa. Day after day I expect to hear them, and day after day I am disappointed.

But then, towards the end of the month, a different sound reaches my ears: the delicate, tuneful tones of the first singing blackcap. If the chiffchaff marked the moment when spring is almost here, the blackcap perhaps marks its genuine arrival.

APRIL

AS I GET older, I see April increasingly as a series of natural appointments to keep. This month sees the great inrush of migrant birds.

At first their arrival may be stuttering: a swallow around the local stables, or a solitary willow warbler braving a cold shower. But as the winds move in their favour, the drawbridge drops and millions of migrants pour on to our shores and infiltrate every corner of the countryside.

Each has to be savoured, songs re-learned and plumages pored over. And I need to seize the day. Some birds are destined to move on and won't breed locally – the common sandpiper teetering on the edge of the canal is merely feeding up for the next part of its journey to a bubbling upland stream. The ring ouzels that clatter on local hilltops like tumbling scree cannot be ignored during their brief stopover because in a week or so they might be singing on a snowbound Swedish fell.

Not all migrants make it back and their absence hurts. Cuckoos are no longer annual birds on my local patch, hardly surprising given a 70 per cent national decline in the last two decades. Turtle doves used to be regular in the last week of April, but they too have gone locally, probably for good.

But every day now brings a first of some sort. A gaudy orange-tip butterfly meandering along the hedge-line; palmate newts egg-laying in a forest ditch; even the scarlet splash of a lily beetle poised to ravage the garden fritillaries.

All mark the acceleration of the wildlife year and I pay homage to each as proof that, in the words of Ted Hughes, 'the globe's still working'.

B.W.

T.S. ELIOT, WITH characteristic bleakness, dubbed April 'the cruellest month'. For today's naturalists, this is all too true: April is the month during which – in Britain at least – we witness the impacts of the changes to the world around us. This applies especially to the growing spectre of global climate change, which threatens to alter every aspect of the natural world, mostly for the worse.

For now, April is above all a month marked by unpredictability, which makes it tremendously exciting, if sometimes a little frustrating. In fine, early springs, we in the south of Britain enjoy balmy temperatures, sunny days and an outpouring of life after the long, occasionally bleak winter. Flowers bloom, insects buzz, migrants return, and all around us is a sense of frantic activity as – for our resident birds at least – the breeding season reaches its climax.

Some years, though, spring never quite seems to burst through. Chill, easterly winds bring temperatures more like February, and we shiver; not, this time, in delicious anticipation, but from the cold and our sheer impatience at the delays in nature's calendar. Migrant birds stay firmly ensconced on the other side of the Channel; woodland and hedgerow plants hunker down as if trying to retain a trace of warmth from the soil; and the sight of a butterfly is a major event.

Such cold, late springs are certainly becoming less and less frequent, as the advance of global climate change shifts the onset of this welcome season forward by two or even three weeks in some years. But at what cost? In the short term, we enjoy the adrenaline rush of birds and bumblebees, bluebells and butterflies; and yet in our hearts and minds we know that something is wrong. When April feels more like May, or even June, the planet has definitely gone awry, with potentially devastating consequences for our wildlife and its habitats.

So what I wish for most is an April like those of my childhood: with showers, sleet and the occasional flurry of snow. Whether I shall ever see such a month again, I cannot tell. But I hope so.

S.M.

WOODLAND VIOLETS

1 April

The purple glimmer of violets in a woodland glade is one of the high-lights of spring for me. On our sandy soil in this corner of north Worcestershire we see fewer sweet violets, but plenty of dog violets which complete the triple spring palette along with yellow celandines and white wood anemones. Not only are violets beautiful – they are vital to some of our most spectacular insects.

Although their sultry flowers are easy to find, their scent is fleeting. Violets play tricks with our olfactory sense. A compound in violet scent called ionone binds to our scent receptors and switches off our ability to smell, so that after a few draughts from the flowers we lose the ability to savour them. Leave them for a while and the perfume returns afresh.

Sweet violets have creeping stems (known as stolons), which form large patches in hedgerows and woods. Dog violets lack these, but also grow in woodland clearings as well as in short turf on clifftops or down-land. There are two widespread species: the common dog violet, which has a creamy spur, and the early dog violet – badly named because it often flowers at the same time as its relative – which has a purplish spur. When woods are coppiced and light floods into the glades, the violets colonise the cleared ground for a few years before shade reduces the numbers of flowering plants.

Their population dynamics are important to butterfly conservationists. Violets are the food-plants of several spectacular fritillary butterflies including the pearl-bordered fritillary, which is becoming very local, in part because of the decline in coppicing. Its spiky black caterpillars prefer violet leaves growing in the sunniest spots, so woodland coppiced in a regular cycle provides a dependable larval buffet. Not for nothing was one species, the heath fritillary, known in the heyday of coppicing as the woodman's follower.

Sunshine also encourages insects, which pollinate the violet flowers. But when the trees re-grow and their leaves blot out the sun, the violets don't shut up shop and shrivel away: they have another trick up their sleeve. They can produce flowers that have no petals or pollen and never open; they don't need to be pollinated externally, because they are self-fertilised. It's a trick that violets have mastered better than most other British flowers and although there are genetic risks in keeping it in the family, it means that even during the darkest times violets can be sexually self-sufficient.

WOOD ANTS
2 April

The Caledonian pine forest at Eastertime. As a light fall of sleet floats down through the trees, it feels far more like winter than spring. This far north, there are no wild flowers to be seen at all, and only the relentless chorus of chaffinches and wrens tells me that the season is under way.

Yet if I look down, rather than up, there is something to see. That mound of earth in the clearing between two stands of Scots pines: is it a natural feature of the landscape or perhaps man-made? Actually, it's neither, as I soon discover when I approach. For this is the nest of the hairy (aka northern) wood ant.

A wood ant colony is one of the most bizarre objects I have ever seen in nature. Built up over years, even decades, using soil and plant material such as pine needles, it is the ant equivalent of a major metropolis, providing everything its many thousands of inhabitants need to survive.

As I kneel down to take a closer look, the clouds above part fleetingly, the sun emerges, and the nest – which until that moment has been virtually inert – springs into life. Hundreds, perhaps thousands, of ants swarm on to its surface, each carrying a tiny fragment of twig or pine needle. Like a speeded-up film of a building site, they pass to and fro, each one looking as if it knows exactly where it is going. This may appear random, but there is a definite purpose: the ants are air-conditioning their home by opening up tiny tunnels to allow cool air into the heart of the mound. When the sun goes in, as it often does at these northerly latitudes, the process goes swiftly into reverse as the ants close off the entrances to keep the heat trapped inside.

These are no ordinary ants, as I can tell by their size. Indeed they are the largest of almost forty species of ants in Britain, growing to between eight and ten millimetres long.

Like other ants they produce formic acid, which they can spray at any intruder that threatens the safety of their colony, including curious human beings. Yet woodland birds such as jays sometimes deliberately allow the ants to spray acid on to their plumage, as it enables them to get rid of troublesome parasites such as feather lice.

Some species of wood ants, including the rather disturbingly named blood-red slave-maker *Formica sanguinea*, have evolved to parasitise other kinds of ant. They do so by fooling the worker ants into carrying them inside the colony, at which point they kill the incumbent queen and take over. Finally they turn the resident workers into slaves.

But despite this antisocial behaviour, I can't help but be fascinated by these little creatures, as they go about their business blissfully unaware of my presence just a foot or so away.

TOOTHWORT

3 April

We are used to plants being green. That's because their cells contain chlorophyll, which – as we all learned in biology lessons – helps the plant to photosynthesise, turning sunlight into chemical energy.

In Britain, only a few plants break this convention: one of them is the toothwort. Each April, I look for its pallid spikes on the banks of the Dowles Brook in the Wyre Forest in Worcestershire. At this time, they are often mud-stained from floodwater, and lie like huge drowned caterpillars among the hazel roots.

Seen clearly and in pristine condition, this is one of the most bizarre British plants, with sepulchral flowers that would suit the grim depths of Tolkien's Mirkwood or the gardens of Gormenghast Castle.

Toothwort is a parasite on the roots of bushes, especially hazels and willows growing by streams. The stiff flower spikes have a strange elegance and it's hard not to be seduced by their pallor. These are botanical vampires drawing nutrients from their hosts so that they have no need of chlorophyll. They bloom in shady places where flying pollinators rarely venture, though where the woodland floor is blotched with sunlight, I have seen the flowers welcome solitary bees.

Toothwort is named from its scaly bracts on the underground stems, which to our ancestors looked rather like human teeth. To me, the fleshy flower-stalk with the blooms set to one side resembles a jawbone complete with a full bottom set.

It was this similarity to a part of the human body that made toothwort irresistible to medieval herbalists who followed the Doctrine of Signatures, claiming that the Creator had placed clues within a plant's appearance to its uses in treating maladies. With its dental analogies, it was a small leap of faith to ascribe healing properties to toothwort, which they knew as *Dentaria*. These included the relief of toothache and according to John Gerard, coughs and 'all other imperfections of the lungs'.

SWALLOW

4 April

The barnyard next to our home has been silent for six months now; ever since, on a breezy day in late September last year, the swallows circled the skies above for the very last time, and then turned and headed purposefully south for Africa.

But now, on a fine spring afternoon, they're back – and it's as if they've never been away. Twittering fills the air; and though it is sometimes frowned upon to ascribe human emotions to birds, I find it almost impossible not to imagine that these are sounds of joy, happiness and relief. That's certainly what I – and many of us – feel when we see that 'our' swallows are safely back home. For these delicate little birds, each weighing about twenty grams – rather less than an ounce – have flown almost 10,000 kilometres to be here.

A few weeks ago they were sunning themselves in the skies around the Cape of Good Hope at the southern tip of Africa. Then, driven by tiny changes in the chemical processes in their brains, they began to head north.

They crossed the tropical savannahs and equatorial forests, skirted the vast Sahara Desert, and then flew over the Mediterranean Sea and France until they reached the English Channel, almost within sight of home.

Here, bad weather at the very end of March delayed their arrival for a few days; but then the skies cleared, the barometer began to rise, and conditions were finally right for them to complete the last leg of their epic journey.

Until then they had been using the sun and the earth's magnetic field to navigate, but in the final few miles of their voyage they found their way by following familiar landmarks, until they arrived at this Somerset barn; the very place they hatched out less than a year ago. Here they will build their rather tatty nest on a wooden beam, and spend the summer raising a family.

It's no wonder, then, that the swallow is such a potent symbol of the coming of spring; not just here in Britain but all across the northern hemisphere, from Canada in the west to Japan in the east. This goes all the way back to the dawn of human culture; references to the return of the swallow can be found in the writings of ancient Greece and the Old Testament Book of Jeremiah: 'Yea, the stork in the heaven knoweth her appointed times; and the turtle [dove] and the crane and the swallow observe the time of their coming . . .'

So as I watch them reacquaint themselves with their summer home, I can't help but feel that the swallows' return, which I have just been privileged to witness, is little short of a miracle.

MORELS

5 April

Spring, a time for resurgence and new life, isn't a season we usually associate with those autumnal rotters the mushrooms, but April is a good month to search for two similar species, which have very different effects on us.

Morels are odd mushrooms. Looking like chunks of honeycomb designed by Dali, their conical fruiting bodies are pockmarked with deep hollows from which the spores waft in light breezes. Unlike the familiar gilled toadstools, morels are 'ascos', mycologist-speak for ascomycetes, the fungi that release their spores from little cups called asci. Breathe on some of the related cup-fungi such as orange-peel fungus and you can see the puffs of spores as they squirt out.

In my neck of the woods, morels are scarce and sometimes turn up where the ground has been burned; in other places they like neutral or chalky soil, but numbers vary widely from year to year. You could put this down to faddiness – many species vary in numbers each season – but morels seem to have a split personality.

Typically, they obtain their nutrients from dead wood; black morels in particular spring up where woodchips have been used as mulch in gardens. But it seems that morels can also form partnerships with living conifers. The underground mycelial web of the fungus invades the roots of the trees in a mutually beneficial relationship. Fungal threads called hyphae ferry nutrients from the soil into the tree's root system and in return receive other nutrients made by the tree.

Not all 'morels' are as they seem. There are false morels out there. I've only once seen this brain-like fungus, in a friend's sandy garden. It's sinister enough to look at, a rubbery brown walnut-sized fruiting body that if eaten raw can kill. Even when cooked, it attacks the liver and kidneys over a long period so that its effects aren't immediately obvious.

Stick to the real thing though and you can't go wrong: morels are highly sought after by gourmets and second only to truffles in their gastronomic appeal, but do cook them thoroughly to avoid stomach upsets.

WHITE STORK

6 April

The stork proverbially brings babies, but it also brings spring. All over Europe, the return of storks is greeted with the same delight we British reserve for the swallow or, as we once did until it became too scarce, the cuckoo.

So when I hear that a white stork has unexpectedly turned up just down the road from my home, I feel I should pay it the compliment of going to have a look. A bird the height of a seven-year-old child should be fairly easy to find; but it is not.

My search is not helped by the presence of dozens of loafing swans, most of them youngsters from last year – too young to breed, too old to be with their parents; teenage versions of the ugly duckling. Several times I screech to a halt (taking care, like all sensible birders, to check the rear-view mirror first), only to find that the stork-shaped bird I am looking at is a swan with its neck held in the air.

I bump into several fellow searchers, who, as is often the case with such events, turn vaguely philosophical in their musings. We discuss the possibility that the bird has simply hopped over the fence from a nearby zoo; given the lack of southerly winds and spring migrants, this seems at least possible.

I return home, having failed. Half an hour later, a text message tells me the bird is still here – but has moved half a mile or so away, to a far more suitable wetland habitat. Heading down to the local moor, I pass a group of three egrets; one appears shorter and less white than the others, and sure enough, it is the cattle egret that has been roaming the area since New Year's Day.

Half a mile further on, the sight of a birder gazing with great concentration down his telescope suggests that I have found the right spot. I have. The stork – grubbier and less white than the pictures show – is standing contentedly in a marshy field, where no doubt it will find the frogs it likes to eat.

Its upright position reminds me that the connection between storks and babies is supposedly linked with the phallic nature of its stance – hence the name 'stork', which derives from a Germanic word, and according to the *Oxford English Dictionary* refers to 'the apparent stiffness or rigidity in the bird's manner of standing'. As always with an unusual visitor, I find myself wondering what impelled this bird to cross the Channel: an accident, or is this bird perhaps a pioneer, whose spirit will one day enable this species to become a permanent colonist here?

SNAKE'S-HEAD FRITILLARY

7 April

In the Gloucestershire village of Cricklade, a keen wind is scouring North Meadow and vying with traffic thundering past on the adjacent A419. It's best to keep your head down here, not only against the elements, but also to look for flowers at your feet. This flood-meadow is one of the best places in the British Isles to see one of our rarest plants, a flower that blooms here in hundreds of thousands each April, luring pilgrims from far afield.

The snake's-head fritillary is unlike any other British wild plant. Its inverted bell-like flowers, the colour of bruised plums, are wonderfully chequered: fritillary derives from *fritillus*, the Latin for 'dice box', a wooden container that was decorated with geometric patterns. Some of the flowers are white, like vegetable lampshades, inside which orange filaments, the sexual organs, glow in sunlight.

Today there's little sun, but the cold start to spring has delayed grass growth so that the fritillaries stand proud of the sward. So numerous are they in places, that in the foreshortened view through binoculars they create a greyish haze that floats just above the meadow, a botanical mist through which distant photographers wade, pondering the impossible task of deciding on the most photogenic patch of plants.

It is a remarkable sight, countless snake's-heads trembling on grey-green stems, their acolytes kneeling in the keen breeze to capture this unmissable and yet, perhaps, not-quite-British spectacle.

Fritillaries do seem too exotic to be British wild flowers and their nativity is often questioned. In the 1970s and 1980s my botany books informed me that the bulbs were native in a handful of ancient undisturbed hay meadows, mostly in southern England and usually on floodplains. The meadows themselves were unusual survivors because most fertile land had been ploughed up long since. The remaining fritillaries often occur in huge numbers such as at North Meadow, or Magdalen College Meadow in Oxford, and so have presumably taken centuries to attain large populations.

This, and the fact that they only seem comfortable in an ancient habitat, surrounded by other scarce plants, suggests that they are indeed indigenous here.

But doubts creep in. Although snake's-heads were recorded in cultivation in the sixteenth century, the first wild record came in 1736 and they weren't further documented until forty years later, which is very late indeed for such a showy native plant. But they are so alluring and so well loved that, whatever their true origins, we desperately want them to be British.

Should this matter? Not a jot. Poppies and corn marigolds aren't native and yet we relish the splashes of colour they bring to dull fields of barley and wheat. The fritillaries don't harm native plants and are undoubtedly popular with their human neighbours. So, while their nativity is an absorbing conundrum, it shouldn't detract from their appeal. For the moment in North Meadow, I'm just happy to revel in their wind-tossed exuberance.

BITTERN

8 April

It's five o'clock in the morning on a fine April day, and I'm listening for one of the most bizarre sounds in the bird world: a sound like someone blowing gently across the top of a milk bottle, but two or three octaves deeper.

BOOM! When it finally comes, it is unmistakable, and yet impossible to believe that it comes from a bird at all . . .

BOOM! It echoes across – and through – the dense stand of reeds, which ripple in the strengthening breeze as if responding to the sound waves passing by . . .

BOOM! It feels as if the bird is right next to me, though it is quite possible that it is several hundred metres away, for this particular call carries up to five miles – further than any other bird in the world.

It's not hard to deduce that this mystery boomer is the bittern, the smaller, browner and far more elusive cousin of the familiar grey heron. This is a bird that, until very recently, I could never have heard here on the Somerset Levels. Yet this year's spring survey is likely to find close to fifty booming males. When you consider that the bittern disappeared as a British breeding bird little more than a century ago, and as recently as the 1990s was down to fewer than twenty booming males, its comeback has been truly impressive.

The healthy population here on the Levels is something of a surprise, given that two hard winters in a row at the start of this decade should have caused bittern numbers to plummet. After all, like a fine malt whisky, bitterns and ice don't mix: when their wetland homes freeze over they usually fail to find food and die.

One possible reason why the Somerset bitterns have managed to survive is that they live in the same place as the famous starling roost, in which on winter evenings millions of birds gather together to spend the night in the safety of the reeds. The starlings may be safe from land-based predators such as foxes, but the reed-bed provides no refuge from predatory bitterns. It seems that during those cold spells, as soon as the starlings settled down for the night, the hungry bitterns simply walked through the roost picking off sick and vulnerable birds, tossing them in the air and swallowing them whole.

The presence of so many bitterns has attracted lots of people who long to see this elusive creature in the flesh. Some are disappointed: either the birds stay hidden, or they just fly briefly from one reed-bed to the next, flopping through the air with all the elegance of an airborne sack of potatoes, before dropping down out of sight again.

But once in a while they do give really great views. On one such occasion a young visitor was so impressed that in his excitement he coined a new, and highly appropriate, name for the bittern: 'toasted heron'.

RING OUZEL
9 April

The love affair began on a cold April day in 1977. I was walking on the Clent Hills in north Worcestershire, approaching the summit where, from just over 1,000 feet, you can gaze north over the vast sprawl of Birmingham and the Black Country.

That day the wind was shaking the gorse hummocks, bringing curtains of snow, which eclipsed the view. Above the gusts came an unfamiliar sound, like the clatter of disturbed scree. A blackbird arced overhead in the breeze, and then a small flock, their stony calls interspersed with hoarse chuckling, not sounding like blackbirds at all. They pitched into the trackside bushes long enough for me to see their pale bibs – my first ring ouzels. Then with another salvo of clacking, they peeled off into the storm, and were lost to the snowflakes.

Enslaved by memories of that first encounter and progressively more breathless as time goes by, I have pounded up the steep slopes of the Clent Hills in late March and April each year since on ouzelling trips. Many of these are in vain, but in most years one or two birds turn up, occasionally a group of six, though I've never equalled that first day's total of a dozen or more. In calmer weather and for more prolonged views, you need a furtive approach: they are nervy birds and will scuttle under the skirts of gorse bushes if disturbed, or fly off, tack-tacking noisily. But if you conceal your outline and stay patient, they eventually emerge to feed on the sheep-cropped turf.

Ring ouzels used to be known as mountain blackbirds, because they breed on rocky tors and fells, especially where streams carve deep clefts through moorland. The birds that we see in lowland spots in spring are on passage between their wintering grounds in the mountains of North Africa and these upland breeding areas in the British Isles and further north in Sweden and Norway.

Ring ouzels are dazzlingly handsome. The blackish males sport a brilliant white gorget, visible from a long way off. Females and younger birds are much more like female blackbirds but with a paler bib. Even in flight or from behind, though, the key feature to look for is a silvery flash in the wing-feathers, which you see as a thin pale band when the birds settle. That and their stony alarm calls make them easy to identify when they are around.

They share their run-and-tilt habit with blackbirds and are equally successful worm-catchers. But there are more subtle differences too: longer wings give them a looser flight action, more like a fieldfare than a blackbird, and on the ground they look rangier and more alert, as if the sparse living in their native uplands has honed their instincts.

I find them irresistibly watchable, perhaps because our paths cross very briefly each year. For the same reason, ouzels fascinated the eighteenth-century Hampshire vicar and ornithologist Gilbert White, who observed them regularly in spring and autumn near his Selborne parish, and suspected them to be Scandinavian birds driven south by the frost. In April 1769 he shot a cock and hen on passage, finding them 'juicy and well-flavoured'.

For me they are alluring for different reasons: the combination of brief encounters, relative scarcity and striking appearance is a powerful one. That's why this April, as every year, I am making the pilgrimage into the hills, to keep faith.

CAPERCAILLIE

10 April

Even in April, dawn comes ridiculously early to the forests of Strathspey in the Highlands of Scotland. My head feels as if it has barely hit the pillow before the alarm clock goes off, and I stagger blearily out of bed.

It should be worth it, though. For I have come to witness the courtship display, or lek, of the male capercaillie. Imagine a turkey crossed with a peacock and doing a breakdance, and you'll have some idea of what I am hoping to see.

As the first flickers of light filter through the pine canopy, and I see him getting ready to perform, I find myself holding my breath in anticipation. Then he's off, strutting and fretting his way back and forth across his chosen stage. Just like the rutting red deer later in the year, he is trying to impress his harem of watching females. Even in this early morning light I can see the subtleties of his plumage: black at a distance, but full of delicate shades of purple, brown and green when seen close up.

Watching him, I am bizarrely reminded of disco-dancer John Travolta in the film *Saturday Night Fever*. This isn't as odd a comparison as it may sound, for although the bird may appear to be the centre of attention, he is not in full control of his destiny. The females may stand in the shadows like wallflowers, meek and quiet, but they will be the ones doing the choosing. If he fails to impress them, he will fail to breed, and so be unable to pass on his genes to the next generation.

Perhaps this explains why he is making so much effort: giving his all in a performance that culminates in the famous 'champagne-bottle-opened-backwards' sound that brings the display to its climax, and leaves me drained of emotion.

To witness this has been a rare privilege, and one that in a matter of decades may no longer be possible here in Britain. For sadly, for the second time in its history on these islands, it looks as if the capercaillie may be disappearing as a British breeding bird, due to a triple-whammy of habitat loss, climate change and predation.

PALMATE NEWT
11 April

By the forest rides are small seepages where water stained the colour of malt whisky by rotting leaves collects in shallow runnels. Here and there tiny pools form, on whose surfaces whirligig beetles gyrate manically like out-of-control speedboats in a James Bond film. Beneath them, dragons prowl across the muddy floor: this is the courting arena of palmate newts.

Within a few paces of passing feet and forestry vehicles, in just a few centimetres of water, the male newts shimmy for their prospective partners. Newt courtship is a complex affair, a ritual in which the wrong move can bring rejection.

Fanning his tail rapidly in front of the female, occasionally lashing the whip-like end against his body, the male channels his pheromones in her direction. If she accepts him, she will move towards the male and nuzzle his tail, the cue for him to deposit a packet of sperm which she takes up into her cloaca. The whole affair can take place by night or day and even in midwinter if it's mild enough. In December 2015 I saw males circling females in a garden pond at midnight, though without the enthusiastic ardour of spring encounters.

Palmate newts are more tolerant of acidic pools than the commoner smooth newts and can survive in very little water. In high summer I sometimes see minuscule newtlets darting like fish across muddy puddles in forestry tracks. How many of these reach adulthood we don't know, but enough presumably to maintain local numbers.

The fully-grown male palmate newts are handsome creatures, mottled olive and gold with a dark eyestripe and, in the breeding season only, black webbed feet, which our two other newt species lack. Come summer, when breeding is over, both sexes leave the water. Now their skins are silkier than the softest kid-leather, as they wander the forest floor looking for insects, worms and spiders. When I uncover them under damp logs, I quickly re-cover them to protect them from predators and drying winds.

PINE MARTEN
12 April

The robin on the bird-table cocks its head to one side, then dashes off in a whirr of wings. The blue tits on the feeders flee too, uttering high-pitched alarm calls to warn their fellow flock-mates. Something has disturbed them – but what?

Moments later, the cause of all this bother appears. A female pine marten – slightly smaller and lighter than the male – lollops across the lawn and climbs up on to the bird-table with practised ease, like a gymnast mounting the high bars. Flicking her long, bushy tail out of the way, she begins to feed. Sleek and slender, with glossy chocolate-brown upperparts and creamy-yellow underparts, she looks like a stoat on steroids. Her fur is rich and lustrous, as if she has just spent a session at a beauty parlour.

Seeing such a rare creature gorging herself like an American teenager on jam and peanut butter sandwiches is rather disconcerting – even though we are in the heart of its Scottish Highland stronghold. But pine martens are great opportunists, so why would she spend time and effort chasing a mouse or vole, when she can simply shin up a pole to feast on this convenient and tasty snack?

Not everyone is quite so enthusiastic about pine martens as I am. Gamekeepers detest them because these wily animals love the eggs of ground-nesting birds such as pheasants. So for centuries they were trapped, shot and poisoned, and by the end of Queen Victoria's long reign their numbers had plummeted to a mere 1,000 or so, forced back into the wooded northern and western outposts of the Scottish mainland.

Now that persecution has all but ended, pine martens have bounced back, and there are as many as 4,000 in Britain. Although these animals are nocturnal and very hard to see, researchers have tracked their advance by searching for the dark, heart-shaped droppings – known as scats – which the martens use to mark their territory. They have discovered that pine martens are now living on the edge of Scotland's biggest cities, where they regularly feed in suburban gardens. One has even been photographed much further south, in a Shropshire wood, and they have also been successfully reintroduced to central Wales.

The comeback of this sleek and efficient predator is good news, because pine martens prey on the introduced grey squirrel, which they chase down and catch with ruthless efficiency. (The smaller, lighter reds escape by running to the ends of small branches where pine martens are too heavy to follow.)

Back on the bird-table she polishes off the last of the sandwiches, pours herself down on to the ground and melts back into the surrounding forest.

ORANGE-TIP

13 April

The decision to let garlic mustard thrive in a wild part of the garden has just rewarded me with one of my best doorstep encounters. Garlic mustard is a food-plant of the orange-tip butterfly, the epitome of April, a mercurial pilgrim of woodland rides and sunny hedgerows.

The spring males, whose wingtips are dipped in vibrant tangerine, appear distracted in their early flights, darting this way and that, backtracking and sideslipping, but always on the move. They're looking for the plainer, grey and white females, and they travel long distances to find one. Even though they're not resident in my town garden, I can lure wanderers in by planting their caterpillar's food-plants, garlic mustard and lady's smock.

The story began last June, when I found an orange-tip pupa, like a small green longbow, attached by silk threads to the garlic mustard seed pods. Although I hadn't seen an adult butterfly in the garden, one had clearly passed through and laid eggs. How many caterpillars hatched I can't say, but only a few will have survived; orange-tip larvae are cannibalistic. As autumn drew on, the pupa turned brown to match the drying mustard stalk and resembled a seed pod.

Throughout the dark winter months I resisted the urge to tidy away its holdfast and acknowledged it with a casual inspection: I assumed that it might have died. April's here now, and a couple of days ago I saw a dark spot that I hadn't noticed before – a fungal infection marking the butterfly's demise, perhaps? Yesterday it was still there, possibly a little darker. I came indoors to answer a phone call and during those twenty minutes, the miracle had happened. Clinging to the tattered chrysalis was a female orange-tip, her filigreed hindwings still rumpled from emergence, her head and legs thickly furred with pale hairs.

Over the next two hours, her wings stiffened and, work suspended, I waited while she took her first faltering flight – just a couple of metres on to a patch of lady's smock flowers. There she unfurled her proboscis for her first adult meal. We all know of the transformation from caterpillar into butterfly, but the emergence of this fragile insect after months of surveillance, a butterfly I actively encouraged by adding its food-plants to my garden, has given me a pleasure out of all proportion to its simplicity. I feel honoured.

MINNOWS AND STICKLEBACKS
14 April

Few of my childhood memories are quite so evocative as what we used to call 'fishing for tiddlers' – dipping a net into the waters of a pond or stream to catch minnows and sticklebacks, then carrying them home in a jam jar with string precariously fastened around the rim.

Even today, almost fifty years later, I only need to stand on a rickety bridge and gaze down into the clear, shallow waters below to experience an almost Proustian moment of recollection. The signal for this is the time when the light ripples on the water's surface settle for a moment or two, and I can see little shoals of minnows: small and fast, their brownish shade providing perfect camouflage until they flick their bodies and move forward, revealing their presence.

Gathering in these loose shoals may look sociable, but it's actually the best way to avoid being eaten – an occupational hazard if you are a minnow. These little fish are on the menu for a whole range of creatures, including larger fish such as pike, as well as herons, ducks and that master predator of our waterways, the kingfisher.

I gaze again through the surface reflection, and glimpse another, slightly larger fish, with three prominent spines along the top of its back: a stickleback. Later, when I read up about this quirky little fish, I discover that it shouldn't really be here at all: sticklebacks were originally marine fish, but after the last Ice Age became trapped in inland waterbodies, evolving into a separate species from their marine cousins.

Despite hours of pond dipping as a child, I have never witnessed the sticklebacks' rather unusual breeding behaviour. Just like birds, the male defends his territory against any rivals, and builds a tiny nest out of aquatic plants. He is an exemplary parent: caring for the eggs by fanning them with water to provide oxygen to help them develop.

That's when his fatherly duties really begin. At this early stage in their lives the tiny young are incredibly vulnerable, being a tasty snack for all sorts of underwater creatures, including cannibalistic sticklebacks. So in a fine display of paternal care, the male will often suck the youngsters into his mouth and spit them back into the nest, where they can be safe – for the moment at least.

NATTERJACK TOAD
15 April

By day the dunes on Lancashire's Ainsdale coast are dry and inhospitable to amphibians. Wind rustles the stiff skirts of marram grass and sand-devils whirl across the beach. What thin-skinned moisture-loving creature would choose to live in this inimical place?

After dark it is a different story. The night I ventured there the breeze had dropped and I made my way to one of the shallow pools behind the dunes. In the distance was a reedy, pulsing sound, the sound of the natterjack toad.

Individually each toad produces a dry but musical trill, but in chorus the effect, as their calls overlapped and phased with each other, was otherworldly, worthy of a *Doctor Who* soundtrack. No wonder that one of the natterjack's names in this part of Lancashire was the Bootle organ.

We approached the breeding pool in darkness, treading carefully to avoid the toads emerging from their burrows in the dunes. By picking out their sand-trails, we tracked down my first natterjacks, running rather than hopping in the torchlight towards the mating throng. They were small compared with the common toads in my garden and had the same golden eyes, but sported a cream dorsal stripe.

At the pool, the torch-beam picked out several males spread-eagled on the surface, their pale throats ballooning with the effort of song.

There were occasional tumbles and skirmishes between rivals, though none of the unseemly mating balls that accompany the nuptials of common toads. I gawped at the sheer spectacle of it and found it hard to believe that I was looking at a colony of one of our rarest amphibians. Driving home down the M6 that night, my ears still rang with the toads' chorus.

To see natterjacks you need to make an effort. In the UK they are amphibians on the edge, and need sand for burrowing and shallow predator-free pools for spawning. The tadpoles grow fastest in warm shallow water, but there's always the risk of these pools drying out which can wipe out the offspring for a whole season. For this reason natterjacks are disappearing from many of their remaining British haunts and depend on human intervention to create new habitat and prevent their existing pools from becoming shaded by vegetation.

There are a few inland sites on heaths, but most natterjack colonies are near the coast as far north as the Solway Firth, and so are at risk from inundation by high tides. Toad conservationists can rarely rest on their laurels, but without their efforts this fantastical chorus would be much harder to hear.

HAIRY DRAGONFLY

16 April

Few creatures say 'summer' as loudly and clearly as dragonflies. So to come across one in the middle of April – even during an unusually fine, warm and early spring – is something of a surprise.

The good news is that I don't even need to look properly to know which species this is. Only one of the twenty or so British dragonflies is tough enough – or perhaps foolish enough – to emerge quite so early in the year. To do so is a gamble: they beat the competition, most of which appear a month or two later, but they do run the risk of a cool, late spring making their insect food hard to find.

The hairy dragonfly – or as it is sometimes known, the hairy hawker – is one of our smaller dragonflies, and like its cousins spends most of its time either zigzagging up and down the paths alongside my wetland patch, or perching on the reeds. When it does land, I seize the chance to get a closer look through my telescope. The powerful lens gives me access to a whole new world; from just a few metres away, I can see the tiny, downy hairs that cover the insect's apple-green thorax, and give the species its name.

I take this opportunity to examine the structure of the dragonfly closely, too. They really are little miracles of nature: those compound eyes, like something a sci-fi writer would invent; the long, narrow abdomen, coloured in this male's case blue and chocolate brown; and most of all the delicate-looking yet immensely strong wings, each latticed as if traced by a skilled etcher.

Then, without warning, he takes to the air, and zooms off, accelerating through the springtime air like time itself.

MOUNTAIN HARES

17 April

It is an April morning on the heathery slopes of Ladybower Reservoir in the Peak District. At the top, deep hummocks of heather are broken by pale swatches of moor-grass, while hanks of brown cotton sedge mark out the wetter spots; spring arrives slowly up here. I am here with two guides from the Sorby Natural History Society on the lookout for mountain hares.

Past a huddle of pine trees, one of my guides, Derek, points out a moorland ridge that lies within the city limits of Sheffield. We scan for hares and suddenly one breaks loose, jinking this way and that, its tail a white beacon flickering on and off between the mounds of heather. These hares, which have traditionally shed their white fur during spring, are now retaining their brown fur longer into winter as the months become warmer and snow cover more infrequent. We wait and it pauses, pale brown, frosted with white, a pallid dot on the umber moor. It's a snub-nosed, shorter-eared, woollier version of the brown hare and this one is clearly well into the spring moult.

As we wade across the heather other hares zigzag away and the other guide, Val, remarks that the milder winter has helped good numbers survive. They feed on heather, grass and bilberry shoots and are seemingly surrounded by food. Even so we find a corpse, white-furred still, so probably a couple of months old and a reminder that disease and wet winters are the modern enemies of hares in the Peaks. There are other dangers, too. Mountain hares may be reservoirs for the tick-borne louping virus, which attacks grouse, and on some Scottish moors they are shot by moor-managers.

In the Peak District there's clearly a local pride in the hares. Although they were originally introduced for sport in the 1870s they are now indelibly part of the character of this rugged landscape, and that – and the attentions of citizen scientists – may be enough to protect them.

PYGMY SHREW
18 April

A squeal of excitement from my daughter Daisy signals the animal's appearance. Moments later, a tiny ball of fur about the size of a golf ball scoots across the path in front of us and promptly disappears into the long grass.

That is a typical view of our smallest terrestrial mammal, the pygmy shrew. Despite the brevity of our encounter, I can be confident in my identification. That's because we are on the island of Lundy, off the coast of north Devon, and this tiny creature is the only small mammal found here.

If it looked as if it was in a hurry, that's because it always is. Small birds have a tough enough time getting sufficient energy to survive, but compared to pygmy shrews they are leisurely feeders. While a blue tit has to eat about one-third of its body weight each day, the pygmy shrew must gorge on an astonishing one and a quarter times its own weight. If it fails to do so, every single day of its life, it will die.

So you don't often get a close look at this creature, which can weigh as little as two and a half grams – less than a penny. If you manage to do so, the obvious features are the long, pointed snout typical of all shrews, which it uses to sniff out prey such as beetles, woodlice and spiders; the pale, greyish-brown fur; and a tail that may be almost as long as its body.

Their small size means that they cannot do many of the things that larger shrews and rodents take for granted: digging tunnels, for instance, or eating earthworms. Instead they have to use existing burrows, and hope that they don't come across any of the permanent residents there.

Life for a pygmy shrew can be nasty, brutish and very short: they are prey for tawny and barn owls, foxes, stoats and weasels and of course domestic cats. They typically live for just a few months – and rarely much longer than a year.

In the absence of house mice on Lundy, pygmy shrews have moved into some of the cottages there, where they can be seen fighting their way through deep-pile rugs to get across the room. Some, the island's warden tells me with delight, have even taken to a diet of cooked spaghetti.

LILY BEETLE

19 April

As soon as the snake's-head fritillaries flower in the garden, drops of vivid blood appear on their leaves, like clues at a murder scene. These are lily beetles, as bright as a guardsman's uniform and as shiny as Humbrol enamel. I have distinctly mixed feelings about them. Their scarlet brilliance makes ladybirds seem drab and, were they as harmless as ladybirds to garden plants, they would undoubtedly be popular. But lily beetles are alien invaders whose slug-like larvae, disguised by their own slimy droppings, reduce garden lilies to tatters so efficiently that I have given up trying to grow the later-flowering varieties.

For the twenty-first-century naturalist, many insects evoke contra-dictory emotions. Last year I found the rosemary beetle in a nearby churchyard. It's another alien introduction, which eats lavender and rosemary, but is a living jewel striped in metallic greens, reds and violets, a colour scheme that way outstrips the plants on which it feeds. It is deemed a noxious pest by horticulturalists, though like the lily beetle was in fact introduced by them as plants are moved between countries.

And though we blame the insect for its invasive behaviour – and more often than not reach for the spray gun – such change is a fact of life. With mixed feelings as a gardener and a naturalist I reluctantly savour this extra injection of biodiversity in the backyard.

BLACK GUILLEMOT
20 April

There are few more pleasant places to sit and watch the world go by than a Scottish fishing harbour on a sunny April morning. For someone from the south of Britain, like me, this also provides a rare and welcome chance to see one of our most endearing yet underrated seabirds: the black guillemot.

These amiable little birds soon oblige, bobbing like rubber ducks on the surface of the water, illuminated by the ever-changing reflections of the sun shining off the fishing boats alongside them. The effect is, quite simply, mesmerising.

I contemplate that, in its breeding garb, the black guillemot really is one of the most striking and handsome of all our birds. A glance through my binoculars reveals that the plumage is more sooty-brown than black – especially in this strong spring sunlight – and is neatly set off by two contrastingly bright white oval wing-patches. One bird opens its gape to reveal a flash of bright crimson, while another dives beneath the surface to search for small fish, momentarily revealing its equally bright-red feet.

I have occasionally seen black guillemots outside the breeding season, when they could hardly appear more different, shedding their elegant breeding plumage and turning a murky, off-white shade.

But for now, they are as stylish as any supermodel; an impression spoiled only slightly when one waddles ashore and squeezes its plump little body into a crevice between two large stones in the harbour wall. For unlike other auks, black guillemots are not colonial nesters, but breed along rocky coasts.

I've even seen them in the busy port of Oban, where passing shoppers and holidaymakers may be unaware of the birds nesting just below them, among the cracks and fissures of the harbour walls.

In the far north of the black guillemot's British range, on Shetland or Orkney, you may hear locals refer to the bird as a 'tystie', which derives from an Old Norse word for the bird's whistling call. This is similar to the official Norwegian, Danish and Icelandic names for this engaging little seabird, reminding us of the linguistic heritage we share with these Nordic nations.

EMPEROR MOTHS
21 April

Out on the moors near Sheffield on an April morning, meadow pipits were rising and falling in their vertical song-flights. But speeding along across our paths were large furry insects, blurs so fast that we couldn't make out any wing-markings or even proper colours.

They were emperor moths and, if they'd stopped long enough to be admired, would have revealed an eyespot on each wing, encircled by interweaving patterns as rich as an oriental kelim.

The first time I saw this gaudy insect – on the cover of a book I read as a teenager – it seemed far too conspicuous and exotic to inhabit our islands. But, the book told me, it revels in the bleak moors where its fat emerald and sable caterpillar munches on heather shoots.

The emperors have an uphill task to find each other in the vast moorland landscapes. The fat grey females squat among the heather like miniature tabby cats and waft plumes of pheromones into the spring breeze. From a radius of 100 metres or more, the males detect this scent cloud with their feathery antennae and zone in on the chance of fertilising her eggs.

What I was seeing on that moor as we barged through invisible ropes of moth-perfume was a frantic search for sex as the male emperors zigzagged their way wildly over the heather, questing for clues that would lead them to the 'calling' female. The emperor's technique has been borrowed by moth-collectors, who rear the females from cocoons and then set them out in open country and wait. It's known in the trade as 'assembling' and soon brings in a crowd of hopeful males. Nowadays they're photographed, but in the past would often end their lives in a killing jar, to be mounted on pins and filed away in cabinets: an unhappy fate for a lovelorn aristocrat.

DAWN CHORUS FEAST
22 April

There's nothing like getting up early to fuel an appetite, especially if you consider breakfast to be the most important meal of the day. So the idea of rising at 4 a.m., taking a score of people on a dawn chorus event, and not eating until gone seven, fills me with a mixture of horror and delicious anticipation.

Fortunately the birds themselves provide enough entertainment to distract me from the rumbles in my stomach. And this morning, at least, they appear right on cue – in the classic order known to all who go out bird-listening at this time of year.

We are on the edge of Long Ashton, a suburban village on the outskirts of Bristol, where a wood of beech and bluebells rises above the houses. It's a good spot, but at this time of year almost any wood or even a city park will provide a suitably loud and varied chorus.

Not surprisingly, the first bird to sing is a robin, closely followed by a blackbird. One of the people with me sings the lyrics to the Beatles' song 'Blackbird', and for the first time I wonder if the bird Paul McCartney heard singing 'in the dead of night' might actually have been a robin. The 'nightingale' singing in Berkeley Square certainly was.

They are followed by the repetitive, comforting sound of the song thrush; the frantic trilling of the wren; and – a mild surprise – a goldcrest carolling its twiddly, high-pitched song from deep inside a conifer.

We venture deeper into the wood, and as the sun begins to illuminate the scene we hear more resident birds: great tits, doing their 'tea-cher, tea-cher' routine; scolding blue tits, which always sound slightly cross; and a distant nuthatch, whose rounded, liquid call fills the morning air.

It is gone six o'clock before any migrants join in: several chiffchaffs, calling out their name with a desperate insistence; and a blackcap, whose song is full of fruity, fluty tones.

By seven o'clock, the chorus is almost over and we descend through bluebell-fringed paths to tuck in to a feast of local produce.

STOAT

23 April

A thin, high-pitched squeak, followed by a blur of movement. I lift my head from the computer screen to see a slender flash of russet brown streak past the window of my garden office.

Thoughts of red squirrels come to mind, but moments later it reappears.

A stoat, carrying a large, grey object in its mouth – a recently deceased rodent. I just have time to register the black tip to the tail – the easiest way, apart from its larger size, to tell it apart from its smaller cousin, the weasel – when it melts into the shrubbery.

A week or so later, on a fine sunny afternoon, I see the stoat again. This time it runs across the garden lawn in stuttering dashes and leaps, before disappearing into a pile of willow branches from the trees that run along the boundary of our garden, and which have recently been pollarded. I wonder if this is why the animal has chosen to come into our garden, for stoats are secretive creatures, and need a place where they can hide away, out of sight. The logpile is the perfect den. And rabbits, the stoat's favourite prey, regularly feed on our lawn, so he won't be short of food.

LAMPREYS

24 April

There are some creatures that a naturalist will never get to see without a certain amount of detective work. Lampreys were, for me, firmly in this category, until one April day when I travelled to Ripon to meet naturalist Brian Morland, who has taken a special interest in lampreys in the River Ure.

We were a little too early for the adult lampreys, which spawn in writhing clusters in gravel-beds, but, undaunted by this, Brian seized a stout wooden-framed net and began probing in the riverbank. After a few purposeful jabs, he hoisted a mass of mud and rotting twigs from beneath an overhanging willow.

As we examined the ooze, small eel-like creatures wriggled below its surface. These, said Brian, were lamprey larvae and they were my first sightings of these extraordinary proto-fish. There is something utterly primeval about these blind, translucent, pig-nosed creatures: I was hooked.

Adult lampreys are indeed primitive creatures armed with large sucker mouths ringed with rasping teeth. Their lack of a jawbone, or indeed any bones – they are cartilaginous, like sharks – and the presence of a pineal eye on the top of their heads, which registers only light, has led some biologists to wonder if lampreys should be classified as fish at all.

For years they lurk in darkness until their final transformation into adults when their true eyes appear and their suckers form. Clearly built to last, lampreys pre-date the dinosaurs by hundreds of millions of years, but are now in decline over much of the UK. A surfeit of lampreys was supposed to have done for Henry I in 1135 – he is said to have fallen ill after he ate a number of them against his physician's advice – though some say that's a euphemism for more fleshly pursuits. Lampreys still retain a royal connection – Queen Elizabeth II was presented with a dish to celebrate her Golden Jubilee in 2012 – but most of us commoners need actively to look for lampreys if we want to see them.

Key to this is getting to grips with their odd life cycle. The brook lamprey is our commonest species, growing to around fifteen centimetres and staying in freshwater throughout its life. The related river and sea lampreys spend some of their adult life at sea, returning to freshwater to breed.

Brook lampreys need clear streams where they spawn in gravelly beds. The young lampreys or ammocoetes that I first saw in Ripon live in burrows in silty riverbanks, where they filter tiny animals such as diatoms by channelling water through their mouths, securing prey on a mucus thread. Each year, they grow a little larger, taking five to seven years to mature, after which they become transformers. Mouthparts become suckers and the skin over their eyes recedes.

River and sea lampreys now turn into parasites, heading downstream and out to sea to latch on to marine fishes. Their last act is a return to freshwater to spawn and die. Brook lampreys don't feed as adults though: they are breeding machines whose adult life is over in a few months.

Inspired by my experiences in Yorkshire, I commandeered some friends to help me look for lampreys in the River Severn near my home. Plunging a net into a carefully chosen mud bank near Bewdley, on the first attempt I was amazed to see three lamprey larvae wriggling in the silt. All were eyeless, and one seemed to be in its pre-adult year. After much cheering and general euphoria, we photographed them in a portable tank and released them back into the Severn where they plunged arrow-straight into the mud.

For decades I'd driven past this stretch of river without realising that these antediluvian creatures lived here. Now my world is that bit richer for knowing that they are there, filtering away anonymously in the ooze.

ST MARK'S FLY
25 April

A country walk towards the end of April, when the sky is filled with small but conspicuous insects, which appear to have forgotten how to fly. I fix my eyes on one, and notice that it heads a few feet forward, then appears to stop in mid-air and plummet downwards, before somehow recalling its purpose and flying upwards to gain height once again.

These are St Mark's flies, also known as black gnats, hawthorn bugs and love bugs. The latter name comes from their tendency to mate in mid-air, each clinging on to one another for dear life as they desperately try to chart a course across the spring sky.

When one does finally land, perching on a blossom-filled hawthorn twig, I at last get the chance to take a closer look at this peculiar insect. This is a male: black, with a rather furry thorax; the females are bicoloured, pale and dark.

Of more than 7,000 different species of fly found in Britain, perhaps only the crane fly or the bluebottle are quite so obvious as this tiny harbinger of spring. So named because they traditionally appear on 25 April, the feast day of St Mark, these flies may emerge as early as the final week of March, and can be seen right the way into June.

But now, towards the end of April, they are at their most abundant and annoying, bumping and crashing into me as I try to negotiate their airspace.

I don't mind, because the appearance of these pesky flies is also the signal that the flood of returning migrant birds is now arriving from Africa. For birds such as swallows, chats and flycatchers, these billions of easily caught insects are a much needed source of food and energy. So however annoying St Mark's flies can be, they are also a very welcome sight.

YELLOW WAGTAIL
26 April

Some birthdays are more memorable than most – and not just because, in this case, it was my landmark fiftieth. Even as we were taking the children to school, the birds had an unexpected surprise for us. We came across a flock of eleven whimbrels feeding in a field behind our house; they had dropped in for refuelling en route from their West African winter quarters to their Scandinavian breeding grounds.

Later that morning, more treats – this time on Tealham Moor, an area of rough grazing a few miles to the south. Lapwings hurtled across the sky, their high-pitched cries tearing into the firmament as if they were trying to shatter it. A cuckoo called in the distance, as a pair of buzzards sky-danced above our heads. Then, the bird we had come looking for: a yellow wagtail, shooting between the legs of the cattle to pick up tiny insects in its slender bill.

Its loud 'sweep' call is the best way to locate this summer visitor as it migrates. Follow the sound with binoculars and you may pick up the bounding lemon dot in a blue sky as the wagtail heads for pastures unknown. Sometimes when they land to catch furry dung-flies at the feet of cattle, they become darting splashes of sulphur among the dandelions. Sadly, this is a less and less regular sight in the country-side, for yellow wagtails – like so many summer visitors from south of the Sahara Desert – are becoming more and more scarce in recent years.

Finally, as the air began to warm, so came the swifts – that classic sign of spring. When I lived in London, they used to appear during the first few days of May; but now, in Somerset, I usually see them on or just after my birthday. I couldn't wish for a better present.

BLOODY-NOSED BEETLE
27 April

How some creatures survive seems a mystery. Without the benefit of speed or camouflage or aggression, it is hard to imagine how insects like the bloody-nosed beetle have managed to last as individuals or, indeed, as a species.

As they stumble drowsily over short grass on downland, heaths and clifftops, their dozy, bumbling shapes look like obvious targets for birds and small mammals. Although their smooth, black wing cases are separated by a groove, they are actually fused and so, unlike many beetles, they cannot fly from danger.

In its defence, the bloody-nosed beetle is encased in tough armour, a layer of chitin that protects it from casual nibblers. If this does not deter them, the insect exudes droplets of reddish liquid from its jaws. These are highly unpleasant to predators and can cause blistering sufficient to discourage larger mammals such as foxes. Even the beetle's bloated blackish larvae wander around on the turf with impunity, the Jabba the Hutts of the insect world.

But what the beetle's noxious fluids can't do is to protect it from larger forces like habitat change. Bloody-nosed beetle grubs feed on bedstraws, so-called because they smell of new-mown hay when dry and were once used to stuff pillows. Though these plants are still common, where hedgerows are sprayed and shaded and grassland is over-grazed, they soon decline and with them goes the bloody-nosed beetle.

'SEA' SWALLOWS
28 April

I gaze out to sea on a hazy April day as a fork-tailed bird passes in the far distance. It flies over Steart Point, across the Bristol Channel, and past the sandy island at the mouth of the River Parrett. Heading northeast, it eventually disappears out of sight.

A sea swallow, I think. Not a tern, which are often called 'sea swallows' because of their elegant flight and forked tail, but a *real* swallow, which just happens to be flying across the sea.

Looking again, I see another, and then another – a steady stream of individual birds that together form an invading army of returning migrants. One comes much closer – only yards above my head – so close I can see the individual feathers in its tail.

The wind is against them today – it has blown persistently from the north-east for days – but the impulse to continue on their journey is far stronger than mere weather can put a halt to.

So they carry on: up the Bristol Channel, across Britain, to end up in Scotland perhaps, or maybe even as far as Scandinavia. Watching these distant travellers, I am reminded that once I stood on the Icelandic island of Surtsey – a lump of rock that emerged from beneath the waves in 1963, and so is younger than me – and watched a lone swallow hawking for insects against a gin-clear sky.

Swallows do not even breed in Iceland, so that bird was a hardy pioneer, seeking out new lands to colonise. Who knows, the birds I am watching now may do the same. I trudge back to my car, re-entering the earthly realm, having glimpsed for a moment or two the world of these global voyagers.

SLOW-WORM

29 April

For a creature called a slow-worm, a tiny island in the Bristol Channel populated by a large colony of gulls doesn't seem the safest place to make a home. Exposed to the elements, not to mention hundreds of stabbing bills and with nowhere to run, you'd think that Flat Holm was the last place to find these legless lizards. So when the warden lifted a huge wooden board to reveal some of the longest slow-worms I've ever seen, I was flabbergasted.

This remote island six kilometres off the Welsh coast, and washed by the muddy waters of the Severn, is home to specimens much longer than those on the mainland; these were near the upper size limit of forty centimetres and some had blue spots which increase in size as the animals age.

I saw my first slow-worms as a teenager in Dorset on the heaths around Studland Bay and learned the hard way why the reptile's scientific name is *Anguis fragilis* – literally 'brittle eel'. Catch it by the tail and the slow-worm 'autotomises' – casts off its tail, which then squirms revoltingly and allows the reptile to escape. It's a trick that many lizards, legless or otherwise, have perfected and about half the slow-worms I see have performed this partial self-sacrifice at some point in their lives. The re-grown tail is never as elegant and whiplike as the original, but this is a matter of survival, not aesthetics.

April is a good time to see basking slow-worms glinting in the spring sunshine, on heaths, in hedge banks and in the hidden corners of churchyards. Their smooth scales are burnished, seemingly by the friction of sliding through rough undergrowth. They are slow movers and will often allow a close enough inspection of their eyelids; unlike snakes, which can't blink, slow-worms and other lizards can close their eyes. They like old allotments where they perform the valuable task of munching the small greyish slugs that can devastate spring shoots. So many have been found in gardens in Worcester, not far from my home, that the city has been declared the British slow-worm capital and when allotments there were partially developed for housing, many slow-worms were airlifted to safer spots.

Usually when I see a slow-worm, I can't avoid the sympathetic ache for their vulnerability in a crowded world. They are no match for traffic, cats and pheasants or worse: I recently found a large one salami-sliced by a strimmer in a picturesque Devon churchyard. But the help they've received in Worcester and the reverence with which they're regarded on Flat Holm shine a ray of light on the future of the brittle eel.

MIGRANT RUSH
30 April

By the last week of April, anything can happen. Today, after overnight rain, it's hazily sunny and as I tread a familiar route around my local patch, the sound that confirms the tenure of spring is a scratchy song from a bramble clump.

In between songs, a bird nags me from deep in the thorns, where it seems instantly at home although it may only have arrived overnight. It's the same spot where I heard the first whitethroat last year and it's staggering to think that this might be the same bird that has flown across the Sahara Desert to hold territory in this anonymous field-corner. Then again, it may be the best whitethroat habitat locally: first come, first served.

Along the lane, the pasture grazed by English longhorn cattle has a scatter of sprinting wheatears on passage between Africa and – who knows – Greenland? I feel an unjustified sense of pride that they've chosen my patch for a touchdown, even if only for a day.

There's a fresh surprise around every corner. A dapper male whinchat with orange chest and brilliant white eyestripes is flirting along a barbed-wire fence, occasionally sallying to snap up drifting St Mark's flies. Spring whinchats are rare locally and although a pair bred regularly in a grassy valley in the 1980s, they are now strictly passage migrants, bound for rougher, wilder terrain.

I complete today's circuit by climbing a woodland path with close views of the urban Black Country to the north and, far to the west, the murky contours of the Shropshire hills. Dreaming of Housman's 'blue remembered hills' lost in the haze, I don't immediately recognise the sweet rattling song in the tops of the sycamores.

But among the opening salmon-pink buds is a small shape flitting high amid the canopy. It flashes a fiery tail while its mate sings – a pair of redstarts. This is the first time that I've seen a spring pair here and they may not stay – so it's important to seize the moment. I lie back on the slope and watch their madcap pursuits through the network of twigs high overhead. April has done it again.

MAY

WHEN A NATURALIST dies and goes to heaven, they must pray that the calendar is firmly stuck in the month of May. For us, Groundhog Day in November would be a vision of hell, while March would represent purgatory, as we wait for all eternity for spring to arrive. But May represents true paradise: the migrant birds are back, insects are buzzing, wild flowers are in bloom, and all is right in the world.

Back in reality, there is just one problem: May contains only thirty-one days for us to immerse ourselves in this burgeoning world of life. So wildlife-watching in this month takes some careful thought and planning: should I head north to Speyside, west to the Hebrides or Wales, east to Norfolk, or south to the New Forest? – all fabulous places to witness the high point of spring.

During my life I have spent at least part of May in all these places, but as time goes on, I find myself increasingly drawn to my home patch. After all, the more time I spend away from Somerset, the more I am going to miss. So while exotic wildlife has its place, there is nothing quite like enjoying the peak season close to home, where you can appreciate the subtle distinctions from day to day, week to week and year to year.

Greedily, I now have two local patches. One is in a hidden corner of the Somerset Levels, where few people ever venture, and where in May I can hear the songs of up to ten different species of warblers. There are also booming bitterns, marsh harriers gliding low over the reed-bed, and the occasional egret – little or great white – flying overhead. Here the reeds sway in the spring breeze, the oak leaves provide cover for singing birds, and by now the ground is just about dry enough underfoot to leave my wellies at home.

My other patch is a larger area near the coast, where three rivers – the Brue, Parrett and Huntspill – meet before pouring their muddy waters into Bridgwater Bay and the Bristol Channel beyond. It's a strange place – people I have brought here either love it or hate it – but for me the big skies, acres of mud and wonderfully variable tides bring a welcome touch of unpredictability. May is marked here by the chuntering song of reed warblers, along with the call of their nemesis the cuckoo, the latter bringing a sharp note of impending doom to an otherwise serene, sunlit scene.

S.M.

FOR NATURALISTS MAY is a cornucopia, an explosion of activity when everything happens at once and time is short. Lacking the Moss discipline at planning my month, I take the easy road that leads into the woods.

Woodlands are where I'm happiest and I dive into them at every opportunity, but in May they're at their supreme best and a simple stroll through the trees just isn't enough. I need to become utterly immersed – and I notice that Stephen uses the same word – in the prime of the year, to slake a thirst for spring and all it promises.

Walking as far from the car park as possible, I burrow deep into thickets, and sit, sometimes for hours, drinking in what H.E. Bates called 'the lofty miracle of light and leaf'. Sunbeams striking through paper-thin beech leaves over a flood of bluebells produce a breathtaking kaleidoscope of greens, purples and blues. There's an unreal quality to the woodland scene in May, a sharpness that highlights the fringing hairs on each sunlit leaf, honeyed by the rays of the sun.

I have my May idylls, set pieces that epitomise the month for me. Bluebells and sunlit foliage are more than enough but if I crave acoustic stimulation, there's birdsong everywhere. A wood warbler trembling with the effort of its coin-spinning song, the garden warbler's rivulet of sound trickling through a glade of birch saplings, a cuckoo far off and high in a stag-headed oak tree, a rattling redstart. In open coppices, flame-coloured fritillary butterflies flicker over clumps of lime-green wood spurge.

It's a scented month too. Down in the mossy forest dingles, I'm engulfed by the pungent aroma of wild garlic, which I can't help crushing however gingerly I tread. Wrens chide from mossy banks, a grey wagtail flutters after a rising mayfly and the outside world seems far off. Why would I be anywhere else on a fine May morning?

B.W.

NIGHTINGALE

1 May

A warm, spring evening on the edge of a Norfolk wood; the perfect place to listen to the remarkable song of the nightingale. As I approach, a delicious shiver of anticipation runs down my spine: the knowledge that I am about to hear a truly great musical performance – not just the greatest of any British bird, but arguably of any of the world's 5,000 or so species of songbird.

Yet even though the conditions seem perfect for a recital from this legendary songster, the star of the show fails to turn up, and I trudge back disappointed through the dark.

Disappointed, but hardly surprised. That's because over the last few decades nightingale numbers have fallen by more than 90 per cent. The chances of you hearing a nightingale in London – as Keats did in his famous ode, in which he tells of how the nightingale 'singest of summer in full-throated ease' – are now virtually non-existent; yet the species can still be found in woods and heaths in parts of Essex and Kent, Norfolk and Suffolk. Here, males hold territory and sing by night – and sometimes also in broad daylight – from late April until early June.

Nightingales have always appealed to us, for their song seems to reach the parts that other songbirds, no matter how tuneful they may be, simply cannot reach. When you do hear a nightingale, it is like nothing else in the bird world. A combination of stunningly tuneful passages interspersed with more free-form improvisations, all delivered at an ear-splitting volume.

But unfortunately for me, this spring sound has disappeared from Devon, and almost vanished from my home county of Somerset, where just a handful of birds now return each year. Unless something can be done – and very soon – this iconic species will soon be making an undignified exit as a British breeding bird.

So why has this skulking little bird declined so dramatically? As with many migrants, it seems to be a combination of changing conditions in its African winter grounds, and habitat loss here in Britain. The nightingale's woodland habitat is affected by the rise in the numbers of roe deer and muntjac, which browse the scrubby understorey of woods and forests where the bird makes its nest. No scrub means no nightingales. So unless we take the tricky decision to cull the overpopulation of deer, we stand to lose our nightingales – and soon.

To find out exactly why these birds are in trouble when they leave our shores in July, scientists have been fitting them with tiny geolocators, which track exactly where they go. Whether this will help us prevent the nightingale disappearing from Britain is as yet uncertain; we can only hope that it will. To lose a bird so central to our culture would be little short of a tragedy.

SAND LIZARD

2 May

The sound that makes my breath catch and tugs me back forty years is a soft rustle in the pathside heather. Something is moving in the spring sunlight on this Dorset heath and instantly I am fourteen again, frightened to make a sudden move, yet straining to see the minutiae of patterns that mark out a male sand lizard. Now instead of flinging myself bodily upon the creature – age and conscience rule that out – I watch from the path as the lizard moves jerkily into view and flattens its ribcage to soak up the sun.

This one is mosaic-basking, warming up the parts of its body that the sun can reach through a filigree of sheltering heather. Without question he is one of the handsomest British vertebrates, supremely camouflaged in his heathland home and at his sumptuous best in the few weeks following hibernation.

His old skin has rubbed away in scurfy patches and his flanks are beaded with leaf-green and chocolate-brown scales. Along his back are chains of darker eyespots or ocelli, each with a whitish highlight. He is big-headed and square-jawed – all the better for fighting rivals or grabbing a mate.

Sand lizard courtship falls into the 'treat 'em rough and they'll love you' category. Soon he'll grab a passing female, bite the base of her tail and perform his reproductive duties. She will lay her eggs in a burrow that she excavates in the soft sand bordering the heathland paths; in midsummer the young lizards tunnel their way to the surface.

Sand for warming and incubating their eggs is vital to these reptiles and the best places to see them are the heaths of southern England and the dunes near Formby in Merseyside. There's also an introduction scheme, which helps lizards recolonise old sites from which they've been lost. Above all, this is *the* reptile of Thomas Hardy country and flourishes on the heathery 'wastes' around Poole Harbour.

As a young teenager, I spent family holidays on the Sandbanks peninsula, where the most evocative sound to me was the clanking of the Sandbanks ferry chains and the throb of its engine as it hauled its way across the harbour mouth towards Shell Bay and Studland Heath. Here sand lizards skittered among the dunes, marram grass pricked my bare feet and I could fossick to my heart's content. I wasn't always content to observe: they had to be caught, which involved graceless and painful dives into gorse clumps.

Now the lizards are rightly protected from young herpetologists like me, but this shouldn't deter interest in them. They are emblems of their heathland habitat and share their homes with nightjars, stonechats and many scarce wasps and beetles, all reliant on this precious landscape.

BEECH WOODS

3 May

Is there such a thing as a perfect moment in the British natural history year? There are many contenders, but for me the most delicious is an early May day among beeches.

The beech leaves, which until now have been impossibly crammed into the tight, pointed buds, shuck off their papery brown scales and unrumple in the spring sunshine.

Each translucent leaf is fringed with silky hairs, which catch the sunlight filtering down through the strata of foliage, so that walking in a beech wood is like walking underwater. Their acid-green delicacy is a perfect foil for the flood of bluebells lapping against the beech trunks. Timing is important and the full experience doesn't happen every spring; in some years, local bluebells peak early and beat the beech to it; in others the trees have the edge, but there's usually enough overlap to be able to sit in their sub-marine shade and soak up the scene.

Improvement is almost impossible, but there is one extra ingredient that takes the experience to Elysian heights. Somewhere among a million leaves is a shivering trill followed by a mournful, down-slurred whistle: a male wood warbler. An animated beech leaf himself, in moss green and yellow, this summer visitor from the west African rainforests is the perfect bird of the May woods, blending in so well that you need to search for his silhouette, trembling high overhead as he pumps out his delicious song.

Once mated, he will stop singing: wood warblers have only one brood each year. Song, bluebells and the fragile beauty of the unfurling beech leaves are over for another twelve months.

GREAT NORTHERN DIVER

4 May

I usually catch up with our largest diver, the great northern, on a bitterly cold winter's day, as I gaze across the choppy waters of my local reservoir to see a bird looking like a giant, pale cormorant diving repeatedly beneath the waves.

But once or twice I have seen great northern divers in full breeding plumage, floating just offshore on the deep, blue-black seas off the north-west coast of Scotland. This comes as something of a shock, for they could hardly look more different from the way they appeared just a few months ago. Gone is the drab plumage of autumn and winter, replaced with a jet-black head and neck, and a chequerboard pattern of white squares on the bird's dark back. These, combined with the diver's rather dignified posture, are strangely reminiscent of an elderly gentleman dressed for a black-tie dinner.

These birds are about to head off on the last leg of their journey north, to breed on remote lakes and pools in Iceland, Greenland or even Arctic Canada. So they are already pairing up, and on fine days I have heard their haunting call.

This sound must have long been heard here in the Western Isles, for the local name, 'bunivochil', derives from the Scots Gaelic meaning 'dumpy herdsman': a reference both to the diver's shape and the simi-larity of the bird's sound to the traditional way of calling to herds of cattle. The official name is far more recent, having been coined as late as 1843 by the Victorian ornithologist William Yarrell.

If you are lucky enough to come across a flock of great northern divers, check them carefully. Another, far more elusive species also migrates off our north-western shores each spring: the white-billed diver, as its name suggests, has a huge, slightly upcurved, ivory-coloured beak, which led one watching birder to dub it 'Big Banana Bill'. I've never seen one, but I am determined to do so one day.

OIL BEETLES

5 May

It pays to watch your step on the steep cliffs of the south Devon coast. Not only because of the slippery turf or the outcrops of rock that could send you head over heels Atlantic-wards, but because you might tread on an oil beetle.

On sunny spring days they lumber across paths, black sausage-shaped insects, their bloated abdomens swelling from their ridiculously small wing cases. Their odd appearance reminded the French entomologist Jean-Henri Fabre of a 'fat man's coat that is too tight for its wearer'. They may look vulnerable and helpless as they crawl in full view on open ground, but they're not known as oil beetles for nothing. If attacked by a small mammal or bird, the beetle will exude oily droplets of fluid called cantharidin from its joints, a toxic cocktail that is enough to deter most predators.

On this particular stretch of rocky coast there are four out of the five British species, making south Devon an oil beetle hotspot. Some species, such as the violet and black oil beetles, are more widespread on downland or moorland as far north as northern Scotland. But oil beetles are not as common as they once were and their strange life cycle holds the key to their decline.

The oil beetles stumbling across this turf are mainly larger females, looking for a place to lay their eggs in a burrow that they dig out. When the hundreds of tiny larvae emerge, they look nothing like their parents: they are slim, pale and fast-moving and immediately swarm up flower heads, in search not of nectar, but a free ride. On each leg they have three hooks, and because of this are known as triungulins, from the Latin for 'three claws'. They wait on their chosen flower until a solitary bee comes along and when it does, they grasp its fur and hitch a lift back to its burrow. Here they eat the bee's egg and feast on the pollen store that the bee has collected, before pupating and eventually emerging in autumn or spring.

Oil beetles parasitise solitary bees, but not honeybees or bumblebees. Many solitary bees need flowers for nectar and soft open ground in which to burrow, but short flowery grassland is in short supply in many places and so solitary bees have declined – and with them, the oil beetles. Buglife, the invertebrate conservation trust, has been monitoring the insects and has found that apart from the violet oil beetle, they are commonest in the south-west of England and have almost disappeared from the east. A discovery of oil beetles anywhere is a strong guide to the good health of local flowers and bees too.

LESSER HORSESHOE BAT

6 May

At first glance, it appears as though clusters of plums are hanging down from the ceiling of this ancient outbuilding. But as I blink in bafflement, one of them unfolds its wings, stretches for a moment or two and then, with a quick flick, detaches itself from its upside-down perch and flies away.

It is followed by another, then another; their wings coming so close I can feel the rush of air as they fly past my head. It's a fine spring evening, the sky is full of invisible insects, and the lesser horseshoe bats are leaving their roost to hunt.

The insects may be tiny, and invisible to us in the deepening twilight, but for the bats, a full breakfast buffet is laid out before them. Midges, beetles, spiders and small moths are all on the menu, each located using the bats' superhuman radar. Then they are snatched out of the air with sharp claws and transferred to the animal's mouth, where even sharper teeth will make short work of them. The bats need to feed because, having hibernated throughout the winter, they must put on as much weight as they can while this good weather lasts.

Like their much larger relative the greater horseshoe bat, lesser horse-shoes have an unusually shaped flap around their nose, which enables them to echolocate more effectively, and gives the species its common name. Their scientific name, *Rhinolophus hipposideros*, translates from the Greek and Latin as 'crested-nosed iron-horse', which suggests that nomenclaturists have rather fertile imaginations.

As well as that bizarre nose, both horseshoe bats have another unique feature: they can wiggle their ears, enabling them to pinpoint their prey more accurately as it flies past in the darkness.

Both species of horseshoe bat are rare and localised in Britain: the lesser horseshoe is found mainly in the south and west, from Devon and Cornwall through Somerset, Gloucestershire and the Welsh borders to Anglesey. They spend spring and summer days roosting on the ceilings of outbuildings and stable blocks, before emerging at dusk to feed along the edges of woodland where small insects are most abundant.

PEARL-BORDERED FRITILLARY

7 May

As I wait at a Wyre Forest car park for friends to arrive, a woman walking her dog stops me to complain about the fifty oak trees that are being felled. There is apparently a buzz in nearby Bewdley about this act of 'vandalism' and some local people are up in arms. I ask her if she's noticed the bright orange fritillary butterflies on her spring walks and she says that she enjoys seeing them. When I explain that felling the trees will encourage the violets on which the fritillaries' caterpillars feed, she is genuinely interested. I hope she spreads the word.

The butterflies in question are pearl-bordered fritillaries, at their best here in late spring, when they flit over bluebell patches like living embers, a flickering leitmotif along rides and through the dappled recesses of older coppice. On a sunny day, you may see tens, even hundreds during a forest walk. When the sun doesn't shine they sit demurely on trackside plants, allowing a close approach when you can inspect the stained-glass patterns and silvery 'pearl' spots on their underwings.

Felling trees is the key to their survival. The fritillaries lay their eggs on violet plants growing in the warmest, brightest areas and these spring up soon after coppicing. Within three years or so, the violets are shaded out by taller growth and so the fritillaries need to move on. Once, when woods were coppiced to provide timber for building and fencing, or in the case of Wyre, for charcoal-making, the butterflies had a continuous supply of open spaces. The 'Dark Ages' of high-yield forestry in the 1960s and 1970s, locally dominated by conifers, saw numbers plummet, almost to extinction here.

Now, thanks to local partnerships backed by the Forestry Commission, Butterfly Conservation and others, the Wyre fritillaries are returning, but their future will depend on more tree felling and that is still a contentious subject. So widely have we promoted tree planting and protection that it's hard for many people to accept that the removal of some trees is not vandalism, but the best hope for a wide variety of wildlife, including one of our scarcest and most rapidly declining butterflies.

GREAT CRESTED NEWT

8 May

As dusk falls on a muggy May evening, a strange crowd of people gathers around a pond, somewhere in lowland Britain. Sporting wellington boots and head torches, they have come in search of our largest and most impressive amphibian: the great crested newt.

During the breeding season, from April to June, the male sports a magnificent crest along the whole length of his back and tail, which rises up when the animal is underwater so he can use it to display to his rivals.

Great crested newts are the top dog of the amphibian world: growing up to sixteen centimetres long, they have a rough, warty skin, are dark above with tiny white spots, and orange below with darker blotches.

That underside pattern is not just distinctive, it is also unique; one group of scientists from the University of Kent uses photography to identify individual newts, which are then given the names of Hollywood stars – not out of any resemblance, however.

Like their namesakes, great crested newts often appear in the news-papers, though for a very different reason. Tabloid journalists often rail against the perceived insanity of a colony of these amphibians bringing a busy building site to a halt, or thousands of pounds supposedly being spent to relocate them. And perhaps they have a point: after all, most of us have never even seen one and in fact they are fairly common and widespread in Britain, which holds a good proportion of the European population. But it says a lot for the British love of wildlife that we don't just safeguard glamorous and showy species, but shy, gawky ones too, and these adaptable little creatures can usually be relocated without any harm.

Incidentally, although the proverbial phrase 'pissed as a newt' has entered the English language as a crude euphemism for being drunk, newts spend only about half their lives in water. Outside the breeding season they are far more likely to be found on land, in damp areas of woodland, farmland and grassland. One explanation for the phrase's origin is that when walking, newts have a rather unsteady gait, similar to the side-to-side wanderings of a drunken man.

By the end of the evening, the pond's newts have been caught, checked and released, adding another few pieces of information to our knowledge of this, our biggest and most colourful amphibian.

LONG-HORNED MOTHS
9 May

A still day in a woodland clearing. Sunlight warms up tender oak shoots, still flushed orange with the tannins that protect them from insect attack before they harden. Just above the oak saplings are clouds of metallic-bronze insects. These are mating flights of green long-horned moths, a small but strikingly beautiful insect, at its peak in May.

In this swarm of fifty or so, several have settled on the leaves, holding their lustrous wings apart to reveal furry black bodies. Their antennae are ridiculously long, like slender white threads three times the length of their forewings. They are slightly reflexed and wave slowly, as the male moths scan for scent pheromones from females. Now and then, they rise to advertise themselves, fluttering weakly above the oak leaves, though steering and agility can't be easy with such enormous appendages to manage.

Even more spectacular is the yellow-banded long-horn moth, which has proportionately the longest antennae of any British insect, four times as long as its forewings and is found in similar places in late spring. Its wings are streaked with gold and copper and slashed with a custard-yellow band. Excluding its 'horns', it's just over two centimetres long but, writ large, would outshine any of our butterflies.

Mating over, the female, whose antennae are half the length of the male's, lays her eggs, but precisely where remains a mystery. After hatching the caterpillars build a protective sleeping bag made from fragments of dead leaves and hide on the woodland floor eating leaf litter. They spend winter as pupae and on a fine spring day emerge for their mating dances in woodland glades or parkland. Sometimes they will congregate around favourite spots such as an oak tree in old hedgerows and in spring 2016 they even brought a flash of brilliance to my urban garden.

TROUT

10 May

A Hampshire chalk stream on a calm, still May morning. The water barely shimmers with the gentle flow, on its leisurely and unhurried journey downstream. Then the surface momentarily breaks: a tiny insect – a mayfly – is emerging to begin its brief life.

But even before its body has fully left the confines of the water, its life comes to an abrupt end. From below the surface of the water a movement breaks the glassy stillness as a fish emerges, grabs the unfortunate insect and descends back into the water. Yet another mayfly has fallen victim to the classic creature of these idyllic southern streams: the brown trout.

Later that day, however, the boot may be on the other foot. For trout attract anglers, and few anglers are so single-minded, so eager to outwit their target, as those who pursue this aristocratic fish. Indeed so obsessed do they become with their quarry that they devote their lives to fishing for this one species, fashioning complex 'flies' out of feathers to lure the trout on to their hooks.

Like their larger relative the Atlantic salmon, some trout lead a double life: having been hatched and raised in rivers and streams, they head out to sea before returning some years later to spawn. But the brown trout found in these Hampshire streams stay put for their whole lives; and given the abundance of food and places to breed, why wouldn't they?

Sitting quietly by a chalk stream on this fine spring day, I watch the trout as they feed: I can just make out their dark, menacing shapes as they bob up towards the surface. The larger fish don't just eat mayflies, but also prey on the chicks of ducklings and moorhens, and even young water voles.

Further north, in the deep, murky, acidic waters of Loch Ness, there are trout that have gone bad. These giant fish, known as ferox trout, are cannibals, seeking out and feeding on the young of their own species. They weren't always like this: as youngsters they live on the usual diet of aquatic invertebrates; but once they reach a certain size and weight they switch to feeding on fish, enabling them to grow as heavy as fourteen kilos. Whether this makes them a separate species is still up for discussion – but they certainly behave very differently from their southern counterparts.

SCARLET LONGHORNS
11 May

The excitement began one March evening when householders noticed two blood-red beetles crawling over a basket of logs in their living room in south Worcestershire. They'd never seen them before and, being interested in wildlife, sent the insects to a local entomologist, who identified them as scarlet longhorn beetles, a rare species of old oak woodlands. As this was potentially the first Worcestershire record it was vital to find out where the logs were cut.

This turned out to be over thirty miles to the north-west and, frustratingly for Worcestershire entomologists at least, across the county boundary in the Shropshire part of the Wyre Forest. More frustrating still, the beetles had never been seen there in the wild. So it was that in May the next year, a few friends and I found ourselves inspecting the vast timber-store at a forest farm on the Worcestershire side of Wyre.

Scarlet longhorns are very beautiful insects, with softly hairy, ruby-coloured wing cases, black legs and long, segmented antennae. Once they were confined to a few sites in the Welsh Marches – hence their alternative name of Welsh longhorn – but now, for reasons that aren't clear, they appear to be increasing and are turning up in woodlands in several places in England and Wales. Indeed, we soon found a score of the newly emerged beetles wandering across the cut logs.

While inspecting log-piles – always from the ground, as they can be unstable – it's best to look on oak timber that has been cut within a year or so or on the bark of dead oaks; on warm days I've seen the males flying in, using their long antennae to detect the scent of cut timber, and of the opposite sex.

You may come across other wood-loving longhorns, which are some of our most attractive insects. Wasp beetles are not only banded black and yellow to fool predators, they also move as jerkily as wasps, but are completely harmless. On warm spring days the beautiful black-spotted longhorn crawls so slowly over logs that if you wanted to you could pick it up. These beetles have blackish wing cases thickly dusted with golden vermiculations and a dark eyespot on each, and are around from mid-April until June. Like the longhorns, never ignore the scent of freshly cut timber.

PIKE

12 May

As I gaze beneath the surface of a gravel-pit, something moves. It's big – *really* big. The creature floats towards the surface and I see that it is a huge fish: long and slender, with a tapered head and marbled markings along its sides, providing camouflage as shafts of sunlight dapple and perturb the water.

A pike. This mighty fish is named, appropriately, after the long medieval weapon (whose name in turn derives from the Middle English for 'pointed'), and the fish is an equally efficient killer. The pike is one of the most fearsome of all underwater predators, whose streamlined shape allows it to accelerate rapidly from a standing start when pursuing its prey, before grabbing it in its huge mouth and despatching it with razor-sharp teeth.

Few creatures have quite the same air of menace about them as this enormous fish. The poet Ted Hughes was a keen angler, and as a young man often fished for pike, which he later commemorated in one of his best-known poems. He tells of how he once came across two dead pike, one jammed down the other's gullet so far that the aggressor had choked to death.

But pike have a softer side, too. After mating, the males hang around and guard their offspring; this is a sensible strategy, as pike are cannibalistic, and will feed on these tiny fish if they can.

Pike are also responsible for more urban myths than any other fish. Monster pike – alleged to be more than two metres long and weighing up to forty-five kilos – are often claimed to stalk the waters of Britain, allegedly attacking anglers and even eating small dogs. But this is entirely fanciful: the largest pike ever caught in Britain tipped the scales at less than half that weight, a mere 21.7 kilos. Even so, at just over a metre long, this was still one of the biggest fish ever caught by rod and line in British waters.

GREEN HAIRSTREAK
13 May

The quickness of the wing deceives the eye. Some of our smaller butterflies fly so haphazardly and so fast that they are little more than hallucinations, a flicker of motion at the edge of our field of vision, making us question whether we've seen one at all.

Small coppers do it and so do small blues, blurs among meadow flowers. Like the poet Emily Dickinson's hummingbird, each insect is a 'route of evanescence', a brief thickening of the air then gone, faster than the eye can follow. But the master of this disappearing art is the green hairstreak, a Scarlet Pimpernel among butterflies. I know experienced naturalists who've never seen one, though of course they may well have, but didn't realise it.

The secret of the green hairstreaks' disappearing act lies in their colour scheme. Their hindwings are a rich emerald, verging on turquoise in some lights, while their upperwings are mouse brown. As they fly rapidly against a backcloth of leaves and twigs, they are almost impossible to follow: only when they settle do they allow a closer approach. They often tilt their closed wings at an angle to the leaf to avoid casting a shadow so, even at rest, can be cryptic.

Green hairstreaks are pretty widespread throughout the British Isles, where their caterpillars feed on broom, gorse and other members of the pea family, but also on bramble and dogwood. To see one, choose a wide woodland clearing or an open area with light scrub. May and June are the best months and sunny weather is essential. On my own local patch I have noticed them just twice in forty years, though because they are sedentary insects I'm grudgingly forced to concede that they have been there all the time. This year, I promise myself, I will try to track them down and prove that they're breeding. That said, I know that it's a hit-and-miss affair and the hairstreak holds all the best cards.

DUKE OF BURGUNDY

14 May

A Kentish hillside on a fine May morning. As the sun begins to warm up the ground, butterflies emerge to feed on an array of wild flowers. Among the usual whites, brimstones and small tortoiseshells, a smaller specimen flutters low over the grassy sward, straight towards me.

Purplish brown in colour, with pale rusty-orange markings on the forewings, it could easily be mistaken for the common and familiar speckled wood. But something about the way it flies marks it out as a different butterfly, and indeed it is: one of Britain's rarest butterflies, the Duke of Burgundy.

Butterfly enthusiasts sometimes refer to the Duke of Burgundy as 'His Grace', but the aristocratic origins of its unusual name are lost in the proverbial mists of time. All we know is that it is a relatively recent coinage: back in the early eighteenth century this butterfly was called 'Mr Vernon's Small Fritillary', after William Vernon, an early collector.

However, this is not a fritillary, but the only British member of a huge family of more than 1,500 species worldwide, known as the metalmarks because of bright spots on their wings.

Just fifty years ago the Duke of Burgundy was a common sight in rough grassland and woodland clearings – its two preferred homes – throughout southern Britain. But numbers have since plummeted, as both traditional farmland and woodland habitats have been neglected or destroyed.

Yet here on the North Downs, conditions are still suitable for this fussy little insect. I watch as this male lands on a cowslip, one of two food-plants favoured by its caterpillars. From his vantage point he will defend this territory against any rivals while waiting – and hoping – for a passing female to fly by and mate with him.

Elsewhere in southern England, His Grace can be found in a very different setting: woodland clearings produced by regular coppicing. Here the dappled sunlight allows clumps of primroses – the other of the Duke of Burgundy caterpillar's food-plants – to grow on the forest floor.

Ironically, the means of salvation for this rapidly declining butterfly may turn out to be climate change. Normally the Duke of Burgundy emerges only in the spring, and is on the wing for just a few weeks between late April and early June. But recent early springs, followed by fine, warm summers, have sometimes led to a second batch of adults hatching out in August, boosting the butterfly's tiny population, and giving hope to its many admirers.

WILD FLOWER MEADOW

15 May

A friend of mine advises me to 'never go on a picnic with an ecologist', because all ecologists do is point out how good things used to be. Gazing over the wooden gate this afternoon, I remember his words. No lush green meadow this. The small, hedge-lined field is a sea of purple and yellow, tinted by clusters of cowslips and countless thousands of green-winged orchids, the hallmark plant of lowland 'unimproved' pasture and the surest sign that this is a very special place. The other sign belongs to the meadow's modern owners, Worcestershire Wildlife Trust, whose volunteers have mown a narrow path through the flowers.

Gingerly, I pick my way between orchids no more than twenty centimetres high, each spike a different shade of pink, from rich magenta to pale rose. Down at their level, the variety of foliage is astonishing: the kidney-shaped leaves of sorrel whose spikes, like miniature rhubarb and as refreshingly sour, are beginning to rocket upwards. They jostle with the saw-toothed leaves of yellow rattle, a hemi-parasite that, by drawing some of its nutrients from the grass, reduces its strength and makes room for herbs. Everywhere there are the lance-shaped leaves of ribwort plantain, whose dense blackish flower heads can be popped off between fingers and thumb: its old name locally was 'Grandmother, Grandmother jump out of bed'. Perhaps those old names are dying out with the meadows themselves.

George Peterken, who has celebrated the history and natural history of our meadows, admits that these traditional grasslands have no part in modern commercial farming. They are relics of an age before the Second World War when meadows were mown by hand tools and fertiliser was applied sparsely. The great productivity drive of the 1940s and since has seen these 'weedy' pastures either ploughed up or enriched with fertiliser, which encouraged grass rather than meadow flowers. A few hardy buttercups and dandelions remain, but, in most cases, lush green deserts of grass prevailed.

The well-worn figure usually quoted is that we've lost 97 per cent of our traditional grasslands since the 1930s. It doesn't mean much until you see the riot of colour that is a hay meadow in late spring and summer. It will be a haven for bees, butterflies and a host of other invertebrates: skylarks will nest among its grass-tufts and maybe even a pair of lapwings or curlews.

It is an anachronism, a rural museum piece, but more valuable for that than any cruck-framed barn or historic dovecote. Some of the best old meadows are in the hands of concerned private owners or conservation organisations which recognise the value of cherishing and managing them, not just for the benefit of wildlife, but because their sights, sounds and fragrances make us feel good too. Otherwise where would ecologists go for their picnics?

SWORD-LEAVED HELLEBORINE

16 May

It's mid-May and the bluebells – always late here – are still at their best in Worcestershire's Wyre Forest. I'm with friend and fellow Wyre Forest Study Group member Rosemary Winnall and we're counting the numbers of a much more reclusive flower.

The sword-leaved helleborine is a graceful orchid, a little larger and taller than a bluebell, with long leaves and a spike of snowy flowers as exotic as any hothouse corsage. It's very local in the British Isles, found in only a handful of places, and Wyre, a mainly acidic oak woodland, is an atypical site. In 1998, when Rosemary first began monitoring the two known populations here, there were only about fifteen plants and extinction loomed.

Since then, she and others have discovered many more sites, some in unexpected places. Several are on the fringes of well-used forestry tracks where they relish the extra lime content in imported stone. Others have appeared in a sheep pasture and one forced its way through the tarmac on the drive of a private house.

Even if you know where to find it, this orchid is a fickle flowerer and may skip a year or more. Those flowering spikes that do appear can be nibbled by deer or slugs, crushed accidentally by forest machinery or mountain bikes, or walked over: the perils of living in a modern, open-access woodland. However, one of the main enemies of the orchid is shading and so Rosemary and her colleagues are working hard in partnership with Natural England and the Forestry Commission to ensure that there are open glades for mature plants and their seedlings.

Today, with permission from the owners, we're inspecting flowers in a private garden, where some large flowering spikes have bloomed in a lawn. Deer regularly visit their garden and the owners also have livestock, so the orchids are enclosed in wire cages, which we lift for closer inspection. They are truly magnificent – a couple of them with over thirty tulip-shaped flowers on each inflorescence. The urn-like flowers are held horizontally away from the stalk and don't open completely, but tease us with glimpses of the bright yellow lip within the hollow of the white petals.

As I replace the cages over the plants, I have mixed feelings. Pleasure of course from seeing them, and gratitude that the house-owners have agreed to protect 'their' orchids, but sadness that this is what it's come to for one of our choicest plants: incarcerated at its finest hour. In Wyre, surveyors like Rosemary are working to improve the lot of this beautiful orchid across the whole woodscape, but until that has happened – and it will be a long process – the cages are our best way of preserving the finest blooms.

COW PARSLEY
17 May

In his classic *The Englishman's Flora*, published in 1955, Geoffrey Grigson notes the cow parsley 'whitening the road verges' in June. Now, in the southern half of the British Isles at least, you're likely to find it in full bloom a month earlier. Here in the West Midlands, the more precocious plants are flowering by late April, some on the wane by early summer.

Whenever it appears, it's an emollient plant, screening the roadside litter with its ferny leaves and softening the raw ends of flailed hedges behind foaming masses of bluish-white flowers. Their delicate appearance is the reason for the name Queen Anne's Lace, though Grigson speculates that it was probably St Anna, the mother of Mary the Virgin, who provided the derivation. Not that the plant has a universal saintly reputation. Devil's meat and devil's parsley are some of the folk names it has gathered, possibly because of its similarity to deadly hemlock.

If it's allowed to bloom before the verge-cutters arrive, it can transform a rural landscape, filling the seams of hedgerows and fields. Many of our smaller hedgerow plants are declining, not always because of early cutting, but because deposits of nitrates from fertiliser used on agricultural land are encouraging coarser species like nettles and cleavers to grow more vigorously and to crowd out more delicate ones. But cow parsley grows tall enough and early enough to shrug off this competition and as a result we have a wild plant that still colours farmland for a few weeks in late spring.

WALL BUTTERFLY
18 May

At first, I assume it's an early meadow brown, that most dull and ubiquitous of summer butterflies. Then I realise that it is the middle of May, at least three weeks before that species emerges. Other brown butterflies run through my mind: gatekeeper? No, far too early – they appear towards the end of July. Speckled wood? But didn't I see a hint of orange? Could it be a fritillary of some sort? Not orange enough!

As it flies past me and lands on the stony path, and I see the cuboid orange shapes on the brown wings, it finally dawns on me that I am looking at the oddly named wall butterfly. This easily overlooked creature used to be called the 'wall brown', to match the meadow brown and the old name for the gatekeeper, 'hedge brown'. But whereas these two have thrived in the modern countryside, the wall has become increasingly scarce, especially in the south.

In Somerset, I've only ever seen the wall along the coast – where I am now. It seems to like the dry, rocky areas battered by onshore winds that most butterflies shun, but is that because it really prefers these marginal habitats, or has it simply been driven away from farmland by the increased use of chemical pesticides?

Certainly it used to be far more widespread – my old friend John F. Burton, who studied wildlife on the Somerset Levels back in the 1950s and 1960s, remembers it being quite common; yet since I moved down here I have only seen it three times: twice on the coast and once on top of the Mendips, at Crook Peak.

So I take time to have a good look at this subtle but rather handsome insect: a combination of orange and light brown, with two prominent 'eyes' to deter predators, and a second row of smaller 'eyes' along its hindwings. Then it flutters up into the air and is carried away on the spring breeze; the end of my encounter with one of Britain's most over-looked butterflies.

BLUEBELLS

19 May

No other flower holds quite the same place in the nation's hearts as the bluebell. Like our favourite bird, the robin, and our best-known tree, the oak, it has become a symbol of what it means to be British.

This is appropriate, given that globally the bluebell has a very limited range, being confined to the western shores of the great Eurasian land-mass, where the Atlantic-influenced maritime climate – generally mild and wet – allows this little flower to grow in profusion.

The name 'bluebell' seems to have been with us for ever, so I am surprised to learn that it first appeared in print barely 200 years ago, in the last decade of the eighteenth century. The name was used much earlier, but it was applied to a completely different plant, the harebell, a flower that tends to prefer sunnier, more open settings.

Poets have been much taken with the true bluebell: Keats called it the 'Sapphire Queen of the mid-May', while Tennyson also waxed lyrical, comparing a carpet of bluebells to 'the blue sky, breaking up through the earth'. But even this is topped by the poet Gerard Manley Hopkins, who in his journal for 1871 wrote of bluebells 'in falls of sky-colour washing the brows and slacks of the ground with vein-blue'.

Sadly, these spring carpets of bluebells are now under threat from two flanks, both, ironically, a result of our very British passion for gardening. Bluebells are extremely vulnerable to people pulling up the bulbs to replant in their gardens – an act that is now illegal as well as selfish. And wild bluebell displays are often infiltrated by stands of Spanish bluebells, a popular garden variety with stiffer, less drooping flowers, which freely hybridises with our native plants.

Fortunately there are still enough displays of pure British bluebells for us to enjoy: all the way from Cape Wrath at the northern tip of Scotland to our southernmost outpost, the Isles of Scilly. And on a sunlit May morning, as I am serenaded by birdsong, it's hard to imagine a more classic wild flower experience than a bluebell wood in full flower.

SKUA PASSAGE

20 May

North Uist, in Scotland's Outer Hebrides, is remote, bleak and windswept; what *Dad's Army*'s Private Frazer would have called 'a wild and lonely place'. But for anyone wanting to witness one of the great bird migration spectacles off our coasts, this beautiful island is a key destination.

Many years ago, in the middle of May, I visited North Uist, and found myself in the right place at more or less exactly the right time. The weather forecast predicted strong westerly winds blowing straight off the Atlantic Ocean, which meant that I had a good chance of seeing squadrons of skuas fly close inshore on their way to their breeding grounds far to the north.

To do so, however, needed time and patience. I also had to endure what the locals call 'four seasons in a day', as wind, rain, mist and sunshine sweep in from the ocean, one after another. Compensation came with the surrounding flower-rich 'machair', home to redshanks and oystercatchers, piping away in a constant soundtrack to spring.

What I was really hoping to see was not the common-or-garden Arctic and great skuas, both of which breed in northern Scotland, but two far scarcer species: pomarine and long-tailed skuas. These spend the winter thousands of miles to the south, off the Atlantic coasts of Africa and South America. So to get to their breeding sites on the Arctic tundra, they must fly right by the coasts of Britain.

Waiting for their arrival involves a mixture of anticipation and fear, for they usually pass two or three miles offshore, out of sight to any land-based watchers. But after several hours I finally got lucky: a tight little flock of pomarines, like a squadron of Spitfires, hugging the tops of the waves. Their powerful wings carved effortlessly through the air, and they came so close I could see their distinctive twisted tail-feathers, like two tablespoons, sticking out behind.

Soon another group appeared, and then another, until the sea was dotted with dark shapes. But the real prize was the even rarer long-tailed skua: a slimmer and more delicate bird than the 'poms', with a buoyant, tern-like flight and an impossibly long tail. Though I wasn't there at the right time to witness a really big passage, I did see a couple of smaller groups, heading north as quickly as they could, to take advantage of the brief but fertile northern summer to breed and raise a family.

ELDERFLOWERS

21 May

Back in the late 1960s, when I was first becoming properly aware of the natural world, my mother would take me out picking elderflowers. Not for some bouquet, or to make into cordial, but for something altogether stronger and more daring: home-made white wine.

You don't have to go far to find elderflowers, at least not in May in south-east England, and we would wander along the hedgerows plucking great clumps of the huge, creamy, honey-scented blossoms and stuffing them into a carrier bag. Once we had picked what seemed to me to be far too many, we would head home; and my mother would begin the strange alchemical process of turning the flowers, along with water and sugar, into wine.

The resulting beverage was a deep straw-yellow colour, rather like stale urine. It would sit in five-gallon bottles known as demijohns, alongside those containing the deep purple elderberry wine made from berries collected the previous August. I tasted some once: it was foul – perhaps because I was only nine years old, but possibly because home-made wine always is.

While collecting the elderflowers, I would notice how many tiny insects were perched on top of the florets. These had to be shaken off before bagging, as my mother drew the line at drinking anything that could fly. I like to think that as the sun beat down from a deep blue sky, I was aware that the elderflowers were a sign that summer was just around the corner; but this is probably just a middle-aged reworking of my memory, almost fifty years on. Today they blossom in my garden, bursting out each May as a welcome reminder of years gone by.

MAYFLY DANCE

22 May

A trip westwards with fellow naturalists to look for river skaters on the Teme. These giant leggy water-bugs skate across the surface film of gently flowing water without puncturing it, feeding on dead and drowning insects. Here, west of Tenbury Wells, they flirt with the boundaries of Herefordshire and Worcestershire and we were keen to claim them for both counties. As it happened, though, other insects took centre stage.

The Teme has sluggish pockets, but is a fairly fast-flowing river with occasional gravel-bars, riffles and deeper pools. Where sunlight pierced the bankside willows, we realised that a mayfly emergence was under way. Thousands of the fragile pale-bodied insects were rising from the water where they had spent their lives as larvae, in burrows in the river mud.

Unlike other insects, mayflies have a flying sub-adult stage which anglers call duns and many of these were resting on the water surface. Ethereal and flimsy, they soon fly to a perch on riverside vegetation where their skins split and the true adult or spinner emerges. Neither dun nor spinner can feed because their mouthparts are not fully formed, but eating is irrelevant. Adult mayflies live to mate. The swarm we saw was of a typically short-lived species called appropriately *Ephemera danica*, the largest and one of the commonest British mayflies.

Synchronising their emergence increases the mayflies' chances of finding a mate, but with no way of replenishing the energy in their powerful flight muscles, they need to act fast and so the males attract attention by dancing. Fluttering upwards a metre or more, at the highest point they relax their wings into a shallow V and gently parachute back down to their previous level. Each mayfly repeats this process many times: the effect of hundreds of insects rising and falling as if being manipulated by invisible puppeteers is mesmerising. Females attracted to the swarm are soon waylaid by males and they couple in mid-air, after which the females return to the water-surface to lay their eggs.

Admiring their vitality, the glittering wings and delicate tail-streamers, it was easy to forget that this was a dance of life and of death. Those already spent were swirling downriver where, in the quieter eddies, their revolving corpses would be snapped up by the river skaters.

BLUE DAMSELFLIES

23 May

They look like multicoloured matchsticks, their dazzling blue markings gleaming in the early morning sunshine as they perch on bankside vegetation. For me, damselflies mark the height of spring in the wetlands near my home on the Somerset Levels. Even on dull days, they gather in huge numbers, and fling themselves up from the path ahead of me as I struggle through the ever-growing plant life.

To get to grips with three very similar 'blue' damselflies I need a sunny day, a magnifying glass and a degree of patience that might test a saint. Seeing them is easy: they are very conspicuous insects, which on fine days may appear in their hundreds – even thousands – along the cuts, rhynes and ditches in my neighbourhood.

But even telling the commonest two species apart takes real effort. Both the azure and common blue damselflies are incredibly abundant and widespread, and can only be definitively separated by close examination of the exact pattern of black on the segments of their abdomen.

Still interested? Well, take a look at the top of the abdomen, just below where the wings meet the body, and you'll notice a distinctive black marking: in the common blue this is shaped like an oak tree, and in the azure is an elongated 'H', rather like the symbol used by the car-maker Honda.

I have noticed that the common blue peaks in numbers a few weeks later than the azure, and is also a more intense colour: as the saying has it, 'common blue is really blue'. But it took me almost a decade before I finally caught up with the third, much scarcer species, the aptly named variable damselfly. From a distance, this insect appears to be rather more black than blue, but to double-check I did a swift sweep with my butterfly net, and was able to confirm that the mark at the top of its abdomen is shaped exactly like a wine glass.

BEE HAWKMOTHS

24 May

This was a moment of utter concentration and I could hardly believe my eyes. Hurtling towards me, zooming low over the grassy ride, was a small fluffy sphere. A sweep of the net and the creature was neatly fielded: hearts racing, we all knelt down to worship the prize.

That was my first heady encounter with a narrow-bordered bee hawk-moth, a rare and attractive insect that we believed no longer existed in this area of the West Midlands. One had been seen the season before in this woodland, but surely there wasn't much chance of repeating the miracle? Yet here, against all the odds, was the fluffy, quivering evidence.

There were two big reasons to celebrate. First, 'bee hawks' are exciting creatures. The two species, broad-bordered and narrow-bordered, are bumblebee mimics, which explains their squat furry bodies, day-flying habits and wings that lack most of the coloured scales that characterise most other moths.

The narrow-bordered bee hawk looks like an outsize common carder bee, its thorax cinnamon above, pale beneath, with a black cummerbund around its plump abdomen. Our specimen had settled demurely in the

folds of the net, allowing us to admire its transparent wings with chocolate borders and its dark clubbed antennae.

Second, this was a discovery in an area where they'd not been seen
for decades. Bee hawks like large areas of open, flowery grassland, which
must contain their caterpillar's food-plant, the devil's bit scabious. As
the plant declines through ploughing or scrubbing over, the moth inevitably disappears. It is now very scarce and its range highly fragmented,
but our find was proof that it could return given the right conditions.
Later searches revealed that the fat green caterpillars, the size of a child's
thumb, were feeding along the rides.

But the discovery was on private land and part of the ride was used
by the owner's son for quad biking. Hundreds of pheasants are released
for shooting nearby and the birds love fat caterpillars. Local moth-lovers
heard about the site and many wanted to see the insects. A larva was
found squashed accidentally underfoot, by whom we can't be sure.
What we do know is that a combination of threats could easily wipe
out this vulnerable new colony. In a crowded countryside where so
many demanding species are localised, the reality is that they need
extra care and attention. I fervently hope that the narrow-bordered bee
hawkmoth survives: no one means it any harm, but sometimes that
isn't enough.

BAT BIOBLITZ

25 May

I've just been back to my old school in Birmingham to take part in a
Bioblitz. Until a few years ago I wasn't even sure what a Bioblitz was.
The idea originated in the USA and is an intense wildlife survey of
a particular area, usually over twenty-four hours.

It may be a small garden or part of a National Park, but wherever you
hold one, the aim is to find out what species occur there and – most
importantly – to encourage people who wouldn't normally record wildlife
to have a go, helped by experts. Conservation bureaucrats call it 'public
engagement', but it's really about having a good time and making discoveries on your doorstep.

This particular event in the grounds of King Edward's School in the leafy Birmingham suburb of Edgbaston was organised by the school's biology masters, excellent naturalists and enthusiasts too. My role was to point out plants and to enthuse the sixth-formers about the delights of botany. A challenge that turned out to be a pleasant surprise, as within half an hour they were identifying hybrid Spanish/British bluebells with minimal tuition, no mean feat for beginners.

But the real scene-stealers appeared in the final acts. Next to the school is an urban nature reserve and golf course, which includes a lake, wooded on two sides. Forty years earlier I'd seen my first smew here: earlier still Bill Oddie and other founders of the school's ornithological society had ringed woodland birds. Today, as dusk approached, the line of boys, parents and teachers stood on the dam, watching dark shapes flickering high above: noctule bats.

Younger ears could pick out their high-pitched echolocating calls but for the oldies bat detectors were essential and also alerted us to common pipistrelles using 45-kilohertz and soprano pipistrelles at 55-kilohertz frequency. As the sun set, its dying light picked out Daubenton's bats skimming low over the water surface, feeding on emerging midges: all this just over a mile from Birmingham city centre.

It was an unforgettable, shared experience. One British Asian mother said she didn't know bats lived in the UK. Her son was utterly entranced by them, asking brilliant questions of all of us. As darkness fell, he had to be prised away. Although the younger generation is widely touted as being disconnected from the natural world, provide the opportunities and interest is soon sparked. This is the power of the Bioblitz and we need more of them.

DEMOISELLES

26 May

They appear as if by magic on a fine day at the end of May, thronging the rhynes and ditches around my Somerset home. I'm always struck by just how stunning they are: the body glowing like burnished metal, while their wings flash in the morning sun.

Known also as 'water butterflies', for their habit of gathering in groups by the edge of a slow-flowing river or stream, banded demoiselles are

– along with their cousin the beautiful demoiselle – the largest of our damselflies.

Their wings are, as their name suggests, banded alternately light and dark, whose regular flashing gives me the distinct impression that they are sending a signal. Actually they are, though not to me, but to lure in passing females and entice them to mate.

When they do so, it is a truly remarkable sight. First the female – whose body is bottle green and whose wings lack the dark band of the male – settles at a suitable place for her to lay her eggs. Then the male lands on her wings and grips her head, and the pair copulate for more than a minute. Once mating is over, he guards her jealously to ensure that the eggs laid are fertilised with his sperm, and not by another passing male.

I don't often see the beautiful demoiselle, as they are less widespread than their banded cousins, being found mainly in acid waters on heathland or moorland. The males' wings are completely dark, while their bodies are a deep shade of blue-green, with coppery tints revealed when the insect basks in the sunshine, as they often do.

Like his relative, the male beautiful demoiselle guards the female after mating; during which time she will lay up to 300 minuscule eggs, bobbing up and down as she deposits each one on clumps of aquatic vegetation. Once hatched, the larvae remain submerged for two whole years, before eventually emerging as adults on a fine spring day, to delight us once again.

EMPID FLIES

27 May

With over 7,000 species of British flies, it's no wonder that even hardened naturalists baulk at the challenge of identifying them. For many, a microscope, a firm grasp of technical terms and an intimate knowledge of genitalia is essential. A few decades to spare would be useful too.

Dipterology, the study of the two-winged flies, is taking off and guides to the more conspicuous groups such as robber flies, horse flies and hoverflies are easy to find. Many other flies are not only common and widespread, but also relatively easy to recognise.

In May, one of my favourites is the dance fly *Empis tessellata*. Dance flies are a large family, which includes those madcap insects that you see whizzing erratically over the surface of small pools and puddles. *Empis tessellata* is a much statelier insect, bigger and more slender than a housefly with long legs and a stork-like beak used for probing flowers. It's greyish but the bases of its long wings are suffused with orange highlights.

Empids appear in late spring, and feed on flower nectar. They're fond of May blossom and you'll often see their leggy forms crawling sluggishly over the flowers. But although nectar is a favourite food, empids are not strict vegetarians, especially at mating time.

When the male goes a-wooing, he seduces prospective partners with a wedding present. Without a gift he will almost certainly be rejected, so to be sure of a successful consummation, he spears another fly, maybe a St Mark's fly or a bluebottle, which is often as big as he is, on his beak-like proboscis, then hauls it off to a waiting female.

If all goes to plan, she will accept his prize and seize it in her bristly basket of limbs and begin draining its life-juices. While she's occupied, he takes his chance to mate. The act itself is an astonishing feat of strength: hanging on to a leaf by just the tips of his front legs he supports not only the weight of the female, but also the huge fly she carries. Each spring I look out for hanging trios of empids and their prey. It looks an impossible feat and I can't pass by without marvelling at their strength and tenacity.

'CABBAGE WHITE' BUTTERFLIES

28 May

A bright, sunny day towards the end of May and, after a spell of cool, rainy weather, my garden is suddenly flooded with white butterflies. They fly frantically from flower to flower, eager to get to the energy-giving nectar before their rivals suck the plant dry.

Because these insects rarely settle for more than a moment or two, I can never get a really good look at them. For this reason, gardeners have long known the large and small whites simply as 'cabbage whites', so named because of their preference for laying their eggs on brassicas, members of the cabbage family.

The first of the two to emerge in my neck of the woods is the small white, which generally appears in early April, though I have seen them on fine days in late March. A week or two later, I see its cousin the large white, though the main emergence comes in May. Telling the two apart is trickier than you might imagine: the size difference is not all that great, and the variation in upperwing pattern between males and females of each species can be confusing.

That's even before I take into account a third species, the green-veined white. This butterfly can look very similar to its cousins, but the overall impression is of pure white (rather than off-white) upperwings and, when perched, the underwings show a pleasing pattern of dark veins on pale yellow, hence the name.

Fortunately green-veined whites, which can be just as common as the other two species, avoid cabbages when laying their eggs, their caterpillars preferring to feed on lady's smock (cuckooflower) and garlic mustard. In spring, the adult butterflies often emerge in damp, marshy fields where lady's smock grows in profusion, fluttering up from the pale flowers as if the petals themselves were taking wing.

BLACK TERN AND LITTLE GULL

29 May

Staines Reservoirs, on the outskirts of Heathrow Airport in the west London suburbs, is not the most attractive place to watch birds. But over the years, the two concrete basins bisected by a ramrod-straight footpath have turned up a stunning variety of rare species. The reservoirs are also the best place in south-east England to look for certain specialities rarely seen elsewhere.

So despite the place's lack of aesthetics, birders flock here at certain times of year. They come to see smew in January, black-necked grebes in August and, towards the end of May, to catch up with two scarce passage migrants – birds that although they do not breed in Britain, pass through regularly on their migratory journeys in spring and autumn – black terns and little gulls.

Little gulls are, as their name suggests, the smallest species of gull – not just in Britain but in the whole world. Barely the length of a blackbird (though bulkier and heavier), they drift through the air with an effortless ease on their rounded wings, giving them a rather tern-like appearance. In autumn, the juveniles appear, with their kittiwake-like wing-pattern, as if someone has stencilled the letter 'w' in black on their upperwings; but in spring I have sometimes seen stunning adults, with their smoky-grey underwings and dark bills.

Little gulls may be graceful – at least compared with their larger relatives – but they are eclipsed by black terns. Mainly black – as their name suggests – these tiny birds float above the water, occasionally diving down to grab a morsel of food off the surface.

Both the little gulls and black terns are only here for a day or two before heading away to the east to breed in the Low Countries and around the Baltic. Why none stay here to nest (or at least very rarely do so) is a bit of a mystery – we would appear to have plenty of suitable habitat. Maybe having glimpsed the urban sprawl of the M25 corridor they simply decide that anywhere else would be nicer; and they may well be right.

SKYLARKS ON A GREEN ROOF

30 May

The vast expanse of brownish green stretches off into the distance, as a small brown bird rises up from the ground in front of me and begins to sing. A skylark – hardly a surprise, perhaps, given this is the middle of May and I am in the heart of the Sussex countryside. Except that I am not in a field, but walking across the roof of the Rolls-Royce car factory.

When Rolls-Royce decided to build here, planning rules meant that they were required to make the structure blend in with the surrounding countryside. The site they chose was an old quarry which enabled them to construct a low building whose profile would not protrude above the skyline, and so have less visual impact. But the designers went one step further: they covered more than eight acres of the factory roof with plants, creating the largest green roof in Britain. The plants they chose were mainly sedums, whose fleshy leaves can store water, enabling them to grow in dry, exposed places. As an added bonus, sedums also provide plenty of nectar for insects such as wasps, hoverflies and bees.

Walking across the factory roof is an unusual experience. The aspect means that it really does feel like you are in a normal field, a perception reinforced when I startle a pair of red-legged partridges, which take to the air on whirring wings, uttering their call like a puffing steam train. All around me, I can hear the song of dozens of skylarks, which have readily taken to nesting on the roof, where they can be safe from predators such as hedgehogs, stoats and foxes.

In the wider countryside, skylarks are in big trouble, having declined by well over half in the past few decades (guess why? – that's right, modern industrial farming). Even for those that have survived, each brood has only a one in three chance of fledging and so a green roof such as this is the ideal option, enabling the birds to have a far better chance of success than in their usual home. It's also a fine example of how many companies are now incorporating the natural world into their ways of working.

ADDER'S-TONGUE FERN

31 May

There's a comedy sketch in which, dressed as a stereotypical naturalist, Lenny Henry visits a field where unseen and undescribed rarities lurk in the grass. As he delivers his commentary on the threats to their survival, each step he takes crushes one of the creatures, which expires with a pathetic squeak.

Minus the sound effects, searching for adder's-tongue ferns is a similar experience. These most un-fernlike of ferns are very hard to spot in the turf of the meadows where they survive. Their small shoe-horn leaves are the colour of spring grass and easy to dismiss as young docks or sorrels.

Only when you bend down to take a closer look do you see the sporangium, looking more like a rattlesnake's tail than an adder's tongue. This spore-bearing spike is as green as the sheathing frond and the effect is of a small, emerald Lords-and-Ladies flower. It is relatively short-lived and will be eclipsed by grass blades in a month's time, after which it yellows. By late summer it is gone.

Finding adder's-tongue is a sign that you are in unimproved grassland

– unimproved for modern agriculture that is – and hay meadows in May are always a good place to look. The plant's underground network of rhizomes allows it to persist in undisturbed spots, but ploughing will destroy it and now that most of our ancient meadows have been ploughed or turned over to monocultures, or else are over-grazed, the adder's-tongue has declined in many places. But it can still be spotted along broad, woodland rides and on commons that are not too closely cropped by sheep and ponies. In 1983 it even turned up in Buckingham Palace gardens.

Nowadays, though a relatively scarce plant and it might be hard to find enough to produce a potion that speeds the process of healing, according to the herbalist John Gerard writing at the end of the sixteenth century, it was 'a most excellent green oyle or rather a balsam for greene wounds'. Adder's tongue was also said to be a cure for tumours if it was plucked at the falling of the moon.

It's hard enough to find by day in grassy meadows, so this story says a lot for the persistence of its searchers. It also tells us that it was a much commoner and more familiar plant than it is now.

JUNE

FOR ME, THIS is a time when insect-watching takes centre stage. Just as April bustles with arriving migrant birds, June can be a riot of wings, feelers and legs as the insect season gathers pace.

Although some spring butterflies begin to wane at this time of year, the first meadow browns, large skippers and ringlets appear. Moths can be abundant on warm nights and dragonflies and damselflies glitter over lakes and rivers.

The real pleasure in looking for insects, and indeed other invertebrates such as spiders, is that you can make significant discoveries for your neighbourhood, your county or even for the whole country. Compared with our knowledge of birdlife, what we know about the distribution of many of our insects is still patchy and there are relatively few people out there in the field, looking.

Recently friends and I have been able to find insects that are new to our home county of Worcestershire or which haven't been seen here for over a century. That doesn't mean they weren't here all along of course, but that no one has been looking for them. Tracking them down in the right habitat and at the right time is exciting detective work.

To see many insects, timing is vital. Some flies and beetles for example have a very short adult season and so are easy to miss especially if the weather is poor. Numbers vary from year to year too, but it's very likely that many species are far less rare than we think. An inspiring group of naturalists known as the pan-species-listers aim to identify everything they find and their efforts have increased our knowledge of many species. There are some excellent guides available in print and online and many societies devoted to recording and identifying invertebrates, so there's never been a better time to focus on them.

The sheer number and variety is daunting at first, but if you concentrate on a particular group or certain species, then I guarantee that the summer will fly by and your discoveries may even help to rewrite the field guides.

B.W.

FLAMING JUNE — or the usual washout? In the past few years the latter seems to have had the upper hand: the weather forecasters may tell us that temperatures are higher than the long-term average, and I'm sure they are; but when day after day dawns cloudy and damp, that's not much consolation.

It seems such a pity to waste what are the longest days of the year, so I usually make the effort to go out and see what I can find. June can – even when sunny and warm – be a rather capricious month, as butterflies tend to disappear in what lepidopterists wryly term the 'June gap', between spring species such as the orange-tip and those of high summer, such as the gatekeeper and meadow brown. But by the end of the month these are finally on the wing.

Many birds are winding down their breeding season; and as a result, can become far more elusive. Birdsong drops away from mid-month, while newly fledged young birds can be hard to find, as they skulk in vegetation to hide away from predators. June is, however, the peak month for calls to the RSPB saying, 'There's a baby bird on my lawn – what can I do to help?' The answer? Nothing! Either its parents will find it, or a predator will, and there's nothing you should or can do, so don't interfere!

But as bird activity declines, so wild flowers and insects begin to reach their peak: the hedgerows around my home are so stuffed with vegetation they look as if they might explode; while on a welcome warm, still evening, the hum of insects gives way to the silent flight of moths, chased expertly across the darkening sky by bats.

June is also the month to head for the far north: Speyside or the Hebrides, or even Orkney and Shetland – where the sun barely sets before it begins to rise again – and where you may encounter some of the rarest wild creatures and greatest wild spectacles Britain has to offer.

S.M.

CUCKOO

I June

Not long after we moved down to Somerset, in a conversation with the daughter-in-law of our local farmer, I was lamenting the lack of cuckoos in the village.

'But we hear them all the time,' she said, looking at me with that combination of kindness and pity that Somerset folk save for incomers from London, like me. 'One sits on the roof just outside my bedroom window; I hear it all year round.'

Now it was my turn to be kind. 'I'm afraid that might be a different bird . . .' I diffidently ventured. 'Did it go "coo-coo-coo"?'

The answer was affirmative.

'In that case I'm afraid what you are hearing is not a cuckoo, but a collared dove. They do sound very similar . . .'

So much for the widely held notion that country folk know far more about wildlife than townies. Though to be fair, she's probably too young to have heard a real cuckoo, with its distinctive syncopated call.

Later that day, I went out on my bike in another vain search for cuckoos. It's not as if there aren't enough reed warblers, one of the cuckoo's favourite host species, here – their harsh, chuntering, song echoes around the lanes from late April through to June. Yet despite the abundance of this elusive summer visitor, I have yet to hear a cuckoo in our parish.

The reason for the decline of the cuckoo, that classic harbinger of spring for generations past, is something of a mystery. It hasn't happened everywhere: Scottish cuckoos, which mainly use meadow pipits as their host, are doing rather well, having held their own while the English population has declined by almost two-thirds in the past twenty years. The latest research suggests this may be because the two populations take different migration routes.

One suggestion for the cuckoo's decline – the loss of habitat on its wintering grounds in Africa – cannot be to blame, or at least not completely so. A more likely reason is the massive decline in the availability of the cuckoo chick's main food, the caterpillars of our larger moths, which have suffered catastrophic falls in the south of Britain.

After searching the lanes around my home, I give up, and head down to the Avalon marshes, where there are still a few cuckoos. But even when I finally hear that classic call, my joy is tinged with sadness.

STAG BEETLE
2 June

Few species from the Biodiversity Action Plan – a programme that includes stone curlew, ladybird spider and greater horseshoe bat – occur regularly in gardens, let alone urban gardens. The male stag beetle, with his antlerish mandibles, is an exception, though this huge insect often goes unnoticed, except in June when the adults emerge from their larval tunnels in timber and see daylight for the first time in what may be as many as six years.

Chestnut and black with ferocious-looking jaws, the male stag beetle isn't easy to miss. And at a whopping seventy-five millimetres long, it is also our largest land beetle. Yet the beetles rarely feed as adults, fly only on the warmest evenings, and live for just a few weeks.

Despite its size and ferocious appearance, the stag beetle is strangely vulnerable. Occasionally, we find these magnificent insects lumbering drunkenly on pavements or crushed by suburban traffic, having mistakenly relied on their armour, which, although tough, is unfit for the world we've created. Commonest in the south and south-east of England, often in the heat islands of towns and cities, London has nearly a third of all Britain's stag beetles, which is why there is a Biodiversity Action Plan to save it there.

Awareness, you might think, is hardly an insurmountable challenge. That may be true for the beetles that reach adulthood, but the real threats are when they are at their most vulnerable, hidden for years as fat white grubs in dead wood.

Stag beetles mate on warm summer nights and the females, which have no 'antlers', lay their eggs in old timber. Dead trees are favourite spots, but they will also use fence-posts and gateposts. Most people, who aren't necessarily conservation-minded, can't resist burning or clearing out dead wood, and with it goes a generation of stag beetles and other insects. A friend of mine with a log fire is convinced that he can hear the popping of small invertebrates above the roar of the flames.

It's hard to change habits and a special challenge to conserve insects, especially large and formidable-looking beetles. But saving the stag beetle is a relatively straightforward matter. Rather than stump grinding and burning old wood, all we have to do is create a loggery in our gardens or leave that old gatepost standing . . . and in June and July look carefully where we tread.

ARCTIC TERN

3 June

When I want to get really close to nature, the best way to do so is to walk through a seabird colony at the height of the breeding season.

No other natural spectacle is quite such a total assault on my senses: the sight of thousands of birds gathered cheek-by-jowl in one place; the sound of the cacophony of calls, as they seem to be raising their voices to be heard above the wall of noise; and of course the smell: an indescribable but instantly recognisable odour that fills my nostrils the moment I arrive.

On the Farne Islands – by far the best place to see breeding seabirds in Britain, if not the whole of the northern hemisphere – there is another sensation: fear. For one particular seabird chooses to defend its chick in the best way possible: by aerial attack.

Like Tuesday's child, Arctic terns are full of grace. They take stylishness to an extreme, their long, slender wings and forked tail lending them a buoyant beauty few can match. But don't be fooled by this elegant exterior. They are also full of naked aggression. Any intruder into their colony is swiftly attacked and punished, as the birds descend from the summer's sky like drones, targeting the scalp of any hatless visitors with their dagger-like bill.

Having managed to survive the tern attack, I usually spend a few minutes simply sitting and watching their antics. Even a short time watching them is better than hours poring over books on bird behaviour. And the subtleties of how individuals cope with living so close to one another – a situation forced on these ocean-going birds by the necessity of finding a safe place to nest – make it easy to draw parallels with another species whose individuals are often forced into close proximity: us.

I'm not the first person to make that comparison. Seabirds were among the earliest living creatures to be studied in the field, rather than in museums or laboratories. Pioneers such as Niko Tinbergen, who first observed lesser black-backed and herring gull behaviour in the years before and after the Second World War, found that by simply watching and noting down the behaviour of these birds, he could discover that they are far more complex and fascinating than was ever thought possible.

This in turn led to the new science of ethology – the formal study of animal behaviour – now the staple of every university course in biology or zoology, and indeed the wildlife TV programmes that are so popular and enduring. It seems that by holding a mirror up to nature, we may at the same time learn something about ourselves.

CLUB-TAILED DRAGONFLY

4 June

It was one of those days. We walked and walked along the banks of the River Severn, praying for the weather to turn and allow at least a glimpse of the sun. We did see a range of commoner dragons and damsels: bulky four-spotted chasers, matchstick-thin azure damselflies and the odd banded demoiselle. But our main target species for the day remained stubbornly unseen. Until, that is, we returned to the car park.

There, perched on the damp foliage of a spring hedgerow, was one of our scarcest and most elusive insects, the club-tailed dragonfly. We almost missed it: the yellowish-green and black markings blended surprisingly well with the foliage in the background, and only the shine from its newly minted wings revealed its presence.

This distinctive insect, about the length of a man's thumb, had presumably emerged from the nearby River Severn just the day before, after spending as long as five years living underwater in its larval form.

But whereas most dragonflies are showy creatures, buzzing around the edge of the water like miniature First World War biplanes on a reconnaissance exercise, these shy insects normally head away from the water, seeking out woodland clearings far away from the river where their life began.

The club-tailed dragonfly is the only British representative of a group of medium-sized dragonflies, named after their distinctively enlarged, club-shaped 'tail' – actually the end of their abdomen. It is known to odonatophiles (a fancy word for dragonfly enthusiasts) as *Gomphus*, a

Latin word deriving from the Greek for 'tooth', as that's what the tip of the abdomen resembles.

They are fussy little creatures, found only on a few large, slow-moving rivers, including the middle reaches of the Thames and Severn in England and a handful of rivers in Wales. Ironically, though, the club-tail is one of the few dragonflies not affected by the huge increase in pleasure-boat traffic on the Thames, because the adults do not need to use emergent vegetation when they appear from the waters for the first time.

The sighting confirmed a belief long held by my wife Suzanne, who spotted this elusive creature: that the very best wildlife is usually found in the car park.

SWALLOWTAILS

5 June

I'm not sure that I will ever get used to swallowtail butterflies, even if I were lucky enough to live among them. Yet here they are fluttering tropically over the Sweet William flowers in a cottage garden. All three of us are enraptured as we gawp at the borders of a cottage next to the RSPB's Strumpshaw Fen reserve in Norfolk.

The owners, Martin and Barbara George, generously invite passing visitors to enter their garden to take photos. It's a touching gesture and we lose no time in taking up the offer.

For most of us, happy to see a small tortoiseshell or a painted lady in our gardens, the sight of Britain's largest butterfly fanning over the borders is as unlikely as a phoenix on the bird-table. We are mesmerised by the swallowtail's flickering custard- and coal-coloured wings, the insects so preoccupied with nectar-seeking that we can almost touch them. Against the lipstick-pink flowers, they are so gaudy as to be an outrage against taste, but their presence in this corner of Norfolk is precarious, tied to the remaining fens and to their larval food-plant, the rare milk parsley, which grows only here.

But there may be changes afoot. The 'British' swallowtail is a separate race called *britannicus*. It is very similar to continental swallowtails but, isolated from them by the North Sea, has evolved thicker black veins on the wings and so looks slightly darker. The larger continental *gorganus* swallowtails are much less fussy about their food and their caterpillars will feed on several members of the wild carrot family.

The continental variety rarely arrive here in any numbers, but in the hot summer of 2013 several were seen in southern English counties where they laid eggs in gardens. Stripy caterpillars became pupae and produced butterflies in spring 2014. Will they settle here? With a run of hot summers and mild winters, it's not impossible that continental swallowtails could set up home permanently and grace our gardens far beyond East Anglia. How they would interact with 'our' swallowtails we can't be sure, but it's likely that they would have a wider range and might even interbreed.

SEA KALE

6 June

For the last three Junes I've travelled on location with *Springwatch* to the RSPB's reserve at Minsmere on the Suffolk coast. The avian stars are the bitterns, whose low thumping calls you feel as much as you hear, and the pied avocets, living logos that compete with black-headed gulls for nest-sites on the brackish lagoons.

But there are botanical treasures here too. The stretch of flinty shingle between scrapes and sea is home to a spectacular plant, sea kale. In late May and early June, its mounds of creamy flowers resemble sheep huddling on the pebble ridges. They foam above the glaucous leaves, ruched and tinted with lilac, some of the most spectacular foliage of any of our native plants. These leaves are smooth and waxy to the touch, resisting dehydration and the regular sandblasting that's inevitable along these windy North Sea coasts.

They're also edible, the stems tasting rather like a cross between asparagus and celery. Sea kale is a brassica, a member of the cabbage and mustard family and was once highly prized by Victorian collectors, who piled stones around the plants' roots to blanch the new shoots, before harvesting them. So great was the trade in sea kale that wild plants were eliminated from some beaches; on others the populations declined so that although widespread, the plant is now distinctly local.

It doesn't help that many kinds of kale are the latest culinary must-haves and that foraging is chic once again. It is not illegal to take small amounts of sea kale, but the plant is a landscape feature, on parts of the Suffolk coast for instance, and so its reduction would be a pity. We can only hope that commercially grown sea kale will be enough to satisfy the market.

MARSH FROG
7 June

An impossibly loud chorus of quacking sounds comes from a water-filled ditch. But as I peer down, the expected family of mallards are nowhere to be seen. Then it starts again – sounding rather like someone is laughing raucously at me. This is no practical joke, but the call of one of our most bizarre amphibians, the marsh frog.

If I am patient, then a careful scan of the edges of the water should reveal a greenish head poking just above the surface, eyes staring back at me. As I watch, the creature's cheeks suddenly begin to bulge out, like two spheres of bubblegum being blown by a surly teenager; and that extraordinary sound begins all over again.

The story of how the marsh frog came to be here in Britain is a strange one. Back in the 1930s a dozen frogs were brought over from Hungary, and released on to Romney Marsh in Kent. From that tiny population the creature has now spread throughout much of south-east England, including the London Wetland Centre, and also as far afield as the Somerset Levels.

Fortunately, it does not appear to compete with our native common frog, as the marsh frog is a more aquatic species, preferring to live in steep-sided dykes and ditches rather than ponds. So unlike other non-native invaders it is accepted more as a curiosity than a pest. If you get a decent view of one, they are usually greener than common frogs, and some have a distinctive yellow stripe running down the centre of their back.

And yet soon after these curious amphibians first arrived here, during the Second World War, one nervous local resident reported the sound as coming from a group of Nazi spies plotting with one another beneath a bridge; amusing now, perhaps, but more understandable at the time given the proximity of Romney Marsh to the European mainland.

POPPIES
8 June

The potency of poppies is never as obvious as on this June day, in the Severn Valley at Bewdley in Worcestershire. Crowds jostle for position behind a makeshift tape strung up to prevent trampling the sea of scarlet. Lions groan distantly in the nearby safari park and engines from the Severn Valley Railway trail white pennants of steam.

This floral spectacle has been provided unintentionally. A few years ago, Worcestershire Wildlife Trust acquired three arable fields next to important heathland. By ploughing these sandy fields and reducing the fertility remaining from when cereals were grown there, the Trust hoped to encourage heather and other species to colonise from the adjoining heath. But ploughing unearthed millions of poppy seeds, programmed to respond to this sudden burst of sunlight and they germinated so thickly that by June the fields were vast red blocks that drew in crowds from far and wide.

The timing, close to commemorations for the First World War centenary, couldn't have been better. Locals walked the short distance from the town to a hastily erected viewing platform. Schoolchildren came to sketch the flowers and regional BBC news made a film. National broadsheets and, aptly, redtops, splashed the poppies across their pages and suddenly the three small fields were an international event. A Korean TV channel applied to the Trust for permission to film, while coachloads of visitors from Japan and China (where red is an important and lucky colour) arrived in their finest outfits to have their portraits taken with the flowers. Newly-weds posed for their albums and there were rumours that a local photographer had snapped his wife in the nude.

This outpouring of public affection is understandable: the resonance of Flanders fields is impossible to ignore. Few flowers have the power of poppies to move us – as was proved by the installation of almost a million ceramic poppies at the Tower of London in autumn 2014.

Their resurrection after decades of dormancy in the soil looks like a miracle. But perhaps the short-lived bursts of flowers also remind us of our own impermanence. Poppies are fragile, their petals what botanists describe as fugacious, falling after a day or so at the first breath of wind. Their gaudy delights need to be enjoyed immediately. Or is it that poppies meet a need in us for wildness; a need that isn't catered for by green deserts of sown grass or fields of commercially planted yellow rape?

Certainly visitors miss them. As nutrient levels have been reduced to allow heathland to take over, the poppies have dwindled. Some people are disappointed and have complained to the Trust that the flowers are not being looked after. Heathland, however, is a much rarer commodity hereabouts and a priority for conservationists. But the event – there is no other word – has exposed a genuine affection for the natural world, neatly encapsulated by this parade of scarlet poppies.

MEDITERRANEAN GULL

9 June

A flock of gulls rises up from their breeding colony, filling the air with wings and noise. Superficially they look like the common and familiar black-headed gulls: but something about that jet-black head, contrasting with broad, snow-white wings, just isn't quite right. These are Mediterranean gulls, the forgotten success story of our modern avifauna.

Only sixty years ago, the Mediterranean gull was a scarce visitor to Britain from its breeding grounds on mainland Europe and western Asia. Even there it was never common: indeed as recently as 1960 it was feared that this elegant gull might be heading towards the exit door, on the way to becoming globally extinct.

But the late twentieth century proved to be a good time for gulls of all species, including the 'Med gull', to use birders' shorthand. Numbers began to increase at the existing colonies, and the species started to expand its range northwards and westwards, towards Britain.

In the summer that England won the football World Cup, 1966, a handful of Mediterranean gulls turned up at a breeding colony of black-headed gulls in Hampshire, just opposite the Isle of Wight. Two years later, a pair nested there – the very first time this species had been recorded breeding in Britain.

Meanwhile other new species, such as the black redstart, little ringed plover and Cetti's warbler, were also colonising from mainland Europe, causing plenty of excitement among the birding fraternity. But perhaps because of our general disdain towards all gulls, the Mediterranean gull was largely ignored by many birders, even as numbers grew and it began to expand its range. Today more than 1,000 pairs breed in Britain, mostly in southern England but some as far north as Cumbria and Northumberland, as well as in Wales and across the water in Northern Ireland.

The species is also a regular sight in winter: scan through a flock of gulls on any park or playing field and you may pick out this haughty-looking bird as it steps daintily across the short turf. I sometimes see one down on the coast near my home; and once, memorably, one flew over my garden.

MEADOW BROWN
10 June

Although June is a vibrant month, the height of the breeding cycle for much of our wildlife, there's often a period when things seem to stall. After the onrush of bird migration, the dawn chorus and the spring explosions of insects and flowers, there comes a lull, the fulcrum of the year held in what Gilbert and Sullivan called equipoise.

Lepidopterists notice this particularly as the 'June gap', the hiatus between the disappearance of spring broods and the emergence of the summer generations. Overwintering species such as peacock, comma and small tortoiseshell can often be elusive now. Orange-tips and pearl-bordered fritillaries are over in my local woods, and ringlets and gatekeepers are yet to emerge. Even speckled woods may be scarce.

The midsummer saviour is the meadow brown, whose bobbing triangles appear in early June in fields and road verges. Although still common, and indeed Britain's most widespread butterfly, my impression is that it doesn't occur in the large numbers I used to see. Their name says it all – they are butterflies that relish old-style hay meadows. Now most of my local grassland is monoculture or has its flowers considerably reduced. On top of this, the silage is cut in early June, leaving little nectar for the emerging adults, which tend to disperse along hedgerows. They may struggle to find alternative sites with a variety of grasses and wild flowers, and so meadow brown colonies tend to be smaller and more isolated than they once were.

There is hope in town, though, if we can persuade local authorities, gardeners and other landowners to forsake the tyranny of the mower and strimmer. As a boy I used to spend hours on a tiny patch of waste ground near my home where meadow browns were really abundant, the 'bread-and-butterfly' on every knapweed and thistle flower. Although at the age of seven I was unaware of the term sexual dimorphism, I was smug enough to distinguish the brighter females with their orange-haloed wing spots from the drabber, sootier males.

Meadow browns shun tidiness, but flourish in these uncut fragments of wasteland. It's a perilous existence: good habitat one summer may be under an office block the next. With very little effort and tolerance, we could leave areas in our parks or on the edge of playing fields and in school grounds uncut, and maybe even picnic among buttercups, ox-eye daisies and clouds of meadow brown butterflies. It's not a lot to ask.

BADGER

11 June

One way to know how well an animal is doing in the wild is by the rather grisly process of counting roadkill. Thus we know that over the past couple of decades one familiar creature, the hedgehog, has gone into a sharp decline, while another, the badger, has enjoyed a population boom. I can hardly drive for more than a mile along the lanes behind my Somerset home without encountering yet another sad-looking badger corpse.

Once only glimpsed on wildlife TV programmes such as *Springwatch* (and even there, badgers were often, to the frustration of both the production team and the audience, absent from their sett), badgers are now far more frequently seen in the countryside – alive as well as dead.

Since they are nocturnal animals, it does take a bit of effort to find them; but if I wander along a wooded drove where I know there is a sett, I sometimes come across three or four of these animals, snuffling around among the bracken. If I keep still and quiet, and am downwind of the creatures, they seem reasonably happy with my presence. Watching them, as they snuffle in the earth for something to eat, I am reminded of more exotic creatures such as anteaters or warthogs.

British badgers have a reputation for sociability. One theory for this is that our generally damp climate provides a ready supply of food in the form of worms and beetles, which means that instead of leading a solitary lifestyle, wandering far and wide, badgers are able to live in larger family groups.

If you don't know where your local sett is, then enterprising naturalists and conservation organisations have set up regular 'badger watch' events, some building hides next to setts to allow visitors to enjoy seeing the animals without disturbing them.

But although many of us have a powerful affection for this bumbling creature – a legacy, perhaps, of the wise and kindly Mr Badger in *The Wind in the Willows* – badgers are certainly not popular with everyone. Dairy farmers, whose livelihood may be threatened by the arrival of bovine TB in their herd, have long called for the badger population to be artificially reduced. In the past few years the government has responded by conducting trial culls in parts of the West Country.

This is not the place to discuss the merits of such a policy, apart from to point out that scientists have long suspected that culling the badgers tends to make things worse: the survivors then disperse and spread the disease elsewhere. And the badgers were, of course, here first.

So where does this leave the animal itself? Having gone against the grain and successfully adapted to life in the modern countryside, the badger is now paying the price for its success, both in the ire it arouses in farmers and the danger it faces on our rural roads. Meanwhile, most badgers are content with simply going about their business, emerging like clockwork at dusk to search for food.

HOUSE MARTINS

12 June

Bird sounds can conjure vivid images, even if they're only subliminal. Few respectable radio dramas set outdoors in a British summer would leave out the gritty calls of house martins. You may not recognise the birds that made them, but they're as evocative of a warm summer's day as Tennyson's doves moaning alliteratively in immemorial elms. Hear the doves and martins and you can picture the cloudless June skies, smell musk roses in the borders and taste the Pimm's.

With their neat white rumps, snowy underparts and blue-black wings, house martins are beguiling birds to watch as well as hear, whether they're gathering pellets of mud from roadside puddles, or rising and falling in pursuit of insects. As a child I remember putting down news-paper under the eaves of my grandparents' house to catch the droppings from several nests. It was a minor chore and well worth the pleasure of seeing the young birds bunched expectantly at the entrance to their nests, waiting for their parents to return with beaks full of flies.

Fixing the nest successfully to a vertical surface depends on establishing a safe holdfast. The eighteenth-century Hampshire parson Gilbert White was an acute observer of his local martins, watching as they braced themselves against a wall with their tails to apply the first pellets of mud. Because the stability of these foundations is all-important for holding up the structure, he noticed that 'the provident architect has prudence and forbearance enough not to advance her work too fast; but by building only in the morning, and by dedicating the rest of the day to food and amusement, gives it sufficient time to dry and harden.'

Observation of this precision over the centuries has enlightened us about the lives of house martins. As a child watching the birds over summer I had no idea where they went after they left the eaves. Fifty years on, I'm pleased to say, I'm still in ignorance. Ornithologists can't be sure where house martins spend the winter – beyond knowing that it is somewhere in the vast continent of Africa, south of the Sahara.

But as radio-tracking devices become smaller that question will soon be solved. Research is likely to confirm that the birds spend their time away from us floating high above the vast rainforests of the Congo where, invisible to human eyes, they hawk insects under the searing tropical sun.

WOOD WHITES

13 June

A walk through a wood on a June afternoon can be a surprisingly quiet affair. Birdsong has all but ended: the adults are busily feeding their hungry broods of young, and have little or no time for singing. Butterflies are thin on the ground too: I think about giving up and heading home.

But in a small clearing, where the sunshine filters through the canopy to scatter the ground with golden shafts of light, I see two pale butterflies. One is quietly perched on the stem of a plant, while the other flies up and down as if trying to attract its attention. And that's just what it is doing; for this is a male wood white paying court to a shy and apparently reluctant female.

Had I not known what to look for, I might easily have mistaken these for mere 'cabbage whites'. But although they look superficially similar, the wood white could hardly be more different in behaviour from its brash and conspicuous cousins. Shy and retiring, it lives in the sunny, open rides and clearings in a handful of our ancient woodlands, from the Welsh borders and the Midlands down to Devon and the Surrey/Sussex borders.

Sadly, numbers of wood whites have fallen dramatically in recent years; mainly because our woodlands are no longer being actively managed. Without regular coppicing, the rides and the clearings the butterfly needs are becoming overgrown.

Nor can the wood white easily move home: its flight is so weak that it is unable to get from one piece of habitat to another, so it cannot take advantage of opportunities presented by a warming world to extend its range northwards.

It was thought that wood whites were thriving in Ireland, though, and this reclusive creature was confidently named as Réal's wood white, which is widespread in mainland Europe but curiously absent from Britain.

Then, in an unexpected twist, in 2011 it was announced that the Irish butterflies had been misidentified. It turns out that they are not Réal's wood whites at all, but belong to a completely different, third species, appropriately named the cryptic wood white.

The new species does appear to be far more adaptable than its cousins, being found along roadside verges and railway cuttings, and even thriving in sand dunes, instead of ancient woodlands.

If you find a wood white, it's no use trying to identify it by appearance: the only way to tell the three species apart is to examine their genitalia under a microscope. But although invisible to the human eye, the difference in the shape of their underparts is far from trivial – indeed it is what keeps them as separate species, as it means that even if their paths were to cross they would be unable to interbreed.

GLOW-WORMS
14 June

We've all read *Pride and Prejudice* and *Oliver Twist*. Or have we? Like those books we feel we've read, glow-worms are insects that we think we've seen at some time, maybe as children. It's an easy mistake to make: glow-worms are with us from an early age, in stories and illustrations. Inevitably, the idea of the glow-worm shedding light into the world is a powerful one laden with symbolism. Underneath it, the real beetle hides incognito.

We've burdened the nightingale with the same cultural baggage. It's hardly surprising then, that the two meet in an eighteenth-century poem by William Cowper, in which the nightingale, having sung lustily for some time, decides it feels peckish. The glow-worm, foreseeing its own demise, puts up a robust defence, arguing that just as it has admired the bird's lyrical prowess, so the nightingale should respect its powers of illumination. Convinced by this logic, the nightingale flies off to eat another hapless grub and the insect lives to light another day – or night.

The truth is that to see glow-worms you need to make an effort. Most are mature in June and July and so a nocturnal visit is best, preferably to an area with low light pollution. Warm evenings are better than cold ones and places with shortish grass such as downland or churchyards tend to be more productive. For most of us, travelling by car at night or walking on urban streets, the glow-worm will remain unseen. That's also why it's hard to say whether glow-worms are declining: it may simply be that fewer of us are out and about after dark in midsummer.

A few years ago, staying with my sister and her family in south Devon, I happened to mention glow-worms and wondered if there were any in the local lane. No, they'd never heard of any. My niece and nephew liked the idea of roaming the countryside though, so on impulse we all went for a midnight walk and found nearly a dozen glow-worms almost on the doorstep, a revelation for us all.

Glow-worms are well worth a search. Their 'earthly stars' as Pliny described them, are soft greenish-gold pinpricks among the grass of old road verges, along woodland rides and on downs. These ethereal lights are produced by the wingless female beetles, which can light the last two segments of their abdomen with a compound called luciferin, which produces bioluminescence, but no heat. Inverting her tail to display the light, she waits for a winged male to fly in. Once mated, she extinguishes her lamp, lays her eggs and dies.

'Out, out, brief candle' applies to the short-lived adults, but the young glow-worm can be two years in the larval state. They are bizarre, primeval-looking creatures – dark greyish with pale orange highlights – and feed on snails, paralysing them with a bite and sucking in the resulting snail soup. Sometimes you will see a youngster by day scurrying across a woodland path, but that's often the only sign that glow-worms are about.

GRASSHOPPERS AND CRICKETS
15 June

What is the true sound of summer? It can't be birdsong, for that is mostly over by the end of June. The buzzing of bumblebees, perhaps; or the humming of hoverflies? For me it is a suite of insects that, although often overlooked, play a crucial part in keeping our grasslands in a healthy state: grasshoppers and crickets.

When I first came across these small but noisy insects I used to get confused, but I have since learned that they are quite different in their appearance, habits and behaviour.

First, take a look at their antennae: if they are longer than the body, the chances are it is a cricket; if shorter, a grasshopper. Crickets also tend to be crepuscular (from the French word for 'twilight'), which means that if you hear singing during the day it is likely that you are listening to grasshoppers.

They produce the sound they make very differently, too. Crickets rub their wings together, while grasshoppers rub their long hind legs against their wings. Finally, they have different diets: crickets are omnivorous, and will prey on smaller insects, while grasshoppers, as their name suggests, feed mainly on grass.

When you hear these familiar buzzing sounds, a constant accompaniment to long, hot summer's days and muggy evenings, you can be sure that this particular part of our countryside is functioning as it should. But nowadays, when the sound is missing from so many rural landscapes, we know that something has gone badly wrong, and that the rough grassland these insects need has been replaced by intensive farming of monoculture crops.

DOWNLOOKER FLY

16 June

It's asking a lot for a fly to possess charisma, but one of my favourites appears in June in damp bushy places or in open woods. And yet, despite being fairly common, our knowledge of them remains rather limited.

As big as house-flies, though much sleeker and more elegant, with longer legs and mottled wings, as their name suggests, downlooker flies can often be found resting with their heads downwards on tree-trunks and fence-posts, often in the company of several others. No one knows quite why they do this, though it does allow them to dart off sharpish, rather like a flushed snipe and this, together with their mottled brown coloration and liking for marshy spots, may account for the family's common name, snipe-flies.

They are often well hidden, sitting in the shade cast by overhanging foliage, and swim into view as you peer at the tree-trunk, materialising before your eyes. What they feed on is also a mystery, and though they might take honeydew and sap secretions, fame and possibly fortune awaits the entomologist who can reveal the downlooker's diet.

Their larvae, which live in damp soil or rotten wood, are definitely equipped for a carnivorous life, sporting hooks and saw-toothed mouth-parts for slicing into prey which could include other grubs or worms.

As with so many of our common and widespread insects, the detail of their lives is still uncertain and the fascination of flies, downlookers or otherwise, is in their almost infinite adaptability. There's hardly an ecological niche that flies haven't colonised: they ride as bloodsuckers on birds or feed deep in the heart of rotting trees or in dung heaps. Many feed on live plants: others share our homes – the tiny fruit flies for example, which have told scientists so much about our own genetic make-up.

Some flies such as tsetse flies and mosquitoes bring disease on a tragic scale: others such as hoverflies pollinate fruit and vegetables. Many are beautiful insects – look into a horsefly's eyes and you'll see a rainbow. The downlooker is easily overlooked but is harmless to us and has its own subtle attraction, a good introduction to this vast group of insects.

LARGE BLUE
17 June

Butterflies don't, as a rule, attract crowds. Whereas a thousand or more avid twitchers might travel to see a rare bird, each focusing their optics on the unsuspecting creature like a firing squad preparing to shoot, a scarce butterfly can generally go about its business unobserved.

Apart, that is, from the large blue. For this is a true 'box office' butterfly, whose emergence each June is greeted with all the excitement of the paparazzi at an awards ceremony. In this case, the winner is not just Britain's rarest butterfly, but also one that has come back from the dead. So the crowds that gather down the road from me each year, on Somerset's Collard Hill, come in devout pilgrimage to witness what can only be described as a miracle.

Back in the 1970s, the large blue was in big trouble. No matter what conservationists did, its numbers were dropping through the floor. And finally, in 1979, came the news that the last British colony, on the edge of Dartmoor in Devon, held no more large blues: the butterfly had become extinct in Britain.

But the hardcore lepidopterists were not going to give up. And their determination was boosted by something they had learned about the extraordinary life cycle of this little butterfly. They had discovered that when breeding, large blues depend on a particular species of red ant.

After hatching out, the large blue caterpillar emits a pheromone that fools the ants into taking it into the underground nest and looking after it until, almost a year later, it pupates and then, on a sunny June day, it emerges as an adult butterfly.

But in turn, this ant needs short, cropped grass. During the post-war era, the shortage of rabbits brought about by the disease myxomatosis meant that in much of the large blue's habitat the grass was simply too long for the ants to survive, and so the butterfly began its irrevocable decline.

Having discovered this, the next step was to introduce grazing animals into the large blue's former haunts, to allow the red ants to thrive. Then, in 1983, a small cohort of large blues from Sweden was released into a series of secret sites in south-west England. Progress was slow but steady, and by the first decade of the twenty-first century there were as many as 10,000 large blues on the wing each year between mid-June and mid-July. The rabbits are back too, helping keep the grass short for the ants and butterflies.

And so now, each summer, hundreds of butterfly enthusiasts descend on the Polden Hills near Glastonbury in Somerset, not to attend the famous music festival, but to have a celebration of their own. They are here to witness the return of one of our most delicate and beautiful butterflies, a rare conservation success story in a troubled world. And as we gaze on this surprisingly small, powder-blue butterfly, its wings etched with black, we can all join in the celebrations for its return.

BIRTHWORT

18 June

Godstow Abbey, on the Thames just outside the city of Oxford, is not the place I would expect to find one of Britain's rarest wild flowers. And yet I have been told that among the ruins of this twelfth-century religious building grows a modest but fascinating plant, with pale yellow, trumpet-shaped flowers and heart-shaped leaves: birthwort.

And here it is – hardly worth the journey, it occurs to me, were it not quite so scarce. Yet looking around this fairly standard grassy habitat, similar to many places in lowland England, it's easy to wonder why it chose this particular spot.

Of course it didn't – this spot chose the plant. A clue to this mystery lies in the name: birthwort was traditionally used to help facilitate childbirth, by quickening the birth process and purging the womb afterwards, reducing the chances of mother or child dying, and helping to stave off infection following the confinement. Nuns, who lived at the abbey, traditionally performed the role of midwives; which would explain the fact that birthwort was planted here. But might there be another, more sinister reason for its presence so close to this ancient nunnery?

Given to a woman earlier in her pregnancy, birthwort has a more dramatic effect: inducing the foetus to be aborted. In the wry words of the late botanist Richard Fitter, the plant was the source of a drug 'used to save peccant [sinful] nuns from their misbehaviour with peccant monks'.

BROOMRAPES

19 June

Broomrapes first seduced me in my late teens, when a colony of these eerie plants turned up in a flowerbed in the front garden. Their stiff spikes of snapdragon-like flowers, the colour of bruised flesh, contained no hint of green, a sure sign that they didn't depend on sunlight for sustenance. Broomrapes have sidestepped the need for photosynthesis using chlorophyll by battening on to the roots of green plants and hijacking their resources; in quantity they sometimes kill their hosts.

My broomrapes hung around for many years, attached to the roots of a shrubby yellow daisy called *Brachyglottis*. Although they are called common broomrapes, they are scarce plants locally and so when I hear about the discovery of hundreds in ornamental flowerbeds at a retail park in Kidderminster, I head down there. Once again they are freeloading on *Brachyglottis*, this time in a busy superstore car park. It's an unglamorous location for a plant that most people ignore.

Common broomrapes would win no prizes for beauty. They have no leaves, only stout flowering stems up to a foot tall. From a distance it's hard to tell whether this colony is dead or alive, but as I approach I detect succulence in the fleshy stalks. Closer to and cooled by the slipstream of shoppers' cars, I can see the stamens, protruding from the mouths of the purplish-brown blooms. They remind me of miniature versions of the triffids created for an early 1980s BBC TV series. At ground level, cohorts of purplish buds like demonic asparagus spears are erupting from the soil.

Common broomrapes are the most widespread of the dozen or so species found in Britain. One of the largest is the greater broomrape, a statuesque plant up to a metre tall, which parasitises gorse and broom plants. It's rare now, but was once more common and gave the plants their name. The 'broom' half derives from its host and you'd think the 'rape' was self-explanatory given its habits. But the broomrape has a bulbous root that reminded botanists of a small turnip, for which the Latin name is *rapum*, as in oilseed rape.

Different species choose different hosts. Ivy broomrape is common in some southern towns and cities, where its pale spikes appear among ivy leaves on wall-tops and in gardens. Others are much choosier, even though their host plants are everywhere. The thistle broomrape grows only on a small area of Magnesian limestone in Yorkshire, and is protected by law, while its host is a noxious weed that should legally be destroyed: an interesting conservation conundrum. For most of us, though, they are botanical oddities, overturning our notions of what wild flowers should be.

LUNDY CABBAGE

20 June

Lying off the coast of north Devon in the Bristol Channel, the island of Lundy is one of Britain's classic wildlife sites. And yet among its puffins and pygmy shrews, Manx shearwaters and sika deer, there is one plant that trumps them all for rarity: the Lundy cabbage.

As its name suggests, this unprepossessing member of the brassicas is found here on Lundy, and nowhere else in the world. But despite its great rarity, it's not much to look at.

I come across it almost immediately after disembarking from the boat, as it flowers alongside the path up from the quay to the famous Marisco Tavern, the island's only pub. My first impression is of a gangly, bushy plant, which reminds me of oil-seed rape, with hairy, pale-green stalks and leaves topped with four-petalled, custard-yellow flowers – slightly less 'electric yellow' than rape, and altogether more pleasing on the eye.

I bend down and take a closer look using my magnifying glass, and notice that among the usual crop of insects are two smaller ones – almost too tiny to see. These are just as rare and unusual as the cabbage itself for, as their names suggest, the Lundy cabbage flea beetle and the Lundy cabbage weevil are also endemic to the island, and indeed only found on this particular plant.

So how on earth did this unusual trio get here in the first place? Some botanists believe that they must have arrived on a ship stopping off at the island, which had perhaps come from Spain or North Africa. But others point to the fact that the plant has two unique insects living on it, their co-evolution suggesting that it must have been here far longer – maybe as long as half a million years.

Knowing that the plant is related to wild cabbage and sea kale may tempt you to have a taste, but beware: although the Lundy cabbage is technically edible, it is said to smell rather like rotten eggs when cooked. I decide, this time at least, to give it a miss.

BRAVE WEASEL
21 June

Returning home by car along a very busy A-road I saw a streak of russet flash across the tarmac ahead. My relief that the weasel had made it on to the verge turned to horror as she reappeared and launched herself back into the path of an oncoming lorry. It looked suicidal, but there, quivering on the central white line, was her motivation: two tiny weasel-kits, trapped by the traffic rushing by on both sides. A move either way would have meant obliteration.

I slowed to a halt and cars built up behind me as she raced over to one trembling youngster, snatched it up in her jaws and, narrowly avoiding the wheels of another lorry, carried it into the roadside grass. Immediately she returned for her other baby. By now I was transfixed as she darted into the road, then retreated to avoid a speeding car.

Weasels and stoats regularly move their youngsters around as they grow. Their nest, which can be in an old rat burrow or mole tunnel, may become too cramped or may inherit an infestation of parasites such as mites or fleas from the previous occupants. When the youngsters are born they are hairless and blind, but soon develop a covering of white down and by four weeks old are miniature versions of their mother.

The kits I saw being carried must have been about a month old. Undaunted, the mother weasel tried again and again while horns behind me blared, the small crisis unimportant to frustrated drivers with appointments to keep. But not all: in the nick of time, the driver of an oncoming truck realised what was happening and slowed down. The short window this gave her was enough: she seized her remaining youngster and ferried it to safety.

The drama – all ninety seconds of it – was over, but my hands gripping the wheel were shaking as I drove away. Foolhardiness, or extreme courage? Powerful maternal instinct, or the workings of the selfish gene? Whatever impulse drove her to protect her young, it was a lesson in the urgency of life and the memory of it, thirty years on, is as strong for me as ever.

RED VALERIAN

22 June

Not all classic wild flowers are native: I can enjoy the sight of butterflies on a buddleia bush in the full knowledge that the plant is an import from the Himalayan foothills, brought back by Victorian explorers; or marvel at a display of snowdrops on a freezing February day, even though I suspect that they came to Britain from mainland Europe in Tudor times.

Another accidental tourist appears from the middle of June onwards, its deep magenta flowers bursting out of walls and along roadsides all around my home.

The red valerian also arrived in Britain in the Tudor era, bringing a splash of gaudy Mediterranean colour to formal gardens. Inevitably, perhaps, it escaped, and began to spread rapidly across Britain. Like other invaders it took advantage of the fact that it can survive in dry, rocky habitats where native plants cannot compete, such as dry-stone walls; the plant is a common sight in country villages, especially here in the milder south and west.

Despite its alien origins, red valerian has been in this country long enough to earn a varied assortment of folk names, including American lilac, bouncing Bess, fox's brush, gypsy-maids, kiss-me-quick, Queen Anne's needlework and scarlet lightning.

But whatever we choose to call it, there's no doubt that this attractive and prolific plant has become a firm favourite in its new home – a classic sight of midsummer. Maybe we like it because the shade reminds us of the rich colours used in interior designs. Butterflies and bumblebees love it too, not least because the long, narrow flowers make it inaccessible to smaller pollinating insects such as wasps. For me, it signals that moment when spring slips unfussily into summer.

AESCULAPIAN SNAKE

23 June

The banks of the canal near London's Camden Lock are the source of the latest wildlife scare story. According to one tabloid, there are 'six foot' snakes living there which could 'take out a small dog the same size as a young child'. The *Daily Mail* has stretched the snakes and maybe readers' incredulity even further by claiming (inaccurately) that they can reach a length of eight feet. There are mutterings of a cull of these introduced serpents to prevent them from becoming invasive.

It is frustrating. Just when we need more understanding of the wildlife that shares our cities, amid fears of urban dwellers becoming disconnected from nature, we're subject to this kind of irresponsible sensationalism. Even the grandly titled London Invasive Species Initiative (LISI) has included the snakes on its list of species 'of concern', though quite why we should be concerned about the small and very slow-growing population of thirty or so snakes isn't made clear. The rats they feed on are infinitely more dangerous to us than the reptiles.

A few facts. Aesculapian snakes are native to continental Europe and are named after Aesculapius, the Greco-Roman father of medicine, around whose staff a serpent is traditionally entwined.

In theory, they can grow to two metres long, but in highly populated, traffic-ridden Europe, few of them get the chance. They are non-venomous, whip-like snakes with shining brown scales and a hint of mustard yellow on their throats and faces. Unlike our native snakes, none of which penetrate this far into central London, they can climb and in summer will drape themselves over the branches of shrubs. Shy and retiring, they are unlikely to be seen unless you go looking for them and even then are far from guaranteed.

So how did they find a home in London? One account suggests that they derive from a deliberate release following the closure of a study centre in 1986. Breeding was suspected within ten years and has been proved in 1999 and in 2010 when youngsters were found in the basement of a building near the Regent's Canal.

This is the first time that any non-native snake has been proven to breed in the wild in Britain. About thirty snakes have been recognised from their individual head patterns, so any increase since the 1980s has been very slow. Indeed the fact that any have survived given the level of traffic locally is remarkable.

Technically, it is illegal to allow any foreign snakes to spread or escape into the wild, but in this case that particular horse has bolted. Maybe this is a chance to put aside our narrow views on what is native and what isn't, and admire this wonderful reptile that, against overwhelming odds, has established a quiet toehold in the capital. It's harmless to us, doesn't compete with our native snakes – there aren't any here to compete with – and eats rats and mice.

There is one other population in the UK, in North Wales, where a few escaped from the Welsh Mountain Zoo in Colwyn Bay in the 1970s and have grown modestly since then into a small population of a few hundred at most. At the edge of their climatic range in the British Isles, they're unlikely ever to cause a problem to anything other than the odd rodent or nestling bird. Long may they flourish in relative obscurity.

MIDSUMMER CUSHION

24 June

Midsummer's Day, which usually takes place on or around 24 June, coincides with some of the richest and most colourful displays of wild flowers in our meadows and hedgerows. The lanes around my home are awash with great willow-herb, a splash of pinkish-mauve among the cow parsley.

Today, we are generally discouraged from picking the blooms; but our ancestors had no such qualms, and would frequently bring flowers into their homes to add a vivid note of colour to their drab interiors.

Writing almost two centuries ago, my favourite nature poet John Clare told of an old custom among his fellow villagers, to 'stick a piece of greensward full of field flowers and place it as an ornament in their cottages . . .' The name of this display? A 'midsummer cushion'.

Clare was so taken with the custom that he wanted to use it as the title for his new collection of poetry. But by then the novelty of this 'peasant poet' was waning among the London literati, and he failed to find enough subscribers for the work. It languished forgotten for almost 150 years, until it was finally published in 1979. I remember reading it a year or so later, and being astonished by the direct way in which Clare wrote about ordinary nature in the places he knew best.

Today, long after Clare's death in 1864, local schoolchildren in his home village of Helpston in Cambridgeshire lay their own home-made midsummer cushions on his grave each year; though not on Midsummer's Day but on 13 July, the anniversary of the poet's birth.

GHOST MOTH
25 June

As dusk falls on a sultry early summer's night, the moths begin to emerge, their silent wings flickering in the fading light as they take to the wing; tiny movements in the growing darkness.

But as I sit outside sipping a beer on this unexpectedly warm evening, I notice that one bright, white and noticeably larger moth has a very different flight path to these randomly active insects. Instead, it is methodically quartering a small patch of lawn, as if conducting an aerial survey of its territory.

I realise that it is a male ghost moth: a pale, white insect with a yellowish head, and among the most bizarre and bewitching of all our 2,500 or so different kinds. And he is on a mission: to find his potential mate, a golden-yellow female hidden somewhere in the grass below, out of my sight.

Like the females of so many wild creatures, she is teasing and tantalising the male by releasing a chemical pheromone to attract him – but she's not going to make things easy, as first he has to prove that he's worth it.

I've heard that sometimes, as he swings like a manic pendulum to and fro, he is joined by one or more rival males, each eager to win the right to mate with the female. Thus what was a simple one-on-one courtship turns into a lek – a display involving several males, each trying to impress the female.

Lekking is rare in nature, but found among a surprisingly varied collection of species, including grouse, hummingbirds, antelopes, walruses and even fruit bats.

Finally the female puts her suitors out of their misery, and reveals herself, allowing the winner to mate with her. The other males slink off, disappointed, into the darkness of the night.

GOLDEN-RINGED DRAGONFLY

26 June

A stiff rustling sound, like starched muslin, from a small forest seepage is the first sign that our longest insect is about. Unlike their relatives, which cruise over ponds and lakes on sunny days, golden-ringed dragonflies make relatively short flights low over the ground on wet heaths, moorland and damp clearings in woods. With their black abdomens encircled with waspish yellow bands, they are impressive, all the more for suddenly appearing in a shady glade or over a shallow trickle through sphagnum moss.

They are huge insects, the females nudging nine centimetres long, which breed in shallow streams and rills, sometimes in places where their spiny nymphs are barely covered by water. Camouflaged in the mud, this 'trickle tiger' seizes smaller invertebrates in its powerful jaws.

The adult dragonflies emerge in late May and are on the wing until September. They're also powerful predators and will eat insects as large as hornets and bumblebees, which they munch in flight or carry to a perch, grinding their way through their victim's stiff exoskeleton with muscular mandibles.

While most dragonflies are hard to approach, the golden-ringed is often confiding and makes short flights along linear features such as streams and small valleys, so is easy to follow. A specimen I once tried hard to photograph insisted on using my camera hand as a perch, apparently unaware that there was a living human attached.

FALLOW DEER FAWN

27 June

In the forest, I startle a fallow deer hind in a ferny clearing. It's hot, and droneflies are pinned to their mid-air hovering stations just above head-height. The only birdsong is from a chiffchaff, listlessly calling out its own name.

Usually when surprised, the local fallows bound away, but this one hesitates, unwilling to leave the spot, a sure sign that her fawn is couched among the bracken stalks. At this time the fawns are vulnerable to off-lead dogs, so the mother is right to be wary. Like most of the local fallow deer she has a dark brown coat with paler markings. Her fawn – though I hardly ever see one clearly, so well are they camouflaged – carries a constellation of white spots on a clean russet coat, a dark line along its back and a pure white scut, the undertail we see as deer move off through the shadows.

Fallow deer are one of the main public attractions of this forest. They fulfil visitors' expectations of the ancient wildwood as they prance across rides and melt into the trees. But these are relatively new inhabitants whose ancestors escaped from a nearby deer-park in the late nineteenth century when a wall collapsed.

Nor are they actually native, though they have been here a good while. All fallows in Britain are introductions, the earliest probably brought from continental Europe by the Romans. As beasts of the chase they were hunted by the nobility and poached by commoners and were also decorative attractions to parkland.

Here in Worcestershire, the duskier forms are most frequent, but there are some known as menil with strongly white-spotted coats in summer. There are even a few pure white specimens.

But though they are a popular attraction for visitors, the growing numbers of deer are a concern. When deer graze the forest in large numbers they create a browse line, below which there is no foliage on low branches. They also suppress wild flowers and regenerating trees. With no natural predators – though each year at least forty animals from a population of around 250 are killed on forest roads – unless their numbers are reduced they will alter the woodland structure, affecting plants, the insects that depend on them and the birds that feed on those insects. Culling is a controversial business and a tragedy for the individual, but it ensures that some deer will always remain to quicken our pulses on woodland walks.

The fawn lying doggo just a few metres from me is invisible but knows I'm here and so I back off to allow its mother to re-join it. They will spend the rest of the year together and after the autumn rutting season, which ends in mid-November, does and fawns form separate herds apart from the bucks.

CUCKOO BUMBLEBEES
28 June

'See that lemon flash? There, at the base of its white tail . . .'

I can still remember the day, a decade ago, when my naturalist friend Harry Green pointed out my first cuckoo bumblebee. With that identification, he unlocked a treasure chest – suddenly I began seeing these insects everywhere. It was a lesson, not only in identification, but also in the value of sharing knowledge in the field: no amount of reading and googling can compensate for seeing things for yourself.

Now, in the middle of fieldwork for a county bumblebee atlas, I'm testing that experience. Although there are only six species of cuckoo bumblebees in the British Isles, they are a tricky bunch to distinguish: males and females often look different and some have odd colour forms.

At least there are no workers to identify. Queen cuckoo bumblebees don't need them, because, like their avian namesake, they usurp the nests of other bumblebees and lay their own eggs there. After killing or dominating the resident queen, the cuckoo bee lays her own eggs, which are tended by workers from the usurped colony. Any cuckoo bees produced will be males, which die soon after mating, or queens, which will overwinter.

Each of the cuckoo bees specialises in different hosts and some are hard to tell apart. As a rule, female cuckoo bees tend to have shinier bodies with less hair than other bumblebees and their wings are often darker brown when fresh. But the telltale sign is their lack of a pollen basket or corbicula on their hind legs. Worker and queen bumblebees have a shiny bristle-fringed patch on which they accumulate a mixture of pollen and nectar. On cuckoos, this area is rounded and matt with shorter hairs. They don't need to bring in food: that's what their hosts are for.

As I found out from Harry, their markings are subtly different. One of the commonest, the vestal cuckoo bee, looks very like its white-tailed bumblebee host, but has citrus-yellow flashes at the edge of its white tail. By contrast, the huge hill cuckoo bumblebee is jet-black with a fiery orange tail and looks remarkably like the red-tailed bumblebee whose nests it invades. But cuckoo bumblebees aren't serious enemies

of bumblebees: they evolved probably as a result of competitive struggles between rival queens over occupied nests. For me, they are also
a reminder of the years when I went around the garden blind to their
presence, and of the importance of learning from wildlife mentors
like Harry.

BURNET MOTHS

29 June

As a child any moth that you could catch without a net was a bonus.
That's how I became intrigued by the blundering shapes of burnet moths
as they droned, apparently impervious to danger, over a patch of rough
grass near my house. I remember the day that I first connected them
with their cocoons, which were placed at eye-level, for a seven-year-old,
on grass or thistle stalks.

The caterpillars spun these strange creamy pods as protection while
they pupated. They were utterly outlandish, especially after the moths
had emerged and the black remains of the pupa complete with legs and
mouthparts were left protruding where the moth had erupted from its
case. Now when I see them among the grass stalks they remind me of
the monsters from the *Alien* films.

Nearly half a century on and a few miles away, I'm on an urban verge
near my home in the West Midlands. It's starred with ox-eye daisies and
bright with bird's foot trefoil and red clover, sown to soften the impact
of a new road. Five-spot burnet moths are whirring drowsily over the
flowers. I snatch one from the air – no stealth or athleticism needed –
and in the darkness of my closed hand, the moth is quiescent, pulling
in its legs and playing dead.

It's not relying on camouflage to save it, but its gaudiness. The scarlet
splashes on its glistening bronze-black forewings are a warning to birds
that eating this moth would be a serious mistake. Both adult moths and
their caterpillars can release hydrocyanic acid, distasteful at best, but
potentially fatal. By displaying warning colours, the moth advertises its
dangers and is avoided by birds.

There are several species of burnet moths, many of them rare and
local, but the commonest have five or six red blotches and are easy to

find on open verges and patches of waste ground, where their black and yellow caterpillars feed on clovers and trefoils. In June and July their whirring flight over sunny banks is the essence of high summer.

HORSEFLIES

30 June

Few of Britain's insects are able to inflict real pain on human beings but, along with wasps and honeybees, horseflies are a notable exception.

Like mosquitoes, leeches and Count Dracula, female horseflies require a diet of blood to reproduce; and unfortunately the easiest way to obtain blood is to bite a large mammal – horses, cattle or us. The bite is very painful, and can leave a nasty swelling behind.

Along with many other familiar insects, horseflies have acquired a suite of country names, including deer flies and clags or clegs. The latter became the source of some amusement when the similarity was noted between its name and that of the Liberal Democrat leader and former Deputy Prime Minister, Nick Clegg.

But like other so-called insect 'pests', horseflies play an important role as pollinators of flowers too, as the males feed mainly on nectar. They also provide food for birds, though they have to be agile to catch these highly manoeuvrable insects in the air.

And like so many other insects, horseflies are in decline because the traditional ways of farming cattle out in open fields are rapidly being replaced by indoor facilities, which the flies cannot enter.

JULY

HALFWAY THROUGH THE year, and in some ways the best of nature is behind us. Birds are coming to the end of their breeding season, and once the chicks have fledged and left the nest their exhausted parents take advantage of the warm weather and plenty of available food to undergo their annual moult. So woods, parks and gardens that until recently resounded with birdsong have now fallen silent.

Meanwhile many wild flowers are past their peak, and although the summer insects are out in force, the spring butterflies are long gone.

But if you know where to look, July can be a fabulous month for watching wildlife. The days are still long, which allows you to be out in the field from dawn to dusk, in a range of habitats.

For me, this is the time of year when my attention turns to 'dragons and damsels' – the various species of dragonfly and damselfly that cruise along our waterways in the summer sunshine. On a sunny day, the classic summer butterflies, mostly brown or orange in shade, are out in force; while as dusk falls, the moth trap yields some amazing results, especially on moonless, muggy nights.

July is also your last chance to visit one of Britain's greatest spectacles – our seabird colonies around the northern, western and eastern coasts – with the added bonus that marine mammals are at their most abundant at this time of year. Towards the end of the month, the first signs of autumn migration begin to appear: notably green sandpipers heading south from Scandinavia to sub-Saharan Africa, and stopping off on little waterways en route.

S.M.

BLOWSY AND WANTON, July is a month of excess as summer beds in. Hogweed heads and bindweed trumpets buzz with bumblebees. Most colonies are now producing a flush of males, which cluster in bachelor parties, sipping nectar on thistle heads, after fertilising the newly emerging queens, who will go on to found their colonies next spring, relying on sperm stored this summer. The males last a few weeks; hedonism has its price.

The 'June gap' between spring and summer butterflies is over: now the high-summer species begin to appear in force. Gatekeepers are the insect symbols of July for me, crowding around bramble blossom on rides and in hedgerows. My local woodlands are being managed for silver-washed fritillaries, flame-coloured beauties that accompany me along sunny rides. If I'm lucky they'll be joined by soaring white admirals and, flickering in the oak-tops, purple hairstreaks.

In the forest, birds are harder to find than butterflies. Occasionally I stumble on a party of newly fledged great and blue tits fussing through the foliage, the youngsters paler and yellower than their parents who look dishevelled, as well they might after rearing two demanding broods in the last three months. With them are tag-along warblers, coal tits and long-tailed tits, all seeking safety in numbers. Searching for them involves looking up, but be careful if you are doing this near forest ponds as there are probably toadlets scrambling by your feet.

Not all birds have fledged. Out in the fields, sadly in fewer and fewer places nowadays, yellowhammers and corn buntings are pumping out their lazy midsummer songs. Males are still singing to defend their territories, because they may be guarding females with very young fledglings even this late. For me, growing up near an organic farm, the crackle of a corn bunting's song on a sweltering July day is the essence of high summers long gone.

B.W.

PURPLE EMPEROR

1 July

With a rapid shake, butterfly expert Matthew Oates unfolds the crisp, white tablecloth on to a trestle table. He then carefully places three silver salvers on the cloth: one containing a lump of oriental shrimp paste, the second filled with a glass of fine red wine and, on the third, a neat deposit of fox poo. The summer's picnic is ready.

The maître d'hôtel steps back to admire his handiwork, and to await our first guest; a guest so noble, so regal in his bearing that grown men are moved to obsession by him. The object of all this attention? Not a human being, but a butterfly: the purple emperor.

The purple emperor is an enigma among insects. Second only to the swallowtail as Britain's largest butterfly, it is also one of the most striking and colourful; and yet despite its beauty it rarely reveals itself to human eyes.

Whereas other butterflies flit from flower to flower to find nectar along the forest rides, the purple emperor spends its life out of sight: high in the wooded canopy, where it feeds on the sticky honeydew produced by aphids.

Thus of all our butterflies it is one of the most elusive. This perhaps excuses the Victorian butterfly collectors, who praised and extolled this creature in the most effusive terms, coining the name that is still used by purple emperor fanatics to this day: His Imperial Majesty.

Imperial he may be, but the purple emperor has a pretty peculiar taste when it comes to food. So the bizarre banquet Matthew has laid out before us today, here at Fermyn Woods in Northamptonshire, has been designed to tempt these winged creatures down from the trees.

Moments later, not so much fluttering as pulsating through the thick, fetid air, I watch as the first emperor – a splendid male – descends from his lofty throne. As he flies past me he looks black, though I do catch flashes of white on his upperwing and a hint of rusty orange below. But when he lands and opens his wings, he reveals his true splendour. As the light catches the surface I see a dazzling, blazing flash of purple iridescence; a colour so rich, so splendid, it leaves me open-mouthed in awe.

Then he rather spoils the magic of the moment by extending his long, straw-coloured tongue and beginning to feed on a lump of fox excrement, greedily sucking up the juices and minerals he cannot get from honeydew alone. Another, and then another butterfly join him, and soon there is a phalanx of these beautiful insects perched on the silver salvers, enjoying their malodorous meals.

Finally sated, they take to the wing once again, heading to the tops of the forest canopy – out of sight. Matthew clears away the tablecloth, and the feast is over.

WHITE ADMIRAL
2 July

Of all our butterflies, the white admiral feels the most exotic. Not for its relatively sombre colours – it is, on the upperside at least, an almost monochrome insect, its blackish wings slashed with white bands – but because it flies like many tropical forest butterflies, using thermals and eddies around trees to glide and float with exquisite ease.

It is a restless insect, flickering through sun-dappled glades, vanishing and reappearing as it flirts with sun and shade. If you see one land, on a bramble flower perhaps, the closed wings reveal rich mahogany highlights.

White admirals fly in mid-June and throughout July through open airy woods, mainly in southern England, though they scrape into east Wales. They're a good-news story among the gloom that is modern butterflying, in that their range has increased since the 1970s, when they were rather local. Whether this is because of climate change or woodland management isn't certain: unlike many woodland butterflies whose caterpillars thrive in sunny places, the white admiral likes shady spots in which to lay its eggs on the honeysuckle that festoons the trees.

As coppicing has declined, some woods have become more overgrown, which may suit the caterpillar's needs. The weather in June is important to the white admiral: if it's warm the caterpillars and pupae develop faster and are less likely to be eaten by birds with youngsters to feed; but cold Junes delay caterpillar growth and so fewer butterflies emerge in July.

As long as food for the larvae and nectar for the adults are around, you can find white admirals quite easily within their range. They can even tolerate conifers and I regularly see them in a local pine plantation, which has a smattering of birch trees draped with honeysuckle. Although they're woodlanders, they will travel in hot weather in search of new sites. A few years ago I was astonished by a visitation from one in my very urban garden, a brief encounter that left me dreaming of July forests.

PIPISTRELLES

3 July

Imagine if scientists had just discovered that there are two completely different species of robin breeding in Britain, separated by subtle differences in the pitch of their song. Or two different species of blackbird, badger or fox? For such common, widespread and familiar species, that would simply be unimaginable.

Yet that's exactly what happened when, in the final year of the last millennium, bat enthusiasts found a major difference in the frequency at which pipistrelle bats were using echolocation, the sonar technique that allows them to find their way around without bumping into things, and catch prey in complete darkness. While one group of pipistrelle bats were echolocating at a frequency of 45 kilohertz (kHz), another was doing so at a significantly higher frequency, 55 kHz.

The two species – renamed common and soprano pipistrelle, or '45 pip' and '55 pip' – also showed other small but significant differences in their appearance, behaviour and ecology. Yet they had been under our noses, as it were, for centuries, without anyone realising that they were living completely separate lives.

Thanks to some rather expensive survey work done when we demolished an old outbuilding in our Somerset garden, I have recently discovered that both species of 'pip' are living here. Actually I had already suspected that this was the case, as I had ventured out on warm summer evenings with my trusty bat detector. Twiddling the knobs as if tuning an old-fashioned radio, I found bats echolocating at both the higher and lower frequencies.

As they flew over my head in the gathering gloom, I found it hard to credit that these rival the pygmy shrew for the title of Britain's tiniest mammal. As they flit, swoop and dive overhead, they appear quite large, yet they weigh as little as three and a half grams (about the same as a one penny coin). I love watching them: few other flying creatures are quite so fast and furious, especially when they stop momentarily in mid-air to grab an unsuspecting insect.

There is a third species of pipistrelle in Britain too, though sadly not in my neck of the woods. Nathusius' pipistrelle, named after a nine-teenth-century German zoologist, is marginally larger and heavier than its commoner cousins. But being so similar, this mysterious bat is easily overlooked, and so may be more widespread than we think. Astonishingly, the native British population is boosted each winter by migrants from continental Europe, which fly all the way across the North Sea to be here.

WEEVIL-HUNTING WASPS

4 July

In July the sandy cracks between paving stones in the garden are irre-sistible to wasps. Although we have several species of social wasps, which rasp away at wooden fences to provide papier-mâché for their magnificent nests, these traditional picnic-disrupters are way outnumbered by the solitary wasps.

There are several hundred species in Britain and, unlike bees, they provide fresh meat for their growing grubs. Some paralyse spiders, others extract froghopper grubs from their cuckoo spit foam baths, or ambush flies, but the ones I look out for now are the weevil hunters, *Cerceris arenaria*.

Although they're as long as a worker common social wasp, the female weevil-hunters are much slimmer, their slender abdomens neatly ringed in black and yellow. I usually see them early in July in the herbaceous border, where flowers are both a fount of nectar and a hunting ground.

The male weevil wasps are mating machines and only live for a week or so. The larger females run over leaves and flowers, their antennae quivering frantically as they try to detect the weevils hiding among the foliage. When a female wasp finds a weevil, she stings it between its abdominal plates to paralyse, but not kill it, then flies with it slung beneath her body to the nest-hole that she's excavated in sandy soil.

Along this deep tunnel are individual cells, each containing an egg which she provides with its own weevil. When the grub hatches, it feeds on the weevil, then pupates over winter, and emerges the following summer.

Sometimes a female wasp will drop or 'mislay' her weevil as she enters the nest-hole and if she does, she won't pick it up again. It seems a huge waste of effort, but her caution is prudent. Around the nesting burrows, especially in the south-east of England, lurk iridescent red and green jewel wasps that sneak into the *Cerceris* nest-holes and lay their own eggs there, eating not only the paralysed weevil, but the wasp grub or pupa too.

If a weevil is abandoned for just a few seconds, a jewel wasp could lay its egg on the victim's body. For the weevil wasp then, it's better to catch fresh prey than risk taking the enemy's egg down into the nursery.

SUMMER BUTTERFLIES

5 July

For several weeks now, the number of butterflies in my Somerset garden has been woefully low. But then, fluttering across my lawn on a fine summer's morning, I see the first of a quartet of high-summer butterflies: a meadow brown. This is the Ford Focus of butterflies: ubiquitous, taken for granted, and perhaps a little dull.

Since I first moved down to Somerset, every summer I would try to turn the dark male meadow browns into their more localised relative: the ringlet. It took the sharp eyes of my youngest son George, then aged five, to spot one: as he put it, it's the one with hula-hoops beneath its wings. Once we'd spotted one ringlet, they seemed to be everywhere; only later did I discover that 2010 was the best summer for years for these attractive, velvet-brown butterflies.

The third of the quartet, the gatekeeper, is a common sight in our garden and along the surrounding paths and roadsides from mid-July onwards. It was once known as the hedge brown, and got its current

name from the habit of basking near gates and stiles. Here the impact
of constantly passing feet has kept the grass shorter, and so the ground
is marginally warmer, enabling the insect to get to its optimum temperature for flying more quickly. Gatekeepers are smaller, brighter and neater
than their cousins, and one of our most attractive butterflies. So it's
always a pleasure to spot the first of the year, a few weeks after the
meadow browns appear.

The final member of the four, the grayling, has yet to appear in my
garden, and probably never will. This is a creature of dry, sandy soils;
the nearest suitable habitat to us is on the south-facing slopes of the
Mendips.

Even there they can be tricky to find, for graylings perform a clever
conjuring trick. When you disturb one it flies strongly away, gliding on
powerful wings; but as soon as it lands it seems to disappear. A closer
look reveals that the butterfly has simply shut its wings, hiding the
distinctive 'eye' and using its mottled underwing pattern to camouflage
itself on stony ground.

URBAN FLOWERS

6 July

Returning home from Birmingham by train, I'm surprised by summer
blooms, none of them deliberately sown, clustering at the edges of the
tracks where the sun warms the clinker. In the edgelands bordering the
line, they sprout from the walls of disused workshops and burst from
the exposed floors of abandoned factories, a floral tribute to the decline
of local manufacturing.

Most of these fly-by-night flowers are dismissed as weeds, only fit to
be sprayed: by July their encroachment on to the tracks has been halted
in places, as yellowing patches testify. But there are more than enough
to admire. Buddleia, or the butterfly bush, is king of these raw places,
gaining a holdfast in almost soil-less rubble or probing mortar seams
with thirsty roots that are adapted to rock fissures in its native Himalayas.
The long sausages of purple flowers are a magnet for butterflies, but
also attract hoverflies, bees and, in a good year, hummingbird hawkmoths.

Very little grows under buddleia thickets though. The grasses and nettles that our urban butterflies need to sustain their caterpillars are either shaded out or discouraged by compounds that the butterfly bush secretes from its roots. The butterfly bush is only good for adults and not their offspring.

Even from a moving train, you can identify some plants with confidence. The egg-yellow splashes of common toadflax above their willowy, glaucous leaves are easy. They often rub roots with purple toadflax, a close relative that's jumped the garden fence.

The mulleins, or Aaron's rods, are botanical skyscrapers, delighting in the sunniest, driest areas, where their towers of yellow blooms can reach two metres or more. Mullein hates shade and wet, but avoids too much water loss in these parched places by coating its stem and leaves with a woolly pelage of thick, star-shaped hairs: from a carriage window, the plant looks frosted. This doesn't protect them entirely and many plants are nibbled by the gaudy black, white and yellow larvae of the eponymous mullein moth, which sit openly on the leaves, confident in the security of their warning colours.

Now teasels are in bloom, their spiny stems topped with tridents of bristling flower-clusters: when dried these were once used to raise nap on cloth, including the baize used on billiard tables. The paired leaves meet to form a vase around the stem in which rainwater collects and in which insects often drown. This has led to speculation that the teasel may be an incipient carnivore, which can absorb nutrients from the entomological soup that collects in its leaf axils. I'm not sure if it's just a rumour, but as my train pulls in to the junction, I'm intrigued by the idea that vegetable killers may be crowding the platform edges as I alight.

MONTAGU'S HARRIER

7 July

Twenty years ago, I invested in what is now one of my most treasured possessions, a painting by the renowned bird artist Bruce Pearson.

In subtle shades of yellow, buff, blue and green, it shows a summer scene, with two birds locked in mid-air, one dropping a small object down towards the other. They are Montagu's harriers, and Pearson has depicted them at the exact moment when the smaller, greyer male drops a food parcel – perhaps a vole or a meadow pipit – to the browner female, as she rises up from her hidden nest on the ground below. He catches this moment of time with absolute perfection: the birds' grace and beauty, the balletic intimacy of their behaviour, and the searing heat of that endless summer's day.

I have been privileged, just once, to witness this conduct for myself. It was so rapid and brief that it left me wondering if I had dreamed the whole thing. I have since learned that this behaviour has both a practical and symbolic function: by bringing back something to eat, the male allows the female to stay close to her nest and its precious eggs or chicks. But the giving of food also has a higher purpose – as of course it does in our own culture – strengthening the pair bond between the two birds.

Male Monties, as birders call them, are the poster boy of the raptor world. They float nonchalantly across arable fields on long, pearl-grey wings with inky-black tips, held in a shallow V-shape above the head.

Montagu's harrier was named as a tribute to one of my heroes, the pioneering eighteenth-century ornithologist George Montagu, whose story is one of the most scandalous of all British naturalists.

Having led a blameless life as an army officer until his mid-thirties, Montagu went through what would now be called a mid-life crisis. He embarked on an affair with a fellow officer's wife, was court-martialled and thrown out of the army, and fled to Devon with his mistress Eliza Dorville. They then devoted the rest of their lives to the study and classification of British birds, including the harrier that now bears his name.

Sadly, this bird is now a very rare sight in Britain, as fewer than a dozen pairs breed here each year, mainly on arable land in southern and eastern England. The harriers are entirely dependent on the goodwill of the landowner, as if the crop is harvested too early, before the chicks are old enough to fledge, they will perish between the blades of the combine harvester.

Most sites where this elusive raptor breeds are, understandably, kept secret to avoid disturbance from birders and photographers, or to combat the small but determined band of egg-collectors for whom a clutch of British-taken Monties' eggs would be a prize indeed. But each year the RSPB usually opens a watchpoint so that people can see these elegant birds as they fly to and from their nest.

TOADLETS
8 July

Today, on a field meeting, we tread with care. There are amphibians abroad, hundreds of russet toadlets, clambering through the dock-leaf jungles along the bridle path. They've emerged on this humid day from a nearby pond, where they've spent two or three months as tadpoles and so we're forced to pussyfoot around them as they plod determinedly through the grass blades, intent on dispersing throughout the local countryside.

At this age they are no bigger than bluebottle flies, and utterly vulnerable. Those that turn the wrong way when they leave the pond are doomed: they will never make it across the busy A-road. Those that brave the bridleway face hooves and boots, the mandibles of roving ground-beetles, the beaks of pheasants and crows and the iron-tipped teeth of shrews. Everything, it seems, eats a toadlet. The adult toads contain bufotoxin, a poison that deters many predators, but whether these youngsters contain enough toxin to keep them off the menu, I'm not sure.

It's not all about being eaten. Toads are moisture-loving and the hot summer sun can be merciless. I once saw hundreds of minuscule corpses piled next to a local canal on a dried-up overflow where there was no cover. Within minutes of emerging, the toadlets had simply dehydrated on the hot stone, just a few metres away from shade and safety.

This is a lesson we can all learn: if we have garden ponds surrounded by paving slabs, it's a good idea to provide shade by planting overhanging vegetation or by placing a few broken pots or pieces of bark near their emergence sites to give the young amphibians a surer start to life on land.

Many will perish for other reasons. Frogs and toads play the numbers game, and of the thousands of tadpoles that swam in our ponds this spring, only two or three will reach adulthood. It's easy to dismiss these losses as evolutionary strategy, but if you get down to their level and look one of these brick-red toadlets in its beady black eyes, it's hard not to be seduced.

SUMMER MOTHS

9 July

Drinker, pebble hook-tip, riband wave,
Figure of eight, dusky thorn, willow beauty,
Swallow prominent, buff-tip, rosy footman,
Flame shoulder, setaceous Hebrew character, pale tussock,
Lesser broad-bordered yellow underwing, clay, uncertain,
Burnished brass, gold spot, scalloped oak,
Dark arches, spectacle, silver Y,
Light emerald, pebble prominent, muslin,
Ruby tiger, coronet, snout.

Could there be a more evocative collection of names than this list of our summer moths, a recitation worthy of any poet? Yet despite their bizarre and exotic names, these moths are not only fairly common and widespread, they have also, at some time or another, turned up in our garden moth trap.

Emptying a moth trap, the morning after the night before, is like opening a dictionary at random, and then picking the oddest combination of words you can find. And this is just the tip of a very large iceberg: these are only a few of almost 1,000 different species of 'macro-moth' found in Britain and Ireland. There are also about 1,600 'micro-moths', many so small and similar to one another they can only be reliably identified by closely examining their genitalia under a microscope.

Victorian naturalists – who, judging by some of the names they chose, must surely have been overdosing on hallucinogenic drugs – gave many of these moths their extraordinary monikers. Who thought of 'uncertain', 'true lover's knot' and 'toadflax pug', for goodness sake?

But the names are just the start. The sheer variety means that with moths there is always something new to discover. When you bear in mind that the average suburban garden has more species of moth than there are different kinds of butterfly in the whole of Britain, it's clear that you really don't have to look further than your own backyard to find a wide range of moths.

Moth trapping is surprisingly simple: you can use a professional trap with a mercury vapour bulb, but an old white sheet and a powerful torch work just as well. A few years ago I invested in a 'proper' trap, from which my family has had hours of entertainment, as we open it to reveal the night's catch; then try to attach a name to each specimen.

I have to confess that I struggle to identify some of the moth equivalents of 'little brown jobs', those very similar and rather dull-looking creatures that have you scratching your head as you try to tell one apart from another. But others are easy: the elephant hawkmoth, whose lime-green and pink coloration mimics the fuchsias on which its caterpillars feed; the silver Y, which has a Y-shaped mark on each upperwing; and the buff-tip, surely the most extraordinary of all the moths we find in the trap. Looking exactly like a lichen-covered birch twig cut off at one end with a sharp knife, the buff-tip is guaranteed to produce shrieks of delight from my children, and remind them once again of the infinite variety of the natural world.

SILVER-WASHED FRITILLARY
10 July

It's a hot morning in the forest and the pathside oaks are powdered with dust from the wheels of forestry vehicles. There's no birdsong on this still day, just the squeaking of tit parties in the oak-tops.

A blur of brilliant orange speeds past at head-height, a butterfly so large and powerful that it can only be a silver-washed fritillary. It's a typical encounter with this mercurial insect that always leaves me wanting more. And as I stroll around the wood, sure enough, there are many more brushes with this butterfly. In high summer it's a link between open rides and shady dingles, its fire unextinguished even by the darkest coppice.

This tolerance of shade may have saved the silver-washed fritillary from the sharp declines experienced by its fussier British relatives. Even during the 'Dark Ages' of forestry in the 1970s, when sunlight was at a premium as conifer plantations matured, the butterfly hung on. Since then it has welcomed management to provide more habitat for its food-plant, the violet, and for the brambles and hemp agrimony whose flowers it probes for nectar. It's thriving over most of southern England and Wales too, in open woods where violets grow.

A bank of brambles allows me to soak up the butterflies' magnificent colours. The male fritillaries are spectacular, a rich effulgent orange and easily recognised by the dark lines along the veins of their forewings. These are scent brands, which contain a kind of love-dust – modified scales known as androconia, doused in pheromones to lure in the slightly larger and more chequered female. She also produces pheromones, which she exudes from her abdomen in a wonderful roller-coaster display flight. Her eggs fertilised, she lays them, not on the food-plant, but in the crevices of tree-bark. Once I saw a female ten metres up a spruce trunk, carefully probing cracks and fissures for a safe niche. If the eggs survive the attentions of tits and treecreepers, the tiny young descend to find the nearest violet plants.

The silvery lines on their underwings give these butterflies their name, but there is a form of the female called *valezina*. It doesn't seem to occur in these Worcestershire woods, but I've seen it in the south of England: when fresh it is a striking butterfly, the greyish upperwings overlain with a sheen of green or blue depending on how the woodland light falls. It can be common in some seasons in the New Forest, hunting ground of the Victorian lepidopterist F.W. Frohawk, who was so enchanted by this form of the butterfly that he named his third daughter Valezina in its honour.

QUAIL

11 July

The sound seems to come from the very earth beneath the waving corn. A soft, liquid, three-note call – usually transcribed as 'wet-my-lips, wet-my-lips . . .'. The call of our most elusive, indeed an almost invisible, bird: the quail. I can hear it – but I know I have virtually no chance of seeing it.

No other British breeding bird is quite such an enigma as the quail. Our smallest game bird, hardly bigger than a sparrow, it parachutes unseen into our countryside each summer in a seemingly random way. They can be present in a particular place one year, and absent the next; and even when they are there, quails are hardly ever seen, and only rarely heard.

Quails arrive back from Africa in May or June, and can be heard almost anywhere in lowland Britain right through July and into August. Unlike other farmland birds, which have declined as intensive arable farming has increased, they thrive in these vast prairies of wheat and barley, so long as there are insect-rich flowers along the field margins to provide enough food for them and their tiny young.

But what's truly extraordinary about quail is that the ones that breed here in Britain may themselves be only a few weeks old. They hatched out in North Africa or southern Europe back in March and, able to fly at just eleven days old, flew north to reach here in midsummer. Having bred in July and August, they all then head back to Africa to spend the winter. That much we know; but we still have so much to learn about the quail's curious lifestyle.

So as I sit by a field of ripening barley on a warm summer's evening, and listen to a calling quail, I reflect that however much we think we know about Britain's birds, there are still some puzzles that remain to be solved.

SUNDEW

12 July

It's become a custom for travellers and gardeners stopping by the road across the common to gather handfuls of sphagnum from the edges of the tiny acid bog to line their hanging baskets. That is how the last of Worcestershire's sundew disappeared, not in Victorian times, but about fifteen years ago.

I remember the last sundew stronghold well, though stronghold isn't really the word for the spatter of reddish rosettes that clung on in the few damp gaps between the tufts of purple moor grass. Nonetheless it was my county's only insectivorous plant and a miniature marvel, each spoon-shaped leaf bristling with soft red tentacles, topped with a glistening drop of mucilage. If you go to a wet heath where sundews are really common, the stroboscopic effect of these massed droplets shimmering in sunlight is dazzling.

Beautiful to us, but deadly to invertebrates. Creatures as large as damselflies and butterflies are snared in its sticky clutches along with smaller flies and other insects. All this carnivory allows the sundew in its nutrient-poor bogs to enrich its diet with insect flesh. Each mucus drop is a powerful mix of ingredients: glue to block the victim's spiracles, through which it breathes, and a cocktail of enzymes to break down its tough exoskeleton and digest the softer parts. Once snared and enfolded in the leaf's embrace, there is no escape.

It would be counter-productive to assassinate your pollinators though, and so the sundew holds its white flowers high above the leaves where insects can visit safely. There is even a plume moth whose caterpillars feed with impunity on the sundew leaves.

If you want to enjoy sundews at their best, go in high summer to an acid mire on a moor or heath as the sun rises, and watch the first rays splinter in a myriad of droplets. But don't come to Worcestershire, where the sundew is botanical history.

SEABIRD SPECTACLE

13 July

At the end of the path, next to the bright, whitewashed walls surrounding an old lighthouse on Inner Farne, I reach the clifftop. Looking down towards the sea-battered rocks below, I am once again assailed by a deafening wall of sound combined with the not unpleasant, rather sweet smell of seabird guano.

The most recognisable sound is that of the kittiwakes calling out their name: 'kitt-i-waaake, kitt-i-waaake!' as each member of the pair signals to the other in their complex, formal and highly endearing courtship display.

Kittiwakes are often dismissed as 'just gulls', yet that is unfair to both gulls and kittiwakes. Gulls are fascinating and beautiful in their own right, but kittiwakes are the Kate Moss of the gull world: poised, elegant and immaculately dressed in gleaming white and pearl grey, set off with their jet-black legs and greenish-yellow bill.

Just above them, on the rocky top of the cliff, sits a rather less attractive, though just as charismatic, bird: a shag. Named after its prominent crest, the shag is the smaller cousin of the cormorant, with an oily-green plumage and a more maritime lifestyle.

Being as close as this – I am perched on a rock only a few feet from the nest – allows me to take in every last detail as the bird pants to lose heat under the baking summer sun. Its staring, emerald-green eye fixes me with a look of undisguised disdain.

Hidden beneath the adult bird is a scrawny chick, trying to get some relief from the baking sun. Looking more like a reptile than a baby bird, it's not the most photogenic creature I've ever seen. As I always do when I come to these islands, I shoot off a couple of dozen photographs of the kittiwakes and the shags, endeavouring to get just the right combination of a posing bird and a suitably aesthetic, out-of-focus background.

It strikes me how quickly I have got used to what, just an hour or so earlier, was one of the most extraordinary sights I have ever witnessed. I notice that after a while visitors tend to lose interest in the astonishing array of behaviours going on all around them. Instead they lie down and close their eyes for a brief sunbathe, or chat, or unpack a picnic, almost oblivious to the birds they greeted so recently with loud exclamations of delight. But then a puffin waddles right past them, and they show their appreciation once again in a volley of camera shutters.

ROSEMARY BEETLE

14 July

Our perception of beauty in the natural world is a complicated business. The aesthetic appeal of a plant or animal is altered by perspective. The peacock, for example, is almost excessively attractive, a bird so profoundly exotic as to seem mythical, and yet we still complain about its harsh cries. There's an entomological peacock slowly sweeping through Britain now, but few are interested in its delights: it's widely labelled as a pest.

I saw my first rosemary beetle last summer. I'd been shopping and did a double-take as I walked past the town centre churchyard. A single lavender bush overhung a low wall and there, nestling between the flowers was a metallic bud-sized sphere: my first ever rosemary beetle.

I went back later and, to the bemusement of shoppers, took a few shots. Captured on screen and magnified, the beetle was a revelation. Glinting in the sunlight, lustrous green banded with rich purple stripes, it looked like a miniature Christmas tree bauble.

Rosemary beetles first turned up in the British Isles in the gardens of the Royal Horticultural Society at Wisley in Surrey in 1994 and began to find their feet after the turn of the century, when they established themselves in London and across south-east England. They're native to southern Europe where their plump grey larvae munch on rosemary and lavender plants, but seem to be able to cope well with our winters and have steadily spread or have been introduced to Scotland, Wales and Northern Ireland.

My sighting was one of the first for the area and so I was especially pleased to see it in the flesh. The welcome from gardeners has been chillier, even though the beetles were almost certainly brought in by the horticulture trade. Already there's no shortage of websites advising us how to get rid of the insects, though using pesticides on flowering lavender or rosemary, which bustle with bees in summer, is not a good idea.

So far the beetles are not causing a problem in my neighbourhood, but they will continue to spread and their reputation as a pest is unlikely to endear them to most people. Our reaction to the rosemary beetle is ironic given that a very similar, native species, the rainbow leaf-beetle, which lives only on a few mountain slopes in Snowdonia where it feeds on wild thyme, is strictly protected by law and cosseted by conservationists. For the equally striking rosemary beetle, aesthetic appeal is not enough: to be really appreciated you need rarity and nativity on your side.

WHALES

15 July

A summer ferry crossing over the English Channel towards the Bay of Biscay is not, you might think, a likely place to come across the second largest creature that has ever lived on Planet Earth – bigger even than the largest dinosaur.

But as I stand on the deck, clinging on to the handrail and trying not to be blown off my feet by the freshening wind, my eyes are fixed on the sea ahead. I am hoping to see a dark, blue-grey island breaking the waves; which might just turn out to be a fin whale.

At up to twenty-six metres long, the fin whale is second only to the mighty blue whale as the world's largest mammal. Yet despite their huge size, fin whales can still be very hard to find in the vast open sea. They rarely come to the surface for long, and in choppy waters it is easy to miss the moment when a triangular fin briefly breaks the waves. We eventually had brief glimpses of a pod of these enormous creatures – just enough to see what looked like small islands rising momentarily above the waves, before they sank once again.

Yet sightings of these massive beasts are definitely on the increase. They have long been seen to the south of Britain, but there is now evidence that pods of fin whales are heading further north to feed, perhaps as a result of warmer seas caused by global warming. As the seas warm up, the fin whale's main food source, huge shoals of tiny fish, head northwards too, so the whales are simply following them.

On this particular crossing, we have distant, frustrating views of what is almost certainly a pod of fin whales. But even a fleeting sighting of these mysterious creatures is worth the discomfort, and we reach land relieved and happy.

RABBITS

16 July

Tonight out late looking for barn owls, I'm struck by the numbers of rabbits grazing in the sandy pastures, a sight I associate more with the Suffolk Sandlings or Breckland than my patch in the West Midlands.

It's obviously been a successful breeding season and among the sixty or so in this field are a black youngster and a few sandy individuals, which look golden in the fading light. Around here these two varieties are quite common, but I never see animals with white patches as I have on islands such as Shetland, where piebald rabbits burrow into the cliffs around Sumburgh lighthouse.

Musing on the sheer quantity of rabbits this summer, I wonder whether there's a term for rabbit biomass. Bunnage, perhaps? There don't seem to be many local controls other than the shotgun. Stoats are pretty scarce here, though the summer before last a rabbit shot between my legs as I walked along a bridleway, quickly followed by a stoat that flowed down a hedgebank in hot pursuit. The rabbit escaped. Not so the youngster I saw in spring, in the mouth of a vixen heading back to her earth in the distant wood. Rabbits are probably more important at sustaining predators than my happenstance observations suggest.

Rabbits sustain other species here too. The sandy soil in which they burrow supports locally rare plants such as spring vetch and cudweeds, which need regular disturbance to survive. These plants can't stand competition, so rabbit grazing is perfect for micro-managing small areas by nibbling taller, coarser vegetation.

Burrowing bees and solitary wasps also like bare sand and so the rabbit provides them with habitat too. It may be an introduced species, but the health of the local rabbit population underpins a web of plant and insect life.

FOX

17 July

A few summers ago I got a job in London, which meant that I needed to move back to the capital for a few months. It was then that I realised just how far I had strayed from my urban origins.

For a start, I gave a friendly greeting to the people I met as I walked down the street – definitely a no-go. Then I said sorry if I bumped into someone on the Tube; again, right out of order. But my biggest faux pas came when I saw a fox strolling casually towards me one July evening. Instinctively I froze, hoping I hadn't frightened him. But to my surprise, he walked straight by, turning to look at me with a mixture of aloofness and contempt.

What a difference from his country cousins. On the rare occasions when I encounter a rural fox back in Somerset, it sprints away the moment it sees me. Instead of the urban fox's self-assured swagger, rural foxes are shy, wary and frightened – as indeed, given the attitude of most of my neighbours towards them, they should be.

If you wanted to choose one animal that typifies the town vs country divide in Britain, it would be the fox. Foxes not only behave completely differently in urban and rural settings, but so too do our attitudes towards them vary dramatically.

Many of my city friends welcome the presence of foxes in their gardens. They put out food, marvel when a female chooses to make her den beneath their garden shed, and delight in the appearance of the playful cubs on a sunny spring afternoon. This may well be because the fox is – along with the introduced grey squirrel – just about the only mammal that can regularly be seen in the urban jungle, bringing the thrill of the natural world into city-dwellers' lives.

This benign attitude would cause my rural neighbours to shake their heads in disbelief. For them the fox is a cruel and pitiless killer, causing devastation in the henhouse and to newborn lambs, and warranting no more than what is always due to 'vermin': a death sentence to be carried out whenever and wherever the animal crosses their path.

And yet are town and country foxes really so different? Both are highly adaptable creatures, always on the lookout for an opportunity to feed and breed. Both are sociable animals, living in loose family groups – youngsters born the previous year often stay around and help to rear their new generation of siblings. And both have given rise to a whole range of urban and rural myths, which persist despite a large body of contradictory evidence.

So although foxes have been demonised for entering people's homes and attacking young children, the tiny handful of occasions when this has happened is dwarfed by the thousands of attacks by pet dogs each year. Foxes also rarely raid rubbish bins – the culprit is far more likely to be a domestic cat.

But as the human population of these islands continues to rise, it is inevitable that encounters between foxes and us will increase too. Whether we can learn to live alongside this handsome animal, and accept its behaviour as part of the natural world around us, is now in the balance as never before.

DROWSY BUMBLEBEES

18 July

Suddenly, after a slow start to the bumblebee season, there's an explosion of them, every thistle-head and mop of creamy meadowsweet crawling with the insects. But not all of them are the paragons of industry that we expect. In fact slothful, drowsy and tipsy are adjectives that come to mind as they stir gently on the flower heads, languidly raising a leg to ward off predators.

Many of these apparently sleepy bees are males, which with practice you can identify from their markings and their slightly longer antennae. Unlike the females – the queen and workers – they don't have pollen baskets because their role is not to take pollen back to the nest. All the males have to do is to fertilise the founding queens, which are emerging now and which will overwinter before starting new colonies next spring.

But not all the bees you see sitting sluggishly on vegetation are males lounging about on flowers, sipping nectar and looking for sex. Sometimes you will see drowsy bumblebees, often workers, early in the morning or at dusk, that have not returned to the nest. It's tempting to think that these dew-spattered bees have been caught out by cold weather, but often there's a far more sinister reason for their reluctance to seek shelter.

Buzzing around the flower heads on summer days, you may see a rust-coloured fly with a yellow face, which shadows the bees as they forage for nectar. This is a conopid fly called *Sicus*, which has a muscular abdomen that it carries partly curled beneath its body. When it seizes a bee, it grapples its prey and uses its abdomen tip like a bottle-opener to prise apart the plates under the bee's body. Once it has enough leverage, it inserts an egg and the bee's fate is sealed.

The egg hatches into a maggot, which begins to feed on the bee's internal food reserves, maybe directly from the bee's gut. But rather than eat its host quickly, the maggot needs to slow down its own growth rate by keeping cool; otherwise it will eat itself out of house and home. We don't know how exactly, but it forces the bee to stay out at night away from the warmth of the nest, which is why we often see drowsy bees crawling sleepily over flowers at dawn or dusk.

Throughout the day, the bumblebee continues to forage for nectar and pollen as normal, until the maggot approaches pupation and is ready for the final act. Pushing its narrow head through the bee's waist and into the thorax, it eats the wing-muscles. The game is up for the bumblebee. As a final twist, the conopid maggot persuades its host to dig its own grave, and pupates in the bee's husk, where it spends the winter and emerges next summer.

EMPEROR DRAGONFLY
19 July

On a warm, sunny July day, just as our village pub opens its doors for the passing lunchtime trade, so our largest and most impressive dragonfly takes to the air. As it passes me by, flying low over the surface of the broad, clear waterway to patrol its territory, I catch a flash of sunlight from its translucent wings.

The emperor is well named: few if any of our insects are quite so huge, quite so majestic, and indeed quite so imperial in appearance as this feisty blue, green and black dragonfly. With a body length of over three inches and an even longer wingspan, it is considerably larger – though not quite as heavy – as the stag beetle and the great green bush-cricket, and so perhaps deserves the title of Britain's biggest insect.

The emperor is not just big, but very successful too. The clean-up of Britain's rivers, and the creation of new wetland habitats, have been good news for this charismatic creature. Thanks to this, and the advantages conferred by global climate change, the emperor is now rapidly extending its range. Once confined to the lowlands of southern England and Wales, in the past couple of decades it has moved north like an invading army. You can now see them in North Wales, northern England and even some parts of eastern and central Scotland.

Big though the emperor may be, it is dwarfed by the world's largest dragonfly, a Malaysian species with a seven-inch wingspan. And even this mighty insect pales into insignificance compared with a 300-million-year-old fossil dragonfly discovered in 1979 in Derbyshire, whose wingspan reached an incredible sixty-five centimetres – about the same as a pigeon. Now that would be something to see flying past me on a fine summer's day.

HORNET HOVERFLY
20 July

It's hard not to be startled when you meet the hornet hoverfly. My first encounter was in Bristol, when one droned in and began mopping up spilled lager from the table outside the BBC bar. Not only was it huge, but there was something unreal about its orange-tinted cellophane wings, and bright yellow Bakelite face – a fly too vivid to be at large in Britain. The felted abdomen banded like a hornet was clearly a warning not to mess this with insect.

But these enormous, unmissable flies are completely harmless and are spreading fast. They arrived naturally from continental Europe in the late 1930s (they are powerful fliers) and initially colonised south-east England. Since then they have spread north and west, probably in tandem with the hornet, which has increased its numbers possibly due to climate change.

The two species not only look alike: their lives are intimately entwined. Hornet hoverflies enter their hosts' nests, apparently unscathed and probably cloaked in disguising pheromones. Here, in the dark catacombs of the wasps' cells, they lay their eggs. When the grubs hatch they scavenge on the detritus in the nests, but not on the young wasps. After pupating they emerge unchallenged by their hosts to begin the cycle afresh.

Its dramatic appearance makes the hornet hoverfly an ideal subject to monitor. The Hoverfly Recording Scheme has been asking for records from its members and from the public to chart its progress through England and into South Wales; the insect has yet to reach northern England and Scotland where hornets are scarce or absent.

Citizen science helps us learn more about this fly because it seems very fond of gardens, especially those in towns – areas that are normally closed to public access. Since I first saw one in my garden in 2006, greedily drinking from buddleia flowers, I see it each year and anticipate its appearance as if it has been around all my life.

EEL

21 July

A muggy July night by a quiet West Country river. At first, the clouds passing across the moon make it hard for me to see more than a few inches in front of my face; but gradually my eyes adapt to the gloom and the pale, slowly flowing water takes shape between the dark, earthy banks.

A small group has gathered, bringing along a tin bath, a couple of metal poles and several balls, each about the size of a grapefruit, and they look as if they are made from elastic bands. Then the surface of one of the balls begins to writhe, and I realise that it is made up of dozens of earthworms, threaded together to make a tight sphere. The ray balling is about to begin.

Ray balling – also known as clodding – was once a common summer pastime here on the Somerset Levels. It's just one of many different ways our ancestors came up with to catch one of our most mysterious fish, the eel.

Originally the worms were threaded on to a length of worsted (a strong kind of wool), and then the ball was suspended from a stick of newly cut hazel and dipped into the river.

Today we use metal poles, but the aim is the same: to entice a hungry eel to grab hold of the worms, and then – because its teeth grow inwards – get caught by the thread and be unable to escape. A quick swing of the pole across the river and – hey presto! – the eel lets go and falls into the tin bath.

Eels caught in this way were once an important source of protein for people in this mysterious watery land, well into the post-war period. But like so many country pastimes, ray balling has gone out of fashion nowadays: too much trouble, perhaps, for too little reward, especially as there are far fewer eels in our rivers than there used to be.

The life cycle of the eel is both complex and extraordinary. Having spent much of its life in a British river system, at some unseen signal an eel will choose to head out to sea, cross the whole of the Atlantic Ocean, spawn and then die. Its tiny offspring – known at first as 'glass eels' and then as elvers – swim all the way back to Britain, up our rivers and start the cycle over again.

Along the way they face untold hazards, including changes in ocean currents, overfishing at sea and barriers as they try to swim upstream. No wonder that tonight we catch just a single, immature eel, which after examining we release. It sinks invisibly back into the waters to continue on its lonesome journey.

GREAT DIVING BEETLE
22 July

Asked to name the deadliest predator in the garden, I have no hesitation in plumping for the larva of the great diving beetle. The adult beetles are large handsome insects, their blackish-green wing cases bordered with gold. They're common in pools of all sizes and, on warm summer nights, fly between waters. Sometimes they crash-land on shiny car bonnets or moonlit puddles.

They can create mayhem for moth-trappers when they blunder into light-traps with all the grace of a hovercraft crashing into a ballet school, reducing delicate specimens to mush in their efforts to escape.

But once these beetles were insatiable larvae prowling the depths of our garden ponds. Fully grown they look very un-beetle-like, as long as a baby's finger and tapering at each end. They breathe through their bottoms, hanging from the surface film where they gather air, before sinking below to prowl the weed-jungles where they actively hunt prey.

Each larva's head is armed with a formidable pair of curved mandibles, which pierce its prey and inject digestive enzymes. Their victims are often soft-bodied tadpoles and newt larvae, but they will tackle creatures much larger than themselves, such as adult newts and unwary stickle-backs. Other insect larvae are fair game too.

The enzymes soon break down their victim's tissues and the larva turns from blow to suck, drinking the resulting soup through its mandibles, soon reducing its prey to a husk. As soon as it has finished one meal, this voracious pond-tiger is on the prowl for another and several of them in a garden pond can make a serious dent in the amphibian fauna.

That said, frogs and toads produce huge numbers of eggs, because so few will reach maturity, and I know from experience that the beetle larva is one of the most popular creatures in a pond-dipping session. Just make sure to keep it away from any other life you want to study.

BATHING BONXIES
23 July

We may regard great skuas as both fierce and fearsome, especially when they are heading towards us at speed to chase us away from their nest. Their feeding habits leave a lot to be desired, too: they spend much of their time harassing smaller seabirds, such as terns and kittiwakes, to make them panic and regurgitate their food, which the skua then grabs in mid-air. But they do sometimes reveal a surprising grace and beauty.

I remember one July evening twenty years ago, on the Shetland island of Fetlar, where a flock of great skuas had gathered a mile or so inland to bathe on a small lochan. I watched enraptured as these huge, ungainly birds sat in the shallows, twisting their bodies from left to right, then up and down, coating their entire plumage with the fresh, clear water. It was one of those special moments when you look at a familiar bird in a whole new light, and find grace and beauty in the most unexpected place.

ELEPHANT HAWKMOTH
24 July

It was the silky-smooth feel of the thing that most impressed me; that and the black and lilac eyespot. And the strange head, extending like a tiny elephant's trunk. And the stiff horn on its backside. Then there were the prolific cuboid droppings that it produced relentlessly from its rear end. Heck, the whole creature was unfathomable.

Aged seven, I had no idea where to place it in the Great Chain of Being. I suppose I knew deep down that it was a caterpillar of some sort, but this dark-brown sausage was an outlandish size, thicker and longer than my thumb with two pairs of fearsome eyespots on each side of its head. When picked up (it had a grip like sticky tape) it contracted its head accordion-style to create a fearsome hooded shape like a small cobra.

But what was a cobra doing on a patch of wasteland in my road? Back home it came under further investigation. This was the first elephant hawkmoth larva that I'd seen and left more vivid impressions on me than any other creature. I was captivated by its strangeness and, as I learned more, by its shape and colours. It was a living lesson. This huge moth larva was pretending to be a snake to scare predators: my first awareness of the powers of mimicry. It was also here because its food-plant, the rosebay willowherb, flourished on waste ground that had been created by Second World War bombs: history as well as natural history.

I was reminded of the power of big insects many decades later by the brilliant entomologist Roger Key. Despairing of our attitudes to them, he told me of a newspaper report about a magnificent privet hawkmoth caterpillar, a harmless, horned, green and purple wonder that had allegedly terrorised a Leicestershire family who'd found it in their garden. The offending insect was flushed down the loo, a sad indictment of our attitude towards wildlife we mistakenly interpret as threatening.

GREEN SANDPIPER
25 July

Piles of black peat tower forbiddingly over dark, glossy pools, fringed with rushes and the occasional splash of colour from swathes of purple loosestrife in full bloom. It is a high summer's day on my local patch.

Feeding unobtrusively along the water's edge there is a single wading bird. Bobbing up and down like a fidgety child, its reflection is mirrored in the pool below. From a distance it appears black and white, but a closer look reveals dark, greenish-brown upperparts, with a distinctive white ring around the eye, which for me gives it a permanently surprised expression.

It's a green sandpiper; and although the day's heat suggests that summer could go on for ever, its appearance is evidence that autumn is already waiting in the wings. Green sandpipers rarely breed in Britain, with only a handful of pairs nesting each year in the Scottish Highlands. So when one turns up here, on the Somerset Levels, it is likely to have come rather a long way: from the wet woodlands of Scandinavia or even as far as northern Russia.

Green sandpipers are notoriously jittery, and soon as this bird catches sight of me it takes flight, warning any other birds nearby with a fluting crystal-clear whistle, and towering off into the blue. As it dashes away, its snow-white rump contrasts with its dark wings, making it look rather like a giant house martin.

The vast majority of green sandpipers I see here from July through to September are passage migrants, our paths temporarily crossing as they stop off to refuel on their journey south. A cautious few will stay here, though, spending the winter hidden away in a muddy ditch or freshwater pool, where they dine on aquatic invertebrates and their larvae.

But not this particular bird. In three months' time, as the temperatures in Britain begin to fall, it will be beside an East African waterhole. Walking daintily between the hooves of giraffes, elephants and wildebeests, it will pick tiny insects off the surface of the drying mud – a far cry from both the forests of Scandinavia and the ditches of Somerset.

COMMON STINKHORN

26 July

Walking through hot pine woods, I catch a whiff of carrion, a sweet stench emanating from a hidden spot under the bracken fronds. I don't claim to be a connoisseur of rotting corpses, but this one is overlain with a cabbagey aroma that betrays it as a stinkhorn, a fungus that so ashamed Victorian naturalists that they wouldn't illustrate it in many of their books.

For a generation that reputedly covered piano legs to prevent moral corruption, the stinkhorn must have presented the ultimate horror. Not only did it assail your senses with its foetid stench, but its appearance was so suggestive that Charles Darwin's daughter Henrietta (known as Etty) went into the woods at fruiting time and, following her nose, hoiked all the offending fungi into a basket with a stick. Back home her noisome harvest was burned secretly on the drawing-room fire behind locked doors to protect 'the morals of the maids'.

No such niceties for the herbalist John Gerard who called a spade a spade: to him the fungus was the 'pricke mushroom'. Its Latin name has more than a whiff of indecency: *Phallus impudicus*, the shameless male member.

But if the stinkhorn's appearance affronted innocent Victorians, it compounded the offence by attracting clouds of blowflies to the sticky miasma on its cap. This goo, which is brown in colour, is called the 'gleba' and contains the spores that the flies obligingly distribute. It's also a laxative for them, ensuring that the stinkhorns don't travel far from their favourite spots. So efficient is the pong at attracting dispersers that when you search for the stinkhorn, often all that remains is the white honeycombed stalk and cap like a rocket nosecone.

You'd think that the last thing anyone would do is eat a stinkhorn, but you'd be underestimating our sense of adventure. Apparently, and I have to take this on trust, the early egg-shaped fruiting bodies are edible, though the slimy texture alone must be off-putting to all but the hardiest epicure.

HUMMINGBIRD HAWKMOTH
27 July

On a sultry summer's day, the buddleia bush in my garden is covered in fat purple tresses, each composed of hundreds of tiny, yellow-throated flowers exuding a cloud of sweet, musky scent. Through the air drift butterflies, heady with nectar: small tortoiseshells, red admirals and peacocks unfurling watchspring tongues to probe the irresistible fluid.

As I stand and watch, from the very edge of my vision an orange blur intrudes, moving purposefully towards the plant like a guided missile. Its wings are whirring faster than any human eye can see, at up to eighty beats per second – hence this creature's name, the hummingbird hawk-moth. It even looks like a hummingbird: with a gingery tinge to its body, large, prominent eyes and a distinct 'tail' (actually the end of its abdomen).

Just like a hummingbird, this amazing insect can hover forwards, backwards, up and down, and from side to side, manoeuvring itself in order to find the optimum place to feed. Once it is satisfied with its position, it extends a long, thin proboscis, which penetrates the heart of the flower and sucks out the nectar. Then it simply flicks its wings and moves on to another clump of blossom.

As a migrant from Spain or North Africa, this exotic-looking creature used to be scarce and unpredictable in Britain, seen mainly in the extreme south-west of the country during spells of warm, southerly winds.

But now, along with many other species of moth, it is appearing more regularly and at different times of the year – not so long ago one was photographed in winter in Birmingham, taking nectar from a snowdrop. They have even bred in this country; the fat green caterpillars feed on bedstraws and, if they become moths, may just have time to make it back south before fatal autumn frosts arrive.

Both the name and the appearance of the hummingbird hawkmoth cause confusion for the unwary, with frequent reports of 'hummingbirds' in local newspapers and radio bulletins. Sadly, hummingbirds themselves are confined to the Americas, but for those lucky enough to encounter this fascinating insect on a warm summer's day, the hummingbird hawkmoth provides ample compensation.

COMMON RAGWORT
28 July

This part of north Worcestershire and south-west Staffordshire is a sandscape: graze the dry topsoil and you see New Red Sandstone glowing just beneath the surface. Its friable blocks have been used to build local churches and, in the nearby village of Kinver, sandstone outcrops were excavated as homes for troglodytes until as late as 1961.

Such a well-drained landscape becomes parched by midsummer if there's no rain and, away from gardens, wild flowers are scarce. The grassland is heavily grazed too on the margins of suburbia, dominated by 'horseyculture'. Out in the fields, some pony-keepers have succumbed to their seasonal bout of panic and are uprooting ragwort. Removing ragwort also removes an important nectar source for bees, butterflies and a host of other insects and its removal is a matter of great concern to entomologists.

It's disappointing to see this annual ragwort cull because the risk to horses is actually very low. Although ragwort is undeniably toxic and contains alkaloids, which can lead to cirrhosis of the liver in horses and cattle, cases locally are extremely rare and indeed the stables that don't uproot the plant have reported no incidences of poisoning. On one farm where ragwort isn't pulled, the horses stand hock-deep in a golden sea of the flowers, which they leave alone. Fresh ragwort is of little interest to them because it tastes bitter: the risk comes when the dried plant is eaten among hay. Little hay is taken from these sandy meadows, which are zero-grazed year-round, and so the ragwort displays are effectively harmless.

In recent years the panic has worsened. Highways managers spend large amounts of money uprooting ragwort by hand from road and motorway verges in case its seeds blow into nearby fields. Even wildlife trusts and county councils are removing it from nature reserves, though there is no statutory duty to control its spread. The result is that we have the nonsense of conservationists removing important nectar sources on which our late summer insects depend.

SPARROWHAWK ENCOUNTER

29 July

Being a low-flying predator, flying into glass windows and doors is an occupational hazard for a sparrowhawk. Sadly this usually results in a fractured skull, followed by a rapid death. And so when my twins George and Daisy dashed in to tell me that there was a hawk in our greenhouse, I feared the worst.

Fortunately, this aerobatic predator had managed to slam on the brakes just as it entered the open door and realised its error. Now it was cowering angrily in the corner of the greenhouse, unable to find its way back out.

As I approached, the hawk stared back at me with piercing, yellow eyes. For a moment I was taken aback: no other bird – apart perhaps from the sparrowhawk's larger cousin the goshawk – looks at you with what appears to be such single-minded hatred and contempt. I crouched down and put my hands around him, marvelling as always at how light even large birds are, thanks to their adaptations for flight.

Taking him back outside, I decided to check him for injury, so handed him to Daisy, who took hold of the bird very gingerly. He was unharmed and so we passed him over to George to release. As we did so, the sparrowhawk shook free and darted off, at eye-level, straight into the distance. We stood and stared, silenced by our close encounter with this beautiful – and fortunately fit and healthy – predator.

BULLHEAD

30 July

In midsummer, when water levels in the forest streams are low, we – the members of the local study group – flip over stones to look for whatever's lurking beneath. Within a minute or so, someone will find a bullhead, marvellously camouflaged against the pebbly stream-bed, its pectoral fins shielding the toad-like head. This flattened head-shape has prompted an alternative name, miller's thumb, because breadmaker's thumbs were traditionally broad from kneading dough. Isaak Walton in his *Compleat Angler* called it 'a fish of no pleasing shape'.

Few fish are show-offs, but this is one you need to look for especially carefully because it rarely swims in open water. Bullheads secrete themselves in the cracks between stones or beneath them, usually where the current breaks into fast-flowing riffles rich in oxygen. The joy of fossicking for the fish is not only in picking out their mottled shapes on a bed of gravel, but because the search takes you to sun-dappled places where kingfishers call above the conversation of the stream, water licks around the larger boulders and swags of moss wave lazily in the currents. Suddenly you're back to childhood, a state most naturalists are reluctant to leave.

Childhood has little respect for fish. In my case, the tiddlers in question were invariably sticklebacks that perished in jam jars, deprived of oxygen. Bullheads with their reptilian skins, frog's eyes and huge mouths deserved better treatment. I first saw them on an early crayfishing trip and knew that I couldn't replicate the rippling waters in which they lived, so I reluctantly let them swim free.

Afterwards I read that in spring the male oxygenated the eggs he'd sired by fanning them with his large pectoral fins as they clustered under stone overhangs. A model of parental behaviour, apparently, though I didn't know then that he would eat them if he became peckish. Bullheads are nearly all mouth and the animal behaviourist Desmond Morris noted that the male's simple response to an intruder is to bite it. If it's prey, it's eaten; if it's an enemy, it's spat out; and if it's a female, it's propelled into the nest he's prepared.

CROSSBILL IRRUPTION
31 July

Some birds migrate in spring and autumn; others stay put all year round. But a handful of species do neither – instead they make a single annual journey from one feeding area to another, then stay put to breed the following year in their new home. These are known as irruptive species, and the best known of these in Britain is the crossbill.

Crossbills are curious birds. Uniquely, the top mandible of their bill crosses over the lower one, creating a pincer-like structure that enables them to tease out the tiny seeds of conifer cones, which they then swallow using their long, fleshy tongue. Back in the thirteenth century, a monk named Matthew Paris noticed a flock of strange birds in the orchards around his Hertfordshire monastery, and noted: 'They had the parts of the beak crossed . . . by which they divided the apples as with a forceps or knife.'

Paris was witnessing an annual irruption of crossbills, which usually occur in midsummer, after the birds have finished breeding. Many have come south from northern Britain, but some may have travelled across the North Sea from Scandinavia.

I've witnessed crossbill irruptions from time to time, in some unexpected places, ranging from a crag overlooking Morecambe Bay (where I was searching for, and eventually found, the rare northern brown argus butterfly) to the North Uist Hotel on the Outer Hebridean island of the same name. Whenever I find them, it is their call that alerts me first: a deep 'chup chup', quite different from the usual chaffinches and greenfinches.

My best crossbill sighting, though, was a single bird hopping along a dry-stone wall in Village Bay, St Kilda. I assume that, having taken a good look round, and discovered the complete lack of trees – pine or otherwise – he turned and headed back to the mainland, to more congenial surroundings.

AUGUST

WATCHING A LOCAL patch teaches you how strong and reliable natural timetables can be. August in my corner of the English Midlands is symbolised by the arrival of redstarts flashing flame-coloured tails among the elder bushes lining local horse-pastures. Every year I see them in the ragged hedges and wonder where they've bred and how they will reach the Sahel region south of the Sahara Desert where they spend the winter. They're joined by spotted flycatchers, which no longer breed on 'my' patch, and lesser whitethroats sneaking through the bramble clumps, white breast feathers daubed with purple juice.

Migration is well under way everywhere now and muddy margins of lakes and gravel pits are home to Arctic and northern waders: green and wood sandpipers mingle with little stints and elegant spotted redshanks, all heading south.

The insect world continues to flourish. August is cricket season when many species including dark and great green bush-crickets are maturing and advertising to females. In my neighbourhood there are two recent arrivals, the long-winged conehead and Roesel's bush-cricket, but I need a bat detector to hear them well. I can still pick out grasshoppers though and August is their heyday.

Flowers are declining, but one at its peak this month is Himalayan balsam, whose tall flowers on succulent stems pulse with honeybees and bumblebees. It's a plant with few friends, but is a staple nectar source where I live.

On the local heaths, the slim, blackish shapes of newly born common lizards dart across paths and skeeter off logs as I approach. Sand-wasps patrol the bare patches for caterpillars and bee-wolves return to their burrows like miniature Lancaster bombers, their honeybee cargoes slung beneath them.

B.W.

FOR ME, AUGUST is always redolent of those long, hot summers of my childhood, when the sun always seemed to shine and all was right in the world. Of course, it wasn't really like that at all: however exciting the prospect of weeks and weeks off school might have been in anticipation, in reality we soon grew bored.

August can be a quiet month for wildlife too. For birds, the breeding season is now over, birdsong is silent, and many are hiding away to moult and replenish their energy reserves before either migrating or preparing to stay put for the autumn and winter to come. Many plants have finished blooming too, yet there are still plenty of wild flowers – and their attendant swarms of insects – to satisfy even the most demanding naturalist.

Around our coasts, beaches are thronged with holidaymakers; but head inland and our meadows, moors and heaths attract far fewer people. They also support plenty of fascinating wildlife, with dragonflies and damselflies, reptiles and amphibians, bumblebees and butterflies, all making the most of the summer heat and glut of available food to reproduce.

Later in the month, bird migration begins to accelerate, as waders and warblers, flycatchers and chats all begin to appear. So, as Brett does on his local patch, keep an eye out for them as they stop off to feed before continuing on their long journey south.

S.M.

BALEARIC SHEARWATER
1 August

Seasickness and sunburn are an unusual combination. But these are the hazards I face if I wish to encounter some of our most elusive and sought-after species, by taking a trip into the unknown. I'm on a sea-going trip to catch sight of rare seabirds on the *Scillonian* passenger ferry, heading out of Penzance, past the Isles of Scilly, and into the Western Approaches.

Birders call this 'going on a pelagic' (from the Greek *pelagos*, meaning 'sea'), and it is a true test of stamina and psychology. Hours spent staring across an empty ocean can be soul-destroying, while the weather brings either baking sunshine or wind and rain, neither of which make the experience any more bearable.

Then the boredom swiftly turns to excitement, followed by gut-wrenching fear, as a bird is sighted in the far distance. Will it approach the boat or simply fly straight past, leaving its identity unknown? Is it just a common species – a Manx shearwater or storm petrel perhaps – or could it be something scarcer, a Cory's or great shearwater, Leach's petrel, or even Sabine's gull?

Or (still my beating heart) could it be a true 'mega' – birder terminology for a once-in-a-lifetime bird, one that makes the hours of vomiting worthwhile? Thoughts of a red-billed tropicbird, a black-browed albatross and Fea's petrel come to mind, before I dismiss them as mere fantasy.

To my delight, it turns out to be a Balearic shearwater: a coffee-coloured version of the more familiar Manxies that are often seen flying low across the waves around our coasts. But although this species is regularly sighted off south-western Britain in late summer and early autumn, it is nevertheless the rarest bird, from a global perspective, that I shall ever have the chance to see in this country.

As its name suggests, the Balearic shearwater breeds only on the Balearic Islands in the western Mediterranean, including Mallorca, Menorca and Ibiza, where beach-loving holidaymakers may sometimes catch sight of them as they pass offshore to and from their feeding grounds.

After breeding, they go 'flyabout', heading from their Mediterranean home out into the North Atlantic, and spending the autumn and winter months circumnavigating that great ocean before returning the following spring.

Seeing this bird off the coast of Cornwall on a sunny August day is something akin to finding the haystack-based needle, given that there may now be fewer than 10,000 Balearic shearwaters remaining in the world. Threatened by tourism development, cats and rats, this modest-looking seabird may not pass by our shores for very much longer.

ROCKPOOLS

2 August

An August day by the seaside: seagulls hanging in a clear blue sky, sand between my toes and the remnants of an ice cream dripping down my chin. What better place to lie back and relax as the children build a sandcastle?

But instead I decide to get up and join them, to explore the two very different hidden worlds inhabited by miniature creatures whose lives are governed by the twice daily changing of the tides. For as the tide begins to ebb, and the water drains out of the moat around the sandcastle and races back towards the sea, the rockpools begin to appear.

We scramble gingerly over the dark black rocks, taking care to avoid slipping on the shiny clumps of bladderwrack seaweed, and stare down in wonder at this temporary realm. At first we see nothing; then Charlie spots a tiny shrimp, its tentacles poking out of the sand as it decides whether it is safe to emerge and begin to feed.

As it finally does so, a larger creature about the size of a human thumb crosses its path, causing the shrimp to beat a hasty retreat. It is a blenny: a small fish, mottled greenish brown in colour, with a large head and tapering tail, and fins running along its back and at its sides. The blenny shouldn't really be here – it has become trapped as the tide rushed out, and will now have to wait until the waters rise and it can swim back to sea.

Around the sides of the pool we find plenty of limpets: pyramidal shellfish that look as if they are stuck to the rocks for ever. And yet in a few hours, when the sea finally covers the rockpool once again, they

will go walkabout: wandering around to find food, before returning to
the exact same spot and re-fixing themselves with the natural equivalent
of superglue, as if they never went away.

More permanent rockpool residents include colourful sea anemones,
distant relatives of corals and jellyfish. When they extend their tentacles
and wave them in the water, the resemblance to their floral namesakes
becomes clear. But these are no shrinking violets: they are predatory
creatures that can give a nasty sting, and so we decide that, discretion
being the better part of valour, we will leave them be and return to our
sandcastle.

WALL LIZARD

3 August

A few summers ago I stopped off in a disused roadside quarry on the
Isle of Portland in Dorset to take a break from driving. But I soon
discovered that I wasn't alone: there were four other people prowling
furtively among the blocks and columns of dark stone. My first instinct
was to head straight back to my car, but then I noticed that two of them
were carrying long sticks from which hung a loop of fine material. They
crept slowly as they carefully scrutinised each sunlit boulder.

I was so intrigued by their activity that I almost missed the shadow
that slithered across a rock: a lizard as dark as basalt, but longer-tailed
and more streamlined than our native common lizard. I remembered
reading that there were escaped or introduced wall lizards in this part of
Dorset and suddenly I had an inkling as to the activities of the mysterious
prowlers. Chatting to them, I discovered that they were from Oxford
University and were studying the provenance of Portland's wall lizards.

If you've ever taken a holiday in the Mediterranean, you'll have seen
wall lizards skittering over old buildings or basking on walls. They are
attractive and very variable reptiles, mottled in various shades of green
and brown. In England, wall lizards are all introductions or escapees
and survive in only a few warm places in the southern extremities: there
is a flourishing colony in the botanical gardens at Ventnor on the Isle
of Wight, for instance, where I've seen them basking among Mediterranean
cistus bushes; they also live on the cliffs at Bournemouth.

Catching a wall lizard among rocks is well-nigh impossible, unless you lasso it with a noose at the end of a pole, and that's precisely what the Oxford University team were doing. Having caught a lizard, they'd persuade it to shed its tail, providing them with a nice dollop of DNA, which would help to assign the lizard to a particular species or subspecies. From that they could then work out approximately where the population came from: these dark-brown Portland specimens seemed to be Italian wall lizards: the greener Ventnor lizards, which have been there for over a century, are probably French.

Lively and sun-loving, wall lizards bring a touch of the Riviera to our rain-sodden shores and I am always thrilled to see them. Not everyone agrees. Some herpetological organisations worry that illegal introductions may bring disease to threaten our native sand lizards. Given that the wall lizard will probably only ever have a claw-hold on the warmest and driest parts of England, I hope that these concerns are misplaced and that through the reptiles we can at least pretend that we live somewhere hot and sunny.

CHALKLAND BUTTERFLIES

4 August

The butterfly perches on a wild flower just a few millimetres above the close-cropped grass. Wings closed, he is tricky for me to see: a delicate pattern of black, white and orange blotches on a pale-brown background help break up his outline and allow him to blend in with the surrounding vegetation.

Then he opens his wings and, as if a spotlight has come on, a stunning flash of cobalt blue the shade of a summer sky dazzles my eyes. This is the aptly named Adonis blue, arguably the most beautiful, and certainly one of the most striking, of all our butterflies.

Few wild creatures are quite as indicative of high summer as the butterflies of chalk and limestone grassland. Along with the Adonis blue (named after the Greek god of beauty and desire), there is also the chalkhill blue, whose subtler, powder-blue shade makes it harder to spot; and the brown Argus, which despite its name is actually a 'blue', albeit chocolate brown in colour with a row of tiny orange markings along the edge of its upperwing.

All these butterflies depend on 'unimproved' (i.e. unsprayed and unfertilised) grassland, an increasingly uncommon habitat here in southern England. Today I'm at Barbury Castle, an Iron Age hill fort just outside Swindon, where the remains of the earthworks dug by our ancestors provide a sheltered suntrap for these attractive insects.

They are fussy creatures: their caterpillars feed only on a limited range of food-plants – in the case of the Adonis and chalkhill blues just one, the horseshoe vetch, which is itself becoming scarcer as more and more land goes into intensive food production.

Whether we can afford these choosy little butterflies in a nation determined to produce ever-more mountains of cheap food is a moot point; but when I watch a male Adonis blue flashing his wings on a sunny summer's day it's hard not to agree that they are, quite simply, priceless.

URBAN RIVER SAFARI
5 August

Rediscovering our rivers is a welcome twenty-first-century trend. I've celebrated a couple of recent summers by joining friends to fight our way along a stretch of overgrown river, fraught with submarine dangers and as dense and impenetrable as an Amazonian backwater. In three hours we travelled half a kilometre and were forced to keep popping up above the dense stands of Himalayan balsam to work out where we were – in the heart of Kidderminster.

Kidderminster in north Worcestershire was once the centre of British carpet-making: the River Stour, which flows through the town, ran red or blue on alternate days, depending which dyes were being used. Until recently, this heavily polluted river, which rises in the industrial Black Country west of Birmingham, has itself been brushed under the carpet, banished below ground to allow development of its banks and reduce the smell from its waters. But now thanks to tighter controls on pollution, the Stour is cleaner than for many years and is at last being uncovered.

One result of this cleaner water is that damselflies – including beautiful demoiselles that gleam tropically in summer sunlight – have returned along with greater fish numbers. Best of all are the otters, which hole up beneath the town's shopping centre. Queuing for the bus or trundling shopping trolleys through the streets, Kidderminster's shoppers might be just a few metres from a slumbering otter.

In search of otter signs, our tortuous trip upriver, dodging underwater shopping trolleys, bricks and broken bottles, took us past a supermarket car park and into their coffee-shop. The (Morrisons) superstore was granted planning permission in return for their contribution to uncover the Stour and re-plant waterside species such as yellow iris and purple loosestrife. In a corner of the car park, shoppers load their car boots near an artificial otter holt hidden by a screen of Himalayan balsam.

Back in the river and thigh-deep in roiling brown water, we struggled into town and stopped under a converted carpet factory, now a nightclub. Traffic rumbled overhead as we ran our torches over a small bank of smelly sediment. There were shopping trolleys here too and all manner of rubbish, but there were also four-toed footprints in the drying silt and dark droppings – otter spraints – on a pile of bricks. Unobserved, an otter had been here within the last day or so. It was a glorious reward for the hard work being done to re-expose the river and improve water quality.

Later that month, helping out at a District Council wildlife awareness day, I saw a procession of children gaze adoringly at a dog otter, sadly a road casualty from nearby which had been expertly stuffed by an experienced taxidermist. Dead or not, the affection for this animal, one that they'd never seen in the wild, was palpable. One small boy was captivated by it, talking to it and stroking it as he would a family pet. Parents and children went on special otter walks, looking for otter-poo on stones and footprints in the mud, bubbling with enthusiasm as they saw their town centre anew. Like me, none had seen a live otter locally, but knowing that they were here beneath our feet and thriving among us was enough.

BANDED SNAILS

6 August

For a bunch of kids straight out of inner-city Bristol, the Somerset Levels might as well be on the far side of the moon. Here on their summer camp on the Avalon Marshes, and armed with nets and collecting pots as weapons, like an invading army they swipe and swoop at anything that moves. Butterflies and damselflies, beetles and bugs, even the occasional tiny froglet, are caught and incarcerated, then held up as trophies to squeals of delight.

But of all the creatures caught by these urban invaders, it is the snails that really intrigue them. Pink and yellow, pale and dark, plain and striped . . . yet all belonging to the same two species: the brown-lipped and white-lipped snails, collectively known as banded snails.

These are some of the most common and widespread of all our snails, yet often overlooked, partly because they have such a varied appearance. Over the years, curious children have dubbed them 'humbug snails' and in the United States (where they were introduced and have become a pest) 'candy snails'.

Yet despite their differing colours and patterns, these snails have a very similar genetic code. We know this because, apart from human beings, we have a better understanding of the genetics of these humble invertebrates than any other species of animal.

They have an amazing sex life. Like other land snails, many of which are hermaphrodites (possessing both male and female sex organs), they use a lovemaking technique known as love darts, in which sharp objects are injected (rather than thrown) from one snail into another during mating. It was once thought that they contain sperm, but in fact they introduce a hormone that enables the sperm to stand a better chance of surviving and fertilising the snail's partner.

At the end of our visit, it takes all my skills of persuasion to coax the children to release their booty. As we leave, I hope that they remember their day out in this fascinating landscape, and the creatures they discovered – including those remarkable snails.

MOULTING BLACKBIRDS

7 August

It's as if a switch has been turned off. The blackbird that has been fluting from the TV aerial has stopped and, apart from the occasional fussing of blue and coal tits, there is silence.

I'm often asked where blackbirds go in summer by people worried that their garden birds have deserted them. The fact is that they have gone nowhere. Cloaked by thick vegetation, most of them are recovering from the business of rearing a brood and are in moult.

Singing and food-finding during the breeding season are energetically costly to both sexes. They're also conspicuous activities: in spring and early summer we can't fail to notice female birds carrying beakfuls of worms to their nest-sites and hear the males proclaiming their paternal rights from the rooftops.

But once the young blackbirds have fledged – and there may well be two broods – their parents are looking understandably worn out. Their plumage is tatty and faded and the care they've lavished on their growing brood has taken its toll on their body condition. To prepare for the arrival of autumn, they need to grow new feathers and feed while there's shelter from summer leaves and plenty of ripening fruits and insects.

So secretive are blackbirds in late summer that the only hint of their presence might be a wheezy chuckle from deep in the bushes or a flurry of wings in the plum tree. They replace their body and wing feathers in stages so that they are never flightless and completely at the mercy of cats and other predators. Even so, while the new feathers are growing – and the moult can take several weeks – it makes sense to lie low and concentrate on getting fit for winter.

ST KILDA FIELD MOUSE
8 August

The archipelago of St Kilda is not just the remotest place in the whole of the British Isles, but also one of the most extraordinary places I have ever visited, anywhere in the world. The unique combination of millions of seabirds, the history of the 'bird people' for whom these were the staple diet, and several creatures found nowhere else on the planet is guaranteed to impress.

Walking along the main street, where tumbledown stone buildings seem to whisper with the sound of ghosts, I found myself thinking of the people who eked out a harsh living here until they were finally evacuated in 1930, having reluctantly decided that the hardships of remote island life were simply too difficult to bear. I was so caught up in my thoughts that I almost didn't pay attention to the tiny movement I spotted out of the corner of my eye as something emerged momentarily from between the stones of the house wall.

I looked again, and was rewarded by the appearance of a small mammal. My rodent identification isn't good at the best of times, but this little creature was easy to identify as a St Kilda field mouse, the only rodent to live on these outlying islands.

This isn't strictly a unique species, but a race of the very common wood mouse familiar to anyone living in rural Britain. Naturalists now believe it hitched a ride here with the Vikings over 1,000 years ago. Isolated on the islands, it thrived – indeed it grew to weigh more than twice as much as its mainland cousins. They survive today by feeding on insects, seeds and whatever the human visitors leave behind.

There used to be a second subspecies of mouse on St Kilda: the St Kilda house mouse, which as you'd expect lived in the homes of the islands' people. Yet only a few years after the people left, this unique rodent was extinct, having been forced out of the now-abandoned dwellings by its bigger and tougher cousin, the St Kilda field mouse. Such is the law of nature.

A SHINGLE LIFE

9 August

South of Worcester, the River Severn meanders sluggishly through fields of corn and pasture. With each flood, its turbid waters gouge the earthy banks and carry a fresh cargo of silt towards the estuary: clear water is rare in this heavily agricultural zone.

Today, though, I'm heading west into the heart of Wales where the river is leaner and faster running. Here, beyond Newtown, a youthful Severn ripples over pebble beds and squirms between banks of shingle. The stones clatter underfoot with the sound of stacking crockery.

Biologists unromantically refer to these shingle beds as ERS – Exposed Riverine Sediment – a description that doesn't begin to hint at their glories. Today I'm looking for two special creatures, both of which are found nowhere else.

As I approach the river through a thicket of gorse I glimpse the pale banks of shingle and hear the sharp calls of grey wagtails, pitched to be audible above the chatter of the current. Two birds loop overhead and with a flash of yellow underbellies flirt on to the stones at the water's edge, their long tails trembling as they begin to pick out newly hatched mayflies from between the cobbles with the delicacy of a dentist probing a tender tooth. A needling call alerts me to a common sandpiper, a visitor from Africa to upland waterways: it flickers upstream on bowed wings, pitching down just out of sight around a bend, as they often do.

No time for avian distractions. I'm here to look for a ladybird, the five-spot ladybird to be precise. Unlike its commoner relatives, the two-spot and seven-spot ladybirds, this is no garden softie, but a beetle found only on riverine shingle banks, which limits its distribution to parts of Wales and Scotland.

No one quite knows why it's so fussy, because when you do see it, it's usually hunting for aphids on nettles, thistles and other plants growing through the shingle. That's exactly what my first one is doing, sitting on a nettle leaf at the water's edge, next to its black and orange larva. This has been easier than I thought.

My next target is more challenging. I've chosen this time of year because the wolf spider *Arctosa cinerea* is at its largest now. Wolf spiders are a large family of fast-running spiders, which include those dark brown ones you see scampering across garden paths on sunny days. They don't spin webs but hunt their prey by running it down, hence their name.

Arctosa cinerea is a giant among wolf spiders: a pregnant female is nearly as large as the house spiders that fall into our baths. Finding her is extremely difficult: somewhere among these countless water-worn pebbles she is lurking in her silk-lined chamber, which can protect her even when the river floods. I turn over a few stones, dislodging beetles and mayflies, but this could take all day, especially as I'm carefully replacing each stone.

Skip forward a couple of hours during which I curse the futility of my quest. But then I turn a stone and something brownish and pebble-like shifts in the gloomy hollow beneath. It's an *Arctosa* and a large one at that. She races into the sunlight across the shingle, but when she stops, disappears. The dark bands on her pale legs break up her outline and her swollen abdomen becomes another polished rock. Another movement and a sudden rush for cover and I now have to strain to keep up. It's a thrilling encounter. Like the five-spot ladybird, this magnificent spider is confined to river shingle, mainly in Wales and northern England. Serenaded by the river music, I'm happy to watch her until she scampers to safety under a stone and I reluctantly crunch back to the real world.

SHEARWATERS AND SHARKS

10 August

An evening boat trip off the Isles of Scilly, guided by local boatman Joe Pender and a team of crack seabird experts. We expected storm petrels – yet only saw a couple, along with the usual gannets, fulmars and a couple of dozen Manx shearwaters skimming the waves.

Then a real surprise, as four larger birds cruised towards the boat. They were visitors from the seas off north-west Africa: Cory's shearwaters, which travel here in late summer to feed in these fish-rich waters.

This seabird is named after Charles Cory, a nineteenth-century US millionaire who as well as being an expert ornithologist was also one of the first Americans to take up golf. At first this naming seems odd, because the species is only a scarce visitor to North America. But it arose because Cory, in his early twenties, on a visit to Cape Cod, Massachusetts, shot one of these large shearwaters and realised it was a bird he had never seen before. Later, the name was given to the bird in his honour.

Most of those aboard the MV *Sapphire* were less concerned with the origin of the birds' name than with their presence. Cory's shearwaters are one of those birds you can only add to your British List by taking a trip offshore, so several of the passengers were delighted to finally catch up with this long-winged seabird.

I'd seen them several times before, so after taking a good look I focused on another unexpected creature: a blue shark, which thrashed around the bottom of the boat while it was tagged as part of a scientific study of these mysterious ocean-going fish. Like all sharks, it had that glassy-eyed stare that is so disconcerting, especially at such close quarters. Once successfully tagged, the shark was released back into the deep blue sea, where it instantly vanished.

HIMALAYAN BALSAM
11 August

Today the valley is impassable. For the first time ever, this sandy fold in the surrounding farmland has been overwhelmed by greenery and pinkery. Rain earlier in the year has allowed Himalayan balsam to flourish and the plants now tower three metres and more above the public footpath they have obliterated.

Pushing through the succulent groves of hollow stems, it's hard not to admire this controversial escapee, our tallest annual, which was brought here from the Himalayan foothills in 1839 as a colourful addition to Victorian gardens.

Himalayan balsam is a plant for the senses. Underfoot, the sappy stalks crunch loudly, releasing a cloud of antiseptic smells: cool, clammy leaves brush your hands. Overhead are clusters of pink, pouched blooms alive with bees, pulsing like the throats of toads. Here in north Worcestershire where late summer flowers are scarce and where ragwort, one of the few that does flourish on the acid soil, is grubbed out by horse-worshippers, the balsam is valuable bee-fodder. Watch a flower closely and you'll see the bees reversing out, floury with white pollen. In places, the plant is known as bee-bums and locally as poor-man's orchid, modern folk names that reflect a grudging acceptance.

But, conservationists point out, for all its flamboyance Himalayan balsam is an invasive alien that can swamp more delicate natives. This is undoubtedly true along riverbanks and in wetlands where it occupies bare ground with ease. The seed pods, like small ribbed gherkins, ripen in September sunshine until, taut with pressure, they curl back explosively, flinging the black seeds up to a metre away: it's not called *Impatiens* for nothing. The spring-germinating seedlings establish beachheads on bare riverbanks and may encourage erosion by preventing perennials from colonising. But in this fairly dry valley, bluebells flower and fruit before the balsam has grown tall enough to shade them out, so it does little harm.

Here, balsam is a boon to bumblebees and honeybees. Pioneering a path through the jungle of towering stalks is almost a wilderness experience – was this how early explorers felt? Like them, you never know what you might find. Once I stumbled on a conspiracy of cannabis plants deep in a balsam thicket whose convenient canes cloaked a spot of illicit horticulture. Today there are tunnels where Labrador-sized muntjac deer have barrelled through the greenery. Their asymmetrical slots mark their paths as they do in their native Asia where balsam also thrives – two strangers reunited thousands of miles from home in this corner of the English Midlands.

PURPLE LOOSESTRIFE

12 August

On the rough ground alongside the pools left behind after tonnes of peat have been dug out, the summer greenery has reached new heights, depths and volume; surely there can't be room for any more foliage.

And yet in the middle of August the banks here are alive with clusters of tall, deep purple flowers: a sure sign that summer has reached its zenith. The purple loosestrife is in bloom.

This tall, elegant plant is a distant relative of henna (long used to dye hair red) and the pomegranate. It has a statuesque beauty, lending a splash of vibrant colour to the summer scene in and around wetlands, swamps and bogs. It is also a clear indicator of where not to tread if I want to avoid a boot full of mud, as this plant usually grows on the very edge of the water.

Like so many plants, purple loosestrife has a deep symbolic importance. In his painting of the drowning Ophelia, the nineteenth-century artist Millais depicted Shakespeare's tragic heroine floating in a stream surrounded by what Hamlet's mother Gertrude calls 'long purples', a common country name for the purple loosestrife. However, scholars now believe that the playwright was actually referring to a very different bloom: the early purple orchid. But this did not trouble Millais, who famously arranged all the flowers for his artwork (including purple loosestrife) in a Surrey river, and then painted the poet Lizzie Siddal – who posed for him shivering in a cold bath – in his London flat. Lizzie contracted pneumonia as a result, but fortunately survived her ordeal.

I take a closer look at this plant's complex structure, with stalkless leaves arranged in opposing pairs or groups of three up the lower part of the stem, and the pinkish-purple flowers above. They can appear any time from June onwards, and usually stay in flower until late August or early September, when the colours slowly begin to fade, leaching the colour out of the landscape as summer comes slowly to an end.

HOLLY BLUE

13 August

Ice blue on a hot August day, the holly blue is always a refreshing sight in the garden. Unlike our other blue butterflies, which prefer wide open spaces, the holly blue enjoys life in town. But how many you see in any one summer will depend on the intimate relationship the butterfly has with one of its parasites.

These are diminutive butterflies, which fly erratically. While they will take nectar from flowers, they are just as happy crawling over the surface of leaves where they mop up honeydew, the sticky secretion produced by aphids.

Holly blues have two generations which breed on different plants. The spring blue emerges in April and lays its eggs on the flower buds of holly, on which the caterpillars feed before pupating and emerging as a summer generation from mid-July onwards. Sometimes they last well into September: in 2015 I even saw them as late as the first week of October. These summer holly blues lay their eggs on ivy flower buds; they spend the winter as pupae and emerge as caterpillars the following spring.

In some years, though, holly blues can be hard to find, whereas in others they seem to be everywhere. These fluctuations, over a cycle of five or six years or so, are caused by a small parasitic wasp called *Listrodomus*, which injects the caterpillar with a long sting-like ovipositor. The *Listrodomus* grub lives inside the caterpillar, but keeps it alive long enough to allow it to pupate, emerging later from the chrysalis. As wasp populations increase, they reduce the holly blues. Fewer butterflies mean fewer opportunities for the wasps and so, in turn, wasp numbers fall too. This allows the butterflies to build up again, and that's why over a span of several years our sightings of holly blues go up and down.

LULWORTH SKIPPER
14 August

For a brief period at the height of summer, one of Britain's rarest butter-flies takes to the air, fluttering along the Dorset coast in tens of thousands. So why, when I visit the picturesque village of Lulworth in search of its eponymous skipper, do I find it so hard to see a single one?

After all, conditions do seem ideal. It's the middle of August, the height of the skippers' short flight-season. The weather is fine: after a grey start, the sun has come out and the temperature is warming up nicely. The wind has dropped – like many butterflies, Lulworth skippers tend to hide out of sight during a stiff breeze. And other grassland butterflies are already on the wing. Chalkhill blues flit over the flower-rich clifftops, while strikingly piebald marbled whites bob over bird's-foot trefoil, stopping from time to time to feed.

I walk slowly up the hillside, focusing my eyes firmly on the cropped grass a few feet in front of me. For the Lulworth skipper is not only small, but also much harder to see than its larger, showier cousins. Like all the 'golden skippers' it looks very like a moth, and holds its triangular wings flat when perched, which makes it easy to miss.

Finally I spot a skipper. But the wings are too plain, too pale and too even in shade. A closer look confirms that this is a small skipper, a common species found on rough grassland across much of lowland England and Wales.

I trudge onwards and upwards. As I reach the top of the slope, the sun disappears behind a cloud, and a gust blows across the grass like a wave over the open sea. My chances of seeing the Lulworth skipper are fading fast. But then, another tiny butterfly sweeps past me, and lands. I fumblingly focus my binoculars on this darker, olive-coloured insect. At that moment, with perfect timing, the sun emerges, and illuminates the classic 'sun-ray' pattern on the upperwings. I've found the object of my quest.

Sunshine is a recurring theme in the life of the Lulworth skipper. Although widespread in continental Europe, in Britain the species is only found along this short stretch of the Dorset coast. Here, the warmer, sunnier microclimate suits both adults and caterpillars, which, once hatched, feast on the tender young blades of tor grass, before pupating.

Originally identified in Germany, it was first found in Britain when a wealthy entomologist, James Charles Dale, stumbled across it at nearby Durdle Door in August 1832. A year later, the lepidopterist John Curtis christened it the Lulworth skipper. Although unsuitable, the name stuck – indeed the Lulworth skipper has the distinction of being the only British butterfly whose name has remained unchanged since it was first given.

Literary lepidopterists might appreciate a tantalising reference in Thomas Hardy's *The Return of the Native*. The troubled hero Clym Yeobright takes solace by labouring in the summer fields, among 'strange amber-coloured butterflies which Egdon [a heath to the east of Dorchester] produced, which were never seen elsewhere'. I like to think that these 'strange butterflies' were indeed the Lulworth skippers, which continue to flutter across Hardy's Wessex landscape, well over a century later.

TERRAPINS

15 August

When I was growing up, we had the usual pets: a Scottie dog and a series of goldfish, each of which seemed to die even more quickly than its predecessor. So when my mother agreed that we could keep terrapins, I wasn't particularly hopeful that they would survive.

But they did. And like Topsy, they grow'd and grow'd: initially on flakes of fish food from the local pet shop, but soon on slabs of raw meat taken from the dog's dinner.

Years later, I came across terrapins again, this time not in a tank but in the wild. Walking around my local patch by the Thames Boat Race course, I noticed what looked like a large green dinner plate floating in the water. Curious, I took a closer look through my binoculars, and was suitably stunned at what I saw. Staring balefully at me was an adult terrapin; more specifically a red-eared slider, as this species is known back in its native North America.

As it dipped its head in and out of the water, I could make out the scarlet patches on the side of its head that give the creature its name. It looked rather benign and harmless; but the headline in the *Brighton Argus* tells a different story. 'Killer reptiles eating ducklings in Ditchling' leaves little to the imagination, and is not entirely inaccurate: these creatures are sometimes partial to a duckling or two, though they usually feed on aquatic invertebrates or pondweed.

But where did these apparently wild terrapins come from? It all began back in the late 1980s, at the height of the *Teenage Mutant Ninja Turtles* craze. These were characters from a children's TV series, improbably named after four Renaissance artists: Raphael, Michelangelo, Donatello and Leonardo. All over Britain children begged, cajoled, wheedled and whinged at their parents, pleading to keep terrapins as pets. You can see why: when young these reptiles are intricately marbled with shades of green, and those narrow yellow markings along the sides of the neck look like go-faster stripes.

Unfortunately, terrapins don't stay small and cute for long, and you can't keep a creature the size of a dinner-plate in a tiny plastic tank. So long-suffering parents soon decided to rid their homes of these bad-tempered reptiles, some dumping them straight into the nearest pond.

These creatures, whose native home is the Mississippi Delta and the Gulf of Mexico, might have been expected to perish in the chilly British winter. But they are tougher than they look, and have managed to survive. Today, more than a quarter of a century after the *Ninja Turtles* craze came to an end, they can be found in waterways up and down the country.

As I watched this animal sunning itself, I suddenly remembered what had happened to my own pet terrapins. When they grew too large for comfort, my mother heard that a major frozen food manufacturer just down the road was offering to take the animals and put them in a tank in the foyer of its HQ. That may well have been true; all I can say is that I never ate another fish finger again.

GIANT HOGWEED

16 August

Among the pages of the *BSBI News*, the members' magazine of the Botanical Society of the British Isles, you don't expect to see postcards of bikini-clad young women. The sirens in this case were draped among the stems of giant hogweed on an island in northern Scandinavia, advertising the delights of holidaying near the Arctic Circle. Their charms were lost on the *BSBI* editor, who drily remarked that these beauties had clearly not heard of photo-allergic reactions.

It's a fair point. Giant hogweed stems and leaves contain toxic compounds called furocoumarins, which react when exposed to sunlight causing weals, blisters and eczema-like rashes on human skin. For this reason, the plant is listed as a threat to human health under the Wildlife and Countryside Act 1981 and it is illegal to introduce it into the wild.

When you first see a grove of these enormous plants in full bloom, with stems than can reach five metres high, supporting the cart-wheel-sized clusters of flowers, it's hard not to be impressed. That sense of awe has probably eclipsed giant hogweed's ability to cause the rashes, technically known as phyto-photodermatitis. Certainly the condition seems to have been glossed over by the Victorians. Instead they were seduced by the plant's architectural splendours and it was imported from its native Caucasus in the early eighteenth century as a dramatic orna-ment to large gardens and country estates. A single plant can produce 100,000 penny-sized seeds, so its cultivation was hardly a problem, but containment certainly was. Although the first record of giant hogweed in the wild was in 1828, it didn't become widely established until the early twentieth century, by which time its blistering effect was attracting more attention.

Now this botanical colossus is well naturalised throughout the British Isles and has so far resisted attempts to control it. Recent research shows that we have not one, but two species of giant hogweed at large here. Together they are among the most wonderfully theatrical plants in our countryside and good nectar-providers for pollinating insects too. With the help of a stepladder it would be good to find out which bees, wasps and other pollinators were visiting the hogweed: but please, don't try this in swimwear.

BOTTLENOSE DOLPHINS
17 August

The *oohs* and *aahs* from the crowd are almost reverent in their air of suppressed excitement and delight, as the dolphins leap right out of the water before plunging back down with a mighty splash. But this is no circus act or marine park – but real, wild bottlenose dolphins chasing salmon in Scotland's Moray Firth. The crowds that have gathered here with me on a fine August day have come to witness one of the most impressive wildlife spectacles anywhere in Britain.

At least 130 bottlenose dolphins live here in the Moray Firth, the most northerly resident population of this species anywhere in the world. They are also the largest of their kind, reaching lengths of four metres, far longer than the usual two and a half metres. They're also noticeably plump, because these dolphins need a thick layer of blubber beneath their skin to keep them warm in these chilly North Sea waters.

The best moment to witness the display of these mighty cetaceans varies from day to day, as it is governed not by time, but tide. Roughly an hour after low tide, just as the waters begin to surge back in from the sea and up the Moray Firth towards Inverness, the dolphins start to appear. They are attracted by shoals of Atlantic salmon, which they catch by chasing them down in teams, as befits such an intelligent creature. I have once seen the dolphins shoot vertically out of the water and dive back in, as if celebrating their success at hunting, but today I make do with more standard views of them breaching the waves like giant penguins.

They aren't the only marine mammals found here: I've seen common dolphins, harbour porpoises and once just missed an elusive minke whale. But the leaping bottlenose dolphins remain the star attraction – and are well worth the journey.

BEE-WOLVES

18 August

Climate change provokes mixed feelings among naturalists. While northern or mountain species risk being pushed out by climbing temperatures and changing weather patterns, the picture is very different for southern species that are now colonising the British Isles. One of the most charismatic of these is the bee-wolf.

Bee-wolves are black and yellow solitary wasps about as long as the social wasps that annoy us at picnics, but more slender and with bigger heads. As recently as the 1970s they were among our very rarest insects,

confined to a handful of southern sites. Since then, they have spread as
far north as Lancashire and Yorkshire and west into South Wales and
are now well established over large areas.

To my delight, bee-wolves turned up on a local common in the late
1990s where they dug their burrows in the warm, red sand. A circlet of
excavated sand marks each burrow, which is dug by the female and is
about forty centimetres deep. Several chambers open off the main burrow
and in each of these the bee-wolf would lay an egg. Many females dig
burrows in favoured areas of well-drained light soil: last summer they
even chose a sandy lawn by a main road opposite a local hospital in the
heart of town.

I waited for a wolf to fly in. Its speed was slower than I'd imagined,
but I soon discovered why. Slung beneath its undercarriage was a
honeybee weighing as much as itself. It had ambushed the bee by waiting
cat-like on a nearby patch of flowers. After delivering a paralysing sting,
it had sucked any residual nectar from its victim's jaws and was now
about to stock its larder. After a few aerial circuits, the heavily freighted
wasp found its burrow and was gone. Below ground, it would lay one
egg, maybe two on the living but paralysed bee and seal the chamber.
When the wolf-grubs hatched they would feast on their huge meal,
spending winter and spring dormant, ready to emerge in high summer.

Bee-wolves intrigued the great animal behaviourist Niko Tinbergen,
who was eager to know how the wasps found their own burrows in
Dutch heathland colonies where the landscape was fairly uniform. By
placing objects near nest burrows, he discovered that the insects were
using landmarks, such as pine cones or large stones as guidelines. In
one experiment he placed a ring of pine cones around a burrow during
wet weather when the wasps were underground. When the wasps first
emerged they reconnoitred the area before they went hunting. After they
left, Niko and his researchers moved the ring of cones away from the
real burrow. Most of the returning wasps came back, not to the nests
they'd left, but to the ring of cones, proving that their latest recce, in
one case as quickly as six seconds, was enough information to allow
them to re-find their burrows.

Bee-wolves have little if any effect on the health of a beehive: all their
hunting is done among the late summer flowers where Niko Tinbergen
found that they recognise honeybees by sight and scent. Wasp-watching

may not catch on, but it deserves to; if you're lucky enough to live near a colony, it's addictive.

BUTTERFLY INVASIONS

19 August

On a warm summer's afternoon, most garden butterflies either flit from flower to flower, or perch momentarily to reveal their identity. So when a butterfly zooms straight past me, going hell for leather before disappearing into the far distance, I immediately realise that it's something out of the ordinary.

I catch a flash of custard colour as it vanishes behind the hedgerow, helping me to identify it as a clouded yellow. Soon afterwards a smaller, more elegant butterfly flashes past too: a painted lady. Both these are, like the red admiral, migrants, coming all the way from Spain, Portugal or even North Africa.

Sometimes they do stop to feed, and I can take a closer look. The clouded yellow, as its name suggests, is butter-coloured – gaudier, darker and richer in tone than our only other yellow butterfly, the brimstone – with black edges to its wings.

The painted lady looks like a more elegant, subtle cousin of the red admiral, with paler, more restrained tones of orange, white and black, and longer, narrower wings, enabling it to fly thousands of miles with apparent ease.

Both these butterflies flitting across my lawn began life several months ago, somewhere around the Mediterranean, where they hatched out of their pupae and began to feed on nectar in the spring sunshine.

Then, in response to some unseen signal, they headed north, crossing continental Europe before reaching the Channel. This is no barrier to them, as they are easily able to cross even broad stretches of water on their delicate-looking but deceptively strong wings.

But these two, unlike the red admiral, which turns up regularly each spring, are fickle little creatures. During most summers, I may see only a handful of either species. But once in a while they invade in their tens of thousands – or in the case of the celebrated 'Painted lady summer' of 2009, in tens of millions. During that glorious August, these beautiful creatures were simply everywhere. Then, as summer turned into autumn, they disappeared: some flying back across the Channel, while the rest eventually perished. Like a dream, that memorable summer was over, and the next year painted ladies were, as usual, few and far between.

DODDERS

20 August

A fuzzy red tangle among gorse on a heath or pink threads draped over riverside nettles catch the eye, but don't immediately suggest a plant. A web made by a particularly large spider, perhaps? Or an especially virulent fungal infection? In fact, these are dodders, an unruly mass of writhing stems and nodes that could have been designed by pop-artist Ralph Steadman, and are some of the strangest plants in the British countryside.

Dodders, known in the US as strangleweed, love vine and devil's hair, have no green pigment. They don't need it because they draw their nutrients from the stems of their host plants. On heaths, the common dodder attaches itself to gorse or heather. By lowland river valleys, the rarer greater dodder feeds on nettle-stems, but will ramble from its holdfast to suck the sap of neighbouring plants too. There is also an introduced yellow dodder from continental Europe, which feeds mainly on clover: I've only seen it once, looking from a distance as if a cotton-reel has unspooled in the middle of a field. Harmless here, but in parts of North America dodders can be a pest of crops such as tomatoes.

Look closely at the Gordian knots of stems and you'll see the tiny scale-like leaves and clusters of tiny whitish flowers. Dodder seeds can survive for decades in the soil, germinating when they sense the presence of a suitable host. The young seedlings have to find a home within a few days or they will die.

Speeded up by time-lapse photography the thread-like young plant gropes wildly in search of a host. When it finds one, it lassos it with a couple of stabilising coils and starts to put down foundations. Root-like structures called haustoria invade the host's tissues and tap into sap streams. Once the union is complete, the dodder's roots shrivel and it becomes entirely dependent on its new support system.

In the quantities we're likely to meet them in the British Isles, dodders don't seem to damage their hosts and indeed are declining in many places so finding a patch of these incredible string plants is a cause for celebration. Look for them in late summer and early autumn as you stroll over a local heath or along a riverbank.

LONG-EARED OWL

21 August

One of the joys of birding is that however experienced you think you are, birds never lose the capacity to surprise. So it was that on a warm, muggy August day I had one of the strangest avian encounters of my life.

I was sauntering around my coastal patch, where the three rivers of the Brue, Parrett and Huntspill meet. Just back from the coast, a long strip of grass had been allowed to go to seed, forming an ad hoc wild-flower meadow, which on a sunny day attracted a host of grassland butterflies. Among the commoner meadow browns and gatekeepers I detected two smaller specimens, which on close examination with a magnifying glass turned out to be Essex skippers. In a messy patch of hawthorn and brambles I saw a flash of azure and white – a holly blue, accompanied by two or three larger common blues.

While I was looking at these, a sound of urgently twittering swallows made me look up – and just as I did so a male peregrine flew past, giving brief but excellent views. Surely things couldn't get any better. But then they did.

After the peregrine moved on, I had turned my attention back to the butterflies, when a movement at the corner of my eye made me look up again. To my astonishment, an owl was flying straight past me, barely a few yards away. Once again, the swallows went ballistic.

As well as being surprised, I was also baffled. It was clearly not a barn or little owl – too dark and too big; so it surely must be a tawny. But something about its demeanour – the small, compact size, orange fringes to the feathers and overall 'feel' – simply did not compute.

Then it dawned on me. This was a long-eared owl, our most nocturnal member of its family, disturbed from its daytime roost in the dense, scrubby hawthorn hedgerow. It was only later that I recalled that when in flight, long-eared owls flatten their ear tufts, so that their head appears rounded. The bird then flew over the river, pursued by a phalanx of agitated swallows, and plummeted into an equally dense hedge on the opposite bank – never to be seen again.

REDSTART PASSAGE

22 August

At this time of year there's a special place on my local patch that I visit to look and listen for redstarts. It's a suite of narrow pastures, grazed by skewbald ponies and walled in by tall hedges of hawthorn and elder. Ragwort thrives here and white bryony festoons the old bushes.

Within a few minutes of arriving, I've been spotted: there's a penetrating, upslurred whistle – *hoo-it* – that manages to be alarm and query at the same time. It's a sound that I await with anticipation every August: redstarts are heading home.

Although the best places to see these spectacular summer migrants in the breeding season are in the north and west of the British Isles, in late summer and early autumn there's a chance of crossing paths with one almost anywhere. Between July and late September, they filter south and east through a network of hedgerows until they reach the coast, from where they push south through France, Spain and into sub-Saharan Africa.

Today I intercept four of them, flitting ahead along the ragged hedgerow and flirting around the base of a pylon, their fiery tails quivering. There's a controlled urgency in this trembling motion, as if they are bursting with energy, impatient to be on the move. Three are brownish females, but a male is still in summer plumage, his black mask contrasting with a dazzling white forehead, shining out among the bramble leaves like a Davy lamp. They call incessantly, darting to grab insects from the ground, skirmishing with a resident robin, which seems clumsy by comparison. No wonder the writer Tim Dee says, 'the redstart is all I need in a bird'.

Every year, without fail, redstarts will illuminate these hedges, joined once the elderberries ripen by skulking lesser whitethroats and young spotted flycatchers, which sally out from twigs to snap up passing insects. Without ringing the birds, I can't tell how long each individual stays. There might be a steady trickle of redstarts passing through during late summer or some birds may linger for weeks to refuel for the long journey ahead.

What's important is that the overgrown hedgerows are there to sustain them with insects at this important stage of their lives. I don't know where they have bred – far up in a Scottish glen perhaps, or in an airy Welsh oak wood – but their annual appearance in the dog days of summer is as much part of my ornithological calendar as the arrival of swallows in spring or redwings in autumn.

HAWKER DRAGONFLIES

23 August

In mid-morning, as the warmth begins to rise from the ground, I start to see them: singles at first, then duelling pairs, and finally whole squadrons of these huge, streamlined insects, buzzing around the late summer sky like planes at an air show.

They are southern hawker dragonflies: among the largest and most impressive of their kind, with a body length of almost eight centimetres.

Southern hawkers fly fast and high, though they have the good manners to stop motionless in mid-air from time to time to stare at me, as if inspecting this human invader into their territory. This habit gives me the chance to admire the male's apple-green and bright-blue markings, and the female's green and brown ones.

In late summer, the southern hawkers may be joined by their relatives, including the brown hawker, whose delicate golden-brown wings glow in the sunshine like an illuminated medieval manuscript.

But on sunny days at the end of August, the southern hawker takes pride of place. For the next few weeks, as summer nears its end, they rule the skies like majestic birds of prey, cruising up and down in search of insects on which they feed.

As I watch, in a split second one turns, dashes and dives, grabbing a smaller creature in mid-air and despatching it with those tiny talons: as fine an example of hunting skills as you will find anywhere in nature.

WASP SPIDER

24 August

A creature that conflates two of our most urgent fears, arachnophobia and the threat of being envenomed, is spreading through southern England. On heaths and in patches of rough grassland, as summer wanes, the wasp spider spins her web between plant stems.

Spread-eagled and motionless at the centre of its creation, a full-grown female brings you up sharp, enough to produce an audible gasp. It is completely harmless, but even so this wonderful spider provokes in me an atavistic reaction, which I find hard to rationalise. Maybe it's the impressive leg-span and those warning colours that raise the hairs on my nape. Simultaneously I'm thrilled when I see one and jealous of those who have it in their gardens.

With a few exceptions, most British spiders are subdued in colour. Wasp spiders are outrageously marked. Males are small and insignificant, but the much bulkier females, their abdomens up to fifteen millimetres or more across, are as jazzily patterned as 1970s wallpaper, in horizontal stripes of black, yellow and white. They hang head-down in their webs which contain a zigzag weave of denser silk known as a stabilimentum, which some naturalists think reflects light in the ultraviolet spectrum (which insects can see) to dazzle potential prey. Grasshoppers and crickets are favourite foods and so the web is placed at leaping height among the grass stalks.

I saw my first wasp spiders one late August day a few years ago, at a Shropshire nature reserve, where they lurked among brambles and knapweed stalks along a fence-line. They caused excitement locally because at this site, not far from Shrewsbury, they were on the north-western frontier of a rapidly expanding range.

Wasp spiders were first seen in England in East Sussex in 1922, having arrived either as wind-borne spiderlings from France or as accidental introductions. For many years they stayed in the south, but during the 1970s began to move north and west, so that now they have colonised many areas around London and are along much of the south coast as far west as Cornwall and the Isles of Scilly.

Warmer winters may have allowed the eggs in their brown flask-shaped egg-sacs to survive further north, and since the 1990s there's been a swift expansion in range, with spiders reaching Derbyshire. So far, they've skipped over Worcestershire, but at this time of year I prowl the local commons in hope: it's only a matter of time.

ELDERBERRIES AND BLACK TERNS

25 August

I remember the day as if it were yesterday. An August bank holiday when I was eleven years old: hot and sultry, the perfect weather to lounge around in the garden, or go and play football with my mates.

But my mother had other plans. Down at our local gravel-pits, the elder bushes were hung with bunches of berries almost as big as grapes. It was time to go elderberry-picking.

I always rued the fact that while elderberries – plump and purple, and perfectly formed – look temptingly delicious, they are actually bitter and tasteless. Yet my mother had, like others before her, discovered that they make a deep-red wine the colour and consistency of a fine claret. So, just three months after we had come here to pick bunches of elderflowers (to make white wine), we were back with our baskets.

During the next two hours, my fingers became stained with blackish purple as I picked bunch after bunch of the succulent fruits. Pleading exhaustion, I was allowed a short break and, picking up my binoculars, I scanned the water looking for great crested grebes.

As I did so, a pair of birds flew across my view, floating above the water on long, elegant wings before dipping down to grab an unseen morsel from the surface. I realised they were black terns, a scarce passage migrant on their way from their breeding grounds in central or eastern Europe, passing through south-east England before turning left towards Africa.

I watched as these graceful birds – themselves the colour of bruised elderberries – fed for a few minutes before heading onwards. Then I returned to my task, reinvigorated by this unexpected encounter.

BECHSTEIN'S BAT

26 August

A new local mammal is always a big event, especially if it's a native species. As we sloshed along woodland rides, porridgey after rain, there was a tingle in the air. Ahead were points of light in the blackness, the head torches of bat-workers surveying for one of our rarest and most elusive mammals: Bechstein's bat.

No bats are an easy study for the casual naturalist, but this big-eared forest-lover has a reputation for being ultra-secretive. All bats can be frustrating, flickering haunters of the dusk, which usually appear at the limits of our aural and visual perception. We can take an informed guess at identifying some species. Large bats flying high with swifts on summer evenings are likely to be noctules, whereas the tiny, fast-flying species that whizz around the house or along local lanes are probably pipistrelles, though even this, our commonest bat, is now split into two species based on the frequency of its ultrasonic calls.

Bats use ultrasound to locate their prey, which is why they can feed in pitch-darkness. To get to grips with many species, you need a bat detector, which converts the animal's calls into sounds that we can hear. Bechstein's bat doesn't play by the rules though, because it often gleans its prey from the surface of leaves under the woodland canopy and uses low-intensity calls, 'whispering' rather than 'shouting' ultrasonically.

There are about 1,500 Bechstein's bats in England (none as far as we know elsewhere in the British Isles), but until a national survey between 2007 and 2011 their distribution was uncertain, because the bats avoided mist nets or harp traps put up along rides to catch them. The break-through came when bat biologists synthesised the social calls of the bats and played the simulated sounds in potentially suitable breeding woods. These acoustic lures, holding the promise of a liaison, were attractive to the bats, which then flew into the traps.

The wood I visited in Worcestershire is the northernmost Bechstein's breeding wood in England, and tonight torchlit shapes huddled along the rides: specially trained Bat Group members poised for action. When the moment of truth arrived, there was little preamble; suddenly a bat flew into a three-storey mist net that towered high into the canopy.

The net was lowered and the animal disentangled: a Bechstein's, its beady eyes peering from between the fingers of its captor. To me, it looked like a long-eared bat, with outsize canoe-shaped ears far too large for such a tiny creature. But, I was told, the ears of a Bechstein's bat meet at the base, whereas those of long-eared bats are separated. That established, my time with this small, quivering morsel was limited: its vital statistics had to be taken and processed quickly before it was released back into darkness.

I may never see another in my life, but I left with a satisfying feeling on that muggy August night, knowing that as a result of the surveys the Bechstein's woods will be managed to provide feeding and roosting areas for generations to come.

PELAGIC TRIP

27 August

While families relax on the beach, soaking up the August sun, some birders find it hard to stay on terra firma. Offshore seabirds are streaming away from their breeding colonies and heading out into the open ocean, and to see them close up, you need to join a pelagic trip.

That's why a few years ago, one August morning I stood shivering on a Penzance quay at 5 a.m. with over 400 other early-risers, waiting to board the *Scillonian III*. The *Scillonian* usually plies between Penzance and the Isles of Scilly but had been specially chartered to take us on a day-trip into the Western Approaches in search of rare seabirds.

As light dawned and we left the harbour, a Force Six was blowing, enough to make some people queasy. One unfortunate birder fell down a flight of stairs and had to be unloaded at St Mary's on Scilly to receive hospital treatment. A few others took the chance to disembark here, but most of us were determined to press on. So far we'd glimpsed gannets and gulls from the heaving deck but not much else.

All changed when the buckets of chum appeared. Seabirds are suckers for fish offal, and while this malodorous mixture does little for churned-up stomachs, it draws in birds from miles around. One of the sought-after species was Wilson's petrel, a tiny black and white bird even smaller than a starling, which breeds in the South Atlantic during our winter.

Its diminutive size and habit of feeding in the open ocean make it very hard to see from land and so it's always a popular pelagic species.

Petrels have a powerful sense of smell and use the large olfactory bulb in their brain to locate offal floating on the sea's surface over astonishing distances. Within a few minutes of the chum hitting the water, the first petrels appeared, sideslipping into the wave troughs and pattering with lowered feet on the crests. Over 300 birds assembled, but all seemed to be storm petrels. A few hopeful birders claimed that a Wilson's was among them, but picking out the square-ended tail and the yellow webs on its feet were beyond me: remaining vertical was the main challenge. Wilson's or not, the assembling of these wonderful birds from a roiling ocean was exciting enough, but there was better to come.

Manx shearwaters and gannets were in constant attendance off the stern and, as we tried to focus on them, breathing in a mixture of rotting fish and engine fumes, two darker shapes materialised among the melee. They had long slender wings and dark caps and had travelled thousands of miles north from their nesting colonies on Tristan da Cunha. They were my first great shearwaters, superb aeronauts, which glided effortlessly among their relatives.

Views were broken every few seconds as the boat lurched downwards, followed by a chance to relocate them when the *Scillonian* found a wave crest. Standing in tiered ranks, we shouted our approval above the roar of the sea. When we reached the shore, fourteen hours later, we were weak at the knees for more reasons than one.

IVY-LEAVED TOADFLAX

28 August

Any plant growing in cracks in a vertical surface is faced with a fundamental problem: how to provide the next generation with a foothold. Heavy seeds will simply fall off a wall on to the ground, and light, flimsy seeds will blow away in the wind.

Some wall plants, like the yellow corydalis, whose toothbrush-like flower spikes nestle among cushions of ferny foliage, have an ingenious solution. Their comparatively heavy black seeds are capped with a pale blob of protein called an elaiosome, which is a delicacy for ants. To enjoy it, the ants carry the seeds to a crack in the wall, unintentionally planting it while they tuck in to the edible bribe.

Another plant native to the Himalayas is the butterfly bush, *Buddleia davidii*, which often escapes from our gardens where we first introduced it in the late nineteenth century. Buddleia opts for quantity over quality: each plant produces a miniature dust-storm of hundreds of thousands of seeds which whirl across our towns and cities. It's a hit-and-miss approach, but by the law of averages some will land in mortar cracks, which are a perfect substitute for Himalayan cliffs and chasms.

One plant, however, which flowers on walls throughout spring and summer, has an apparently perverse, but remarkably successful, way of finding a foothold for its seedlings. Ivy-leaved toadflax is a native of the Mediterranean basin, but was introduced to the British Isles around 400 years ago: some say it was brought in with slabs of Italian marble, others that it was deliberately imported as a rock garden plant. It's certainly an attractive plant, its three-lobed mauve snapdragon-shaped flowers held on trailing stalks above leaves webbed like tiny ducks' feet.

It has spread rapidly and now grows throughout the British Isles. One measure of its popularity is the directory of folk names it has garnered, among them wandering sailor, roving jenny and mother of thousands, all of which refer to its trailing stems, which invade mortar seams by travelling along and under the skin of old walls.

But this continental rock-lover has another dispersal card to play. Most flowers are heliotropic – they lean towards the sun and continue to do so when they seed. But after flowering and fertilisation, the toadflax's flower-stalks elongate as if made of elastic, and turn away from sunlight. This photophobic behaviour takes the seed-capsules into dark cracks in the wall where they rupture and release the seeds to germinate in pockets of moisture and nutrients. It's a neat trick, rare among British plants, but is clearly a successful strategy for this delicate-looking flower.

WHINCHATS AND WHEATEARS
29 August

'I've taken this photo of a bird and I'm not sure what it is.' So said Mick, my new neighbour, not long after we moved down to Somerset.

When I took a look, I could see why he was confused. It was a female wheatear – whose sandy colour and lack of obvious field marks (apart from when she flies to reveal her snow-white rump) can be confusing.

My neighbour seemed pleased with the answer; as was I when he told me where he had seen the bird: only a mile or so behind my home, on Blackford Moor. A few minutes later I had cycled round, to be greeted by not one but three wheatears, including a splendid male with his black bandit-mask.

I was about to return home when I noticed another, smaller bird – plump, short-tailed and perched bolt upright on a hay-bale. Even before I raised my binoculars I knew its identity; no other bird but a whinchat has quite the same pose. As the late August sunshine illuminated the bird from above, I could see the yellow-ochre breast, mottled brown back and flash of creamy white above the eye of a stunning male whinchat. Looking around, there were no fewer than ten of these charming little birds, stopping off to feed on the way south to winter on the African savannah.

A notable gathering; though just thirty years ago whinchats didn't just stop off here on the Somerset Levels: they bred here too, in good numbers. Today, none do so.

It was the mass conversion from hay to silage that did for the whinchat. The earlier harvesting of the grass meant that the fields were no longer suitable for them to nest, as there were far fewer insects on which to feed their chicks. So today we think of the whinchat as an upland bird – simply because the lowlands where they used to breed have become a no-go zone.

I like to think that one day the whinchat will return to breed here on the Levels; in the meantime, we have to make do with the occasional spring and autumn sighting. Yet another way in which our experience of the natural world is being impoverished.

NIGHT WOODS

30 August

Every year, I make at least one night-time expedition into the local woods with friends. We're not bat-watchers burdened with the latest acoustic paraphernalia; we don't even take a moth trap. All we have are hope and head torches.

When the last light has leached away and the jagged outline of the conifer-tops is blunted by the night sky, we are struck by the stillness. These August nights can be very quiet, though at one point we hear a couple of complaining tawny owls.

Unexpectedly, in the darkness we see birds. At first we're mystified by a ball of feathers, at eye-level in a small tree-crevice, which doesn't move as we approach. No beak, wing or eye is visible, but we take a guess at a roosting chiffchaff. It isn't going to budge, so we leave it to its slumber. Under a new bridge over the brook our torch-beams pick out a dipper on a metal support, its white shirt-front gleaming in the light. Rather than fly into the dark, it stays put, even though people are walking overhead. I'd heard stories – and been sceptical – of dipper-ringers in Shropshire who'd claimed to be able to pluck the birds like fruit from their winter roosts and replace them after ringing. Now I see that these tall tales were true.

We tread gingerly along the forest roads to avoid crushing toads. Most we see are very small and were tadpoles a few months ago: they're now looking for insect meals to boost their weight before they enter hibernation. There are plenty of commuters along the tracks. Ground beetles scurry in search of worms and caterpillars. Long-legged harvestmen stilt-walk in our torchlight, casting freakish shadows. On a pile of deer-dung, we find two heavily armoured dor-beetles. These large scarabs feed on dung and decaying material, but are beautifully coloured, their undersides gleaming with metallic violet tints.

The forest is alive with vertical commuters too. Creatures that we rarely see by day are scurrying or crawling up the tree-trunks. Millipedes ascend slowly, their fringe of pale legs moving in a Mexican wave as they rove in search of algae on the tree bark. Slugs are everywhere on this humid night. Tree slugs, also algae feeders, are grey and stripy and climb as high as our torches can pick them out. On a stout oak trunk, we disturb two ash-black slugs in flagrante. These are our longest British slugs and can reach twenty centimetres: like all our land-slugs they are hermaphrodite, which means that every encounter is a potential love-match. It's something we rarely see. Their pale penises emerge just behind the head and are almost as long as the animals themselves. As we watch them entwine tenderly in our spotlights, we feel like voyeurs and so after taking a few photographs we retire, leaving them to the dark.

SWIFT

31 August

Some creatures are defined as much by their absence as presence, and the swift is one of those. Their stay with us lasts barely three months before they head southwards once again on that incredible journey back to Africa.

When I lived in the city, it was hard to connect with nature; so for me the swift was always the perfect reminder that the seasons really do change. Like a bolt from the blue, they would arrive back in the last week of April or first week of May, skidding across the urban skyline as if they'd never been away.

Now that I live in the country, I see fewer swifts; yet they remain my favourite bird – not least because their time with us coincides almost exactly with the natural season that runs from late spring into late summer, and is the most eventful and rewarding time of the year for any naturalist.

Barely a third of the year after they first arrived, they have almost all gone, having mated, nested and raised a family during their short span with us. Famously, swifts are the most aerial of all the world's birds: apart from landing to breed, they spend the rest of their lives on the wing.

So where do they go when they leave our shores? Having crossed the Mediterranean Sea and Sahara Desert they end up over equatorial and tropical Africa, from the Congo basin in the west to Malawi in the east, where they hawk for tiny insects above the jungles and savannahs, before heading back north again next spring.

Now, by late August, the vast majority of swifts have departed, and are already well to the south of here. But on a fine, sunny day I catch sight of a lone straggler, scything through the air as if striving to catch up with those that went ahead of it.

As I see this, the last swift of the year, heading south on its long journey, it's hard to resist the temptation to wave goodbye; for few birds better sum up the brevity of the British summer; and few are more welcome when they finally return, eight months hence.

SEPTEMBER

LIKE ALL MONTHS on the cusp between seasons, September is both fascinating and unpredictable for wildlife-watchers. In some years, it is simply a continuation of the summer, the warmth only gradually waning as we approach the autumn equinox two-thirds of the way through the month. In other years, autumn can arrive in force almost as soon as August ends, with Atlantic gales bringing winds, rain and sometimes floods across the country in a never-ending progression of depressions.

More than ever, you need to be ready to react to these rapidly changing events. Storms can bring unexpected avian visitors: seabirds blown inland or songbird migrants swept across the North Sea. A late summer (or early autumn) heatwave can bring a last flourish of wild flowers and insects, in a replay of Keats's 'season of mists and mellow fruitfulness'.

When it falls between these two extremes, September can also seem very quiet. Clear nights allow migrant birds to pass straight overhead without stopping, while with birdsong at an all-time low, a walk around my local patch can be a dispiriting affair – caught between the time when summer visitors have mostly departed, but the autumn arrivals are still to come. At this time of year, it can be tempting just to stay indoors and wait for the 'real autumn'; but even on the quietest day, there should be something to see – if you know how and where to look.

S.M.

A FLASH OF red 'trousers' marks the arrival of one of my September faithfuls, a sleek hobby hunting the flocks of house martins and swallows that gather to feed on insects around the local stables and are hunted in turn by this summer-visiting falcon. September sees a trickle of migrants heading through, but most, like whitethroats, seep silently away overnight – one morning they're simply gone.

Although absence marks some species, the presence of others becomes more obvious. Skylarks and meadow pipits move around the country in search of food, calling overhead as they travel in loose flocks.

Spiders, always common, but not always prominent, suddenly seem to be everywhere. Garden orb-web spiders sling their complex constructions between plants and indoors amorous long-legged house spiders scamper over the shagpile in search of a mate. Long-legged harvestmen trundle through vegetation and leaf litter and winged daddy-long-legs, properly known as crane flies, probe the meadows as they lay their eggs.

There are few flowers in bloom now but a wealth of berries: elderberries, blackberries, the scarlet chains of white and black bryony in hedgerows and the gaudy pink and orange berries of spindle. Apple trees are laden with fruit and tempt the garden blackbirds back into the open after a few weeks of seclusion while they've been moulting and growing new feathers.

B.W.

WART-BITER CRICKET

1 September

It was the first day of September, gloriously sunny, and my second visit to this sheltered combe in Wiltshire. Among entomologists, this is a hallowed place because it's one of only a handful of locations in the British Isles for wart-biters. These enormous crickets are sun-lovers, and require intensive care to provide the precise conditions they need: old grazed downland that features patches of sun-warmed, bare ground and longer tufts of grass where they lay their eggs, a habitat supplied here by the National Trust.

I'd first been here in 2011 with the Trust's ecologist Matthew Oates to record a radio programme about the wart-biter, but although conditions were fine and we saw Adonis blue butterflies, each one looking like a fragment of the late summer skies, the crickets wouldn't play ball.

Matthew explained why they have such a bizarre name: they eat other insects as well as vegetation and their powerful mandibles were reputedly used in Sweden for chewing off warts.

According to Matthew, wart-biters were scarcer in 'odd years', so the following September I made the trip with an orthopterist friend Gary. We set out with high hopes, treading carefully on sloping sides of the combe as we followed narrow terraces worn by countless generations of sheep.

Livestock numbers here are managed carefully to provide the right grazing for wart-biters – and suddenly there was one, squatting toad-like on the bare track. Its body armour was shiny – almost plastic-looking – the colour of Astroturf flecked with black, so that it looked unreal as it crouched motionless. This was an impressively large cricket, a paunchy Falstaffian insect with a long, scimitar-like ovipositor that identified it as a female.

She allowed us to take photographs – perhaps she was too fat to hop – then we withdrew and listened for others using a bat detector: neither Gary nor I can rely on natural hearing to locate crickets any more, though they're perfectly audible to most people under forty-five or so. The reeling song converted to an audible signal led us to another male and then another, hiding in plain sight in hoof-holes.

In spite of their long hind legs, they showed no sign of athletic ability and I remembered Matthew's warning to look down before I placed my feet: wart-biters rely heavily on their camouflage and remaining motionless is often the best strategy to avoid the gaze of predators: a kestrel was hovering nearby.

We met two other wart-biter pilgrims paying homage and, after swapping experiences, left feeling grateful to have found the insects, but also comforted by the knowledge that they are being cossetted in a few precious corners of England.

ARCTIC WADERS

2 September

I scan a marshy pool on the Somerset Levels, which has been temporarily drained to encourage migrant waders to stop off and refuel on their long flight south. It's worked: orange-breasted black-tailed godwits from Iceland rub shoulders with redshanks, knots and ringed plovers, some of which will winter in southern Britain or France, while others travel all the way to Africa.

But a closer look reveals two scarcer and more special birds, both of which have bred way to the north. Little stints, each barely the length and weight of a robin, have just flown thousands of miles south from their breeding grounds on the Arctic tundra. The larger curlew sandpipers I'm watching have come even further, a full quarter of the globe west and south from the Yenisei Delta in remote Siberia.

I often see little stints and curlew sandpipers together, travelling companions on their epic voyage from the Arctic to Africa. The adults are the first to drop in, as they trickle through Britain during the month of August. The grey and white stints look like tiny clockwork toys, while the curlew sandpipers are more obvious, with their long, decurved bills and patches of brick-red breeding plumage still showing on their breasts and bellies.

But the main influx of these long-distance travellers comes a full month later, in the middle of September. It's now that the juveniles – born earlier this year and on their very first migration – begin to appear. Both species are far commoner in the east of the country than the west, so when I do see them here I'm always momentarily surprised.

I can easily pick out the youngsters by their fresh, neat plumage, each feather overlapping the next to create a pleasing, mosaic-like effect. The little stints have a distinct white 'V' on their back and a white eyestripe, while the curlew sandpipers also sport a white eyestripe, with a pale belly and yellow-ochre wash across the breast.

This is not only their first journey – it may also be their last. Migration has many dangers, not least running out of fuel; and so they feed frantically to build up the energy they need for the long flight ahead.

The stints probe rapidly with their bill like a sewing machine, picking up tiny insects from the surface of the mud. Their larger relatives use that longer, curved bill to probe beneath the mud or water to find worms, shrimps and snails; all of which help these birds put on a layer of fat just beneath the surface of their skin to fuel their journey.

Then, if tonight is clear, and especially when there's a full moon to guide them, they'll head off. Both little stints and curlew sandpipers are scarce in spring, so I probably won't see them again until a full year has passed and these transglobal voyagers stop off here once more.

COMMON LIZARD

3 September

Soaking up the September sunshine are a group of young common lizards. They sidle on to logs and flatten their scaly bodies against the warm wood to absorb the heat, occasionally fluttering their feet as if the surface is too hot.

They were born a month or so ago each within a soft membrane that ruptured immediately. For a cold-tolerant lizard that can survive north of the Arctic Circle, there's no time for incubating eggs: these youngsters need to be active as soon as they see daylight for the first time. One false move and they are gone in a blur, whisking back into the shelter of the heather.

The newborn lizards are black, good for absorbing heat, but as they grow their bodies become rich mahogany with a dark tail. Basking is important because their body temperature is regulated by the temperature of their surroundings: the warmer their blood, the more active they become and so are better able to hunt for prey or evade predators. They eat spiders and insects in the short run-up to hibernation, which will begin as early as mid-October.

The need to thermoregulate – to control their body temperatures – means that the largest numbers occur where they can find sunny basking spots, plenty of prey and cover to hide in. They like heaths and moors, quarries and sheltered cliffs, open woods and rough ground – which can include undisturbed places in town, such as railway cuttings. I often hear reports of common lizards in local gardens, but they invariably turn out to be newts, which can look remarkably lizard-like when they leave their breeding ponds and develop a silky feel to their skins. Unlike newts, which are amphibians, lizards have bead-like scales and sharp claws and are much less common as garden residents.

Common is not the best adjective for these lizards, though, because they avoid farmland and most built-up areas and are declining in many places. They don't travel far from their colony and once a population has been wiped out by development, there's little chance of lizards re-colonising from more than a few hundred metres away.

BROWN HAIRSTREAK

4 September

A sleepy little Worcestershire village on a fine September day, right on the cusp between late summer and early autumn. We walk across the fields from the quirky medieval church to an ancient wood, now being transformed to help one of Britain's most charismatic and elusive butterflies, the brown hairstreak.

The brown hairstreak is a paradox among its peers. It doesn't emerge until early August, later than any of our other native butterflies, and is on the wing until October, its autumnal colours blending in nicely with the season. Yet it can also be found earlier than most other butterflies, as you can come across its eggs through the winter, long before they hatch into caterpillars.

Brown hairstreaks love hedgerows; tidy-minded farmers are their nemesis, as cutting or flailing a hedge will destroy any eggs the butterfly has laid there. The hairstreaks have taken refuge in this wood, studded with oaks and aspens as well as newly grown blackthorn suckers, just a metre or so high, on which their caterpillars will feed next spring.

Looking for brown hairstreaks can be frustrating: their pale brown underwings are a remarkably similar shade to autumnal oak leaves. So we endure several false alarms, not helped by the appearance of both comma and small copper butterflies, both of which I briefly mistake for our prize.

Then a small, pale butterfly flutters up from the undergrowth and lands amid the blackthorn. Binoculars slammed into focus, I can see that this one really is a female brown hairstreak. Her wings held open, she looks rather like a smaller, darker version of the commoner gate-keeper, showing chocolate-brown upperwings with a patch of orange near the tips.

But it is when she closes her wings that she shows her true beauty. As the light shines through it reveals a shimmering golden-brown background with jagged black and white lines – the 'hairstreaks' that give this group of butterflies their name – running across her underwings.

I watch as the female crawls down the stem of the blackthorn, lays an egg, flutters to a nearby stem and repeats the process, the delicate markings on her wings again catching the light as she does so. But she can only lay her eggs with a helping hand from us, for if the blackthorn scrub grows too high she will not deign to visit.

Nearby, we come across a dedicated band of hairstreak enthusiasts, 'gardening' this ancient woodland: cutting, hacking and burning the scrub in order to create exactly the right microhabitat for this fussy little creature.

Recently the brown hairstreak had its moment in the limelight when it appeared as a character in the long-running rural radio soap *The Archers*, where it was used as a key creature in the fight against development of the countryside. But the sad truth is that Britain's farmers are at best indifferent to the plight of this delicate little butterfly; unless we can persuade them to manage their hedgerows very differently, the brown hairstreak will remain scarce and elusive for the foreseeable future.

SPECKLED WOOD

5 September

'Glory be to God for dappled things', wrote Gerard Manley Hopkins, the Victorian poet with a keen eye for the natural world. The interplay of light and shade in a leafy woodland glade on a sunny day is dappling at its finest and even in a small town garden like mine it's quite easy to recreate with a few quick-growing shrubs and plants. I have a silver birch, which rains freckled shadows over a hazel hedge where insects love to bask: the reward for this is a small colony of speckled wood butterflies.

As a child growing up in the 1960s, I don't remember seeing speckled woods locally. I first saw them on a family holiday in west Wales, flitting ahead of me through tunnels of sunlit blackthorn on a clifftop path. Over the last three decades or so, they've spread eastwards and headed north into Scotland, colonising woodlands and leafy gardens on the way.

They have an understated beauty, their khaki wings flecked with cream spots and bordered with eyespots, which make them look alert. Although they spend much time perching on leaves, the males are always on the lookout for rivals and will contest sunny spots with each other. When they clash, they ascend several metres, spiralling together in an aerial dogfight, which usually ends with the territory owner victorious (paint spots on the wings help biologists to recognise individuals). Any notion we have of butterflies being carefree and frivolous quickly evaporates when you watch these vigorous territorial disputes.

In hot sunny weather speckled woods will also patrol the trees in search of females, though as flying cools them down they need to perch regularly to raise their body temperature again. Once mated, the female lays her eggs in clumps of grass in sunny spots, where the caterpillars feed on a variety of common grasses.

I leave a small wild flower patch uncut until late autumn to encourage the butterflies to breed, and it seems to work. The result is that from April until October I have their company in dappled corners of the garden.

MEADOW PIPIT

6 September

Some bird sounds are instantly evocative: the cuckoo's song in April, the screech of swifts in the summer suburbs, and the quavering of tawny owls on a midwinter night.

But for me a much less obtrusive sound signals a change in the seasons. One day, usually in the first week of September, a thin squeak overhead marks the passing of a meadow pipit, the first of the autumn. Although they're common breeding birds in grassy places, on moors or mountainsides throughout the British Isles, these streaky and nondescript little birds are scarce breeders in my part of the West Midlands, and in most places are absent between May and August.

When I hear the flat, barely perceptible 'seep' flight call I could be anywhere: in town, in the garden or out in the open countryside. As the pipits stream south to spend the winter in open fields and on saltmarshes, they call to keep contact with each other. They usually travel in loose parties, with just a handful of birds in each, but on days of heavy passage there can be a continuous thin stream of the birds. Look up when you hear the sound, and there they are, aerial flotsam battling gamely against the cool breeze.

Sometimes they gather in larger flocks and on the Isles of Scilly, where I've spent several autumns, they range over the small bulb-fields and pastures in groups of 100 or more. They demand to be checked because these flocks can contain rarer pipits in their midst. When you scan a flock, you realise what attractive birds they are, streaky as the grass tussocks they probe for insects and spiders.

Although the pipit's call is unremarkable, it's freighted with meaning. For me and many other naturalists I know, it's a sign that summer is nearly spent, a vital ingredient in the autumnal scene. Often the first meadow pipits coincide with a rush of northern air, the ripening of fruit in local orchards and the dance of daddy-long-legs above dew-drenched grass. The pipits' arrival may occur in a blazing 'Indian summer', but is usually a herald of colder weather to come: if I'm in town when I first hear it, I check the price of scarves.

GARDEN ORB SPIDER
7 September

A misty September morning in my garden. As the rising sun slowly begins to pierce the airborne particles of moisture, it lights up a classic autumnal scene: the delicate, geometric web of the female garden orb spider, spread between two dew-laden brambles.

Like many people, my first response is an aesthetic one. How could I fail to appreciate the web's concentric patterns, so perfectly arranged like threads drooped across the spokes of a wheel? I can also appreciate its ephemeral, transient nature; for it is unlikely to last more than a few days, before becoming so damaged that the spider must spin a new one.

I see the spider, sitting plumb in the centre of her web, head facing downwards, and legs splayed across her network of silken threads. Patience is a virtue: she remains motionless until an unwary insect stumbles into the web, setting off tiny vibrations only she can detect. The response is instant: she races towards her prey, grabs it, and then wraps it up in a shroud of silken thread before feasting on its tender, juicy flesh.

This deadly but beautiful arachnid can also be a weather forecaster: if she remains in the centre of her web the coming day is supposed to be fine and sunny; whereas if she is racing up and down and making adjustments to the threads, then rain and wind are on their way. Today, she is calm; and, sure enough, it turns out to be a classic late summer day, one of the last of the year, and all the more special for that.

SILVER-Y MOTHS
8 September

A blur of grey wings among the grass stems, vibrating frantically, is likely to be a silver-Y moth warming up before it careers off to safety. Wait a moment and you may see the metallic Y-shaped mark on its sheeny forewings: its scientific name, *Autographa gamma*, is perfectly suited.

Though silver-Ys are common everywhere in the British Isles, they aren't resident here – our winters are too cold for the caterpillars to survive. Instead they are migrants, which breed across huge areas of Europe and North Africa. Each year the moths head north to colonise new habitats, laying eggs as they go. Between late spring and early autumn, the generations that have bred further south reach us and in some years can seem to be everywhere – in our gardens and parks and on farmland. In other years they are hard to find.

Because their larvae feed on grasses, including cereal crops, in big arrival years silver-Ys can be agricultural pests, so their invasions have been well studied. At Rothamsted Research Station in Hertfordshire, entomologists have been able to track the moths by using beams of vertical-looking radar – or VLR for short – which measure the movement, speed, altitude, time of day and flight direction of moths and butterflies. As well as giving an indication of how many moths are about, the VLR has shed light on the way the insects navigate. Far from being flimsy migrants at the mercy of the winds, the scientists found that silver-Ys are sophisticated navigators, which use air currents to find the fastest and most direct route.

When the wind is against them, they remain grounded, but with the right conditions they can travel faster than migrating birds. How they plan their route isn't known, but, like birds, they probably use the earth's magnetic field as a guide.

The story doesn't end there. These migrant moths aren't wasting their efforts by coming to our cold islands whose winters would be fatal. Thanks to research conducted at the University of York, we now know that large numbers of silver-Ys, which are the children or grandchildren of those spring pioneers, head back south in late summer and autumn: radar tracking has shown that more leave our islands in autumn than arrived in spring. Although their parents or grandparents have died, these newer generations are now heading home on an autumn breeze to enjoy a frost-free winter.

CORNFIELD PLANTS
9 September

As I gaze across a field of gently waving corn on a warm early September evening, the straw-coloured crops look as if they have been daubed with bright-red paint. The corn poppies are in bloom.

And yet however permanent this scene may appear, and however evocative of the British countryside, it is not exactly 'natural'. Corn arrived here from mainland Europe with the first Neolithic farmers roughly 5,000 years ago and the poppies came with it: tiny black seeds smaller even than a pinhead, hidden among the grain.

The poppy may be the gaudiest and best known of these 'arable weeds', but it wasn't the only one. Several other attractive wild flowers, such as the corncockle and cornflower, came too, spreading their way across Europe from their original home around the shores of the Mediterranean, thanks to those early farmers.

For thousands of years they flourished, and even as recently as my grandparents' day they would have been a common sight among the wheat and barley. The cornflower's blue flower heads were once so widespread it had more than two dozen folk names. But only a couple of generations later, this precious flower has vanished from the countryside, hanging on in only a handful of carefully managed meadows.

It's not the only one: the corncockle, whose pinkish-mauve flowers once too graced our rural fields, is now virtually extinct. They have both fallen victim to new and more efficient ways of sorting seeds and grains, and to the widespread use of chemical herbicides.

Apart from the pleasure we used to get from finding these colourful blooms on a country walk, why do these 'weeds' matter? Because their seeds are a crucial source of food for farmland birds such as finches, buntings and especially the grey partridge, which is declining rapidly because its food supply is no longer available.

The one exception to the declines of our arable flowers is the poppy, still a common late summer sight across most of lowland Britain. The reason for its survival is that poppy seeds can stay dormant in the soil until disturbed – for instance by the plough – following which they bloom in their thousands.

This ability to miraculously appear, together with a long history of symbolism going back several thousand years, explains why the poppy is such a potent emblem of the death and suffering associated with the First World War. As the fields of Flanders were turned into a sea of mud, the poppy was one of the few flowers able to survive and bloom again. And so, each November, we wear red poppies in memory of the millions who died in this and other conflicts.

ROESEL'S BUSH-CRICKET

10 September

It takes some time to realise what I'm hearing. The sound I'm straining to catch is masked by the whisper of the breeze percolating through a sea of grass stems. A burst of sunshine and suddenly it's louder, a thin metallic reeling, like the static buzz from overhead power cables. But even now the sound-thread needs unbraiding from the mild tinnitus that's beginning to afflict this middle-aged cricket fan.

This is the cricket season and that high-pitched reel is the love-song of Roesel's bush-cricket, a new and exciting insect to look – and listen – for as summer slides into autumn. It's particularly welcome to people in their fifties and older for whom – like me – high-frequency sounds are slipping away; the tinny bickering of hedgerow shrews and the echo-locating clicks of noctule bats are a fading memory. But with some relief, I defer decline for another day. Roesel's bush-cricket is still audible; my ears haven't deteriorated quite that far and there's life in the old naturalist yet.

For me, living in the English West Midlands, the song is a very modern consolation, an acquaintance built over the last few years. This big glossy-brown insect, with its creamy go-faster stripes, is on the march. Once it lurked in a few eastern saltmarshes, but by the end of the last century it had embarked on a dramatic northward extension of its range. Since then it has come on in leaps and bounds. No one can be sure why, but it's likely that warmer winters are helping the eggs to survive.

Leaps and bounds isn't the whole story though. A small percentage of each Roesel's bush-cricket population have extra-long wings. When things get crowded for the crickets, these macropterous (long-winged) individuals can take to the air in search of new ground. They've reached the north Midlands and west Wales and their progress continues apace in open grassy places or overgrown waysides.

If you can't hear their song, don't despair. At this time of year, most cricket-fanciers over fifty wouldn't go anywhere without their bat detector. Those in the know set the dial at around 22 kilohertz, which converts the sound to a guttural buzzing.

The cricket stridulates by rubbing toothed ribs on its left forewing against the edge of its right forewing, which is equipped with a flat area called a mirror to amplify its song. Follow the sound carefully and with luck the cricket will materialise among low vegetation. Then its most obvious feature is the buttery-yellow piping along its head-shield or pronotum. Armoured as it is, like a medieval warhorse, you half expect it to clank rustily as it shifts through the grass. The only sound, though, is the thin songstream stitching summer to autumn, a song that will be silenced by the first frosts.

ATLANTIC SALMON

11 September

A waterfall by a rushing torrent of water in the Highlands of Scotland on a chilly September day is a fine sight and sound. Yet even this majestic spectacle pales into insignificance next to what I am about to witness: one of the river's inhabitants on its spectacular return journey to the place where it was born.

I endure several false alarms: the sudden appearance of a plume of water flashing in the weak autumn sun as the current strikes a rock. The water's whirls and eddies become almost intoxicating, putting me in a Zen-like trance as I watch and wait.

And then it happens. A flash of silver emerges from the black river like Excalibur, forging upwards until it leaves the waters way behind and flies through the air like a javelin. Onwards and upwards it goes, until the laws of gravity exert their inevitable influence, and it crashes down on to water-splashed rocks, before sliding back into the water. The salmon are leaping.

The Atlantic salmon, as its name suggests, spends much of its life out in the mysterious waters of that vast and mighty ocean. But it was not born at sea, nor will it die there: its life begins and ends in the quiet, slow-flowing waters near the river's source.

This mighty fish began life several years ago, when it hatched out of a tiny egg, one of thousands laid here. It fed, grew and most importantly avoided being eaten, as its brothers and sisters dwindled until there were only a few left alive. Then, in response to some mysterious impulse, it headed downstream towards the open sea, its body changing to cope with a very different way of life in salt, rather than fresh waters.

Years went by, until the salmon was impelled to change once again, swimming thousands of miles back to its original home, guided by the invisible equivalent of a satnav system in its brain.

But getting back isn't anything like as simple as that first journey to the sea. Now it must swim upstream, negotiating barriers such as weirs and waterfalls along the way. It does so by leaping – sometimes twice as high as a human being – using vast reserves of energy to do so.

Only when it finally arrives back in the place where it was born, five or six years ago, does the salmon rest awhile; then mate, after which the female deposits her huge clutch of eggs. Having made such a mighty effort to get here, both male and female are exhausted, and the vast majority die soon afterwards. But their work is done: and soon a new generation of Atlantic salmon will be growing here in this remote and beautiful waterway.

SWAN MUSSELS

12 September

Can you mourn for a mussel? Or feel compassion for a clam?

For me, these are questions that arise each autumn if the weather has been dry over the summer and I pay a visit to one of the local mill-pools, which were created several centuries ago to provide water to drive mill wheels. The wheels powered hammers at forges along the north Worcestershire brooks, allowing their owners to make agricultural implements, but now, with one exception, they are silent, the pools undisturbed. Most of them sit over porous red sandstone and without artificial topping up, their water level soon drops in rain-free autumns, leaving a shoreline of crusting mud and some of our largest British shellfish high and dry.

The evidence is there today as I skirt one pond: dozens of huge, olive-yellow swan mussels, their hinged shells gaping in the exposed mud in a silent cry for help. For these molluscs, it's too late. Having settled down in their chosen position many years ago, they are mainly stationary. Though they have a muscular foot to pull them along, they often fail to reach deeper water when the pond shrinks.

But seeing them, even *in extremis*, reminds me what extraordinary creatures they are. Far larger than any seashells we're likely to see on the beach, swan mussels hide nearly all their lives in mud. Each soft-bodied mussel is protected by a pair of oval shells, up to six inches long. These are lined with a pearly-white layer of nacre or mother-of-pearl. They filter minute food particles through a siphon, which also draws in water from which their gills extract oxygen. Another siphon acts as a waste disposal service.

It's a quiet life, but the swan mussel's youth is a very different affair. Baby swan mussels start life as little larvae called glochidia, minute free-swimming creatures similar to oyster spats. They hatch in winter from fertilised eggs inside the mussel and are released into the open water by the parent. As they swim, they trail sticky strands, which attach themselves to investigating fish. Once they've found a mooring, the young hitchhikers clamp themselves on to the fish to form a protective cyst and suck its blood.

After several weeks they have grown vestigial shells and are large enough to sink to the pond bed and find their own home in the sediment, far from competition with their parents. This co-existence can be very sophisticated. In North American streams there are mussels that protrude part of their own bodies from their shells to imitate the shape of a fish, complete with eye and fins. Real fish coming to check it out or eat what they think is fishy prey are showered with a spray of young mussels.

But some fish, known as bitterlings, turn the tables on the mussel and use the shell of the living mussel as a nursery for their eggs. For what is easily dismissed as a dull mollusc, the swan mussel leads a complex life which is why I mourn for those marooned in the mud.

TIT FLOCKS

13 September

As I walk with my children through a local wood on an early autumn afternoon, things are suspiciously quiet. The only birdsong I can hear comes from the occasional fluting robin or trilling wren, somewhere out of sight; the summer visitors are mostly gone, and the winter ones have not yet arrived.

And then I hear them: a distant note, then another, and soon a whole chorus of tweets and squeaks, cheeps and peeps, trills and little farting sounds, rapidly approaching in the canopy above my head. A tit flock is passing by.

For a moment or two I still can't see any movement; then a flash of wings and a tail disappearing into the foliage signal the first arrival. A head pokes out among the leaves: the smart black, white, yellow and green of the great tit, followed by its equally colourful but smaller cousin, the blue tit.

Deeper in the vegetation there are more movements: subtly different from the brash great and blue tits, somehow more tentative. This time the bird looking back at me shows the soft pink, brown and cream of the long-tailed tit, whose moist little call I have been hearing for the past minute or so. As always, another, and then another follows it; long-tailed tits are famously family oriented, the youngsters staying with their parents all winter long.

All these birds have come together to increase their chances of surviving the rigours of winter: more birds mean more eyes to find food, and to warn against predators such as sparrowhawks. The calls are their way of keeping in touch and allowing stragglers to reconnect with the main flock.

Over the years I have seen other, scarcer birds tagging along with the usual crowd: a random hoi polloi including tiny goldcrests, slender treecreepers and – just the once, more than thirty years ago – a tiny, sparrow-sized, lesser spotted woodpecker.

Often the flock has passed by almost as soon as it appears; but I have occasionally persuaded them to linger awhile by a technique birders call 'pishing'. This involves pursing my lips together and uttering a series of squeaks, hisses and kissing sounds. These are supposed to resemble the alarm calls of small birds, and may lead the flock to come and investigate. What these tiny birds then make of this huge and noisy mammal in their home territory I can only guess.

THORN-APPLE

14 September

This month, I prowl the local potato fields in search, not of an illicit meal, but of one of our deadliest and most attractive plants. Thorn-apples, like potatoes, are members of the nightshade family, and sometimes turn up as contaminants of potato seed. By September, just before the potatoes are dug, they have reached full stature and their large, green spiky fruits, like vegetable maces, stand head and shoulders above the potato plants.

Timing is crucial. If I arrive too late the crop will have been sprayed by commercial defoliants, used to kill off the potato leaves before the tubers are lifted. Early frosts are also fatal to thorn-apples, which are native to North America.

I read about the plants long before I saw my first real one. In Richard Mabey's masterful account of urban wildlife, *The Unofficial Countryside*, he mentions a specimen growing in a railway yard in 1970, which was summarily hacked to pieces and burned once its deadly powers were discovered. Thorn-apple is indeed a dangerous plant, chock-full of chemical alkaloids that induce hallucinations and can kill in large doses, though you'd think its foul smell would limit its appeal.

Apparently not: in the USA it's known as Jimson weed, after an incident in 1676 when soldiers in Jamestown, Virginia, picked the leaves for an impromptu salad and were reduced, in one account, to 'grinning like monkeys and pawing at their companions' for ten days. They didn't suffer any after-effects, though they probably got off lightly. In small doses, Jimson weed is still used by experimental American teenagers in the way that magic mushrooms are in Britain, though the risks thorn-apple poses are not worth taking.

A large thorn-apple can reach a metre high and is an imposing plant with its pinwheel buds and tubular white flowers whose sensual charms captivated the artist Georgia O'Keeffe. For me it's a short-lived wonder, usually cut down in its autumn prime. But each of those spiky plum-sized fruits contains seeds that can survive in the soil for more than a century, and that's why they could surprise us wherever the soil is disturbed, often in town, and might even reveal a hidden history of the site to which the plant has become a modern witness. Was it once grown here deliberately?

Thorn-apple alkaloids, used with care, were taken in the past to relieve stomach cramps, dilate the pupils and stimulate the heart and had an important role in ritual and folk medicine. For example smoke from burning leaves was inhaled to relieve rheumatism pain and steam from water in which leaves were soaked could be used to allay discomfort from haemorrhoids. Although in the wrong doses it was very dangerous, the plant had many uses involving pain relief, so it would have been regarded as a valuable medicinal herb and a mind-altering one too.

SCORPION
15 September

The docks at Sheerness in north Kent, on a chilly autumn evening. As night falls, the bright lights of this twenty-four-hour port illuminate the surroundings, lighting up north-facing walls that have never seen sunlight.

As I peer into the newly lit scene, I see an alien immigrant that has managed to make its home here in the narrow crevices between the huge, black stones. It's a species you might not expect to find anywhere in Britain: *Euscorpius flavicaudis*, the European yellow-tailed scorpion.

Inching closer, avoiding any sudden movements that might alarm this little creature, I can see the classic scorpion shape. It's a long, slender animal with two powerful claws held out in front, and that familiar tail with the mildly venomous sting on the tip, curved back over its body.

But the scorpion has a secret to reveal, which can only be seen where the creature is hiding in the darkness. To discover it, I've brought along a torch that emits ultraviolet light. The beam is invisible to the human eye. But when I shine it on to the scorpion, the creature glows an eerie shade of blue.

Why they do so is a bit of a mystery. Scientists now think that the ability to emit light allows the scorpion to sense when it is heading into or out of a dark place. When it is threatened it can scuttle away into the darkness, where it is more likely to be safe.

This animal looks pretty exotic, so you might suspect it to be a fairly recent addition to our fauna, especially given its limited range. Yet it has probably been in Britain for more than 200 years, having arrived on cargo ships from its native Spain or North Africa sometime during the eighteenth century. For such a tropical animal to have survived here at all is quite miraculous, especially as during the winter Kent can be one of the coldest parts of the UK. But survive they have, earning them a place in the record books as the northernmost colony of scorpions anywhere in the world.

BLACKBERRIES AND BRAMBLES
16 September

We take a family walk along the lane at the back of our home on a bright September afternoon. The children are in turns bored and irritable, seeming unable to enjoy this rare break from their screens.

But once they spot the blackberries, everything changes. Smiles break out, together with a clamour to be the first to harvest them. Plastic bags are miraculously produced (we suspected the fruits would be ready) and the blackberry-picking begins.

Even among townies (as we once were), the annual appearance of blackberries is one of those moments in the calendar we all remember from our childhood; and if we are lucky, still enjoy today.

That exquisite mixture of pleasure and pain – for few of us escape without at least some scratches, and we relish the naughtiness of getting our fingers (and if we are greedy, our mouths too) stained with the dark purple juice – means that picking these autumnal fruits takes just enough effort to make it seem worthwhile.

We debate what to do with the ones we haven't eaten. The consensus is that an apple and blackberry crumble – using the fruits from our own apple trees – would be the perfect end to a September Sunday. And so, later that evening, it proves.

HOUSE SPIDERS
17 September

A blur of motion and a pause. Another blur, then stillness. Something large is moving across the living room carpet and the gaps between movements increase my unease. It's an encounter that arachnophobes dread: a long-legged hairy house spider on the prowl.

In autumn the males enter houses for shelter and mating opportunities. Some fall into baths and sinks and can't escape. Spread-eagled against the porcelain, they are impressive creatures even in their plight.

If you're not keen on them, it probably won't be a comfort to know that there are eight species of large *Tegenaria* – the genus that includes our house spiders – in the British Isles. They're hard to tell apart and some of them hybridise with each other, making microscopic inspection essential.

The males mature in early autumn. Look closely and you can distinguish them from the females by their palps, which are like small boxing gloves at the front of the head. Before wandering off to seek a mate, they make a small web on which they deposit a drop of sperm and, having charged their palps with this, go in search of love.

Female house spiders are bulkier and have larger bodies. They can live for over two years in their lairs of greyish silk, often in the corner of sheds, cellars or garages. They lurk in a tunnel at the centre of these dense webs, forelegs sensitive to every vibration, and rush out to grab prey that becomes entangled. I once saw an exhibition of house spider webs at Bristol's Arnolfini Gallery, each one framed as a grim tapestry in which were enmeshed the limbs of beetles and the bright wings of hibernating butterflies.

Many of us find the jerky and unpredictable movements of the house spider on the carpet unsettling. We're not alone: one species, reputed to have frightened Cardinal Wolsey at Hampton Court, is still known as the Cardinal spider. They certainly can move fast but only in short bursts. The spider expert Bill Bristowe calculated that a female could cover 330 times her own body length (sixteen millimetres) in ten seconds. But if you chase one around a room it will collapse exhausted after half a minute or so. Better to let them proceed at their own pace – after all they're only looking for love and will rid your house of flies and other pests that might be harmful. Maybe their pest-clearing presence is the origin of the old saying: 'If you wish to live and thrive, let a spider run alive.'

SANDERLING

18 September

The beach at Berrow, just down the Somerset coast from Weston-super-Mare, often seems to melt into the sea beyond, making it hard to work out where the sand ends and the brown, muddy waters of Bridgwater Bay begin.

But this morning there's no such problem. A brisk wind is whipping up the sea, so that it curls into white-tipped wavelets, which then crash down on to the beach. This makes life tricky for the flock of waders – a hundred or more strong – that are running swiftly along the shore in that temporary, liminal, ever-changing space between land and water.

Even from the very top of the beach, where I must tread carefully to avoid tripping over the flotsam and jetsam of our throwaway society, I know exactly what they are. That clockwork-toy action, their ghostly pale plumage and the time of year can only mean one species: sanderling.

Having travelled all the way from the High Arctic – the sanderling's nearest breeding grounds are on the tundra, thousands of miles to the north of here – these birds are frantically feeding, refuelling with much needed energy after their epic flight.

For some, this is almost the end of their journey: several thousand sanderlings spend the winter in Britain. But the vast majority continue much further: all the way to the coasts of Mauritania, Namibia or even as far as South Africa.

I look more closely at these birds, wondering at their marathon global journeys, until a dog comes along and they sweep up into the air, heading down the beach until they are finally out of sight.

CRANE FLIES

19 September

There's a persistent urban myth floating around that crane flies – other-wise known as daddy-long-legs – are the most venomous of all insects, and would pose a national threat if only their mouthparts could pierce human skin. It seems to have its foundation in the ability of the daddy-long-legs spider (a similar-looking but entirely unrelated species) to subdue and eat venomous spiders, implying an even more potent poison at work.

By analogy this fearsome reputation has spread to similar long-legged creatures such as harvestmen, which are related to spiders, as well as to crane flies, which are winged insects. It's all tosh of course and is particularly unfair on the humble crane fly whose mouthparts are poorly developed and which doesn't feed at all in its short life.

There are around 350 species of crane flies in the British Isles, and most of the larger ones we see stumbling across the lawn or clinging to windows at this time of year are the tipulids. They're mainly brownish with a single pair of wings and a pair of small stabilising club-like structures called halteres, which help to direct them in flight.

Flight seems a grand term for the aimless, drifting technique that most crane flies use to get around, but they ride on thermals to travel high and far, their outspread legs acting as natural parachutes. On warm September days I've seen hobbies, elegant falcons that migrate to Africa in autumn, plucking the rising crane flies from the air with great delicacy. Holding the insect in its talons, the bird de-wings it in mid-air before swallowing the slender body.

It's a risky life being a crane fly: all manner of predators lie in wait, including spiders, which are especially noticeable now. The crane fly has a useful talent if snared by a web. It simply detaches a limb or two and breaks free.

Females have sharp-ended abdomens, chestnut-coloured ovipositors that allow them to insert their black eggs – like minute caviar – into soil in lawns and meadows. The hard-skinned grubs, known as leatherjackets, nibble at grass-roots and although we may not like them, are valuable food for birds such as starlings, which probe the turf – bills agape – to search for these delicacies, aerating the lawn as they go.

BLACK-TAILED SKIMMER

20 September

Some insects, as the famous advert says, do exactly what they say on the tin. Male black-tailed skimmers have a black tip to their abdomen, and skim low over the water – in this case the murky pools left behind after the peat has been removed.

These feisty dragonflies patrol their tiny airspace with all the zeal of First World War air aces. I watch as they zigzag back and forth, rarely rising more than a few inches above the glassy surface, and hardly ever landing. Where they find the energy is hard to tell, until I see one stall momentarily in mid-air, grab a tiny insect, and fly purposefully on.

Just occasionally, especially on cool early autumn mornings, I come across a black-tailed skimmer in a rare static pose. Needing the heat of the sun to get airborne, they perch on stony ground, or on the wooden slats of the boardwalks thoughtfully provided for the use of visitors – and skimmers – around the various nature reserves in the area.

When I do come across one, I always take the opportunity to have a really close look: that broad abdomen, a delicate, powder-blue shade – almost mauve in some lights – and the lattice-like wings, held forward at an angle from the body, like a biplane about to taxi down the runway. Females and young males are very different in appearance: a wasp-like black and yellow, glinting in the early morning sun before they take flight once again.

CRAYFISH

21 September

When I was thirteen I visited the forest for the first time with a friend and we caught white-clawed crayfish in the main brook running through the woods, turning stones carefully and watching for the swirl of sediment that showed we'd got lucky. But now, that same brook is full of a larger and more vigorous competitor: North American signal crayfish, so-called because of the pale spots at the base of their claws, escapees from a fishery upstream. Until recently we thought that the white-clawed crayfish I'd caught in my childhood had gone for good, but colonies have been found during surveys of smaller streams.

Late summer and early autumn is the time to survey our local white-clawed crayfish. It is a subtle art and under the tutelage of ecologists Graham and Anne Hill we don our head torches and follow the forest's smaller streams, which have incised deep valleys through the oaks. Tonight the water has become a mere trickle, in places only a few centimetres deep, so the omens don't look good. But it turns out we will have a bumper crop of these rare crustaceans: over 600 in this tiny streamlet alone.

The larger North American species has been widely farmed for eating, but is a carrier of crayfish plague, which can't penetrate the thicker carapace of the signal crayfish, but which kills the white-clawed crayfish. Now that signal crayfish are widespread, the white-clawed is severely threatened.

But today, to our amazement, engineering has saved its skin. White-clawed crayfish are smaller than signals and can live in the upper reaches of the rills and rivulets that flow down the wooded slopes towards the main brook. Where these streamlets cross paths, they are channelled through pipes that crayfish can't negotiate, and so any signal crayfish trying to move upstream from the main brook face an impassable barrier. This has effectively kept the plague below the pipes and protected the white-clawed crayfish in their upstream enclaves.

It's a precarious existence. These remaining white-clawed crayfish are very vulnerable, for example to accidental introduction of the plague on someone's boots, and so each year, under licence and with disinfected wellies, we check the numbers to see how many adults and youngsters there are.

Although crayfish hide in overhangs and bank tunnels by day, at night they emerge to feed on the stream-bed and our torchlight picks them out, scuttling like small mud-coloured lobsters over the stones. The lack of rain has reduced some stretches of this rivulet to pools and in one we find several stranded adults. I offer one a piece of apple core and it nibbles delicately at the unexpected windfall. Feeding a marooned crayfish in the darkness of a silent forest is an odd communing, but strangely touching.

These woodland populations, clinging on in improbably small streams, are doing well. The count of several hundred in a single night is impressive, but down in the valley below their escaped relatives carry death through the swirling currents. A misplaced boot carrying the plague could spell the end of centuries of white-clawed crayfish in the forest.

PS: In summer 2016 the event that we'd been dreading happened, and crayfish plague was somehow introduced into their last strongholds. Nearly all the white-clawed crayfish have since died.

MIGRANT HAWKER

22 September

Like many Somerset gardens, mine is long and narrow – a legacy from the days when they farmed the land around here in strips, known as batches. At the lower end, there's a patch of long grass encircled by brambles, above which rise the mature ash and cider-apple trees. On warm early autumn days this quiet, sheltered spot forms a perfect suntrap. It is where, as the sun rises towards the meridian, I look for a recent addition to our insect fauna: the migrant hawker.

The name is a clue to its habits. This striking dragonfly did used to be a scarce visitor from southern Europe. But just as birds such as the little egret and Mediterranean gull have surged northwards in the past few decades, so has the migrant hawker. Indeed it was once known as the scarce hawker, reflecting its rarity for much of the twentieth century.

The recent *Atlas of Dragonflies in Britain and Ireland* – a fascinating volume produced by hundreds of dedicated odonatophiles – shows just how much progress this insect has made. Today it is widespread across much of lowland England and Wales, and is now surging northwards into the Scottish Borders.

For me, this is one of our most attractive dragonflies. Smaller than the mighty emperor and southern hawkers, the males are chocolate brown alternating with sky blue, while the females are brown and yellow. But as in some other dragonflies, such as the scarce chaser, the immature female is the most striking, with delicate mauve markings on the abdomen – subtle, but truly beautiful, especially as they perch in the September sunshine.

DEVIL'S FINGERS

23 September

The aliens have landed. Sprawled like nightmarish starfish in the orchard grass they are unnervingly unfamiliar, completely beyond our comprehension. Stinkhorns we can deal with, but these are fungi from another planet perhaps.

Clathrus archeri – aka devil's fingers – is one of the strangest life forms that we're likely to see in our gardens or, indeed, islands. This outlandish fungus is native to Australia and we can't be sure how it arrived here, though its minute spores could have been brought in accidentally with antipodean goods.

The fruiting bodies appear in late summer and autumn in grassland, gardens and on wood chippings used as mulch. Initially, large off-white eggs appear above the ground, before rupturing to reveal a squid-like shape, usually comprising five to eight tentacles, which are thrust skyward.

Soon they arch over to create a sprawling reddish star, each arm daubed with a dark, sticky slime or gleba that contains the spores. Like their relatives the stinkhorns, devil's fingers have a foul smell aimed at luring in flies, which leave with some of the spore-bearing goo on their feet.

Once a great rarity, in recent years devil's fingers seems to be increasing, especially in places where wood chippings are used, so it's worth looking out for in municipal flowerbeds or along newly coated paths in early autumn.

OSPREY STOPOVER
24 September

The crowd gasps as the bird launches itself off its perch, sweeps majestically across the lake and dives into the water. This time, it fails to emerge with a fish in its talons; but more often than not it is successful. This is the 'fish-hawk' – better known as the osprey – whose fishing skills put most anglers to shame.

This particular bird has stopped off on its long and leisurely journey to Africa on the aptly named Noah's Lake, part of the Avalon Marshes near my home on the Somerset Levels. In spring, ospreys always seem to be in a hurry – if they pause to feed at all, it is usually only for an hour or two, impelled by the need to reach their breeding grounds. But in autumn, things are very different. This bird will have left the forests of Scandinavia – or perhaps the Highlands of Scotland – a few days ago, drifting slowly south and west like an itinerant hobo. Having found a place to feed, it is in no rush to move on; though eventually it will cross the Bay of Biscay towards its wintering grounds in The Gambia or Senegal.

We know this because of the pioneering efforts of conservationists such as Roy Dennis. Every year Roy puts tracking devices on young ospreys while they are still in the nest, enabling anyone with access to the Internet to follow the birds in real time on their long and dangerous journey.

Not all make it – especially the youngsters on their first ever migration – but enough do to allow us to know where they spend the winter; and, almost as important, where they stop off along the way. Like all migrants, ospreys need to feed on their journeys south and north; and with the Sahara Desert continuing to expand, there are fears for their future.

A few years ago I was in my garden, on the phone to a friend, when a commotion in the skies above made me look upwards. There, being harassed by two ravens was a long-winged raptor: an osprey. Dropping the phone, I shouted to my wife and children to come and see the bird as it drifted slowly south, still being chased by the ravens, until it was finally out of sight. When I called my friend back and explained the reason for my abrupt termination of our conversation, he was almost as excited as I was. That's the wonder of migration.

GRASS SNAKES

25 September

Whenever I see what Emily Dickinson described as 'a narrow fellow in the grass' I can't help feeling a delicious shiver of excitement. As a teenager travelling home from school, I used to visit the pet shop in Birmingham market, where tanks of writhing grass snakes, cream-striped variants imported from the Continent, awaited an uncertain fate at the hands of young but misguided enthusiasts like me. Sadly, most were fated to die in cramped conditions – grass snakes are rovers and need space.

But to my delight I discovered that there were wild grass snakes within a short cycle ride from home. Where a pile of rotting hay-bales had been left near fishing pools, huge olive females, bulging with eggs, lay basking.

At that age, possession is everything: it was unthinkable to let a grass snake go free and if you crept up quietly enough you could lunge at the snake before it slid fluidly away between the haystacks.

The thrill of its warm, muscular strength, the black and white tessellations of its underbelly and the dark flickering tongue scenting the air are with me still. Less pleasant memories also linger. Grass snakes don't bite attackers, but defend themselves by voiding the creamy contents of their anal glands over them. It's a pungent cocktail of rotting cabbage, fish and garlic and is difficult to remove even after several washes.

But after this initial protest, the snakes quickly adapted to handling, though they do have other tricks up their sleeves. Cycling home with one in my trouser pocket one day, I felt a warm wetness and stopped to find that it had regurgitated a semi-liquid, but still recognisable, frog. It took some explaining when I arrived home, malodorous but triumphant.

The need to possess snakes soon passed, but as result of those encounters I have an enormous affection and respect for this harmless reptile with its trademark black and yellow collar. In particular, I'm touched by its vulnerability in a crowded landscape. Grass snakes wander widely and are often killed by traffic: roads are a serious barrier to populations. The reptiles are said to be declining and, certainly, the simplification of modern farmland and spread of towns and cities do them few favours.

On the plus side, the creation of fishing lakes and gravel-pits has provided new habitat and, on some nature reserves, grass snakes are doing well. I once went to a Norfolk reserve where the pool frog, a long-lost native amphibian, is being introduced, much to the delight of the local snakes which see the rare frogs as just another tasty meal, to the frustration of conservationists.

There's a lot we can do to help them too. Grass snakes will turn up in gardens, especially in late summer when they lay their off-white leathery eggs in rotting vegetation: the warmth incubates them and speeds up hatching. Compost heaps are favourite locations and, if left undisturbed, will produce pencil-slim youngsters in September, crisply marked in olive, yellow and black. They are as fast as quicksilver when disturbed.

If you're lucky enough to have grass snakes in the area, encourage them by leaving a few patches of longer vegetation and by digging a garden pond: they feed on frogs and newts. Above all, the compost heap is invaluable as a nursery for their eggs, so in August and September, be careful where you stick your fork!

CURLEWS AND GODWITS

26 September

The River Parrett meanders slowly on its journey from Dorset through Somerset, until it finally pours into Bridgwater Bay, where broad mudflats are exposed with each change of the tides. In September, almost anything can turn up, so I take my walk down to the river with more than the usual sense of expectation.

And here, among the wheeling flocks of knots and dunlins, and the loud, insistent calls of redshanks, are some larger waders, each probing the rich mud to find food.

The majority are curlews, whose huge, downcurved bill is the longest of any British wader species, enabling them to reach deep into the mud for food.

The other two look superficially similar: both slightly smaller than the curlews, with long, fairly straight bills, with maybe just a hint of an upward curve when seen in profile. These are godwits – black-tailed and bar-tailed – both of which have stopped here for a day or two on their travels south.

The larger, plainer black-tailed godwit has the shorter journey. They breed in Iceland, and either pass through on their way to overwinter in France or, if they like what they see, simply stay put until the spring. Now that the new reserve has been built across the river at Steart, black-tailed godwits are a regular sight from now until May, when they head north once again. They used to breed occasionally on the Somerset Levels, but sadly they have not done so now for decades.

The smallest of the three waders, the bar-tailed godwit, has a far more ambitious journey to make. These birds do not breed anywhere in Britain; indeed they travel all the way to the High Arctic tundra to raise their family. Having done so, they pass through Britain on their way south to spend the winter along the Atlantic coast of Africa. Watching this bird as it deftly probes the Somerset mud, I find it hard to believe that it will venture so far.

GREENSHANK

27 September

The pool is still, its shallows crusted with mats of drying algae. Hanks of thistledown lie becalmed in a bay where lapwings doze, bills tucked under oily mantle feathers. Occasionally one calls peevishly, but the flock seems too settled to fly on this hot September day. The only movement is from darting dragonflies, skirmishing over the water with a cellophane rustle of wings.

Suddenly the calm of this oasis is ruptured by a ringing 'chew-chew, chew' call. There's a flash of white rump and suddenly a long-billed, greyish wader pitches in, bobbing nervously on the shore, before stalking confidently across the pool: a greenshank, a bird that brings a breath of the north to this ordinary waterway.

I was first introduced to greenshanks by the writings of the ornithologist and enthusiastic nest-finder Desmond Nethersole-Thompson, for whom this wader was the acme of birds. Braving Scottish midges, mists, floods and sometimes violent storms, he and members of his family camped out in greenshank breeding grounds in the northern flow country of Sutherland, where sedgy moors dotted with dark peaty lochans are bordered by stony hills. Above this wilderness, male greenshanks held territory, fluting high over the boggy expanse, while their mates incubated specked eggs in the heather beneath.

I was smitten by his wonderful accounts, but as a young birder had no chance of seeing these birds in the breeding season. But there was hope: greenshanks leave these inhospitable places in autumn when the insects run out, and head south, often stopping at inland pools and gravel pits en route.

Early autumn is a good time to catch up with them and to savour that delicious call, which seems able to harness all the acoustic potential of any site the bird visits: it is a thrilling sound that tugs you north to the vast, boggy mires where greenshanks breed.

Greenshanks aren't colourful birds, though on a misty September morning they have a pale luminosity, white beneath and lichen-grey above with a longish, slightly retroussé bill and greenish legs. Sometimes one will dash through the water after small fish. At other times they wade chest-deep or pick their way elegantly through the shallows, scanning for prey. Some remain for days, others stop to refuel for an hour or so on their way to Mediterranean and North African estuaries. A few will winter in southern creeks, especially in Devon and Cornwall, whose oak-lined shores reverberate with their wild triple calls until the birds head back north again next spring.

BLACK GROUSE

28 September

All birders should have a local patch; somewhere they can get away from it all, either alone or with a fellow enthusiast. I share my Somerset patch with Graeme, an expat Scot who commutes from Somerset to Fife, where he runs his business.

But Graeme has his own local patch near his work: a little patch of moorland with a stream running through it in the wilds of Perthshire. Having heard so much about this place, and its very different birdlife, I was delighted to be able to see it for myself on a weekend jaunt north.

Late September can be a quiet time for birding, caught halfway between the summer visitors leaving and the imminent arrival of birds from the north. Yet there was still plenty to see, including species I rarely get good views of down south. Almost as soon as we began along the path the distinctive 'go-back, go-back' call floated across the moor towards me. Seconds later, a pair of red grouse exploded from the heather, followed by several more. It was good to see them in a place that isn't managed for shooting, where one of Britain's most distinctive birds can fly without fear.

The trees along the side of the stream produced both redpolls and siskins, plump little finches that fly together as if connected by pieces of elastic, their calls echoing in the autumn sky. A grey wagtail flew across the stream, while dozens of meadow pipits bounced up from the grass in front of us.

But the highlight came as we turned the corner at the end of the valley to begin the walk back to the car. Three dark, crow-like birds perched on an unsightly electricity pylon; yet something about their silhouette marked them out as a different bird. They were black grouse – three splendid males – one of the classic Scottish specialities, and always one of the delights of a day's birding north of the border.

I've seen these birds in early spring on their lek – a grassy arena where the males compete for the chance to mate with the watching females. But to see them so unexpectedly was a kind of bonus – reminding me that even the quieter times of year always have the capacity to surprise.

PHEASANTS

29 September

Suddenly the lanes are full of scurrying brown birds, looking tatty and confused. Others are already squashed flat, mown down by drivers who expect too much awareness from them.

Pheasants have been released over summer from breeding pens in readiness for the shooting season, which opens on 1 October. The adult male birds, which appear on countless Christmas cards strutting over frosty fields, are quintessential features of the British countryside, but they don't belong here.

The common or ring-necked pheasant is native to south-east Europe and Asia, from Armenia and Georgia east to China, but has been established in the British Isles since around the fifteenth century, though there are records prior to the Norman Conquest. A cock pheasant is an imposing bird with its long barred tail, blood-red wattles and coppery plumage, but so familiar that naturalists often ignore it.

For many of them, the pheasant is merely a rural commodity and, at this time of year when numbers are high, a road hazard too. It is also an alien. Release a grey squirrel you've nurtured after an injury and technically you could be fined for introducing a non-native pest. Allow a terrapin to escape into your local pond and you've committed a crime. But you can flood the countryside with 35–40 million pheasants each year with impunity.

One argument from the shooting lobby is that they are releasing sporting birds that bring in the money and don't appear to do much harm to native wildlife. A study from the Game and Wildlife Conservation Trust has concluded that pheasants don't usually have a detrimental effect on flowers and invertebrates near release sites. But unfortunately the Trust's report didn't consider the fate of reptiles such as adders and slow-worms, which I've seen wiped out in local woods within a few years of pheasants being released. Pheasants kill or injure the reptiles by pecking them and will swallow young adders and slow-worms whole. The upshot is that reptile populations, already weakened by isolation and habitat degradation, soon disappear – never to return.

Making a case for a venomous snake and a legless lizard is tough in the face of the pheasant's contribution to the rural economy. Pheasant-rearers don't intend these consequences and fans of pheasants, or at least of shooting them, point out that our landscape would be less varied without the copses and coverts planted to conserve them. Some of the best finch and bunting flocks that I see in winter are among weeds planted as game cover.

However, in some places, birds of prey have been shot or poisoned illegally near pheasant release pens. In summer 2016 the government's conservation watchdog, Natural England, announced that it had issued a licence for buzzard control – a euphemism for killing – near pheasant pens in north-east England. To me, it seems a nonsense to cull a legally protected native bird of prey to reduce the threat to an alien bird that is being released in such enormous numbers.

But pheasant road casualties are a boon to reintroduced red kites and recolonising buzzards and ravens. It's a complex situation and a practical compromise lies somewhere in there, but I wouldn't hold out much hope for any small enclaves of adders and slow-worms.

CETTI'S WARBLER

30 September

If I had to pick the quietest month on my local patch, on the edge of the Avalon Marshes, it would definitely be September. Most birdsong ended back in late June, with a handful of species continuing to sing into early July. At this point, the vast majority of birds have finished breeding and the adults are hiding away to moult out of their tatty plumage. Even robins and wrens, which now sing almost all year round, fall silent in July and August.

Then, some time in the first week or two of September, these two songsters – the commonest and second commonest birds in Britain – burst into song once again. They always sound, to my ear at least, slightly less enthusiastic than in the spring, though the wren's trills sound almost as frantic, while the robin is a bit more subdued. But my usual walk has another regular musical accompaniment: Cetti's warbler.

This newcomer arrived in the early 1970s and began to colonise wetlands right across southern Britain. Its very name is a reminder of its exotic Mediterranean origins; it is one of only three British breeding birds (the others being Montagu's harrier and Leach's storm petrel) named after a person: in this case an eighteenth-century Italian priest and ornithologist, Francesco Cetti.

Today Cetti's warbler's extraordinary song resounds everywhere in the Somerset Levels; yet it was not until I checked my field notes that I realised that it never misses a month – even singing during the sonically quiet months of July and August, when other birds are silent. But Cetti's warbler simply never stops; on virtually every visit I hear at least one, and even outside the breeding season there are two or three holding territory in the depths of the scrub surrounding the reed-beds.

I still hardly ever see them – Cetti's is a notoriously elusive bird, preferring to skulk deep inside thick brambles for most of the time – but at least I know they are always there.

OCTOBER

EARLY OCTOBER IS a great fulcrum of the natural year during which remnants of summer are balanced against the oncoming winter. The first squalls and easterlies of autumn speed the last swallows and martins on their way, but usher in northern redwings and fieldfares, wildfowl and waders. In sunny orchards, gaudy red admirals and commas feast on windfall fruit, while around them, in a parody of spring flowers, yellow and scarlet waxcap fungi sprout.

October is the fungi month for me, when the pale busbies of shaggy ink-caps appear on the lawn and fly agarics troop beneath pines and yellowing birches. Parasol mushrooms grow in abundance on our local heaths and are a delicious seasonal nutty treat fried in butter. Each year I try to learn a few more fungi, only to find that their names have been changed or that they've been split into several species; a mycologist's lot is a turbulent one.

I can't pass a sunlit ivy cluster without inspecting it for hoverflies, wasps and a new arrival, the ivy bee, which is rapidly moving north and west. On sunny trunks and fence-posts, flies bask in the autumn sunshine and are picked off by hornets, feeding until the food supply runs out; often they and a few dragonflies will still be on the wing at the end of the month, when rashes of harlequin ladybirds break out on fences and tree-trunks.

In the local woods and in parkland across the British Isles, fallow deer are rutting now. Although they are introduced, there's something primeval about hearing the urgent belching groans of the bucks deep in a forest with no one else around: the wildwood beckons . . .

B.W.

THE MIGRANT BIRDS have mostly gone, while the winter flocks of ducks, geese and swans are still on their northern breeding grounds. Yet for a hard core of birders known as twitchers, whose purpose in life is to see rare and unusual birds, October is by far the most exciting month of all. For this is when birds from all corners of the globe turn up at the extremities of our country. So from Scilly in the south to Shetland in the north, crowds of twitchers search for these lost vagrants, hoping against hope to find the Holy Grail – a 'first' for Britain – a species never before recorded here.

For the rest of us, October definitely marks the point when we say goodbye to the abundance of summer and instead learn to appreciate the more subtle charms of autumn. Insects can still be found – so long as you know where to look – while for many mammals, including our two largest, the red deer and grey seal, this is a time to prepare for the most important time of their lives, pairing up and breeding.

Other autumnal delights include fungi, emerging overnight as if by magic in our woods and fields; while our trees and hedgerows also bear close examination at this time of year, as they produce an abundance of fruits, seeds and nuts that in turn feeds so many birds and mammals.

Most of all, October is a month of shifting shades and colours. Gone is the gaudy green of spring and summer, and we are in a world of reds and russets, sepias and chestnuts, yellows and ochres: a dazzling autumnal panorama before the bleak, bare branches of winter.

S.M.

STONE CURLEW

1 October

In a few select spots, autumn is time for the mustering of the goggle-eyed plovers, as they are known in East Anglia.

Over the last decade, scanning a rabbit-grazed heath for some of our strangest birds has, for me, become an annual pastime. Although I don't live within the breeding range for what are more politely known as stone curlews, a trip to the East Anglian Brecklands or the Suffolk Sandlings has, one way or another, insinuated itself into my diary.

Stone curlews are unusual among British waders in that they avoid water, and prefer dry, open landscapes where they nest on the ground. As a result of protection, some survive in specially managed 'curlew patches' in arable farmland, but most breed on short grassy heaths or downs, mainly in East Anglia and Wiltshire.

They belong to the family known as thick-knees, but their wailing shrieks reminded some ornithologists of the curlew's call. It's a thinner and much less musical sound but as far-carrying and startling when it pierces the night air.

Settling down to watch stone curlews needs time and good optical equipment. Active by night, they're often motionless for long periods during the day and if there's a heat haze over the heath, they can be easy to confuse with the shimmering forms of grazing rabbits, which invariably dot the landscape. The same rabbits are a lifeline for the birds because they keep the turf short, providing the stone curlews with nesting opportunities.

Once seen, though, a stone curlew isn't easily forgotten: a stocky, long-legged wader with a short bill and enormous staring yellow and black eyes. By day, as the birds doze, their eyes narrow into slits, but become owl-like when the bird is alert or at night, when they hunt for insects with a plover-like run, stoop and peck technique.

Stone curlew chicks are sandy like the ground on which they crouch. Camouflage is vital: before they can fly they are prone to the buzzards, stoats and foxes that hunt the rabbits.

Once the chicks have fledged in late summer, stone curlews form family groups. In a few places, especially on Breckland heaths, these groups merge to create flocks of up to 150 birds, which feed and roost together for a few weeks before dispersing south into the Mediterranean basin and North Africa for the winter. Catching up with one of these autumn gatherings is a special experience because you could be watching a sizeable proportion of the 300 or so pairs that breed in England.

GIANT STICK INSECTS
2 October

A first trip to the Isles of Scilly can be a culture shock. Naturalists take their cues from familiar animals and plants in typical habitats and so they can usually second-guess what they will see in a particular place, even if they've not visited before. But this archipelago, forty kilometres off the Cornish coast, breaks the rules: Scilly is unlike anywhere else in the British Isles. Because the islands revel in a mild, oceanic climate and frosts – even in mid-winter – are rare, exotic plants from the Mediterranean, South Africa and New Zealand flourish here. On the island of Tresco, where the Abbey Gardens were established in the mid-nineteenth century, you can walk under date palms while admiring giant agaves and exotic South African proteas, none of which could survive for long out of doors on mainland Britain. Here a short walk feels more like a stroll in Portugal or Cape Town.

Look carefully among this exotic foliage and something unexpected might stir. Many plant species came to Tresco from a nursery in Truro, which imported them from New Zealand and Australia. In the soil around their roots lurked antipodean liverworts and the eggs of large stick insects. The first records of wild-living stick insects in the gardens were in 1943, but it's likely that they had been established much earlier than that, helped by the mild climate, which allowed their eggs to overwinter.

The first time I saw one of these monsters was early one October as I waited for the boat from Tresco to the main island of St Mary's. Sitting in a bramble patch by the quay, a lighter green twig resolved into a prickly stick insect, green with small black thorns scattered over its long body. Its legs were well armoured, though one was missing, and so confident was it in its camouflage that I was able to pick it up and allow it to totter along my arm. At about ten centimetres long it was a spectacular sight, one of our longest British insects. This one was green but they can also be brown and are then even harder to find in the bramble thickets on which they feed. Since then, a midnight visit to a churchyard on St Mary's has revealed more prickly stick insects munching brambles between the gravestones.

The prickly stick insect isn't alone on Scilly: it shares the Abbey Gardens with the smooth stick insect, also from New Zealand, which is slightly smaller and lacks prickles. Both smooth and prickly stick insects are around in summer and autumn, but die in winter after egg-laying. As plants have moved between gardens, so these insects have spread to other islands: stick insects are now also at large in Cornwall, Devon and Hampshire, and could spread if winters become milder.

There are two other stick insects on Scilly: the Mediterranean stick insect was first identified on Tresco in 2002 and, amazingly, the Indian or laboratory stick insect, which many of us have kept as pets at some time, has survived the winters here at England's south-western extremity. It may yet become established on this archipelago that has welcomed plants, insects and birds from all corners of the world.

SHORT-EARED OWL

3 October

The sight of an owl flying over pounding seas on an autumn day is not one I'll ever forget. I was on a Norfolk cliff near Cromer when I saw a large brown bird approaching, low over the coffee-coloured breakers. Mobbed by gulls, it looked utterly incongruous, barely skimming the wave crests that threatened to overwhelm it. But rowing on tortoiseshell wings, the short-eared owl sideslipped its pursuers and headed doggedly inland.

It was the first time I'd seen an owl 'in-off', as sea-watchers describe incoming migrants, and though I knew that long-eared and short-eared owls arrived from the Continent each autumn, being witness to this journey was still a surprise.

Part of that wonder derives from being a landlocked West Midlander, living in an area where short-eared owls are comparatively uncommon. Perhaps I'd be more blasé if I lived in their breeding range in northern

England or Scotland, or in their wintering grounds in the East Anglian fens or along the North Sea coasts. That's why I'm always impressed whenever our paths cross. Each owl must be honoured and savoured.

The numbers of short-eared owls we see each year in Britain vary a great deal. Our own breeding populations and the quantity of birds that cross the North Sea from Scandinavia to winter here depend on the natural cycles of rodent populations. Rodent populations have boom-and-bust cycles and owl numbers track those changes, since the amount of voles and mice that the birds can provide for their young affects breeding success. All of which means that in some years short-eared owls are scarce: in others migrants arrive in good numbers and swell the breeding populations.

Short-ears are one of the most watchable of all British birds, and often fly by day over rough grassland or marshes. As one quarters a grassy field, its languid, flapping flight is broken up by wheeling glides and abrupt turns, sometimes followed by a plunge into the deep grass to seize a vole or a mouse. As the owl flies towards you, its rounded head is a clock-face poised between gold-spangled wings; its searching gaze through yellow, black-pupilled eyes drills you to the core. Sometimes several birds will hunt together over a rodent-rich patch of ground.

Flying by day has its risks. Often owls are harried by crows, which will pursue them to great heights. Way beneath a towering owl, you can appreciate the long-winged silhouettes and the deep, labouring down-strokes that power the bird higher and higher.

COMMA

4 October

With one final flourish, the fine weather brings a short-lived (but very welcome) Indian summer and, with it, a last flutter of butterflies. And among the small tortoiseshells and red admirals I find another, less showy creature: the comma.

My children love the comma: it is one of the easiest butterflies to identify, thanks to its raggedy wings, as if someone has torn them roughly along the edges. The upperwings are striking, too: a base layer of rich orange, blotched with black. But when the comma closes its wings, it can be almost impossible to see, so well does it resemble a dead leaf.

Apart, that is, from one peculiar feature. Look closer, and you'll notice a small, white mark on the centre of the hindwing. This is the sign that, thanks to its resemblance to the common punctuation mark, gives the comma its name.

Commas first appear in our garden much earlier in the year. Because they overwinter as adults, hibernating in the dark corners of our sheds, garages and outbuildings, they usually take to the wing in February or March, though a few years ago I discovered one in the middle of January, basking in the sunshine on a south-facing brick wall. Having emerged, they soon get down to breeding, producing eggs that hatch into cater-pillars. Just over half of these develop normally, pupating and then emerging as a second generation of adults in August and September.

Hard though it is to believe, towards the end of the nineteenth century it was feared that the comma might disappear altogether from Britain. Its range had shrunk so much that it could only be found in any numbers around the lower reaches of the River Severn in Herefordshire, Gloucestershire and Monmouthshire.

How and why the comma declined so suddenly – and recovered so rapidly – is something of a mystery. One possible explanation is that this was an early environmental disaster caused by the use of insecticides on one of the comma's food-plants, hops. Since the First World War it has certainly bounced back; and today we can enjoy watching it among the late autumn butterfly bonanza, before winter finally sets in.

SCILLY BIRDS

5 October

Aboard the steamship *Scillonian III* at Penzance bound for the Isles of Scilly in early October, and there's a palpable thrill in the air. Many of the passengers will be toting telescopes and binoculars because migration is in full swing now and there's no telling what may turn up. The islands are a magnet for birds on the move, many of which are hard or impos-sible to find on the mainland. Some touch down, exhausted after a transatlantic voyage, while others linger to fatten up before they brave the ocean crossing to the Iberian Peninsula and their winter quarters in Africa.

It's the archipelago's reputation as an avian crossroads that makes each October on Scilly crackle with potential. In the past a short-toed eagle from southern Europe, a humbug-striped black and white warbler from the United States and that birder's dream, a Siberian thrush, have all turned up at this time of year.

News travels fast. Once, while eating doughnuts at the Longstones Café on St Mary's, a birding friend and I heard that a blackpoll warbler, a scarce North American vagrant, was in the garden at the Admiralty offices in Hugh Town. Swept along in the rush, we boarded an island bus and joined more than 300 admirers grilling (birder slang for closely observing) the bird, which seemed none the worse for its transatlantic trip.

Now, however, I prefer to avoid the crowds of rarity-hunters and savour the species that Scilly delivers each autumn but which I can't guarantee to see anywhere else. A smart Lapland bunting from the Arctic perhaps, hopping along the heathery paths below the lighthouse on St Martin's, or a dotterel holding up play on the greens of St Mary's golf course.

For me, the autumnal gold medal goes to the wryneck. Wryneck sightings are always a thrill for me because the birds no longer breed in the British Isles. Scilly is one of the most reliable places to see them in Britain, en route from northern Europe to sub-Saharan Africa. That doesn't mean they're easy to find though.

Wrynecks are related to woodpeckers and are named from their habit of twisting their heads round at seemingly impossible angles. Their plumage is intricately barred and striped like lichen-covered bark, which makes them hard to detect when perching on a dry-stone wall or lurking in undergrowth. Often as not, you'll glimpse a banded tail disappearing into pathside weeds where the bird has been feeding. On some days it seems that every birder you meet tells you that 'there was one here a few minutes ago'.

But wrynecks can also surprise. One magical afternoon I watched one in a coastal quarry on St Mary's for two hours as it probed the sandy soil with a ridiculously long sticky tongue, seeking ants and the pupae of solitary bees, its favourite food. Watching it shuffle around on the crumbling quarry face, more like an ungainly reptile than a bird, I couldn't picture it flapping over the Atlantic waves and wondered how many of these Scilly wrynecks made it to their winter homes, thousands of kilometres away in Africa.

SHIELD BUGS

6 October

Think like a shield bug and you'll be drawn to the sunniest spots in the garden. A warm October is the final opportunity to soak up the sun before the first frosts arrive and winter dormancy beckons.

In the USA they're known unglamorously as stink bugs, which seems unfair, if accurate. Some species do indeed produce a pungent aroma if handled, but they are all attractive insects, and, like us, are heliophiles, which respond to a warm October day by basking. They're often mistaken for beetles, but unlike most beetles, which have two wing cases, they have a single 'shield' protecting their bodies. This heraldic shape is a useful guide to the larger and commoner species.

The species I notice most often at this time of year is the green shield bug, which likes gardens and hedgerows where it feasts on almost any unripe fruits, including hawthorn berries, rose hips and even runner beans, though it rarely occurs in numbers large enough to do any damage. Like other bugs, green shield bugs have a long 'beak' called a rostrum – comprising their fused mouthparts – with which they pierce plant tissues and suck up the liquids.

Most green shield bugs start October green and end it in various shades of brown, the colour they assume as camouflage over winter. In spring they resume their verdant colours to match the sprouting greenery.

Green shield bugs are not the only members of their family to look for at this time of year. Hawthorn shield bugs are striking insects with a thorny projection on each of their shoulders. They're green but with wine-red stripes and stipples on their shields and when they fly, which they do with a loud buzzing sound, their reddish abdomens gleam in the sun.

A third garden shield bug is a real success story, thanks to our horti-cultural tastes. Juniper shield bugs suck the green cones of conifers, including wild juniper. As juniper has declined in southern England along with the loss of downland, so has the shield bug, but unwitting gardeners came to the rescue by planting ornamental conifers, especially Lawson's cypress and its many varieties and cultivars. The juniper shield bug, which may now need re-naming, has responded by coming to town. So on a sunny day, if you have conifers in your garden or local park, look out for this attractive little green bug with two chestnut boomerangs on its shield.

GREY PHALAROPE

7 October

It happens most autumns: the dregs of a hurricane sweep across the Atlantic Ocean from the Caribbean or Bermuda as if shot from a catapult, bringing howling gales and squally rain to remind us that summer really is over, and autumn is well and truly here.

Usually this doesn't have a huge effect on seabirds; after all, the ocean is their home, where they feel safe and secure. But one scarce species of wader – the grey phalarope – seems especially vulnerable to being blown inland by these autumnal storms.

So it is that I am standing by the yacht club on the banks of Cheddar Reservoir, watching a tiny, pearl-grey bird bobbing on the surface of the water. The view is both incongruous and very exciting.

I cannot help but wonder how it has survived the storm at all. The grey phalarope (its name comes from the Latin for 'coot-footed', because of the webs on its toes that help it to swim) may be slightly bigger than its red-necked cousin, but it is still smaller and lighter than a starling. Yet as it swims in the shallows, picking off tiny morsels of food from the water's surface with its long, pointed bill, it looks surprisingly resilient.

And so it should be: for this little grey and white bird has already travelled from at least as far as Iceland, and probably much further. Grey phalaropes breed all the way across the Arctic from Siberia and Spitsbergen in the east to Greenland and Canada in the west; where, incidentally, they are known as red phalaropes because of their deep brick-red breeding plumage. A handful also breed in Iceland, where I once had wonderful close-up views of them, looking rather like orange rugby balls.

As I watch the phalarope in these oddly out-of-context surroundings, I may fear for its fate. Yet my worries are misplaced: for this bird will soon reorient itself and head back to the open ocean, where it will spend the rest of the winter, hundreds of miles from land.

RED DEER

8 October

A west London park is an unlikely place to come across one of our great natural wonders. And yet when I lived in the capital, on cold and misty October mornings I would sometimes come across the spectacular red deer rut: the stage on which, each autumn, the stags fight for the right to mate with a harem of fascinated but fussy females.

The show begins at dawn. As the early morning sunlight filters through the mist in Richmond Park, it illuminates the tall buildings to the east, whose backlit beauty will only last for a few minutes before they reveal their true concrete and glass urbanity.

In the park itself, a stag lifts his head and bellows towards the slowly rising sun, producing clouds of steam in the chill air. A second male responds with an equally loud sound, like a roll of distant thunder; and the fight is on.

For the next hour, the two big males challenge one another in a literal clash of heads. Antlers lowered, they bash and bosh, bellow and huff, scraping their feet on the soft ground to prepare for the fight like a tennis champion bouncing a ball before a serve, and then rushing headlong towards one another and locking horns. I watch in growing wonder – who will be the first to stand aside?

Meanwhile the females watch, trying to appear studiously indifferent while studying the fight as closely as any sporting commentator; for the stag that eventually triumphs will be the only one with whom they choose to mate. As with most displays of male power and apparent female subservience in nature, it is the females that are really in charge, choosing the winner, as his strength and determination will give their offspring the best chance in life.

Then, as suddenly as it began, the fight is over. The loser slinks away as if in shame; the winner bellows in triumph. By now the early morning commuter traffic is backing up along the adjacent road, and cyclists, joggers and dog-walkers are crossing the grass; but they are all too late.

IVY BLOSSOM

9 October

No naturalist worth their salt ignores an ivy patch on a sunny October day. Just as pussy willows hum with insects in March and April, so ivy acts as an entomological service station in autumn. For many species it is a vital lifeline, allowing them to build up energy before the long winter sleep, or else a last supper. For some it is a chance to seize prey.

Ivy is unusual among our native plants in that it flowers in autumn and produces its blue-black berries in spring. Trailing or creeping ivy has the familiar fingered leaves, but its flowers are produced on woody upright stems whose leaves are entire, not indented. Ivy flowers are borne in globular pale green or yellowish pincushion clusters between September and November. Glutinous with sweet nectar, they are irresistible to insects: an ivied wall on a warm autumn day thrums with a thousand wingbeats.

Many of these visitors will be droneflies, shining chocolate-orange hoverflies whose early lives were spent in wet manure heaps or stagnant mud as rat-tailed maggots, named from the long siphons which they poke up to the surface to breathe. They spend the winter as adult flies and a feast of ivy nectar will help to see them through.

Although stingless, they are remarkably good honeybee mimics and so are less attractive to predators. Real honeybees and wasps also jostle for places on the ivy pincushions. The honeybees will remain active on warm days throughout winter, but for most of the wasps this is endgame; all but the queens will die.

Not so the brilliant butterflies, which also enliven ivy blossom. Red admirals, their scarlet-slashed forewings soaking up the autumn sunshine, are especially fond of the flowers, as are commas and peacocks. All three species spend the winter as adults and stock up on ivy nectar before entering diapause, a period of slow metabolism similar to hibernation in mammals, reptiles and amphibians.

Ivy is a hunting ground as well as a banqueting table. As you peer at the blossom, you might need to stand aside as huge orange and brown hornets arrive, not only for the sugar rush, but for flesh too. They cruise among the leaves, selecting their prey carefully, then suddenly pounce on a fly or a bee, decapitating and de-winging it before bearing it off to their papery nests in a tree-hollow. There it will be food for the last hornet grubs of the season, whose lives will soon be cut short by the first frosts.

Flies and other insects are food for other predators too. Warblers such as chiffchaffs, which increasingly spend winter in the British Isles, regularly feed around ivy clumps: their soft 'hoo-eet' calls have an anxious quality. In southern England, a tiny green spider called *Nigma walckenaeri* spins a web like a coverlet across the ivy leaves and lurks, brilliantly camouflaged, in the hollow beneath. If you look closely you can see the female, being courted by the browner males. Both have matured to coincide with the bonanza of insects attracted to the bounty of ivy nectar.

INDIAN SUMMER

10 October

The sun is shining, insects are buzzing, and all seems right with the world. All the more so, because this isn't August, but October. Britain – well, the southern half, at least – is enjoying an Indian summer.

This final warm fling before the coming of winter has a long and distinguished history. The term was first used more than 200 years ago by a French-American writer, who had observed that a spell of fine and settled weather would give the Native Americans (known in those benighted days as Red Indians) the chance to harvest their crops. This origin is usually now ignored, in favour of some supposed imperial connection with India itself.

The wildlife in my garden loves an Indian summer. Starlings hover clumsily in blue skies, hawking for tiny, unseen insects, which they snatch out of the air with their sharp bills. Meanwhile the last butterflies – colourful, small tortoiseshells and smart red admirals among them – gather to feed on any nectar they can find.

Part of the bittersweet nature of this unexpected warm spell is the

knowledge that it will come to an end; soon the November gales will begin to blow, heralding the start of the winter.

FLY AGARIC
11 October

A quiet mid-October day on my local patch is not one to set my pulse racing. The only remains of summer are a family of five young mute swan cygnets loafing about with their parents in the flooded wood, while the only birdsong comes from the perennial Cetti's warbler, the one bird that sings here all year round.

But as I tramp along the wooded drove, a patch of colour catches my eye: a tiny beacon of red in a season of yellows and browns. I approach closer, and realise that it is a stout fungus, forcing its way up from the woodland floor among the drooping fronds of bracken. Even my limited knowledge of fungi allows me to identify this gaudy organism as a fly agaric – one of the most notorious of all our native species.

If you ask a child to draw a toadstool, chances are they will produce something looking remarkably like the fly agaric. The thick, white stem topped with a bulbous red cap, itself dotted with white blotches, and perhaps with an elf or fairy perched on top. The overall effect is both pleasing and a clear warning: do NOT eat me!

In fact, the fly agaric is not quite as dangerous as it looks: it can be boiled and eaten, though I wouldn't recommend it. For centuries the indigenous tribespeople of Siberia ate the raw mushroom in small quantities, to take advantage of its known hallucinogenic properties. Holy men known as shamans would ingest the mushroom to achieve a trance-like state, while their followers would then drink the shamans' urine to share in their experience.

Fly agaric was also used as an insecticide, hence its name, after its properties were first discovered by the thirteenth-century German cleric and philosopher Albertus Magnus, who wrote: 'it is called the fly mushroom because it is powdered in milk to kill flies.'

I am tempted to pick this specimen and take it home to show my children, but resist – it looks far better here, lighting up the dismal autumn day with its scarlet cap, and adding an unexpected lift to my mood; without any need for its hallucinogenic properties. Nature does that sometimes.

MONARCH

12 October

The hordes of twitchers are beside themselves in frustration, for the ultra-rare bird found just yesterday evening is nowhere to be seen. Then it miraculously appears, and as this wandering warbler sears its image on the retinas of a thousand obsessive watchers, despair finally turns into joy.

And yet these birds are not the only small miracles here on the Isles of Scilly. On a late flowering border in a garden in the island's capital, Hugh Town, a butterfly is feeding, sucking greedily on nectar with its long black proboscis. It is no ordinary red admiral or small tortoiseshell: its huge size and distinctive black and orange markings with white tips on the edges of its wings mark this insect out as something very different – and far more exciting. It is a monarch butterfly, which like the vagrant birds has crossed the whole of the North Atlantic to be here in south-west England.

Monarch butterflies are famed for their annual migration: a relay race of different generations travelling from Mexico to Canada and back again. Like the birds that get caught up by autumn gales, so these butterflies – each weighing less than a gram – are occasionally swept across the ocean, ending up in south-west England. In the peak year for sightings, 1999, more than 300 made it across; though sadly they will have died as soon as the winter came.

But beware: reports of monarch butterflies outside the autumn gale season, or in unusual places away from the south-west, may be due to them having been released as decorative additions to weddings, or by misguided butterfly enthusiasts whose aim is to establish a permanent colony of this beautiful insect here.

LAND CADDIS

13 October

Had you been in the West Midlands on an October night in 2005, you might have heard cries of delight coming from a wood. Had you had the nerve to approach closer, you'd have seen several people hunched around the glow from a moth trap celebrating a landmark moment in British entomological history. In this dark, damp woodland shrine, we were in the presence of the first female land caddis to be photographed in the wild in the British Isles.

Why is the obscure caddis fly so dear to the hearts of a few Midland naturalists and why has it been seen by just a handful of people?

The answer is partly because of its uniqueness and its odd distribution. There are nearly 200 species of caddis flies in the British Isles and their larvae live in water where many build themselves cases of silk which they spin and use to bind together sand, gravel, leaves or sticks. The land caddis is alone among British caddis in living on land, in the humus of ancient woods. Its tubular case, which is slightly curved, is made from silica grains and fragments of vegetation and as the larva grows it builds new larger cases to accommodate it.

In winter and spring the larvae lug their cases over the forest floor, munching decomposing leaves softened by fungi. We find them by gently scraping the leaf litter with our hands and waiting for tiny twiglets to sprout limbs. In a few places they can be common underfoot: one biologist has described them as 'animated All-Bran'. So twig-like are they that wood ants often incorporate them into the thatch over their nest-mounds.

When the heat of summer dries out the leaf litter, the larvae spin a silken cap over the entrance to their cases and dive down into the humus where they spend the summer. In October they cut their way free and emerge for a brief encounter. The smoky-winged males with their long antennae look for the dumpy, wingless females, who presumably waft pheromones through the woods to attract a mate – how else would the males find them? The naturalist's best way to locate the tiny females is to find a group of males in October and search carefully among the leaves. That was our aim on that memorable October night and since then others have managed to photograph a mating pair, again for the first time in the wild in the UK.

Some of the land caddis's secrets have been unveiled, but there's still one burning question. First discovered on British soil near Worcester in 1858 and re-discovered almost a century later, in 1957, by the young daughter of caddis expert Norman Hickin – who found them crawling over her groundsheet on a camping trip – the land caddis is widespread across the Channel in France's oak woods. But in the British Isles, they are only found in Worcestershire, Shropshire, east Herefordshire and the very south of Staffordshire. In these places they occur in old hedgerows or stream sides, but only in ancient countryside. Why are they so localised in Britain?

We may not solve this mystery, but nevertheless the land caddis continues to fascinate us for its wonderful obscurity and – for this caddis fly enthusiast at least – no October is complete without a trip to the woods in search of the flimsy males on their brief, seasonal tryst.

FIRST REDWINGS

14 October

A mild start to October has prolonged summer for a couple of precious weeks. Today, the illusion ends with roiling grey clouds and drenching cold showers.

Most summer migrants have gone, but today they're replaced by autumn's ushers: gangs of redwings tearing across the skies. These delicate, rusty-flanked thrushes have been away for six months in their breeding territories in Scandinavia or Iceland. It's just enough time to blur the memory, so each October their clipped flight action needs learning again to distinguish them from similar-sized skylarks or high-flying song thrushes. Late September and early October always produces its share of 'hoodwinks', but these redwings are the real thing.

The next birds are more unexpected. I saw what I thought were my last swallows, just ten days ago, and there was a finality to that encounter: I'd packed them away mentally for the year. So when six short-tailed youngsters emerge from the storm in that faltering way they have, sideslipping to chase an invisible insect, then regrouping to struggle on, I'm briefly flummoxed.

There's just enough time to savour, for a few final moments, their fluid flight which mocks the autumn gale. In a ragged, yet cohesive group, they labour over the seething crown of the oak wood, still just about in leaf, and vanish. With their passing, summer is irretrievably over.

COMMON DARTER
15 October

The weak, late October sunshine takes a while to warm up the air. As I walk the short distance from my home to my garden office, I notice the familiar shape of a dragonfly on the limestone path just in front of me. I don't need binoculars to know what species this is, for few other dragonflies are hardy enough to survive this far into the autumn: it's a common darter.

Common and widespread though it may be, this small, neat dragonfly is always worth a second look. The males are brick red and the females yellow, so I use the aide-memoire 'rhubarb and custard' to remember this. They usually emerge in the rhynes and ditches around the Somerset Levels some time in June, but unlike the larger hawkers, which dominate the airspace for a few weeks and then disappear, these smaller insects hang around for four months or more.

As I approach, the darter rises into the autumnal air and buzzes away like a Tiger Moth aircraft; a last reminder of the heady days of summer, before the chill to come.

WINTER THRUSHES
16 October

The last swallows and house martins have finally left for Africa; and the autumn skies around my home are almost empty, save for little flocks of starlings and the usual woodpigeons and rooks. Then, soon after dawn on a chilly October day, I notice a ragged flock of birds in the lightening skies to the east: lumbering silhouettes, looking rather like the familiar mistle thrush, but somehow less streamlined in shape.

For a second I am baffled as to their identity, for I haven't seen them since February or March. But a single burst of sound from the leading bird – a repetitive 'chack-chack-chack' – and I realise what they are: a flock of fieldfares.

They are hungry; and so they should be, for they have come all the way across the North Sea from Scandinavia – some even further, from the bleak steppes of Siberia. The smaller birds alongside them are travellers too: redwings, some of which have accompanied their larger cousins across the North Sea, while others have flown south from Iceland.

All are here for the same reason: food. As winter takes a grip on the northern hemisphere, so birds from northerly latitudes must flee the cold and darkness. Staying put would be suicidal, as the snow and ice would soon cover their food supplies and they would starve to death. That's why they come here, to enjoy the winter thrush equivalent of a holiday by the Med. There are plenty of hawthorn berries in the hedgerows along the lanes, glowing crimson in the autumn sunshine; and when these finally run out, sometime around Christmas, plenty of worms in the adjacent fields.

For the next four months or so, flocks of these attractive birds will be my constant companion on walks and cycle rides around my country parish. Only if the cold weather follows them south, and we get a really freezing spell, will they come into my garden to take advantage of more reliable food: windfall cider apples scattered across our snowy lawn.

Then, one fine day in March, they will disappear again; heading north and east back to their breeding grounds, and leaving me bereft. For these birds are as much a marker of autumn and winter as the swallows, swifts and cuckoos are a sign of spring and summer; and I miss them just as much when they go.

JACK SNIPE

17 October

The great talon of Spurn Head in Yorkshire, which clutches the mud of the Humber estuary while presenting its shoulder to the North Sea, is a funnel for migrating birds. Here in autumn you can stand on the narrow spit, just wide enough to accommodate a rough road, and marvel as swallows flicker past at knee height. One grey October day I watched a last pair struggle south, tailed by six whooper swans from Iceland. The message couldn't have been clearer: out with summer, in with winter.

I'd gone to find merlins for a radio recording, but the falcons were characteristically evasive, so I hunkered down in a hide overlooking a sheltered pool. Here moorhens flicked tails and belched in the reeds, while a solitary greenshank studiously probed the shallows. Then from the corner of my eye, I noticed a bobbing shape among the grassy tussocks, so well concealed that without its springy motion I'd have missed it: my first jack snipe of the autumn.

The jack snipe – the diminutive 'jack' reflects their smaller size than common snipe – is a special bird for which bird-hides were custom-built. Prolonged views are rare unless you're prepared to sit quietly for some time and scan the ground with forensic precision. So well camouflaged is the bird that it can skulk unseen and motionless just a metre or two away among dried leaves at the margins of muddy pools.

The bright yellow stripes on its crown resemble wisps of straw and the buff streaks on its body break up its outline among the grass stems. It's shorter-billed than snipe and its back feathers have an oily greenish or purplish gloss in sunlight. When relaxed, jack snipe feed with a strange bobbing motion as if they were balanced on springs. Ornithologists aren't sure why they do this, but suspect that it may help to blur the bird's outline in wind-blown vegetation.

Away from a hide, the birds are even less cooperative. Threatened jack snipe freeze and are invisible until you practically tread on them, when they start up almost underfoot, soundless except for a flurry of wings. After a short parabolic flight, they drop back into cover, unlike snipe, which if disturbed usually fly high and far.

Jack snipe have very different personalities in the breeding season. They don't breed in the British Isles, but in Scandinavian and Russian bogs, where the male turns extrovert in summer, display-flying high over his soggy domain while producing a rhythmic 'clip-clop' song, like a horse cantering over a hard road. In the mosquito-ridden twilight, this eerie sound echoes through the northern skies, but when the breeding season is over and snow covers its breeding mires, the jack snipe heads south to spend autumn in warmer climes.

Some, like my bird at Spurn, make silent landfall at coastal marshes, while others fan out through damp pastures and wetlands throughout Britain where most will evade the gaze of all but the most observant watchers.

BEARDED TITS

18 October

Like September, October can be very quiet and uneventful on my local patch. Caught between summer and winter, as the evenings get darker I struggle to raise the energy to tramp around because, on some visits, I see or hear virtually nothing.

So when I recognise the cash-register pinging of a pair of bearded tits, I feel both surprised and relieved. Hearing these elusive reed-bed birds is one thing; seeing them quite another. At first, all I get is tantalising glimpses of half a tail or perhaps a brief view of a head behind a reed-stem. But if I am quiet and patient, they usually lose at least some of their shyness and begin climbing up the stem and into view.

When I'm asked which is Britain's most beautiful bird, I struggle to find an answer. How can you choose between the dazzling blue and orange of the kingfisher and the lithe, floating flight of the red kite? What about the perky male stonechat, or the stunning firecrest? But if I were forced to choose, it would be hard not to pick the bearded tit. No other British bird has quite such a pleasing combination of colours: my friend and fellow birder Martin Woodcock once told me that the blue-grey head and ochre body are opposite one another on the artist's colour chart, and so are perfectly matched. When you add the male's ink-black moustaches, it's hard to imagine a more handsome creature.

Bearded tits should also win a prize for the silliest British bird name, for they are neither bearded, nor tits. That raises the crucial question: what are they? When I started birding they were considered to belong to the parrotbill family, a group of similar-looking birds found in Africa and Asia. Then someone decided they were babblers. Now, the latest news from the taxonomists is that bearded tits – or 'moustached reedlings', as perhaps we should rename them – belong on their own. They are unique, and as I enjoy their chorus of pings on an autumn afternoon I believe deservedly so.

RED SQUIRREL
19 October

The movement is brief but impossible to mistake. Amid the funereal quiet of a Caledonian pine wood in autumn, the blurred shape heading down a distant tree-trunk and across the forest floor could only be one thing: a red squirrel looking for food.

I stand stock-still, hardly daring to breathe. Has it gone in the other direction, or will I manage to get a view? I'm lucky: it appears from behind a nearer tree, pauses to check that it is safe, then bounds acrobatically through the leaves to pick up a pine cone. Holding his prize expertly between its paws, the squirrel demolishes it in a few seconds, drops the remaining core, and then heads off to search for more.

Today, this red squirrel will find more than enough to eat. Autumn is a time of abundance, with not just pine cones, but also berries, nuts and seeds. But this squirrel knows that the bad times really are just around the corner; so after eating its fill, it takes the rest of its food to a safe corner of the wood, digs a hole, and buries it.

Known as caching, this habit is typical of all squirrels. Contrary to popular belief, they don't hibernate, so need to feed throughout the long winter months. This strategy only works, though, if in a month or so's time the squirrel can remember where it hid its precious store.

Even if it does find where it hid the food, there's always a chance that another creature will have already discovered it. But if the squirrel has worked hard enough during the times of plenty, there will still be sufficient food to get it through the times when snow covers this ancient landscape.

IVY BEE

20 October

There aren't many new species that you can spot, pint in hand, from your local pub-table. But, on a sunny October day, as I sat with visiting friends lazily watching the throngs of flies and honeybees buzzing around the ivy blossom in the beer-garden, we noticed some very stripy bees, about the size of honeybees but with very neat black and orange bands. To our delight they turned out to be ivy bees, an insect I'd been antici-pating here for a couple of years.

Ivy bees colonised England from continental Europe and were first noticed in Dorset in 2001. Since then, hymenopterists – people who study bees, wasps and ants – have been following their progress north as far as the Midlands and west into Devon and South Wales. Each year the insects have increased their range and because there are no similar stripy bees with furry ginger thoraxes about on ivy at this time of year, they are easy for non-experts to identify. Their colonisation is remarkable enough, but even more surprising is that they were only identified as recently as 1993. Before then they were thought to be a similar bee, common in Europe, from which they've now been separated as a new species.

Ivy bees are solitary bees. Unlike honeybees, they don't form social colonies with a queen and workers. Instead each female ivy bee digs her own burrow in soft ground and lays her eggs there, provisioning them with a pollen and nectar cake to be eaten by the grubs when they hatch. Popular sites such as sunny banks often contain tens or even hundreds of these burrows. One of our first local colonies was in a grassy bank in a town centre car park.

Unlike many of our 230-odd species of solitary bees that appear in spring and summer, ivy bees are adult from mid-September until early November and time their emergence to coincide with the blooming of ivy.

The smaller males appear first and wait by the nesting burrows for a female to emerge. As she struggles into the light for the first time, she may be seized by several amorous males until she is lost at the centre of a mating ball of sex-crazed bees. This unseemly scrum is crucial for each male who lives only a couple of weeks or so as an adult and therefore has to seize every opportunity to pass on his genes. Even the adult females only survive for a few weeks, but that's time enough to dig a burrow, collect pollen and nectar and lay her eggs. It's a short, but frenetic life and makes ivy-blossom-watching, in the park, in the garden or even at the local, an absorbing autumn activity.

GOSSAMER

21 October

In autumn 1832 Charles Darwin was aboard HMS *Beagle*, sixty miles off the Patagonian coast, when he noticed the air was full of drifting silk threads. Huge numbers of 'little aeronauts' were invading the ship, landing on its rigging and scurrying about. Looking closer he saw that they were small reddish-brown spiders, not only settling, but also taking off again into the breeze.

His experience of 'ballooning', the aerial dispersal of spiders, is a sight we can share on warm October days. Step out into a field or on to a common on a dewy morning and you may see the grass and shrubs draped with translucent wisps of gossamer, which glint in the sunlight. Sometimes these wisps converge to create shimmering, silken sheets, which ripple in the lightest of breezes. Across a wider landscape, they are impressive, not least because they're evidence of the sheer abundance of spiders.

The spider expert Bill Bristowe once calculated that in an English field at certain times of the year, there were 2 million spiders to the acre. Most of these were the small linyphiids, the family we commonly call money spiders. The mind can only boggle at the quantity of insects and other creatures they need to keep themselves nourished.

Their hunger explains the amount of silk we see. These strands are used not only to entrap prey, but to help the young spiders, which are most abundant at this time of year, escape from their cannibal siblings and set up home in a less crowded neighbourhood.

But first the spiderlings need to get airborne. To do this they climb a bush or a fence-post and, facing into the breeze, tilt their abdomens towards the sky. From the spinnerets at the end of their bodies, they extrude a thread of silk, which is lifted by the wind and quickly carries the spider aloft.

As these pioneers head high into the autumn skies, you can't help but wonder where, if at all, they will touch down. Many will perish or land in unsuitable places. Others are snapped up as aerial plankton by tardy migrants such as late swallows and martins. Although this is mainly an autumn spectacle, in summer too the skies above Britain are full of Darwin's little aeronauts and it's been estimated that adult and young spiders can form 70 per cent of the diet of swifts, which catch all their prey on the wing. The ones that survive can colonise new habitats and remote places by travelling up to several hundred kilometres, an extraordinary feat.

HORSE CHESTNUT
22 October

Naturalists don't much like aliens. I'm not talking about little green men, but invasive plant and animal species from foreign parts which have, by accident or design, ended up on our shores.

Yet for every grey squirrel or Canada goose there are species, like the brown hare, that we have welcomed into our fauna and flora, and now have a central part to play in our culture as well as our natural history.

One such is the horse chestnut. The unusual name comes from a chance observation by the Flemish ambassador to Turkey, who observed that Turkish soldiers fed the tree's fruit – conkers – to their horses. This majestic tree may be a relative newcomer here – the first were introduced in Tudor times – but it has made an enormous contribution to popular culture, both as 'the spreading chestnut tree' of popular song, and of course with the game of conkers. It helps that, in southern Britain at least, the horse chestnut is so ubiquitous, found in parks and woods throughout urban and suburban as well as rural areas.

It is very easy to identify: in spring the snow-white or rose-pink 'candles' of blossom dot the green foliage, while the five-fingered leaves are very distinctive too. And who could fail to notice the conkers themselves: as the spiky green cases break open to reveal smooth, shiny objects, so pleasing to the eye and to touch; which like all fruits also help the tree to propagate itself.

DYKES AND DUCKWEEDS

23 October

The rhynes – or dykes – around my home are frequently covered with a green layer of duckweed. These floating aquatic plants form a layer of lime green, most persistent in summer, but which often hangs around well into autumn, especially in warmer years.

Duckweed is so common and ubiquitous we tend to take it for granted; yet these really are fascinating little plants. Simple they may be – there is no obvious stem or leaves – but they are remarkably good at reproducing themselves: often asexually so that they can spread rapidly, although occasionally reverting to sex, producing tiny flowers in order to do so.

Indeed the smallest flowering plants in the world belong to the duckweed family; those in the genus *Wolffia* measure a mere third of a millimetre long, making them virtually impossible to see.

The ability of duckweed to spread so effectively gave rise to a chilling legend: that of Jenny Greenteeth. This bogeywoman was supposed to live beneath the layer of duckweed, emerging only to lure unsuspecting children into the water, where they would drown. Like many other fairy tales, this had a clear purpose: to warn small children of the potential dangers of assuming that the green layer of duckweed was solid, so that they would not fall through to the water below.

FAIRY RINGS

24 October

Centuries before we had the excitement of crop circle theories, writers speculated about the darker rings of grass that often appear in fields and on downs. The idea that these circles had been made by dancing fairy folk was a popular one and taken up enthusiastically by the likes of Chaucer, Pope, Dryden, Tennyson and many others. A lively hearsay account by John Aubrey, written in 1639, refers to a schoolmaster of his who found himself one night in the middle of a 'faery dance', surrounded by an 'innumerable quantitie of . . . very small people dancing rounde and rounde' who 'pinch'd him all over'.

There were other theories: that the rings were caused by lightning strikes, the assembling of witches or were scorched by dragons. More practically, it was suggested that rutting deer or burrowing moles were responsible, though the fact that rings could run though hedges was unexplained. Such was the power of the fairy superstition that few people commented on the toadstools that occasionally sprouted around the circles, though the Hampshire naturalist Gilbert White came very close when he wrote in 1780 that 'fairy rings' that occurred in turf brought from the downland into his garden sprouted puffballs: not the causers of the rings, but a fungal association, even if White wasn't aware of it.

It was a few years later that the real creators of fairy rings were pinpointed by botanist William Withering, who described their connection with fairy ring mushrooms, a species we now call *Marasmius oreades*. They're common on garden lawns and most types of grassland where the pale brown mushrooms form circles as their underground mycelium spreads outwards. As it travels the fungus produces chemicals to inhibit grass growth, creating a bare or weakened circle. It also produces nitrogen and enriches the grass ahead of it, which is why there's usually a ring of lusher, darker green grass ahead of the expansion zone.

Fairy rings are slow to develop and may last for centuries if the grassland isn't disturbed. Aerial views of Stonehenge show a whole series of rings, spots and curlicues formed by fungi, possibly over many hundreds of years.

Several species of fungi form rings and one of the most spectacular is the trooping funnel, which appears in woodland. Its large greyish-brown mushrooms have stout stems and indented caps – hence the name. It grows in woodland and so its fairy rings are less easy to pick out, but one enormous circle photographed from a plane measured 800 metres in diameter.

ACORNS

25 October

October's conkers may be flash and showy, but acorns have far more uses. Over millennia the fruits of the oak tree have been used as medicines to cure a wide range of ailments, and as food – porridge, nuts, bread and coffee are just some of the many ways in which acorns have been substituted for more expensive foodstuffs.

Today they are rarely used for human consumption, but pigs love acorns, and we – at least the carnivores among us – love the sweet, tender ham that acorn-fed pigs produce.

But the real magic of acorns is that, to quote the famous phrase, great oaks grow from them. These tiny seeds, their bases held safely in an even tinier cup, fall from their parent trees in October. Most are either eaten by squirrels and jays or land on unsuitable ground. But perhaps one in a thousand germinates and grows, producing first a sapling, then a tree, then – in a few cases – the mighty oak that we know so well.

DORMICE

26 October

Thanks to Lewis Carroll's Mad Hatter's tea party, the dormouse is probably best known to most of us as a mammal that sleeps in teapots. Part of the fantasy is true: dormice certainly do sleep a great deal; indeed a local folk name for them is seven-month sleeper.

For this reason, and because dormice are scarce and usually nocturnal, we rarely have the chance to see these elusive honey-coloured creatures in the wild. That's a pity because they are irresistibly cute, a rodent that Disney could have designed, with large lustrous dark eyes and fluffy tails. Even their diet is delectable: they suck nectar from flowers, though they will also eat insects, nuts and fruit.

The first time I saw a live dormouse was during a weighing session organised by the Worcestershire Wildlife Trust to determine whether the animals had put on enough fat before hibernation. Working under special licence, we entered the ancient oak wood to look for the dormouse nest-boxes, rather like bird-boxes, but with the entrance hole at the back to keep out predators.

It was late in October, a time I'd have thought any respectable dormouse would have been in the arms of Morpheus. Our technique was simple: stuff the entrance/exit hole with a towel, place the whole box in a plastic bag and then remove the towel. An exiting rodent is easily seen as it rushes out of the box into the bag.

There were no mice in the first few boxes we checked, in fact no room for as much as an earwig. They'd been used as larders by yellow-necked mice that had crammed them brimful of crab-apples.

Eventually, though, having extricated it from its box, we had our first dormouse in the bag ready for weighing on portable spring scales; all we had to do was clip on the bag containing the mouse, weigh it and then deduct the weight of the bag. Not all the dormice made it to this stage. Far from being drowsy some of them were as slippery as soap, running up our arms in a ginger blur and disappearing high into the trees. But the news was good: not only were they thriving in this wood with its plentiful fruit and hazel bushes, but they were in good condition for the long winter sleep.

But many recent studies of dormice, also known as hazel dormice, have shown that contrary to popular belief this secretive rodent doesn't seem to need hazel nuts. Much to the Forestry Commission's surprise, the mice thrive in mature pine plantations with some ancient woodland containing very little hazel. Phil Rudlin from the Forestry Commission showed me the boxes he and his study team have erected among the trees as summer shelters for the dormice, and explained how they also construct breeding nests in the skirts of dead pine needles which collect among low-growing branches. The mice even eat pine pollen in early summer and leave tiny golden droppings in their summer sleeping boxes. Hibernating dormice build nests of leaves and dried grass on the forest floor.

However now there's a challenge. The conifers are being removed by the Forestry Commission to allow the wood to revert to native broad-leaved trees and if all the conifers are taken out at the same time, the dormice nests and hibernation sites could be destroyed by heavy machinery. So Phil and other researchers have fitted some dormice with tiny microchips to show how individuals use the woodland and how far they travel. Their findings have informed a plan that will see the conifers being removed gradually over several years, which will allow the dormice time to adapt to their changing world.

PECTORAL SANDPIPER

27 October

A muddy pool on the Avalon Marshes soon attracts waders – especially at the height of the migration season. But among the godwits and redshanks, dunlins and ringed plovers, is a pair of birds that – although they are also long-distance migrants – should be on the opposite side of the Atlantic Ocean, heading not for Africa but down to South America.

The pectoral sandpiper – named after the neat pattern of streaks down its upper breast, contrasting with the white belly – is the commonest Nearctic avian visitor to Britain. It breeds in the far north, from Alaska in the west to Hudson Bay in the east; then heads out over the Atlantic on its epic journey south to Chile or Argentina. Caught up in the tail end of hurricanes, or simply swept across the ocean by strong westerly winds, they turn up every autumn; but are always a treat for any birder.

Today I am in the company of Richard Crossley, an expat Brit who now lives in the New Jersey seaside resort of Cape May, arguably the best place to see migrant birds in the whole of North America. For Richard, 'pec sands', as birders call them, are ten a penny, so it doesn't take him long to pick them out.

But it's not these Yankee waders that surprise him, but their supporting cast of birds – a glossy ibis and no fewer than three species of egret: little egret of course, but also the scarcer great white and cattle egrets, all feeding in the shallow water.

Richard can't help but be impressed, and expresses his delight in the broad Yorkshire tones he has retained, despite his decades on the other side of the Atlantic. We nonchalantly pretend that this is par for the course nowadays; yet we too are secretly pleased that we have been able to put on a show for our visiting friend.

BIRD-TABLE PLANTS

28 October

Last October, a naturalist friend was surprised to find himself potentially outside the law by cultivating illegal substances in his garden. Earlier in the year he had unwittingly sprinkled his bird-table with seeds including those of cannabis plants and his autumn reward was a crop of the long-fingered leaves, sprouting among the sunflowers and green blades of young maize.

It's something that's worried many back garden bird-feeders, but there's no cause for alarm – all you'd get from smoking this is at most a headache. Hemp, or *Cannabis sativa*, which was once widely grown for rope-making in Britain, is a common constituent of many birdseed mixes. It is the same species as the plant that provides marijuana, but contains very little of the psychoactive compound THC (tetrahydrocannabinol), which delivers a 'high'.

Hemp is just one of the unusual and sometimes puzzling plants that bloom because their seeds evaded the birds. Sunflowers and maize are common and easily recognised, but in October and November you may also see a tall plant – two metres high or more – with long saw-toothed leaves and brilliant yellow daisy flowers. This is the niger – sometimes spelled nyjer – plant *Guizotia abyssinica*, whose slim black seeds are now very popular as bird-food and have played an important role in the rise of the goldfinch in our gardens. Niger is a handsome plant and worth cultivating, but flowers late and, as it is native to East Africa, wilts at the first touch of frost. The fern-like leaves of ragweed often mingle with it, though their spikes of greenish flowers are much less spectacular and are notorious for their effects on hay fever sufferers.

Another beautiful but tender plant that often grows from birdseed is the shoo-fly plant from South America; it's also known as the apple-of-Peru, from its berry-like fruit encased in inflated green bracts. Don't try eating it though – this is a member of the nightshade family that can bring on hallucinations. In full bloom, it's a handsome plant with lilac-blue, bell-like flowers and it often turns up on rubbish tips. Its relative the thorn-apple – which will sometimes produce its white trumpet flowers and spiky fruits below the bird-table – is also poisonous.

These late-flowering annuals are as short-lived as the darkening autumn days, so if you want to admire them more fully, sow a handful of birdseed in late spring and see what comes up.

GREAT BUSTARD
29 October

There aren't many birds that match the mute swan for size. But there, standing statuesque and upright among the feeding flock of a dozen or so swans, was a great bustard – looking like a Christmas turkey on steroids.

The great bustard is a contender for the largest living creature still able to take to the air. The biggest male bustard ever recorded weighed in at a whopping twenty-one kilos – over three stones, or the same as a six-year-old child. The bird we were looking at was a female, which are both lighter and shorter than their mates; nonetheless, at almost a metre tall, she was easy to spot even at a distance.

A closer look revealed the subtleties of her plumage: mottled black and brown upperparts contrasting with white beneath, with a sandy-brown neck and pale, dove-grey head. I could also see a bright orange tag attached to her wing, bearing the number '15'. This confirmed what I expected: that she was a wandering bird from the Great Bustard Release Project on Salisbury Plain, a short flight to the east of here. The project is a laudable attempt to bring back one of Britain's most iconic lost birds, the last of which bred in Suffolk in 1832. Since then, numbers of this magnificent species have fallen right across Europe and Asia, and nowadays the nearest breeding sites are in Spain and eastern Europe.

I had mixed feelings on seeing this bird. Regret that we lost the species in the first place, through habitat loss and hunting. Excitement as I imagined its reintroduction. And fear that our little island is just too crowded, our habitats too fragmented, and our countryside too intensively farmed for the great bustard ever to thrive again. In the meantime, though, I could enjoy watching the incongruous sight of a great bustard standing in a Somerset field, like a queen surrounded by her courtiers.

EXMOOR SAFARI

30 October

I've done Land Rover safaris in the Masai Mara, the Okavango Delta and the Highlands of Scotland, but never quite so close to home: on Exmoor. So I wasn't quite sure what to expect when we met our guide, Daphne, in the picturesque Somerset village of Dunster.

Our family of five crammed into the vehicle and headed up the road towards the moor. Until then, I hadn't spent much time in this upland habitat and, as October can be a quiet month on moorland, my hopes weren't all that high.

Going anywhere with a local guide is always a pleasure; they point out the subtleties of landscape that the untrained eye can so easily miss, and tell stories that illuminate the history of a place as well as its natural history. Daphne was no exception, and we were soon entranced.

Places like Exmoor do not give up their secrets easily. We drove first along forest tracks, walls of green coming close as we squeezed through gaps in the trees. A stop by the River Barle, a tributary of the larger and more famous Exe, produced our first notable bird: a dipper, doing its usual bobbing action before flying off like a cross between a wren and a torpedo. But the woods themselves were oppressive and silent, and I soon began to yearn for a more open landscape where we had a chance of seeing more birds.

Emerging out of the forest and on to the moor, we stopped and scanned with our binoculars from time to time. The very nature of moorland means that there are very few species of bird, and those that do live here are both mobile and elusive as they quarter this vast area in search of food. Buzzards, of course, were easy to see as they rose on the currents of wind sweeping across this desolate landscape. Other raptors, I knew, would prove harder to find; but, one by one, we eventually saw them. First, a sparrowhawk, its characteristic flap-flap-glide movement making it easy to pick out. Then a peregrine, driving powerfully across the scene on broad, muscular wings before heading off into the far distance.

Later, Britain's smallest bird of prey, a merlin, which treated us to a prolonged close-up view as it perched on a swaying twig in the strengthening gusts of wind. This minuscule falcon, barely the size of a mistle thrush, is suitably mercurial in its habits, and I couldn't remember when I had last enjoyed such a good look.

Elusive as the merlin may usually be, it was positively showy compared with our final raptor of the day. As we returned through the same dark, cheerless woods, a bird of prey materialised briefly just ahead of us. Large, grey and stiff-winged, it floated between the trees and then vanished, almost as soon as it had appeared. But this view was enough to confirm its identity as a goshawk, the most mysterious and hard to find of all Exmoor's birds.

We may not have seen lions or leopards, but our safari had been as memorable as any in Africa, proving that some of our most unforgiving landscapes have the most to offer – so long as you know where to look.

HARLEQUIN LADYBIRD

31 October

Across the pond in the USA, they call harlequin ladybirds Halloween ladybeetles, because around 31 October the ladybirds come indoors to hibernate: in sheds, outhouses and even spare bedrooms. They are now the commonest ladybird in my garden and in October their pupal cases, sometimes in their hundreds, stud the tree-trunks in the local park.

Although they are now very much part of the British scene, occurring from the Isles of Scilly to Shetland, we haven't yet granted them a familiar name, partly because harlequins have only been resident here since 2003 and partly because they have besmirched the reputation of ladybirds.

Our relationship with these colourful beetles has until now been a benevolent one, based on their pleasing, rounded shapes and bright primary colours, but also because several species eat plant pests including aphids and scale insects. Few insects have collected such a catalogue of folk names, from bishie-barnabee to clock-a-clay. The name ladybird is a medieval reference to the Virgin Mary who was famously painted by Leonardo da Vinci in a bright red garment. Our most obvious species is the seven-spot ladybird, whose black spots were thought to represent the Seven Joys and Seven Sorrows of Mary and its red colour suggested the blood of Christ, so the insect was considered blessed.

Not a reputation enjoyed by the harlequin. It's native to Asia, from where it has been introduced deliberately to North America and continental Europe to control aphids and other pests. Since its arrival in south-east England around 2003, it has spread phenomenally fast.

The harlequin's varied menu is its main drawback. Not content with pests, it also munches on beneficial insects including the larvae of other ladybirds. The smaller two-spot ladybird, for example, seems to have declined dramatically in places following the harlequin's arrival. Biologists hope that harlequin numbers will settle down and even reduce once they are on the menu themselves for our native ladybird parasites.

Hungry or not, harlequins are attractive insects, large and vibrantly coloured. They occur in a number of patterns: the red form with eighteen or so spots is most common, but you'll often see shining black specimens with four blood-red blotches. Their large size is usually enough to tell them apart from other ladybirds. Through binoculars I can see several in the high branches of a bush outside the window now: they've done a useful job of eating the blackfly, but even so, as winter approaches, I'll keep the windows closed.

NOVEMBER

No shade, no shine, no butterflies, no bees,
No fruits, no flowers, no leaves, no birds! –
November!

THE NINETEENTH-CENTURY POET and humorist Thomas Hood took a dim view of the penultimate month of the year, and the majority of naturalists probably share his opinion. For many, this is the time of year to be sitting in front of a blazing fire, planning next year's trips around Britain – and to even further-flung places – to see sought-after species.

But for others, including me, November presents opportunities to get close to species that may otherwise be elusive, and also to enjoy some early winter spectacles. Living in south-west Britain, I eagerly await November's new arrivals from the skies: those species of bird that come here from further north and east to enjoy the benefits of a relatively mild winter climate, where food is plentiful and snow and ice are rare.

November isn't all about birds, though they are, as throughout the late autumn and winter, the most visible of wild creatures. Mammals, too, may be more obvious at this time of year: deer are finishing their annual rut, grey seals are giving birth on wild and windswept beaches, and smaller mammals such as squirrels are preparing for the hardship of the season ahead.

And though they may be hard to find, there are still invertebrates on show, if you know where to look, as well as the late appearing fungi, such as the jewel-like waxcaps. So make sure you keep an open mind, wrap up warm and enjoy what this subtly different month has to offer.

S.M.

ALTHOUGH THE HURLY-BURLY of bird migration is largely done, November can still be a busy month. Step outside on a quiet evening, avoiding the firework displays, and you'll hear that urgency in the pinprick calls of migrating redwings, fly-by-nights keeping in touch with each other under the stars.

They're not the only northern birds using the UK as a winter service station. Wildfowl from Scandinavia and Russia are thronging here. Brought up in an area where wild geese, as opposed to introduced Canada geese, are absent, at this time of year I itch for places like the Severn estuary, the north Norfolk coast or the Solway Firth, where the air fills with their clangour.

Geese are birds that define the landscape in which they roost and feed: to see a skein flying overhead is an uplifting experience. I find wild whooper and Bewick's swans irresistible too, as much for their harmonious bugling as for their pale elegance, out on the misty fens and saltmarshes.

Invertebrates – or at least visible invertebrates – are on the wane now and so if I'm not looking skywards, then I'm furkling in the woods for fungi and other surprises. Early in the month, the beeches are golden as they catch the autumn sunlight and there are still green oak leaves on many trees.

Even on cold November days, frost only penetrates the topmost layers of leaf litter. Last year's foliage, now composting in a springy layer underfoot, shelters a wealth of beetles, snails, centipedes and slugs, including the charismatic lemon slug which is not only an indicator of ancient woodland, but also an autumnal yellowish-orange, the exact shade of freshly fallen leaves.

B.W.

UNEXPECTED LATE MIGRANTS

I November

Just when you think summer is well and truly over, it returns for a glorious few hours, before the world shuts down for autumn and winter once again.

We were on a family walk with my stepson and his wife and daughters, climbing Crook Peak, a high point of the Mendips known to us as 'Charlie's mountain' because when we first moved in my son noticed it in the distance behind our garden. It is a lovely walk, giving panoramic views in all directions, though the proximity of the M5 snaking away below does rather clash with the more ancient sights such as Glastonbury Tor.

It was one of those days when you dress too warmly, and then wish you'd brought the sun cream. Coats were soon discarded, and the children romped happily ahead of us towards the distant peak. I expected to see stonechats, and there they were, bobbing up on nearby rocks and cocking their stumpy tails, occasionally uttering the percussive, pebble-like call that gives the species its name.

But I wasn't expecting the stonechat's larger cousin, the wheatear. Yet sure enough, there was one on the short turf a few metres in front of us, bounding along and occasionally taking flight to reveal that classic white rump. By rights this bird should have been halfway to Africa, yet here it was, feeding on tiny insects in the November sunshine.

Enjoyment of this unexpected sighting was mixed with sadness, as I knew it was the last of the autumn migrants I would see this year. A passing common darter dragonfly and a bright-lemon male brimstone butterfly added to my feelings of imminent loss. But I consoled myself with the knowledge that as some species depart or disappear, so others take their place in the ever-changing calendar of nature.

BRAMBLING

2 November

A distinctive, edgy call alerts me to their presence; then, as I flush the little flock of birds from the woodland floor in front of me, a flash of white confirms their identity. Among the common and familiar chaffinches there are a few of their northern relative, the brambling. They have just arrived from across the North Sea in Scandinavia, and will spend the winter here before departing again in March.

Keen to get a better look at these shy birds, I shuffle slowly forward, trying to keep my movements as slow and steady as possible. Lifting the binoculars gently to my eyes, I focus on a splendid male brambling. Like a chocolate-orange version of the chaffinch, he stands out like a sore thumb, with a mottled brown head, face, back and wings, white on the chin and belly and a warm orange flush across his chest. Seeing me, he takes off again, revealing that snow-white rump as he opens his wings.

Once known as the mountain finch (from its Latin name *montifringilla*), the brambling has nothing to do with blackberries, though they do arrive in the autumn. Instead it appears to be a corruption of the word 'brandling', which comes from the same root as 'brindled' and refers to the bird's dappled plumage.

Like other species such as the crossbill and waxwing, bramblings are irruptive in their habits, so that they may be common in a particular place one year yet absent the next, which can be frustrating if you are hoping to see one. Your best bet is to take a close look at mixed feeding flocks of finches, and watch out for that distinctive flash of white.

WAXCAPS

3 November

Though it's early November, the steep grassy bank in front of us is dotted with bright splashes of vermilion and sulphur, which on closer inspection turn out to be waxcaps. 'Fungal flowers' is an apt description of these attractive toadstools, partly because many of them are brilliantly coloured, but also because, like certain communities of flowering plants, they signpost the quality of older grasslands.

One species, the ballerina waxcap, whose rose-pink cap flares at the edges like a tutu, has been declared a fungal flagship species whose presence denotes meadows and commons rich in fungi, flowers and insects. It follows that waxcaps are rarely common on manicured and over-fertilised garden lawns or regularly re-sown grasslands. They're connoisseurs of older, mossy meadows and grazed commons, orchards and churchyards. Visit one of these places on an autumn day and the fungi glow in soft sunlight. Rub the cap of one gently and it has the cool, slightly greasy feel of a candle or cold butter. Some species are slimier, like the parrot waxcap, which glisten among the grass blades like sucked boiled sweets. As its common name suggests, it has a variety of colours including yellow, orange and unusually a fresh spring green. On the island of Lundy in the Bristol Channel, parrot waxcaps occur in a mind-boggling blue form.

On this early November morning I have joined a friend, Rosemary Winnall, to count waxcaps in her Worcestershire garden. Years ago, she and her husband Tony removed a thicket of gorse from an overgrown bank near her house and allowed a local farmer to graze the area lightly with cattle. To her surprise, the bank has sprouted a succession of waxcaps and is now a nationally important site for them, with over twenty species recorded, including one that is new to science. Today we are surveying the ballerinas, each frilly specimen marked with a stick so that Rosemary can compare their numbers from year to year and manage the site accordingly.

At the top of the bank in a flatter area of grassland, she shows me vivid clumps of scarlet waxcaps and the orange-yellow cones of blackening waxcaps, which become streaked with charcoal tints as they age. Everywhere there are drifts of small snowy waxcaps, which often occur in their thousands and are one of the most likely species to see in parks and on garden lawns.

Individually and en masse, these colourful fungi are an autumnal spectacle. Although you can find some species on village greens, commons and even the edges of cricket-grounds, their real strongholds, hosting the richest variety of species, are old, upland pastures. Those in the Welsh Marches and South Wales are particularly rich in waxcaps: growing with them are other beautiful fungi such as the violet coral fungus, which is as striking as its name suggests. Walk on certain hills around Hay-on-Wye or in the Black Mountains and you can have buzzards mewing overhead and fungal flowers at your feet.

RED KITE

4 November

A long journey back to the West Country from East Anglia gives me the chance to take stock of the extraordinary change in status of one of our most charismatic birds: the red kite. These slender-winged raptors have brick-red flashes on their wings, which glow in the sunlight – hence their name.

When I began birding seriously in the 1970s, this was one of Britain's rarest and most elusive species, found only in a few wooded valleys in the heart of mid-Wales. Today, it is a familiar sight from the Black Isle and the Borders in Scotland, through the conurbations of Newcastle and Gateshead, rural Yorkshire, the east Midlands and the Chilterns – as well, of course, as in its native Wales. This is the welcome result of one of the most successful reintroduction projects ever carried out in Britain, in which kites were re-established throughout much of their former range.

Yet I still get a buzz of surprise and excitement when, while stuck in a traffic jam on the M25 London orbital road, a kite floats serenely overhead. There is a sense of this once mythical bird being so common, but also that it is somehow in the 'wrong place', even though kites are clearly thriving here, on the outskirts of the capital.

Motorways are actually one of the very best places to see red kites, as they float high over the verges in search of food – dead or alive – to scavenge or kill. Rodents and rabbits are a key part of their diet, but they also eat plenty of earthworms, especially on damp, mild days like this, in late autumn. I see more as I head westwards down the M4, while the M40 in Oxfordshire is still the best place to see dozens of kites swirling overhead, hanging in the air like the children's toys, their floating namesakes.

But perhaps the strangest thing about kites is our change in attitude towards them. Once so sought after and revered (yet at the same time poisoned and persecuted by a rogue element of gamekeepers), now that they are so common people are starting to turn against these graceful birds. Urban myths of how they can take kittens and puppies (or even children) are fuelled by the sense that birds of prey should be rare and hard to see, not dropping into suburban gardens or visible on car journeys. It's time for another change of attitude – let's celebrate these magnificent raptors, and the fact that, with a helping hand from us, they have finally returned to the places they should never have left.

HEDGEHOG HIBERNATION

5 November

As historically motivated pyromania grips the British Isles, countless bonfires, private and municipal, are lit during early November. There are timely warnings to check them beforehand for hibernating hedgehogs.

However much we profess to love hedgehogs, we have a gift for making life difficult for them. The slow decline that began in the 1950s is rapidly accelerating and in the last decade or so we've lost 30 per cent of our remaining hedgehogs due to, among other reasons, higher volumes of traffic, pesticides, unsympathetic development and general simplification of the countryside. In our gardens, once a bastion of hedgehog happiness, we accidentally injure them with strimmers, tidy up so there's nowhere to build a nest or breed, and imprison them by fencing our own territories so efficiently that the hedgehogs can't explore the neighbourhood.

All of which bad news means that I was delighted recently to see from the corner of my eye an object like a spherical broomhead trundle past the office window in broad daylight. It apparently disappeared between two flowerpots against the office wall and on investigation I was surprised to discover a football-sized pile of leaves wedged snugly between the pots – a hedgehog hibernation site within six feet of my work-desk. Until then I'd no idea that hedgehogs still lived in the garden, though in our row of Victorian terraces they are able to come and go at will.

Suddenly I felt a responsibility for this endangered species on my doorstep. Each time I stepped into the garden I cast an anxious glance in the nest's direction. No movement or any sign of life. Spring came and I grew anxious, because this was now unquestionably *my* hedgehog. Had it survived? I'd given up hope until, one late April day, I noticed that the leaf-nest had collapsed like a punctured football. I assumed that its architect was at large hunting slugs and seeking a mate.

That hedgehog taught me three lessons. The first was that providing a home for hedgehogs is remarkably easy: all they need is dry, undisturbed shelter. Second, that just because you don't see hedgehogs, that doesn't mean they're not around. And finally that we should value the common wildlife as much as the rare: we really can make a difference to the fortunes of animals we once took for granted.

WATER SHREW

6 November

I've always had a weakness for obscure or elusive wildlife. Rarity isn't that important, but a creature that satisfies my need to hunt (harmlessly) is ideal, especially if it's a creature that is widespread but hard to find. The water shrew is a perfect candidate. Nearly 2 million of them inhabit Scottish, English and Welsh, though not Irish, waterways, but it remains one of our least-studied mammals. I can probably list on both hands the number of times I've seen one. All but one of those sightings has been unplanned.

The planned one was for a *Living World* programme on BBC Radio 4 when small mammal expert Sara Churchfield showed us the shrews in a watercress bed in Hertfordshire. Sara had baited Longworth mammal traps the night before, so we were up at sunrise to extract their contents. There were a few water shrews, feisty creatures, which scolded us with high-pitched squeaks when handled.

This was the ideal opportunity to compare them with common and pygmy shrews. Sara pointed out the charcoal fur on the water shrew's topside contrasting with the white pelt beneath; common and pygmy shrews are browner and smaller with less contrast. The water shrew's tail is fringed with stiff hairs, which act as a keel when it dives underwater and doggy-paddles after invertebrates. To subdue its prey, it uses venom. Poisons in its saliva can affect the nervous system of creatures as big as frogs and a shrew bite can cause a burning sensation on our own skin.

Not that I've been close enough to be bitten since then. My few sightings have been happenstance: one plunging into a woodland stream on a winter morning, another beneath a wooden board on a riverbank. Cats are better at finding them than we are and if you're a cat-owner it's worth checking any 'presents' you've been brought to see if there's a surprise among them.

STARLING ROOST

7 November

We stand together in fevered anticipation, like a football crowd waiting for kick-off. There are many false alarms: more than an hour before dusk every flock of ducks or black-headed gulls is greeted with an excited cry. Indeed, there have been so many cries of wolf that when the first tight little flock does pass overhead we almost miss it; only the alertness of an RSPB volunteer enables us to connect with these pioneering birds.

We have come to Avalon Marshes in Somerset for the legendary starling roost. Made famous by countless wildlife TV programmes, and even used to sell a particular brand of lager in a TV advert, this natural phenomenon is rapidly becoming one of the area's major tourist attractions, drawing hundreds of people every winter weekend. It may be a little chilly as dusk falls, but the sight that awaits us is worth a measure of discomfort.

Like so many natural spectacles, the popularity of the starling roost is partly because it is amazing and partly because it is now so unusual. When I started birding there were starling roosts all over Britain: not just in the countryside but also in the middle of our cities. I remember two urban roosts very well: the one at Bristol Temple Meads station, and the one in London's Leicester Square.

In those days, we hardly noticed their presence, even when, as happens when they finally come to land, they explode in an echo chamber of sound. The reason we didn't notice them was that we have a tendency to ignore the commonplace, taking it for granted – until, that is, it stops being commonplace.

That's exactly what happened to the starlings. Today, thanks to declines at home and abroad (wintering starlings in the UK mainly come from Russia), these roosts are now few and far between. Apart from Brighton Pier, Aberystwyth and a handful of other sites, this is now the only place where you can more or less guarantee seeing the starlings in all their aerobatic glory. Even here, numbers are dramatically down: from several million at the roost's peak a decade or so ago to around 250,000 birds now. But there are still enough to delight the crowds and send them home happy.

EVERLASTING TREES

8 November

A pollarded lime tree, cut back decades ago to produce several trunks above cattle-browsing height, has partly collapsed in a local wood. Undaunted, one of the fallen trunks has sprouted a palisade of thinner upright branches along its length, creating a lime hedge within the woodland. Meanwhile the pollarded tree has sent down aerial roots within its hollowed main trunk to brace itself against further strains. Limes are supreme masters of re-invention, splitting, repairing, rotting and rejuvenating over a timescale that puts our lives in the shade.

The sheer tenacity of the trees was brought home to me at Westonbirt Arboretum in Gloucestershire where the tree collection adjoins an ancient coppice named Silk Wood. It's home to a small-leaved lime that is said to be 2,000 years old.

My first sight of this tree was disappointing. I'd expected a vast crumbling wreck of a tree with bark like elephant hide and woody caves in its trunk. Instead I found myself inside a grove of coppiced limes, whose multi-stemmed clusters of trunks, known as stools, formed a loose circle around me.

Eventually, and the astonishing truth took a few minutes to dawn, I realised that this lime grove *was* the ancient tree. Over centuries, the original lime had been repeatedly coppiced to provide young timber and as it aged its main trunk had rotted and split so that the resulting stools spread outwards in a ring that was still slowly widening. Tests on these stools had revealed that they were genetically identical and it seems that this tree has the capacity to live for ever.

Elsewhere limes are equally inventive. At Calke Abbey in Derbyshire there are remarkable 'walking limes' whose lower branches have rooted and sent up vertical stems metres way from the main trunk. Given time and space they will become independent of their parent and march across the landscape.

And this isn't a talent that's unique to limes. Sweet chestnuts are also adventurous trees when we give them permission. A specimen I pass regularly is the Kateshill Chestnut at Bewdley in Worcestershire, which grows in the grounds of a private house, but has its sights on pastures new and sprawls like an octopus down a wooded bank towards a driveway. Its lower limbs embedded in the ground, this veteran of 500 years or so covers a quarter of an acre: its longest branch stretches seventy-seven feet from the main trunk. Sadly, we rarely cater for these arboreal adventurers by allowing them enough space and time to stretch their limbs.

Some everlasting trees are less spectacular, but raise the question of when one tree ends and another begins. Not far from Bewdley is a crumbling sandstone cliff above the River Severn, from which wild service saplings sprout. Wild service is a member of the rowan family and has maple-like leaves and brown berries or 'chequers', once used to settle colic. Although rarely a large tree, wild service is a good indicator of ancient woodland, because it is very persistent and even after woodland clearance it will sprout from old stumps and roots. Here on the friable Severn cliffs, it's doing just that, but on a vertical plane. As the sandstone crumbles, the newly exposed wild service roots produce leaves and become young saplings, while extending more roots back into the remaining cliff-face. Over time, they keep pace with the eroding cliffs and through this process of erosion and regrowth have the potential to survive for many thousands of years.

GOOSE BARNACLE

9 November

By the look of it, the wreck had been on the beach for some time – decades, maybe. Plenty of time, anyway, for the clump of oddly shaped, off-white shells with strange protuberances to make their home.

This encounter, on a Cornish beach in late autumn, was my first experience of one of the most unusual of all our living organisms: the goose barnacle. These curious crustaceans spend their lives in the intertidal zone, one of the most changeable and hostile environments on the planet. They remain there by attaching themselves, limpet-like, to whatever they can find: rocks, bits of wood, or even, as in this case, entire wrecks.

At low tide, they don't do much. But once the waters cover their home, they spring into action, filter-feeding on tiny marine organisms. They are not active feeders; instead they use the twice-daily motions of the tides to bring the food to them.

Also known as stalked or gooseneck barnacles, their unusual name is the result of a strange belief held by our ancestors. The story goes that barnacle geese – which are also black and white in colour – hatched out of these odd-looking crustaceans, a theory that explained their sudden appearance every autumn (though failed to explain where they all went the following spring). As a result, rather conveniently, the plump and tasty geese were classified not as flesh or fowl, but as a kind of fish, meaning that they could be eaten on fast days and Fridays.

We can choose to believe this tall tale; but if we do, we need to regard our ancestors as credulous fools. Is it not more likely that having noticed the vague similarity between the crustacean and the bird, a crafty cleric decided he could use this as a loophole to allow the geese to be eaten?

LOGPILE HORNETS
10 November

A November morning and I'm exploring a local reserve with friends, hoping for photographic opportunities. It's unseasonably mild and we scan for late-flying butterflies – a red admiral perhaps, sampling the juices of mildewed plums in the neighbouring orchard?

Not today. Few birds are around either as we move quietly through a coppiced clearing. Summer migrants are long gone, the winter visitors yet to arrive in force. Apart from a ticking wren, there's a feeling of suspension; that the seasonal cycle is on hold. Bemused by the stillness, we grub briefly in the leaf litter and pore over tree-trunks where spiral snails have climbed and clamped themselves into place.

Around the clearing are log-piles, left for wildlife by the coppicers. Lifting a couple of small logs from the top of one pile, we gasp. Daylight floods the chamber beneath where three huge comatose hornet queens lurk. Next to them is a queen carder bumblebee and alongside her are two slender black ichneumon wasps, parasites on caterpillars.

This dormitory of odd bedfellows has been carefully selected by insects that wouldn't normally associate with each other, but have recognised the perfect spot for a winter shelter. Insects don't hibernate in the sense that mammals and reptiles do: instead they enter a state of diapause in which they become torpid. This gives us the confidence to photograph the hornets, which we'd usually be wary of approaching. Hornets aren't as aggressive as the smaller social wasps that disrupt our picnics, though their sheer bulk can be daunting. I've only once been stung by one, when it flew into my hair in a dark wood and not knowing what it was, I patted it by accident and briefly saw stars.

This slumbering trio is harmless though and, holding our breath to avoid disturbing them, we gather round to admire their rust and yellow armour and shining chocolate-button eyes. They were reared in late summer in a large chambered nest made of chewed wood-pulp, probably in a tree-hollow or bird nest-box. When they were grubs, worker hornets would have provided them with food, but these have now all perished and the destiny of these dormant queens lies in founding next year's colonies. Mindful of this, we take our photos, gently replace the log and back away reverentially . . . best to let sleeping hornets lie.

WAXWINGS

11 November

Above the rattle of trolleys in my local supermarket car park comes an unfamiliar sound, like the ringing of tiny silver bells. This tempts even hardened shoppers to glance up at the swirling flock of starlings as they descend into the rowan trees alongside the road. But these are no starlings: Siberia has come to Sainsbury's, and the waxwings are in town.

At a time when many of our familiar birds are becoming harder and harder to find, it's a pleasure to welcome a bird that actually finds us – and which, despite its distant origins, seems to be at home in the heart of town.

It's doubly pleasing that the species in question looks so unfamiliar. Waxwings are unashamedly exotic: punk-crested, bandit-masked and daubed in custard yellow and scarlet. Spirited in from the forests of Scandinavia and Siberia, they blend strangeness with unpredictability; their trick of illuminating grey winter days is just part of their allure.

But their arrival isn't actually all that mysterious: like the shoppers thronging the nearby aisles, they're here for the food – specifically, in their case, for fruit. The berry crop has failed in their native home, forcing them to flee across the North Sea in their thousands. By a neat coincidence, supermarkets often plant rows of berry trees to brighten up their concrete car parks; and in doing so attract flocks of waxwings.

Look closely as they stuff themselves full of fruit, and you'll see that the waxwing's common name is self-explanatory. Each wingtip is adorned with tiny red blobs, which bear a striking resemblance to old-fashioned sealing wax.

The scientific name, *Bombycilla garrulus*, takes a little more unravelling, though. *Bombycilla* is a hybrid Greek and Latin word meaning 'silken hair', a reference to the bird's smooth feathers, which also gave rise to the folk name silk tail. *Garrulus* translates as 'chatterer', yet waxwings are relatively silent birds, so how did this name arise? It turns out that the bird was once known as the Bohemian jay, because of its resemblance to this larger member of the crow family, whose scientific name is *garrulus*. The connection stuck, and so did the unsuitable scientific name.

In recent years, there have been several large invasions, or 'waxwing winters', as birders call them. When this happens, supermarket car parks may suddenly be packed with telescopes, each trained on these beautiful birds. As I watch them through my telescope, several passing shoppers stop to ask what I am looking at. When I show them, they are doubly astonished: first at the birds' sheer beauty; then at the distance they have travelled to be here.

OAK GALLS

12 November

Oak leaves are often late in falling, but as they drop, all sorts of lumps, bumps and excrescences come to light. Woody spheres show up on oak twigs. Under the fallen leaves are hundreds of small fleshy discs, like flying saucers. Even the acorns are transmogrified: no longer smooth to the touch, but grotesquely ribbed and fluted.

These strange outgrowths are galls and the oak tree alone is host to over fifty species, all of which produce a different response.

Galls occur on many plants and are aberrations of the plant's normal growth form caused by mites, aphids, fungi or, in the case of the more obvious oak galls, by tiny wasps. Those woody balls on the oak twigs, for example, are marble galls and if you look closely you can see small round exit holes where the wasps have emerged. The overlapping pimples, which coat the undersides of oak leaves, are spangle galls and the acorn tumours are knopper galls, both also caused by different species of gall wasp.

Exactly how the galls are created is still a mystery. The Roman historian Pliny believed that oak trees formed 'gall-nuts' in alternate years to acorns and it wasn't until the seventeenth century that the connection was made between some galls and the insects that induce them. But there are still reasons for cecidologists (the biologists who study galls) to scratch their heads. Adult wasps lay their eggs in the plant's tissue, but when the grubs hatch they somehow – and exactly how is a mystery – interfere with the cell formation to create a shelter, which protects the growing larva. The sheer variety of the responses that the oak tree gives is bewildering: a single branch can produce an array of weird growths from cottony masses and ram's-horn prongs to artichoke-shaped buds.

All have the same purpose: to protect the growing grubs from predators. But not all the exit holes on marble galls are made by emerging gall wasps; galls can be mini-citadels for other freeloading insects seeking shelter or – bad news for the gall wasps – prey.

The glamour of galls lies in their variety and novelty. New species are constantly appearing as we move plants around or as climate changes. Even the marble gall, which is common throughout the British Isles, was originally introduced from Turkey and the Middle East in the 1830s to be harvested locally as a source of tannin for conditioning leather and an inky dye.

Marble galls remain on the trees long after their creators have left and knopper galls turn brown with the acorns, but spangle galls detach themselves from the falling oak leaves and continue swelling over winter in the leaf litter. In early spring the young wasps emerge and the gall cycle begins afresh, though with a few differences. These spring wasps lay their eggs in oak buds and their grubs produce currant galls on the oak catkins. The wasps that emerge from the currant galls lay their eggs in the leaves and their grubs create more spangle galls. We know a little more than Pliny, but galls still amaze and confound us with their complexity.

EXMOOR PONIES

13 November

The ponies face the bitter wind as it sweeps across one of the wildest parts of the West Country: Exmoor. Short, squat and dark brown, with a lighter belly and the characteristic pale patches on the nose and around the eyes, they look perfectly suited to this bleak November landscape. Few other large mammals are quite so well adapted to this cold and unforgiving place, straddling the borders of Devon and Somerset, having lived here for thousands of years since the end of the last Ice Age.

Exmoor ponies are – along with their counterparts on Dartmoor and in the New Forest – the nearest we have in Britain to the wild horses that would have roamed across much of Europe in prehistoric times. They may not technically be wild – 'semi-feral' is probably the best description – but they certainly look as if they belong here. Their role is to manage the land, as they have done for centuries, by grazing the rough pasture and stopping it from turning into scrub.

It's often said that Exmoor ponies are rarer than the giant panda – and numerically that is true, with fewer than 1,000 remaining; though this is up from just fifty left by the end of the Second World War, during which many were killed when the moor was turned into a military training site, and the ponies used as target practice. They have also been hunted and killed for their meat, and today face an increasing risk of being knocked down by fast-moving road vehicles.

But the Exmoor pony isn't a full species, but simply one variety of many different kinds of horses and ponies, so the comparison with the giant panda is slightly spurious. Nevertheless, it does have a unique genetic status and should be preserved – if only for its attraction to tourists visiting the moor on a chill late autumn day.

OAK BUSH-CRICKETS
14 November

The song of crickets summons sunny memories of picnics in flowery meadows or blackberry-picking on September mornings. So when I find one beaded with mist on a dank November day it feels incongruous, a mockery of summer.

But these pale green wraiths can be conspicuous as they cling to tree-trunks or house walls in late autumn. Normally oak bush-crickets spend their time in the canopy of trees where they are carnivores, eating caterpillars, aphids and even each other. Unlike most British crickets, which sing by rubbing their wings together, oak bush-crickets can drum their hind legs rapidly on a leaf to produce a purring sound too soft for the human ear.

Oak bush-crickets aren't restricted to oaks and inhabit many trees and tall shrubs in woods, parks and large gardens. They're adult from late July until the first frosts and many last until November or even December – my latest sighting here in the West Midlands is 20 November. Sometimes they fly to streetlights in town and they often come into houses, for some reason seeming to prefer bathrooms – a friend suggests a more appropriate name for them would be the bathroom cricket.

To fly to our bathrooms – or indeed anywhere – oak bush-crickets have long green wings as adults and that distinguishes them from a new arrival, the southern oak bush-cricket. This wingless insect lives in continental Europe but in 2001 was discovered in Surrey. Since then it has established itself in the London area and has turned up as far west as Bristol and north to the English Midlands.

How so many of these fragile, flightless insects arrived here we don't know, but some have been seen clinging to vehicle bumpers and have probably travelled through the Channel tunnel. A Northamptonshire naturalist who suspected they were coming in on freight lorries decided to search his local industrial estates and in three places found thriving populations of these continental crickets in maple trees under which commercial lorries parked. How they will thrive in our harsh winters is uncertain, but they've established strong colonies and seem to be here to stay and may even have arrived in your neighbourhood.

RED-CRESTED POCHARD

15 November

Some birds, however hard you try to avoid it, demand to be compared with human beings. Whenever I see a red-crested pochard, I can't help recalling the fashions of the 1970s, with bouffant hairdos and brightly coloured clothes.

On a blustery November day, a small flock of 'RCPs', as birders call them, has turned up at my local reservoir. Like their close relatives the pochard and tufted duck, they sit high on the choppy waves like a flotilla of small boats, occasionally diving beneath the surface to find food.

Even at this distance, the orange-red headdress of the male red-crested pochard shines like a beacon in the dull afternoon light. The females are less obvious: rather pale-brown overall, with dirty white cheeks and a darker crown, they can confuse beginner birders.

This is partly because of their rather dubious status. Red-crested pochard used to be a rare visitor to Britain from continental Europe, guaranteed to cause excitement whenever one turned up. But during the latter half of the twentieth century a feral breeding population established themselves at the Cotswold Water Park, that curious assemblage of nature reserves, second homes and watersports facilities on a series of disused gravel-pits close to the M4.

Having bred during the spring and summer, in autumn these birds and their offspring disperse – not too far, though: the majority are to be found in southern and eastern England, with a handful turning up in the south-west.

MERLIN

16 November

A merlin is always an antidote to the darkening days of autumn and winter. In the open farmland that makes up most of my local patch, these mercurial falcons provide fleeting but bracing aerobatic displays. A typical brief encounter is of a flickering arrow hurtling low over stubble, occasionally bouncing in the air or jinking from side to side like a canoeist descending rapids. A few seconds of gawping is all I'm allowed and then it's gone, swallowed by the dips and folds of the field.

Some sightings last longer. A shower of liquid chirrups high overhead announces a ragged flock of skylarks, spooked by a merlin. Scanning the periphery of the flock, I soon pick out the falcon, which has also singled out its target. Although the broad-winged larks appear languid in flight, they can be surprisingly agile when the need arises. Few predators test their mettle as a merlin can.

Flying back to the ground would risk death and so the skylark climbs into the comparative safety of the sky until, even through binoculars, it's no more than a speck. Sometimes larks chased by falcons will sing as if in defiance, possibly as a proclamation that they are in good physical condition and are unlikely to be caught. But on this occasion the merlin follows in grim pursuit, towering ever higher and seemingly inexhaustible. Eventually – and my cricked neck is grateful – the pair is enveloped by low cloud. I can't guess the outcome of this breathtaking display, but it dawns on me at last why in North America merlins are known informally as bullet hawks.

This chase began above a favourite merlin valley, its arable fields seamed with fraying lines of ancient hawthorns which make perfect lookouts. In the late afternoon, male and female birds turn up here before heading off to roost, the diminutive males not much bigger than a mistle thrush and slate-blue on top, orange underneath. The larger, browner females can take bigger prey such as woodcock and stock doves.

Where these merlins come from I can't be sure: they could be British birds from northern and western uplands, or migrants from Iceland or Scandinavia. Whatever their origins, their dramatic pursuits are the highlight of these short November afternoons.

DUNLIN

17 November

When I moved to Somerset from London, I was delighted to discover how near my new home was to the seaside. I say 'seaside', but technically that might fall foul of the Trades Descriptions Act – it would be more accurate to say the coast. For along the coast, from Burnham-on-Sea to

Weston-super-Mare, there is neither sand nor shingle, but miles and miles of oozing mud.

Mud may be a disappointment to holidaymakers, but it is ideal for birds – especially those flocks of waders that choose to spend the autumn and winter here on the edge of Bridgwater Bay. Against the backdrop of Hinkley Point nuclear power station in one direction, and Cardiff's Millennium Stadium in the other, they find paradise; helped by what is often claimed to be the second biggest tidal range in the world.

The mud is full of small marine worms and other invertebrates – roughly the energy equivalent, according to scientists, of munching on a Mars bar. So as the tide began to rise rapidly, I watched well over a thousand dunlins in a race against time to feed.

For birds like these, timing is crucial. They only have a few opportunities each day, when the mud is temporarily uncovered, to feast on the energy-rich mudflats. And so when two massive black dogs began romping along the tideline, my heart sank. The birds panicked and took to the air, swirling around like a pale version of the starling murmuration. By the time the flock of birds was able to make landfall, the tide was starting to cover the mud, making it impossible for them to feed. They headed off to roost on the nearby island, hungry, tired and with another few hours to go before they could feed once again.

LEMON SLUGS

18 November

Normally the forest is dark and still. Few people are inclined to visit on a damp November night and the only sound is the distant trickle of a woodland stream. But tonight the slender tree-trunks are criss-crossed by torch-beams and cries of 'Here's one' or 'Wow – a mating pair' break the silence. Excusable behaviour if you're looking for bats or autumn moths maybe, but tonight we are slug-seekers.

I know, I know, bear with me. These aren't your common-or-garden slugs. Lemon slugs are superior molluscs in many ways. Take their colour for instance, a rich glowing canary yellow offset by delicate lilac-grey tentacles. It sounds gaudy, but on the wet shining leaves of the woodland floor it's perfect camouflage.

They're also discerning creatures, not vegetable-garden browsers or ravagers of precious flower borders. Lemon slugs shun modern life. They are secretive connoisseurs of ancient woodland; that is woods that date back to 1600 or earlier in England and Wales and 1750 in Scotland. So close is their relationship with such places that they are ancient woodland indicators, signposting the forest's antiquity. This intimate relationship means that the slugs are commonest in areas of older wooded country-side, such as the Chilterns and the Welsh Marches, north-east England and Scotland.

But why is old woodland so appealing? After all, most slugs are content to follow us around. However lemon slugs are epicures with the discerning tastes of a Roux or a Carluccio. They feed on forest fungi, which explains why they are most obvious in autumn. By day they lie up under bark or rotten wood, emerging after dark to browse, rasping away the fungal flesh with their many-toothed radula. They will eat many fungi, but seem especially fond of those that match their colour such as ochre brittlegills or buttercaps.

It's a hedonistic life but a brief one. After mating – and it's easy to find a mate when you're hermaphrodite – they lay eggs in the autumn before dying, the sluglets feeding underground on fungal threads through spring and early summer.

This November evening, in the depths of the forest, we find several dozen lemon slugs in all their glutinous glory, beautiful – and all the more so for their association with scarce but precious places.

RED-NECKED GREBE

19 November

I love grebes. The very first special birds I ever saw, as a child, were the great crested grebes that lived on our local gravel-pits on the outskirts of London. They built floating nests, and when they went off to feed they used to cover their curiously long, pale eggs with aquatic vegetation to protect them, which turned them a light green colour.

Over time, I caught up with the other four regular British species of grebe: little grebes, or dabchicks, were common on small waterbodies, while black-necked grebes regularly turned up each August on the vast, water-filled concrete basins of Staines Reservoirs. I had to travel to Poole Harbour in Dorset to see their cousin, the elegant black and white Slavonian grebe. That left just one more species, the red-necked grebe, still to see.

For years, I would try to turn young great crested grebes into their rarer relative, but it wasn't until early 1985, almost two decades after I first began serious birding, that I came across the real thing – at Wraysbury Gravel Pits in Berkshire.

If you're imagining a bird looking as if it had a scarlet or crimson scarf around its neck, prepare to be disappointed. In winter, red-necked grebes turn monochrome, losing their summer brick-red feathering and looking like a small, hunched version of their larger relative. Nevertheless, with practice you can pick them out: the yellow, dagger-shaped bill, dusky feathering around the short, thick neck, and a habit of diving more frequently, should all be enough to distinguish the red-necked from the far more numerous great crested grebe.

INVADING BLACKBIRDS

20 November

Opening the back door this morning, there's change afoot. Yesterday the garden was calm. Today the local blackbirds are dashing anxiously from tree to tree, mik-mik-ing loudly as they chase a party of eight other blackbirds, which must have arrived overnight.

Although I can't prove how far these new arrivals have travelled, I'd place a bet that they're from further north, maybe even continental Europe. All seem to be young birds of the year, the females typically dark-brown with rufous highlights, the males sooty-black even down to their bills: immature blackbirds have black bills and dark eye-rings in their first autumn and can be confusing if you're expecting the bright-yellow beaks of the adults.

Continental blackbirds are winter visitors to the British Isles in large numbers when they escape the freezing conditions in their northern breeding territories and head across the North Sea to milder places. Having arrived, they spread throughout town and country, usually unnoticed by us but often detected by local birds. We tend to think of 'our' blackbirds as being the same pair year-round, but the numbers visiting our gardens can be staggering.

For several years, the villagers of Holt in Norfolk kept watch on the individual blackbirds visiting their gardens, each of which had been fitted with a unique combination of coloured leg-rings. During the breeding seasons between 2007 and 2014, Dave Leech from the British Trust for Ornithology caught and colour-ringed 457 adult blackbirds in the same suburban garden, and he estimated that an astonishing total of 750 or more different blackbirds were using the gardens in the village. This gives us a new and dizzying perspective on the dynamics of our wildlife and is a hint of the importance of our gardens to birds from far afield.

SEXTON BEETLE

21 November

Some jobs, once common and widespread, no longer exist. One such is the sexton. These men (and a handful of women) performed a crucial role in every parish: managing the church and churchyard, ringing the bells on joyful and solemn occasions, and, perhaps most importantly, acting as gravediggers, burying the dead.

It is this last duty that led to the name of several species of 'burying beetles' of the genus *Nicrophorus*, known colloquially as sexton beetles. They don't all live in graveyards, though given that these sites are often left unsprayed and unmown, and so are paradoxically full of life amid the signs of death, some do.

Like their human counterparts, sexton beetles do a crucial job in enabling the cycle of life and death to continue. They have a very acute sense of smell, and use this to track down the dead bodies of small mammals and birds. Having found a suitable corpse, the beetle then buries it in a shallow grave, though not before laying its eggs either on the body or nearby. So when the young beetles hatch out, they have a ready-made source of food. Unlike most insects, however, both male and female sexton beetles care for their young after they are born.

I have seen these beetles on only a handful of occasions, but their striking appearance lives in my memory: a shiny black body, with splashes of orange on the wing cases and clubbed antennae. They remind me of the scarabs of Egyptian mythology – though they come from a different family – and, like those, are the undertakers of the insect world.

GREY SEAL PUPS
22 November

Someone had left an old sleeping bag at the top of the beach. Scoured by the biting winds, it lay half under an improvised rope-fence between the dunes and a vast stretch of beach beyond which the North Sea raged. As I approached to within a metre or so, the bag pulsated and it stared at me with mournful eyes.

I stumbled on Donna Nook and its breeding grey seals by accident one late November afternoon several years ago, after an unsuccessful attempt to find a rare steppe grey shrike, an Asian vagrant that had been around for weeks nearby, even perching on birders' heads and telescopes in its bid to be noticed. My visit, needless to say, took place on the morning after its departure, so I drove north along the Lincolnshire coast and found myself among a crowd of sightseers.

Donna Nook is a huge area of coastal mud and sand south of Grimsby, which each autumn becomes a nursery to hundreds of grey seals. Hauling themselves away from the pounding seas, the females give birth on the wide sand-flats and, shortly afterwards, mate with the dominant bulls. Their quavering moans, distorted by the wind, drift onshore towards the crowds who've braved the autumn blasts to see a remarkable spectacle.

As far as the eye can see, seals are slumped motionless or humping maggot-like across the sand. Small white pups and fatter greyish ones are dotted everywhere, seemingly impervious to humans. Some are almost within touching distance. The Lincolnshire Wildlife Trust, whose staff and volunteers manage the site, are there to protect people as well as the wildlife.

Those limpid eyes are beguiling, but seals have powerful jaws and even pups can deliver a fierce bite if disturbed. Not that you'd guess it from this one, lying on its side in a blissful state, eyes closed, languidly scratching its barrel stomach with a flipper.

Although their birth in the howling late autumn winds seems a harsh baptism, they are well prepared for the sandblasting they receive. In their first two weeks the pups can triple their weight on a diet of their mother's milk, which is 50 per cent fat, building up blubber reserves to protect them from the elements. It's also insurance against any shortfall in food: after three weeks their mother abandons them and goes searching for a mate. That pup that gazed doe-eyed at me under the makeshift cordon will soon be left to the mercy of the winter seas, and has less than a fifty-fifty chance of surviving.

WINTERING BLACKCAP

23 November

There is always a pecking order on my bird feeders. Usually the great tits are dominant, followed by the smaller but equally feisty blue tits. Coal tits are only an occasional visitor, but are always shy, while the finches and sparrows are also fairly brash, flying to and fro to grab a sunflower heart, or occasionally dropping to the ground for spilled seeds.

One bird is more reticent than these; and although it breeds regularly in our garden, with up to four singing males in good years, it is scarce and unusual here in winter: the blackcap. About the size of a great tit, the blackcap is slenderer and more elegant, with a dove-grey plumage and smart black crown. Eventually he does venture on to the feeder, snatching his booty before returning to the adjacent trellis to feed.

When I began birding, blackcaps were exclusively what we called a 'summer visitor' to Britain, albeit an early arrival, usually turning up from the middle of March, and departing south in September.

Today, though, blackcaps are present all year round – though not necessarily the same birds. In an extraordinary shift in behaviour, birds from central Europe now migrate west and north-west to spend the autumn and winter here, taking advantage of our recent run of mild winters and ample supplies of food, thoughtfully provided by us.

My friends in Bristol – and in towns and cities up and down the country – see them regularly in their smaller, suburban gardens, because the night-time temperatures there are two or three degrees warmer than here in the countryside. So this bird hanging around our feeders is an unexpected and very welcome sight.

FIRECREST

24 November

We don't have hummingbirds in the British Isles, but here in a rhododendron thicket is the next best thing. Mist hangs in the woodland and on this still November afternoon the silence is heightened by a few splinters of sound. I follow them up and there, hovering beneath the wet leathery leaves, is a jewel.

In autumn and winter, firecrests are serendipitous sightings, too fickle to be relied upon, but with the potential to turn up almost anywhere and always a thrill. Along with the goldcrest, they're our smallest birds, just nine centimetres long and as light as a 20p coin, so finding them among the dense foliage they prefer isn't easy. The thin, needling calls betray them as they fuss through the leaves. When you see one, its diminutive size eliminates all but the much commoner goldcrests. Unlike goldcrests, however, which are dull olive with black-bordered crown stripes, yellow in the female or orange in the male, firecrests have smart black and white eyestripes and brighter moss-green plumage: a mustard half-collar completes the picture.

Although they can be hard to see in dense foliage or high in trees, firecrests appear oblivious to people at times and will flit through undergrowth just a metre or two away. This apparent tameness is really a matter of seasonal priorities: it's better to risk danger than to die from starvation or cold, constant perils for a bird that burns energy so quickly.

Firecrests are almost constantly on the move, hovering to take prey from the underside of a leaf, or inspecting foliage for small insects or spiders. In winter, they prefer evergreens such as conifers, holly, rhododendrons and laurels, all plants that shelter their prey and keep out the cold and rain. Where these trees grow in large gardens, parks and cemeteries, it's always worth checking for a wintering firecrest.

The birds we see at this time of year are a mixture of those that have bred here – more than 1,000 pairs breed in England and Wales – and continental migrants, which pass through in autumn and sometimes stay for winter. Once they've found a sheltered feeding spot, these colourful scraps of vitality will often remain in the same place for weeks.

MANDARIN

25 November

Virginia Water is a classic Home Counties beauty spot: a large, rangy lake with creeks at each corner, set among delightful woodland and more open parkland. No wonder the car park gets very full at weekends and on bank holidays.

But the joy of this place is that most visitors stay close to the entrance, so by heading along the banks of the lake you soon escape the crowds. As a child, I would visit here with my mother: it was here that I saw my first kingfisher, whizzing past and appearing, to my surprise, both impossibly tiny and also more orange than blue.

Later on, my teenage birding companion Daniel and I saw a pair of hawfinches, sporting their huge, powerful bills, high in the branches of a hornbeam – their favourite tree.

But the bird we most associated with this place – for Virginia Water was its British stronghold for many years – was the mandarin. Few birds anywhere in the world are quite as stunning as this diminutive duck, which has since spread to much of England, as well as a few parts of Scotland and Wales.

Named after senior officials in the Chinese civil service, the males sport a delightful combination of colours, including red, orange, white, black, purple and green, set off with two 'sails' sticking up on their back as they float serenely on the water. Females are less brightly coloured, as they need to be camouflaged when on the nest, but they are still very pleasing to the eye, with a dark brownish-grey back, head and body mottled with flecks of white.

As their exotic name and appearance suggest, mandarins are not native to Britain, but hail instead from South-east Asia. It used to be thought that the British population, which descends from birds brought here from the mid-eighteenth century onwards, was globally significant, but recent discoveries of new populations in China mean that the bird is not now threatened.

Unlike most British ducks, mandarins nest in holes in trees, which means that when they have hatched the ducklings have to leap into the unknown to reach the ground. Those at Virginia Water are then taken off to secluded spots beneath the tree roots that line the banks of the lake, where, despite the bright colours of the males, they can be surprisingly hard to see.

BRITAIN'S RAINFOREST

26 November

The rock-strewn oak woods around Borrowdale in Cumbria are among the wettest places in Britain. Today, a heavy downfall has silvered every twig and fern-tip with globules of rain. Urged on by the pressure of countless others, they quiver and fall on to the sodden moss that carpets the woodland floor.

Rainfall here can reach over 350 centimetres – almost 140 inches – every year. The influence of the warming Gulf Stream on these west coast woods creates an oceanic climate, which is the northern equivalent of the tropical rainforests, loud with its chorus of birds and insects. Here at Seathwaite, though, there's only the sonorous croak of ravens above the canopy and the endless drip, drip of the rain on to boulders plush with moss.

Mosses and liverworts – collectively known as bryophytes – revel in the 'oceanicity' (the mildness and moisture) of these western woods, which occur in Ireland and from Devon to north-west Scotland. They soften the tree-stumps and rocks with their brilliant green velvet: two-thirds of all the European bryophytes occur in the British Isles, giving us something to celebrate on rainy days. There are rare and spectacular lichens in these woods too, most obviously the lungwort, whose glaucous brackets sprout luxuriantly from tree-trunks. But one plant here wouldn't look out of place in a tropical rainforest: Wilson's filmy fern.

I saw my first filmy ferns at Kew Gardens where they have their very own greenhouse, a tribute to the affection that Victorians have bestowed on these delicate translucent plants. But it was an affection bordering on obsession and during the Victorian 'Fern Craze' of the late nineteenth century there was such high demand from collectors that British locations for filmy ferns, and indeed many other fern species, were stripped of their plants and have still not recovered. Thankfully Wilson's filmy fern has survived in many sheltered and humid places, including these Borrowdale rainforests.

Today I find them easily in the damp woods, their wiry rhizomes entangled in the moss around an old tree-stump. More like terrestrial seaweeds than ferns, their pellucid lobed fronds, at most a couple of inches long, are only a single cell thick: you can read a field guide through them. They are utterly dependent on the high humidity here and in (rare) dry weather, blacken and shrivel like beached seaweed. On this soggy day there's no chance of that happening.

CHINESE MITTEN CRAB

27 November

We often hear about alien species, which with few if any predators and competitors are able to rampage through our native habitats and their wildlife. But few are quite as destructive as the Chinese mitten crab, which can cause major damage to riverbanks by their burrowing and have a taste for our native fish.

On the River Thames in London, the high mud banks are dotted with holes. They don't look big enough to have been made by water voles or kingfishers, and, besides, it is the wrong time of year for breeding and nesting. Then, as I look more closely, I notice a large, curved claw emerging, soon followed by the whole body of a crab, which then drops down into the murky waters below.

Local conservationists are monitoring these crabs, and so I get a closer look after some of them are caught. I can immediately see how they got their unusual name: each claw is seemingly wrapped in fur, resembling mittens. The crabs themselves are quite large – the carapace is about the width of my hand, while the legs extend another two palm-widths on either side, meaning that a full-grown adult crab is well over a foot across.

Like so many invasive creatures, the Chinese mitten crab is here by an unfortunate accident. Ships need to fill their ballast tanks regularly with water; and in doing so can easily sweep up the crabs' tiny eggs. By the time the ship had travelled from Asia to Europe, and reached its destination, the tanks would be full of crab larvae, which once released would soon colonise their new home.

Once there, they hang around rivers for a few years before, one summer, heading downstream towards the sea. They mate en route in the river estuary, then spend the winter out at sea, before returning upstream the following spring, when the eggs hatch.

So far, we don't seem to have found a way to control the dreaded crabs. But maybe the Chinese themselves have a solution. The mitten crab is considered a gastronomic delicacy, so maybe an imaginative entrepreneur will begin catching them – mitten crab sandwich, anyone?

ERGOT

28 November

Newly graduated in autumn 1982, I wangled a temporary contract surveying and recording the wildlife in Hereford and Worcester County Council's country parks. Asked if there was a group I'd like to know more about, I rashly replied 'fungi' because my ignorance of them was complete and it was late October, when fungi are at their most visible and obvious.

So it was that I spent many damp November days crawling through dripping countryside, trying in vain to identify small beige mushrooms. It was a relief to come across a fungus that I could name with confidence and – even better – one that had a sinister backstory worthy of Edgar Allan Poe.

Ergot is the fruiting body of the fungus *Claviceps purpurea*, which grows in autumn on the seed-heads of wild grasses, replacing the grain with small black clubs called sclerotia. Once you have your eye in for it, in a 'good' season these dark growths seem to be everywhere.

Ergot's sinister history began when people in central Europe and western Russia began cultivating rye around the fifth century. Rye was a staple diet for the poor, and also an important host of ergot. In the year AD 857 in the Rhine Valley, rural people suffered mysterious symptoms including burning sensations, convulsions and loss of limbs through gangrene. Some bit through their own tongues: others complained of a sensation of ants running about under their skin. Many thousands of people died including large numbers of children.

Similar outbreaks of 'Holy Fire' – this burning sensation was thought to be a divine punishment – occurred in France and other parts of Europe where rye was grown. In the eleventh century a French hospital built to care for the victims of what we now call ergotism was dedicated to St Anthony and the affliction became known as St Anthony's Fire. There was no cure and still no inkling of what caused it, though it was widely blamed on witchcraft.

The plague was only linked with the eating of rye in 1670 by a French physician who noticed that it was a mainly rural problem affecting the poor, but not the rich who had a grander diet. Matching the years of high infestations with epidemics of ergotism, he strongly suspected that the fungus was to blame. But farmers rejected his suggestion and it was another two hundred years and many more deaths before the vital connection was proven.

Screening of cereals has removed the threat of St Anthony's Fire in modern times: the last European outbreak was in France in 1951 from infected wheat, and it's always been rare in the British Isles. Nevertheless, I still can't pass a grass stem with its cargo of small black cudgels without thinking of the mystery and misery that this insignificant fungus has provoked.

SECRETIVE BIRDS

29 November

Reed-beds don't give up their secrets easily. In spring and summer, the score or more of reed warblers on my local patch rarely reveal themselves, except by their chuntering, repetitive song. In autumn, long after the warblers have all headed south, the bearded tits living in those same reed-beds are equally elusive, only occasionally popping up for a moment or two to reveal their astonishing beauty, then plummeting down out of sight once again.

But for the true skulkers of the bird world it's hard to beat two larger species: the snipe and the water rail. It's easy to know that the water rails are here: I hear their curious call, known as sharming (which according to the *Oxford English Dictionary* comes from a now obsolete dialect word meaning 'to scream shrilly and vociferously'), and which sounds remarkably like a piglet being killed. But unless the waters are frozen over, in which case desperation will force the water rails to venture into view as they search for food, I hardly ever see one.

The snipe I do see – though not for long, and certainly not clearly. The first sign that they are about comes when I hear a croaking call, rapidly followed by a small bird zigzagging up into the air and disappearing out of sight. No wonder the snipe is, along with its larger cousin the woodcock, considered the hardest of all game birds to shoot successfully.

Sometimes a single snipe is my only reward for trudging around on a dismal November afternoon. Yet at other times I may flush a dozen or more, each seemingly more desperate to get away than the last.

BARNACLE GEESE

30 November

A pall of grey hangs over the Solway Firth at Caerlaverock. November is living up to its reputation and even the high hills across the mouth of the River Nith are invisible. I'm here with *Autumnwatch* at the Wildfowl and Wetlands Trust centre and all attention is on the huge wintering flocks of barnacle geese, which spend their days grazing local pastures and the saltmarsh. Locally known as the merse, its succulent sedges and grass are cropped by tens of thousands of black stubby bills. Today fog veils the estuary: land and sea are indistinguishable and the only visible wildfowl are the teal hunched on the margins of the pond outside the observatory window.

Which makes the appearance of the barnacle geese even more dramatic. It begins as a distant hubbub far out on the saltmarsh, which builds to a loud clangour as more geese take to the air and join the wheeling flocks already aloft. They are still shrouded in mist, but as they fly inland to feed, small yapping skeins materialise from the gloom and pass overhead. The torrent of sound is now wild and urgent and it characterises this special landscape, which is home to 30,000 barnacle geese each autumn and winter.

The sound is thrilling enough, but on a clear day the spectacle of the Caerlaverock barnacles in the air is mesmerising as they drift and inter-weave far out on the merse. On the ground they are dramatic too. I remember my surprise, the first time I rounded a corner near the reserve and saw, from an elevation, the pasture ahead half carpeted in grey: phalanxes of geese, heads down and feeding briskly, packed together so tightly that from above I couldn't see the grass between them. Several kept their heads up, alert for danger – their short black necks and white faces a contrast to the sea of scalloped grey backs slowly advancing across the field.

Seeing barnacle geese at home in this lush landscape it's hard to imagine that these birds were born on rocky crags in the remote Arctic archipelago of Svalbard. Here, polar bears and Arctic foxes scavenge any goslings that don't survive their maiden plunge on to the ground far below.

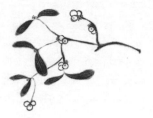
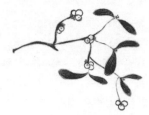

DECEMBER

AS THE YEAR draws to a close, it can seem as if nature is shutting down and so it's tempting to huddle up by the fire with a good book and wait until spring. But if you do, you could miss some of the greatest wild-life-watching experiences on offer. The daylight hours may be short, but December still produces some wonderful winter spectacles: the evening flights of geese and starlings and the flocks of waders roosting at high tide on our coastal estuaries.

The final month of the year can bring surprises, too: the unexpected appearance of a butterfly disturbed from its winter hiding-place; the blooming of an unseasonal plant; and even, if the weather is particularly mild, the start of birdsong and the breeding season.

This is also, inevitably, a time for reflection. What sort of a year has it been for our wildlife – and for us as wildlife-watchers? Has it been a topsy-turvy twelve months, with seasons far earlier or later than they should be? Or have we – and the natural world – enjoyed a rare year of normality, when everything appears on time and in its place? Either way, as the month draws to a close you can look back on the highlights of the past year; and look forward to the next one . . .

S.M.

IN THE FIRST week of December, a ritual has to be observed. I walk to the small park at the top of the street and scan the trampled ground at the base of the lime trees for celandine leaves.

If I spot their diminutive scrolls unfurling among the crisp packets and drinks cans, I know that spring is on its way. It's a sign as sure as returning swallows that the seasons are rolling round and that even though three months will pass before the first golden celandine flowers herald spring proper, these scraps of greenery signal hope for the coming year.

Meanwhile, there's December to enjoy. This is a reflective month in which I plan future trips, look back on the triumphs and frustrations of the waning year and, not as diligently as I should, file records of notable sightings to local or national recording schemes.

There's always time at the year's end to scoop up straggling birds not yet recorded on the 'patch' this year, and to revel in the stillness of a December afternoon. Just as the celandine has become a botanical bench-mark, so too has the barn owl. Checking in with the local pair, never a straightforward matter as their routines are often haphazard at this time of year, has become a midwinter habit. Hard though it is to forsake the hearth at dusk, I venture out to a favourite watchpoint where, hunkered down and shivering in the fading light, I scan the hedge-lines for a pale patrolling shape that will tell me that the owls have made it to, though not yet through, another winter.

It's a sighting that signifies something out of all proportion to its dim obscurity, an affirmation that the stitches haven't frayed completely and that the landscape and its wildlife are still holding together – just.

B.W.

WOODLICE

1 December

Under a plant pot in the garden, I disturb a seething mass of grey-blue woodlice, which trundle slowly away from the sunlight. They're animals I tend to take for granted, but should respect more as highly successful crustaceans, relatives of shrimps and crabs that have forsaken water and adapted to land.

Dry to touch and endearing to watch, it's no surprise that woodlice (an unfair word for harmless creatures that are far from being pestiferous blood-sucking lice) have garnered a host of folk names. Cheese-logs, gramfer-griggles, fuzzy-pigs, wood-bugs, pissi-beds and tiggy-hogs are just a fraction of the long list. When Peter Marren and Richard Mabey were compiling *Bugs Britannica*, they unearthed a roll-call of around eighty different nicknames, over thirty of them from Devon alone, which seems to indicate some affection for these little creatures.

More to the point, woodlice were supposed to be useful medicinally. The shiny species known as pillbugs can roll into a ball and so were assumed to be a sign that, like pills, they could be eaten. Dried and ground into a powder as a cure for indigestion, they were also prescribed as a diuretic and to relieve the effects of ulcers and colic. Their effectiveness isn't recorded, but the doctrine that if it hurts it's working may have been more important than the result: woodlice are rumoured to taste very bitter, and it's rarely I see birds feeding on them.

In my garden, and in most gardens throughout the British Isles, there are several widespread woodlice. The matt grey one with knobbly skin that crowds under pots and in wall crevices is *Porcellio scaber*, whose name means 'rough little pig'. Larger, flatter woodlice with translucent edges to their armour plating are *Oniscus asellus*, which love the compost heap: at night I see them wandering up trees to graze on the algae growing on the trunk. Most woodlice feed on decaying detritus and only nibble the tenderest shoots, so are hardly a garden pest: in fact their droppings add to soil nutrients.

One of the strangest of the forty-plus species of terrestrial woodlice in Britain rejoices in the name *Platyarthrus hoffmannseggii* and lives in the nests of ants. I usually find it when turning over a stone or plant pot under which black ants are nesting. Its delicate, snow-white shape, among the seething ants, is oddly primeval – like an elfin trilobite.

This beautiful species is blind and only five millimetres long and has an uncertain relationship with its hosts. It probably feeds on waste products in the nest and can ward off attacks from the ants by producing noxious chemicals or disguising pheromones: in return, the ants protect it. One of the best places to find it, according to one expert, is to look under flower urns in graveyards, an activity that might not endear you to the verger.

SMALL TORTOISESHELL

2 December

The annual ritual is here again: I venture into the woodshed to unearth the Christmas decorations from wherever we put them last January. As my eyes gradually become accustomed to the murky light, I notice that the spiders have been hard at work: a silken cushion of webs hug every window frame and doorpost, lending the shed a rather spooky air.

Then, as a glint of light pierces the frosted glass, I notice a tiny fragment of colour, as if a piece of stained glass has been caught in the tangled web. I look more closely, and realise it is the wings of a small tortoiseshell: fiery orange dappled with black, with delicate bluish-mauve spots along the edge of each upperwing.

The small tortoiseshell is one of a handful of British butterflies that spend the winter as adults in a state of semi-hibernation before emerging on a sunny day next spring. This long-dead creature ventured inside for safety at the end of the summer, but it was one of the unlucky ones: the place it chose to spend the winter months is shared with spiders.

Yet many – perhaps the majority – do survive. I remember one Christmas shaking out a duvet for guests, from which a small tortoiseshell emerged with a weak flutter of wings – a welcome reminder of summer at the darkest time of the year.

WATER VOLE

3 December

One December day, three years ago, I was patrolling the banks of the River Stour on my local patch at a spot where, like a snagged thread, it shadows the Staffordshire and Worcestershire Canal. I was hoping to glimpse a water rail, a notoriously elusive bird hereabouts, by scanning the river margins a good two metres below me.

Hearing a loud plop, I noticed a patch of exposed sediment was studded with rodent footprints. Surely it couldn't be a water vole? If not, though, what? The marks were too small for a brown rat, the only other likely candidate. Was it possible that an animal I'd assumed was extinct locally was still here, in spite of the mink numbers?

Once, the characteristic plop of a water vole diving into the canal was a feature of almost every walk here. The water vole population began to decline in the mid-1980s and by 1990 I struggled to find any. One of the last I saw was from my kitchen window, a poignant parcel identified through binoculars as it disappeared slowly down the gullet of a grey heron. The water vole was probably the first commonplace creature that I'd seen disappear locally: even grey partridges and turtle doves were still hanging on in the early 1990s. These local catastrophes are now part of wildlife history, mirrored many times over by losses across the British landscape.

In the case of the water vole, the causes are well known. Degraded and polluted waterways have reduced or isolated vole populations, which then become more vulnerable to attack by feral mink. On 'my' stretch of canal, reinforcement with metal pilings has made most of the banks unreachable for the voles, which need access to dig their burrows and create their feeding lawns.

There are very few remaining sites in Worcestershire, but efforts are under way to make those more vole-friendly. In other parts of the country, water voles are being reintroduced and, with the mink retreating in the face of recovering otters, there's hope that Ratty may at last return.

Three years on, I still can't be sure what I saw, but I hope that one afternoon I'll glimpse a plump rounded shape on a sandbank, nibbling a grass stem, before it dives into the swirling waters.

LITTLE EGRETS
4 December

The rhyne at the end of our garden is usually a bird-free zone. It does sometimes play host to a moorhen or two, or a pair of mallards that explode out of the water as if propelled by a cannon when I walk or cycle past. I once even saw a kingfisher there, but otherwise I don't hold out much hope for an ornithological surprise.

So today, the sight of a trio of little egrets is quite an event. On this grim, grey December afternoon they stand out like beacons. Only the black bill, eyes and legs, and daffodil-yellow feet break up the snow-white outline of each bird.

They are here, I suspect, because an overnight freeze-up has displaced them from their usual feeding area, and the steep, grassy banks of the rhyne provide a chance of something to eat. Though as far as I know there are very few small fish, and even fewer frogs, in this narrow strip of muddy water.

If it turns really cold, they will head away from here: usually only a short distance to the estuaries of Devon and Cornwall, where flocks of a hundred or more can sometimes be seen. But if the winter weather really hardens its grip, and all waterways start to freeze, then the egrets will simply hop across the Channel to France, whence they first came to Britain a quarter of a century ago.

PARK DUCKS
5 December

On short grey December days, when I need to escape from the office, I head for the biggest patch of local green space, Mary Stevens Park, Stourbridge. It's a typical urban park with plenty of mature trees, and a newly dredged and re-planted pool, not especially rich in wildlife, but always worth a scan in winter, as its fountain keeps the water from icing over and provides a haven for ducks, coots and moorhens.

We owe its presence, in a sea of houses, to a local pots-and-pans maker, Ernest Stevens, who established the park in memory of his wife Mary in 1925 as a place of 'rest for the weary'.

By which he meant local people of course, but the modern park is also a refuge for wildlife, especially wintering birds. As you approach under the avenue of limes, you can hear the bawdy decrescendos of mallard ducks long before you see them through a flurry of spray as they vie for breadcrumbs. Aloof by comparison, two drake tufted ducks, startlingly black and white with shaggy crests, are diving for shellfish and whatever else they can find in the grey waters. When they bob back to the surface, water droplets roll like balls of mercury from their purple-glossed backs.

Better still is a small flotilla of goosanders loafing out on the water. These long-bodied, saw-billed ducks would have been exceptional here even five years ago. Goosanders are a success story and have spread south and east from their previous breeding range in north and west Britain. They're fish-eaters and not always popular with anglers, but it's likely that reduced pollution and large fish populations have helped them to colonise new areas in summer and winter. Now the bottle-green and white, peach-tinted drakes and rusty-headed ducks are at home on many urban lakes and reservoirs.

These ducks enliven a walk in the park, but as I enjoy their presence on this cold December day, I also wonder where these mallards, tufted ducks and goosanders have come from. They may have bred in the British Isles, but our parks are also a winter refuge for birds from Scandinavia and even western Russia. The home-grown motley of mallards on the park lake might just be rubbing shoulders with ducks from 2,000 miles away.

GREY SQUIRREL

6 December

I never know what to think about grey squirrels. My conservationist head tells me they are vermin: introduced aliens that should never have been brought here from their native North America, and which ideally should be eradicated from our island fauna. But my naturalist head tells me that they are among the most enchanting and entrancing of all our mammals: full of vim and vigour, and able to delight us on even the most dull and dismal December day.

Contrary to popular opinion, neither red nor grey squirrels hibernate, though in very cold weather they do become less active, often spending much of the day hidden away in their dreys at the tops of trees. But in mild weather – and especially in cities – grey squirrels are just as active as during the rest of the year. Watching one scamper up a near-vertical tree-trunk with such consummate ease, I can almost forgive them for the destruction they wreak on young saplings.

They are also – as several observers have pointed out – one of the very few mammals that most urban children (and indeed adults) ever get to see. Apart from domestic cats and dogs, a few deer in the London parks, and the ubiquitous brown rat, they are our city kids' main connection with all things furry.

Many years ago, my colleagues at the BBC Natural History Unit designed an obstacle course for grey squirrels – actually more like an army assault course. At first it was pretty simple, but over time the producers – and keen viewers – constructed ever-more fiendish tests for these agile mammals, each of which they passed with flying colours.

PYLON PEREGRINES

7 December

Growing up as a birdwatcher (that's what birders were called in the 1970s), the idea of seeing a peregrine on my local patch in north Worcestershire was just a pipe dream. That this supreme hunter, the fastest moving creature on the planet, could turn up in my soft West Midlands landscape was a ludicrous flight of fancy. All the bird books informed me that this bird likes to feel rock under its talons, and nests only on vertiginous crags in dramatic landscapes. To see one, I'd need to travel to Cornish cliffs or Scottish peaks.

Forty years on peregrines are a regular sight, their dark, cruciform shapes sweeping across the skies near my home. Their comeback has been swift and dramatic. The organochlorine-based pesticides of the 1950s and early 1960s, which killed them by concentrating in their prey and causing them to lay thin-shelled eggs, have been banned. Public perception of the birds has also changed: peregrines and their nests were actively destroyed along the south coast of England during the Second

World War because they were likely to intercept homing pigeons used for sending vital information – at one point they were even condemned for being 'in league with Goering's Luftwaffe'.

With these pressures relaxed, the peregrine has shown itself to be not a narrow specialist of cliffs and crags, but a highly adaptable bird at home almost everywhere. It has responded by recolonising old haunts, spreading south and east, and, most dramatically, coming into town where our taller buildings provide artificial cliffs for nest-sites and a ready supply of street pigeons for food.

Peregrines are now more widespread in the British Isles than they've been for centuries and a winter day is often enlivened by a hunched shape at the top of one of the pylons that march across my patch. From here the falcon is king: it can survey the surrounding farmland for miles and fix on its target.

One Christmas Eve I watched a stock dove fly heedlessly past the peregrine's lofty perch. Imperceptibly, the pylon shrugged the bird off its iron shoulders and, wings flickering like knife-blades, the falcon powered after its quarry. So rapid was its pursuit that the dove, no mean flier itself, appeared to slow down in mid-air until, just before the moment of impact, it seemed to be stationary. A puff of feathers marked the capture and the peregrine flew on to the next pylon to pluck and eat its prey.

HARBOUR BIRDS

8 December

There's something very special about seeing a harbour from the birds' point of view: not from the land, but the water. And the advantage of a boat is that it can get to many places that simply aren't visible from the coast.

Leaving our mooring at Poole Harbour, we realised this straight away as a large, pale, cormorant-sized bird surfaced right alongside us. It was a great northern diver: a scarce winter visitor to southern Britain from its nesting grounds in Iceland and Arctic Canada. I rarely see these birds at all, and never quite as closely as this – one benefit of being on a boat. The bird's spangled grey upperparts and huge, pale dagger-like beak were easily visible – a far cry from the usual distant silhouette.

I was accompanying a group of schoolchildren on a boat trip to see their local birdlife. The children were suitably impressed by the birdlife on offer, and even more so when a rapid blur swept past the boat and headed straight towards a flock of waders, which wheeled around in panic. The blur we'd seen, we soon realised, was our smallest bird of prey, a merlin. Right on cue it caught a dunlin, and then perched on the mudflats to pluck and eat it, feathers flying as it dug its hooked beak into the unfortunate bird's flesh.

The main reason birders come out on to Poole Harbour in December is to see the wintering flock of avocets, elegant, pied waders that flash black and white as they twist and turn in the bright-blue sky. These birds breed on the low-lying polders of the Netherlands, and then fly westwards in autumn to spend the winter here in Dorset. As they landed they began to feed, using their unique upturned bills to sieve through the shallow water for tiny aquatic invertebrates.

Nearby, on Brownsea Island's tidal lagoon, we came across an even more exciting spectacle: a score of spoonbills, mostly asleep (as they invariably are). Spoonbills – large, white waterbirds with a spatulate bill, also used for sieve-feeding – are an increasingly regular sight along the south coast, but scarce enough to be a treat for me. But sleeping or not, they provided a fine ending to a memorable day – not just for the school-kids, but for us too.

MUNTJAC

9 December

Knee-high tunnels through the russet mounds of bracken betray the wanderings of muntjacs, small Labrador-sized deer that suddenly seem to be everywhere. Just in case I'm in any doubt, sparked by my presence, the wood echoes with their raucous alarm calls, half-fox, half-dog and now an inescapable rural sound. In the soft mud at the trackside I see their neat hoof prints or slots, in pairs, one slot smaller than the other.

When muntjacs first appeared locally in the 1970s I was captivated by their strangeness and exotic origins. These diminutive deer, properly called Reeves's muntjac, are native to China and Taiwan. Introduced around the turn of the twentieth century by the Duke of Bedford, their name is from the Sunda Islands dialect and means 'springing', an apt description as a flash of white undertail fur is often all you see as they bound off through the undergrowth.

Seen well, muntjacs are stocky, barrel-shaped deer. Their short, prong-like, backward-facing antlers and dark facial stripes give them a surly expression, exaggerated in the bucks by tusk-like canines. Both sexes have foxy-brown coats, longer in winter, and when you see them in the open, look rather hunchbacked as they walk, the small head held lower than the ample hindquarters.

A new small deer in the countryside might once have been a talking point, but that novelty has long worn off for many people; as their populations increase, muntjacs are increasingly approachable. As well as being driving hazards and browsing on crops and in gardens, muntjacs are causing havoc among native woodland flowers.

When ancient woodland is coppiced, nowadays mainly for conservation purposes, sunlight floods into the open glades allowing flowers such as violets, primroses, oxlips and orchids to flourish temporarily until the trees regrow and the coppice cycle begins elsewhere. Low levels of deer in the past have had less impact on this regrowth, but as muntjac populations build up in old woodland, the animals browse most of the new young plants and prevent flowering over large areas.

For rare plants such as oxlip and lady orchid, the deer is a serious threat. They also stop smaller shrubs and coppiced trees from sprouting and can remove a complete layer of vegetation from woodland. This layer is important as cover and feeding habitat for birds including that brilliant songster the nightingale, which is already on the decline in England. Grazing muntjac, though attractive, are doing flowers and birdlife no favours.

LOOKING BACK

10 December

The year's turning, when rain beats against the windows and indoors is far more appealing than out, is the perfect time to reflect on the season gone and to send in records.

Over the last forty years or so, I've amassed a pile of fraying notebooks, which record the wildlife I've seen with a reasonable degree of accuracy.

Looking back at the earliest, written in the late 1970s, in smudged ink with a faithful Platignum pen, I can re-live the excitement of those first encounters ('REDSTARTS!' on a local hill recorded in capital letters) or evoke the now barely credible memory of past riches (400 tree sparrows in a weedy cereal crop).

Now I use my notebooks as an aid to cementing knowledge of a species or sighting in my mind, as a record of good times in the field with friends and as a source of records to be submitted to local and national surveys.

Recording is an important part of the modern naturalist's life. Organisations such as the British Trust for Ornithology use their army of volunteer observers to take the pulse of the avian scene, in schemes to monitor changes in birdlife in gardens, on wetlands and nationally in the form of regular atlases. Similarly the Botanical Society of the British Isles keeps close tabs on changes in plant populations and distribution by relying on volunteer botanists. Today when you see the sheer scale of mapping and quantifying of wildlife from moths to mosses and ladybirds to dragonflies, it's clear that there's no shortage of naturalists.

My own notes occasionally feed into national surveys, but usually to my county Biological Records Office, which keeps records of all Worcestershire wildlife. Such records build up an important picture of significant species and habitats and are useful for informing local planning decisions and conservation initiatives as well as monitoring changes in status. Sometimes we conduct targeted surveys to produce a county atlas – one is pending on bumblebees – or to follow the spread of a particular species.

I'm not as diligent as I should be, especially with the commoner species, but the effort is worthwhile. That's why, as the light fades on a winter afternoon, you'll find me, steaming mug of tea at hand, backcombing through last year's notebook for memories and vital records.

WHITE-TAILED EAGLE

11 December

I don't 'do' twitching any more. Like a reformed drinker, I long ago saw the error of my ways, and forsook the joys and tension of chasing up and down the country after rare birds. But just as people fall off the wagon now and again, occasionally I will make a diversion to catch up with an unexpected vagrant.

One such trip took place in the last month before the end of the millennium. Stopping off en route to Norfolk at Cockley Cley to try to see a white-tailed eagle, we arrived to find the usual bunch of disaffected twitchers. As often happens when birders gather together, they were chatting, complaining, indeed doing anything but looking for the bird, which had apparently not been seen since lunchtime. Despite the opinion of the crowd – that we had missed our chance – I set up my scope and scanned the distant row of trees.

On my second or third pan across, I saw what looked like a wood-pigeon perched in a distant tree, silhouetted against the evening sky. Classic shape: small head, plump body and upright stance. But something wasn't quite right. 'I think I've got the eagle,' I said tentatively. My neighbour took a glance through my scope. 'Nah, it's just a pigeon, mate.'

I looked again. A much smaller bird was perched right next to the 'pigeon's' head. 'If it's a pigeon,' I began, 'then why is that magpie about one-tenth of its size?'

At that point the eagle took to the air, and flew away to roost. For the other birders, it was a classic example of not seeing something when it is right in front of them.

Later we discovered that the eagle was probably not one of the re-introduced Scottish contingent, but likely to be a wanderer from Scandinavia. The idea of this huge bird flying slowly but surely across the North Sea reminded me that twitching can sometimes be worth it – especially when you encounter a bird as large and spectacular as this.

SCARCE SPIDERS

12 December

December might seem an odd month to look for spiders, but at a time when few others are on display, a small green species has become something of a local obsession. The spider doesn't have a common name, and its scientific name *Nigma walckenaeri* is a bit of a mouthful: green leaf web spider is as good as anything.

It was first pointed out to me by Harry Green, a naturalist friend who'd spotted it in south Worcestershire. Because, until recently, it was a local species of south-east England and the lower Severn Valley, any records were important, especially as it appeared that the spider was spreading.

Many autumns ago, Harry found the tiny spiders, which are only half a centimetre long, on ivy leaves in his garden. The females are silvery green like tiny chocolate limes and spin a fine sheet web across the hollow of the leaf, where they lie in wait for the insects visiting the ivy blossom. Here they are courted by the smaller, rust-tinted males, though courtship is far too genteel a description: each ivy leaf is an arena where mortal struggles are enacted and it's not always the male who bites the dust.

There must be something addictive about these spiders, because another naturalist friend, Jean Young, has also caught the obsession and has spent many hours photographing their domestic affairs. Her photographs have revealed that cannibalism is common between the sexes and, in a reversal of the traditional roles, males will attack and kill the larger females. In a successful mating, the pair lock their jaws, or chelicerae, in a position that allows the male to transfer his sperm-loaded palps into the female's storage organ or epigyne.

All this seamy stuff could be happening on an ivy leaf in your garden. *Nigma* is spreading into eastern and central England, often in town parks, gardens and churchyards. I've found it by walking my local streets and looking for the delicate sheet web: closer inspection will reveal the pale-green spider lurking beneath.

In mild winters the females can survive until January, not only on ivy but also on the leaves of low-growing evergreen shrubs and often conveniently at chest-height. Harry and Jean's obsession is catching on and now we have a small local army of *Nigma*-hunters who've given us a much better idea of its distribution. Even when the adults have died, with practice, you can spot the small blobs of snow-white silk on the dark-green ivy leaves: buried within are the eggs that will become the next *Nigma* generation.

DESERT WHEATEAR

13 December

It wasn't hard to find the bird, or at least not hard to find the people watching it. A small huddle of binocular-toting birders gathered round like members of a religious sect in the unlikely surroundings of Severn Beach, at the mouth of England's longest river.

The word 'beach' may have given you a false impression. Whoever coined this place name must have had a rich sense of irony; even if it had been the middle of July rather than December, this wouldn't have been a place for sunbathing or sandcastles.

The bird I had come to see was hunched just below the sea wall, too close for my binoculars to focus. A buff-coloured, thrush-like bird with jet-black wings and tail, and a black bandit-like mask across its face, the sandy shade was apt, for this was a desert wheatear – the first I had ever seen in this country. Desert wheatears are a rare but regular visitor to Britain, usually found on deserted beaches in late autumn or early winter, after heading north by mistake. Since the very first wandering bird was shot at Alloa, Clackmannanshire, in November 1880, over a hundred have been recorded.

Most, like this specimen, probably do not survive the British winter, but others may manage to reorient themselves and head back south to their North African breeding grounds. But as it crouched down among the seaweed looking very sorry for itself, I suspected that this would not be one of the lucky ones.

TAWNY OWL

14 December

The sound, when it came, was both completely familiar and utterly incongruous. The classic hoot of a male tawny owl: floating through the air like the notes of an oboe.

There was only one problem. It was the middle of the morning: more suitable for coffee than a cup of cocoa, and definitely not the time I would expect to hear the hooting of this almost entirely nocturnal bird.

He hooted a second time. I was beginning to wonder which of my many birding friends was playing a trick on me. Perhaps Brett had decided to pay an unexpected visit, and was winding me up. But when no one appeared that day or the day after, and yet the owl continued his morning vigil, I realised that it must be the real thing.

A couple of years later, I discovered the reason behind this mysterious behaviour. A paper in the monthly magazine *British Birds* suggested it was because in parts of rural Britain these highly sedentary owls live at such high densities that, each autumn and early winter, the offspring from the previous spring try to kick their parents out of their home. This in turn prompts the incumbent males to defend their hard-won territory, which they do by calling at odd times in the middle of the day. Apparently this has not yet been recorded elsewhere in their European range, so perhaps British tawny owls are evolving a twenty-four-hour lifestyle.

LEAF LITTER

15 December

On winter forest walks, however hard the wind tugs at the treetops, there's always an opportunity to fossick in leaf litter. This natural compost is at its richest under oaks whose leaves decay relatively slowly: mixed with rotting hazel leaves and fragments of birch catkins, they create a moist layer underfoot with a texture like crumbling ginger cake.

The technique is simple. Kneel and gently rake away the top layer of leaves and watch as a teeming invisible world is exposed. Leaf litter life tends to shun bright sunlight so most creatures will scurry or bound away at speed.

The most obvious insects are usually acrobatic springtails, which somersault off in all directions. Many of these have a long springing organ called a furca under the abdomen. When they 'unclip' the furca, the resulting force can propel them several centimetres away from danger, a distance of twenty or thirty times their own body length. Under a hand lens, springtails are engaging and often colourful creatures, though they rarely stay still long enough for you to find out. There are countless springtails in a single wood and their collective grazing on fungi, bacteria and decaying litter helps to create the humus, which underpins the wood's ecology.

Occasionally we find a writhing knot of olive maggots among the rotting leaves: the larvae of St Mark's flies, better known for drifting lazily around in spring. There are slugs here too, including the longest British species, the elegant ash-black slug, which can reach a length of twenty centimetres and specialises in old woods and leafy dingles. Because of this, it has been described by one slug specialist as 'a wonderful judge of scenery'.

With all this biomass beneath the leaves, there are plenty of opportunities for predators. The sturdy violet ground-beetles have wing cases edged in royal purple and lurk under rotting logs or behind loose bark at the base of trees. In winter they're less active and we often find them comatose and snuggled next to potential prey, a slug or an earthworm perhaps, the temporary cease-fire enforced by the falling temperatures.

My own favourite leaf-litter beetle is *Cychrus caraboides*, a tubby blackish insect with a long 'nose', actually the elongated head and pronotum, which helps it reach the parts other beetles can't, in this case soft-bodied snails hidden in their shells. Pick up *Cychrus* and it has another trick: it buzzes briefly like a wasp in a bottle, hence its common name, the buzzing snail hunter.

HOUSEHOLD MOTHS

16 December

A small speck on the living-room curtains in midwinter may or may not be swattable. As I rustle the curtains it takes flight: a moth.

Our centrally heated houses allow many insects to continue their life cycles throughout the year; among them are the dreaded clothes moths which instead of having just a couple of generations outside, can fit in up to seven per year in the comfort of our homes.

Case-bearers are small, dull-brown moths, which skip and wriggle away from danger rather than flying. Their caterpillars munch on carpets and clothes and build small woollen tubes like sleeping bags held together with silk. In the British Isles they much prefer living indoors, but probably evolved in birds' nests where they eat detritus including owl pellets.

It looks as if they're on the increase, in step with our taste for more natural fibres. As a result, sales of mothballs or their modern equivalent are on the rise.

I don't have case-bearers (I hope), but I do see several white-shouldered house moths through the year. Close-to and pre-swat, they're attractive moths, with tabby-patterned wings and very distinctive snowy 'shoulders' – in reality the thorax and base of the forewings, which are thickly dusted with white scales.

These moths don't nibble clothes: instead their larvae feed on all kinds of natural by-products: hair, skin-flakes, insect remains, rotten wood and cereals. Regular use of the vacuum cleaner will keep them in check. It's tempting to reach for the swatter, not because they do much damage, but because they're a salutary reminder to do more housework.

But not all household moths in winter are pests. Two exquisite little insects often come indoors to shelter. The twenty-plume is a peculiar moth with interlocking feathery strips that serve as wings (in spite of its name, it has twenty-four plumes) banded like a hawk's feather in shades of cream, sepia and mushroom. Under a lens it is a very attractive insect and has no designs on any of our household items: its caterpillars feed on honeysuckle in woods and gardens.

The other welcome winter guest is the beautiful plume. Plume moths look very different to most other British moths: leggy and T-shaped with thin narrow wings held at right angles to their bodies. Their shapes and sombre patterns remind you of a scrap of dead leaf or a small twig. Beautiful plumes are masters of camouflage, sitting still until touched. They seem to like the bathroom and I often find one perched on the cistern where I can admire its intricate tortoiseshell patterning against the white enamel. Its narrow forewings even have a white dart at the edge to resemble a tattered leaf. Like the twenty-plume, this moth is completely harmless, and requires a shelter for winter, which I am happy to provide.

PIED WAGTAIL ROOST

17 December

The hordes of Christmas shoppers have just one thing on their mind – to buy all the presents they need and then go home – and so few, if any, think to look up. If they did, though, they might notice a succession of small, slender, black and white birds flying down from the darkening sky and into a tree outside a famous department store. The sound, quiet at first, rises in a loud and persistent crescendo, as the birds settle down for the night.

They are pied wagtails, familiar birds from city pavements and garden lawns, but usually seen alone or in pairs. But on winter's evenings they seek safety in numbers, and this is just one of countless winter roosts up and down the country. I've seen them in reed-beds and motorway service stations, on industrial estates and, as here, in shopping centres. The usual requirements are a safe place to spend the night, free from predators, and close to wherever they will go to feed the next morning.

Most of these locations – apart from reed-beds, which being in water offer their own form of protection – are in well-lit, man-made sites, where any self-respecting predator is going to think twice about exposing themselves to danger.

Urban sites have another major advantage: they are warm. A pied wagtail weighs a mere twenty-one grams – just three-quarters of an ounce – so can lose heat very rapidly. By huddling together in towns and cities, where the winter nights are often two or three degrees warmer than the surrounding countryside, these wagtails give themselves a far better chance of surviving until the following day.

HOAR FROST

18 December

One December day in 2010 I woke to the most spectacular hoar frost. Every bush and tree was furred with ice crystals, where overnight fog had settled on sub-zero surfaces. In places the pelt of frost, which had accreted crystal on crystal, was over an inch thick. A ragged elm hedge became a coral reef, its stagshorn branches sparkling with thick coats of rime. Along the bridleway, the trailing twigs of silver birches had fused into a white torrent. As far as I could see the landscape was ice blue, horses black silhouettes in its midst.

Early on, there was no sun. In the lane, the umbrellas of dried hogweed loomed out of the mist, their spokes clotted with frost as thick as snow. When the sun did appear, its slight warmth dislodged ice crystals from the branches above, sending a splintered rainbow across the garden.

In the stillness, the tiniest movement betrayed a bird, a robin darting towards me and landing with a puff of falling crystals on a twig close by. Today, when the ground is hardened and food hard to find, I have my uses. Robins once shadowed herds of cattle and parties of boar, known as sounders, around forests to snap up the worms and insects disturbed by their progress. Aware of my responsibility, I act like a wild boar and ruffle the leaf litter. Quick as a flash the robin's in there, its large eyes scanning for the twitch of life, which could mean a vital meal in this bleak weather.

Other birds are surprisingly well hidden. This is a waxwing winter, and there's a small invasion of these punk-crested Scandinavian plunderers, gorging themselves on berries on a local housing estate. At first I can't see them in the frosted trees, but a movement in a rowan reveals two, snuggled deep in a grotto of branches. This is a home from home for these hardy inhabitants of the northern forests and as long as there are fruits and berries around, they'll cope easily with our weather.

By midday the sun has broken through, a breeze has picked up and the show is over. As winters become milder, it could be years before I experience another day like it.

COOTS

19 December

Cheddar Reservoir is one of those concrete-banked, water-filled bowls similar to the London reservoirs where I cut my birding teeth back in the early 1970s, though with rather better scenery. Instead of deafening jumbo jets landing at nearby Heathrow Airport, I now have a panoramic view of the Mendip Hills – a great improvement.

If there's one species you simply cannot ignore here, it's the coot: several thousand of them, bobbing up and down on the water like jet-black floats, before diving beneath in a practised arc to find their food. Coots are one of those birds most birders either ignore or simply take for granted, but they are always worth a second look. Their dark grey plumage

– almost black at a distance – is set off with a white bill and face, which gave rise to the saying 'as bald as a coot'.

They may look superficially like the ducks that accompany them, but they are from a very different family: the rails. Like their cousin the moorhen, they have taken to an aquatic lifestyle, and evolved to resemble other waterbirds such as ducks and grebes.

This is one of the largest gatherings of coots in the whole country, and there's no denying it looks impressive, especially on winter mornings when they loom out of the mist like some invading army.

BELLBINE

20 December

A pale trumpet caught my eye today as I drove past a crimson-berried hawthorn hedge. Bone-white against the bare twigs, the bindweed flower looked utterly out of place and unseasonably opulent, an exotic survivor that had continued blooming in the absence of frosts.

Greater bindweed, or bellbine, has always been a favourite of mine. As a child, I was captivated by the vitality of its purple-tinted shoots, which thrust through the base of the compost heap each spring and writhed in unison towards a clump of conifers. Entwining each other, anti-clockwise, the stems plaited to create living hawsers on which they hoisted dagger-shaped leaves and snow-white blooms high into the trees.

My parents' garden was neatly planted, the lawn edges closely trimmed, so I was impressed by the bellbine's anarchy and the way it romped with such elegance and vigour over the neat symmetries of our little patch. I was alone in my admiration and still am. The bind with bindweed of course is that it oversteps the mark and can rapidly take over a garden if not checked: its deep-running, brittle roots are almost impossible to eradicate.

There's an irony in that the same gardeners who wage war on it will spend hours cherishing the tender blooms of its relative, the morning glory, a delicate hothouse annual that has to be cajoled into flowering and protected from frosts and slugs.

In the right setting, festooning an old hedge or embracing a fence-post, bellbine is an exquisite plant, with one of the largest single blooms of any British wild flower. Each virginal trumpet is a favourite with bumblebees whose furry bums are all you see as they nose the flower's extremities for nectar. These deep well-like blooms are gloriously described by botanists as 'infundibuliform' – shaped like a funnel.

Flowering continues from early summer until November and in autumn it's often still going strong when scarlet bryony berries drape the hedgerows. Only when the first frost arrives does it succumb, a fate awaiting my lone December specimen.

GARDEN BIRDS

21 December

When I was growing up, my grandmother regularly fed the birds in our suburban garden. But having lived through two world wars, she was not inclined to give them anything we might be able to eat ourselves, so their diet consisted mostly of suet and stale bread – not guaranteed to attract the greatest range of species.

How very different from today. Some garden birds eat rather better than our children do, with a range of specially chosen, energy-rich foods designed to give them – and us – the greatest bang for our buck. My feeders are packed with the wonderfully named 'kibbled sunflower hearts', which according to the marketing blurb produce less waste and more energy.

And on this, the shortest day of the year, they really need to. There are not even eight hours between sunrise and sunset, and with many of these birds having to eat between one-quarter and one-third of their body weight just to survive – and that's every single winter's day – any advantage I can give them is certainly worth the extra cost.

There is a classic pecking order to the garden bird feeders. Great tits are usually dominant, though flocks of wandering starlings will displace them before moving on to raid another garden. Blue tits are smaller, but they are pretty feisty, so get more than their fair share. Coal tits may be the same size as their more colourful cousins, but they seem far more reticent – dashing out of the cover in the adjacent hedgerow, perching momentarily on the side of the feeder to grab a seed, then dashing off and out of sight.

INDOOR ROBINS

22 December

As I made my way through the packed garden centre to the usual accompaniment of festive muzak designed to soothe my fellow shoppers, what I hadn't banked on was that they would also be playing birdsong. Cutting through the dulcet tones of Wizzard's anthem 'I Wish It Could Be Christmas Everyday' was the wistful song of a robin. Then I realised that it was actually a robin – not a recording, but a real, live bird, perched on a Christmas tree and pouring its heart out with its winter song.

It used to be said that if you hear a bird singing in autumn or winter, it must be a robin. That's no longer quite true: a run of mild winters has encouraged other species – notably the wren – to join in this festive singsong. But by far the most frequent winter songster is indeed the robin.

This is not, as we might think, for our benefit, but because unlike most species both male and female robins hold a territory throughout the winter months, and must defend it against intruders. Yet I, along with many others, still love hearing what feels like an unseasonal sound at this cold, dark time of year.

For robins, living inside a garden centre is a sensible lifestyle choice. These places are warm and snug, free from predators and provide plenty of opportunities to feed. Here, members of staff are happy to point out the robins to their customers, who in turn seem delighted that this classic symbol of Christmas has chosen to live in such an unusual place.

BEAVER

23 December

The surface of the loch is still and calm on this windless early winter's day. Only the occasional leaf landing from above, or the brief movement of a fish from below, ripples the glassy waters. Until, that is, one of our most charismatic mammals chooses to appear.

Full-grown adult beavers can reach well over a metre in length and weigh up to thirty-eight kilos, more than a medium-sized dog, but even so, a swimming beaver creates remarkably little disturbance. They may not be the world's biggest rodents – that honour goes to the South American capybara – but they are still pretty formidable for what is, in effect, a giant rat.

Watching this beaver swimming sedately across a Highland loch is a real thrill. It's like being transported back in time to the Middle Ages, when beavers were still widespread in Britain. Hunted for their fur and a secretion used in the making of perfumes, beavers disappeared from our rivers and streams about 500 years ago.

But now they're back. They may have arrived here by accident (though it is more likely that they were deliberately released by enthusiasts for re-wilding) but they are now making the most of their newfound freedoms. Of course this brings its own problems: beavers do have a destructive side, felling saplings in order to build their dens, but as 'nature's architects' they have the potential to shape our wetland habitats for the benefit of many other species.

I am happy simply to sit and marvel at this extraordinary creature. Just before it reaches the shore it upends and disappears beneath the water's surface, entering its semi-aquatic underground lodge, never to be seen again.

LONG-TAILED TITS

24 December

Only one small bird spends Christmas with its family: the long-tailed tit. At almost any time of day at this time of year, from dawn to dusk, I can hear the telltale twittering calls from the hedgerow. It's a series of tiny explosions, interspersed with a flurry of high-pitched 'see-see-see' sounds that tells me the long-tailed tit flock is back in town.

Then they appear, as if by magic: tiny little balls of fluff with that impossibly long tail sticking out below like a child's lollipop; perched for a moment on bare twigs, then setting off again with that characteristic bounding flight action that takes them just enough distance to reach the safety of the next tree or shrub.

Long-tailed tits are not the only bird to form flocks in autumn and winter: many eyes are the best way to find food and to keep a lookout for predators. But other flocks may contain several different species. Long-tailed tits, by contrast, often stick together, with the youngsters hatched earlier in the spring following their wiser and marginally older parents.

Whenever I come across a flock I try to stay as still as possible as they pass. Often one will pause briefly just a couple of feet away from me – far too close for me to use binoculars – before heading onwards in that constant search for food. As their sound finally fades into the distance, I always feel an immense sense of privilege, to have come so close to an apparently fearless wild bird.

CHRISTMAS MOTHS

25 December

There's something about moths that captivates children from a very early age. Unlike many adults, who associate them with holes in clothes and go into a blind panic when one flutters around their heads, most young-sters love to see them close up, even allowing them to crawl over their hands and arms.

My daughter Daisy has always found moths fascinating. She has a real affinity with the buff-tip, that master of camouflage that looks exactly like a piece of lichen-covered birch twig with the end neatly cut off with a penknife to reveal the wood beneath – until, that is, it opens its wings.

But Daisy has learned, along with the rest of us, that moths are with us from spring to autumn, and not to be expected in the middle of winter.

So when I heard squeals of surprise and delight on Christmas Day morning, back when she was six years old, I assumed that this was simply the usual excitement over presents. Then she came indoors, hands cupped. Opening them carefully, she revealed a pale, buffish-coloured moth.

It took me a while to identify it; leafing back and forth through the field guide to see if any of the hundreds of pictures matched the docile specimen still perched on her palm. Then it briefly closed its wings, and I realised that it was one of the 'thorns', members of the wonder-fully named *Geometridae* family. A quick check of the book again, and there it was: feathered thorn, so named from its delicate, feathery antennae.

Three years later, more or less in the same place on the wall outside our back door, we found another moth: but much darker brown in colour than the previous specimen. When I discovered its name, the reason for its sepia shade became obvious: it was a December moth, one of the few species that habitually emerge in late autumn and can be seen during the winter, and whose dark colour allows it to retain what meagre warmth there is at this time of year.

Both these encounters were a reminder that nature always has the capacity to surprise; and that you should always learn to expect the unexpected.

MISTLETOE

26 December

The last stubborn leaves have fallen, tugged free by December gales. Their absence reveals mustard-coloured balls among the bare branches, like wind-blown seaweed marooned in the treetops. Each tangled mass contains hundreds of paired leathery leaves among which the translucent white berries sit. Locally, in late November, we have a mistletoe auction at Tenbury Wells in west Worcestershire, and the rapid sales show that the plant has lost none of its Christmas appeal.

Bringing mistletoe indoors is a tradition that we've grafted on to our Yuletide celebrations, partly because of a fascination for druidry in the eighteenth and nineteenth centuries. For the Druids, the plant symbolised vitality because in winter it produced green leaves from trees whose own foliage had fallen. The paired leaves and the pale berries filled with sticky white juice were irresistible links to human fertility, which we've chastely transmuted into kissing. In Norse legend, Baldur the son of Odin was made invincible to all things growing in the ground by his mother Frigg, who overlooked mistletoe, which grew on trees. The mischievous Loki persuaded Baldur's brother to kill Baldur with a mistletoe spear. Frigg's tears became the translucent berries and her request for peace after her son's death has associated the plant with harmony and goodwill ever since.

Apple trees are this parasitic plant's favourite host, but it is also commonly found on poplars, limes and hawthorns, and grows on many other species including rowan and field maple. Mistletoe is common in Somerset, the Severn Vale and the southern Welsh borders where the highest densities of old orchards can be found, but what the plant really likes are warm summers and cool, but not cold winters and lately I've noticed more clumps of mistletoe appearing in urban streets not traditionally a stronghold for this curious plant. They're mainly in the tops of limes, though a small rowan in the next street to my home has sprouted a couple of robust tufts.

But why the increase in mistletoe? The sticky white berries are a favourite food of mistle thrushes, which defend their chosen mistletoe trees with loud rattling calls and vigorous attacks, which are usually enough to deter all-comers. The thrush swallows the berries whole and excretes the seed in a sticky string-of-pearls, many of which will not stick to the branches and so won't germinate into new mistletoe plants.

But a much smaller bird, the blackcap, a warbler that was once a summer migrant only, is increasing as a winter visitor in the British Isles. It too is very fond of mistletoe berries, and is able to slip under the thrush's radar and lurk deep in the clusters of leaves. One winter I counted four blackcaps in a single, small, mistletoe-laden orchard. Blackcaps are thought to be more efficient mistletoe planters because instead of excreting the seeds, they wipe them on to a branch before they swallow the berry. This increase in wintering blackcaps may well be the reason that mistletoe is increasing in town and elsewhere.

FINCH FLOCKS
27 December

In winter, when territorial barriers crumble, seed-eating birds such as greenfinches and linnets join forces to rove the local farmland in search of unharvested crops or uncut weeds. Although many finches are declining as breeding birds, and these flocks are smaller and often harder to find, occasionally a large congregation appears, materialising as if from nowhere.

Last winter my local farmland hosted 600 or so linnets, which fed avidly on the weed known as fat hen, because its mealy seeds were once used to feed poultry. It's a downmarket relative of the trendy quinoa, and its tall stems clotted with seed-clusters are magnets for linnets.

I found this flock by ear. The massed twitters of a distant linnet flock sound like a wave breaking over rocks. They're jittery birds, never perching for more than thirty seconds, before rising in unison and swirling, brown on brown, over the spears of fat hen.

The swirl moves closer now, and I can pick out the white chalk-lines along their primary wing-feathers and tail edges, the greyish hoods of the males and here and there a smudge of pink, which is all that's left of their breeding finery. They swarm frantically over the seed-heads and then explode into the air once again, this time with reason as a sparrow-hawk brushes the weed-tips with its blunt wings. This is why the linnets flock together now, reaping the benefits of mass-vigilance and confusing the hawk with their unpredictable flight.

Scanning these flocks is irresistible because there may be other species among them. Today there are a few tortoiseshell-patterned bramblings, northern relatives of the chaffinch, clad in soft peaches, tans and sepias. A streaky reed bunting flits into a hedgerow and sits there, nervously flicking its tail-feathers. Best of all – and I'm amazed I haven't picked them out earlier – there are over 100 lesser redpolls: smaller, neater versions of the linnets, with black bibs and red foreheads and jingling calls like loose change in a pocket.

Redpolls are a taxonomic nightmare: few ornithologists can agree where one species or subspecies ends and another begins. I scan the flocks for larger, greyer individuals, which might indicate rare northern stragglers, but by now dusk is closing in so I leave them feasting hungrily in the last vital minutes of daylight.

DIPPERS

28 December

Water levels are low and a dipper has come to town. Today one is bobbing on the gravelly shores of the Severn below Bewdley's sandstone quays, while shoppers and day-trippers pass by above.

When rainfall is sparse and the forest streams run low, dippers move out on to the main river to take advantage of the exposed shorelines and occasional shingle banks. Some of these birds are youngsters that fledged last spring, others adults, which leave their territories for a while to search for a different food supply. Usually these portly white-bibbed birds are hard to see as they whirr upstream along the wooded brook, but in the open it's fascinating to watch their feeding technique.

Dippers are the only British perching birds that feed underwater and are most at home in the tumbling well-oxygenated becks, burns and rills of the north and west. In deep water, one will swim to the bottom, rowing with its wings and holding on to stream-bed pebbles with its claws as it plucks insects from the stones. When it's finished, it lets go, allowing the air trapped in its plumage to buoy it to the surface.

This one is in very shallow water at the river's edge where it is flipping the stones with its stout bill, looking for mayfly and stonefly larvae. Now and then it seizes a caddis fly, holding it in its beak like a Churchillian cigar. The caddis case of sand grains and sticks is inedible, but by squeezing one end of the case tightly, the bird extrudes the soft grub and deftly flips and swallows it.

If disturbed, it flutters on to a stone and bobs as if on hinges: dippers are rarely still for long. These town birds proclaim their winter territories by singing, an unexpected sound in midwinter. Both sexes sing their bright, apparently unstructured ramble in which melodies are mixed with scratchier notes. A few years ago, one bird took to performing under the concrete arches of the town's bypass bridge, a perfect auditorium for its song, which echoed around the buttresses and was audible above the thrum of overhead traffic.

Winter ends early for dippers, and within a month or so these birds will leave the main river which is too deep and slow-flowing to provide enough food for broods of chicks. Back on the forest streams, they begin building their football-shaped nests among tree-roots or in the overhangs of a steep bank: by early March the female will be incubating her first clutch of eggs.

BIRDS OUT OF SEASON
29 December

The day dawned sunny and mild – had it not been almost the end of December I would have said warm – which seemed a good time to go birding. But despite the fine weather, I hadn't banked on it sounding exactly like early spring.

OK, I would expect to hear robins, wrens and the occasional outburst from a Cetti's warbler. But that trio would normally be the only birds singing.

Yet as I walked, I could also hear the twin-tone notes of the chiffchaff and the hurdy-gurdy song of our smallest bird, the goldcrest. In the distance a song thrush sang its repetitive serenade, while hidden deep inside a bramble bush a dunnock let rip too. The overall effect was of a day in mid-March, not late December.

Birdsong always brings a spring to my step: even though I am well aware that these birds are not singing for me, but to defend a territory and (in spring) attract a mate, it still feels special. Recent studies have now proved that listening to birdsong makes us feel more relaxed and content: something any birder knows well.

Yet even though this was an enjoyable experience, it was tinged with fear and worry. Global climate change is no longer simply a theory, but a firm reality, especially here in southern Britain. Autumn lingers longer, spring starts earlier, and if we have many more Decembers like this one, winter will simply disappear.

Nature does have a balance, and when it starts to go out of kilter there is a real danger that it will become like a runaway train, careering into the future with no chance of returning to the status quo. I may not live long enough to witness the consequences, but my children will; and although it may be a cliché to say so, that worries me more than I can say.

WINTER CROSSBILLS

30 December

A quiet December morning. I can't hear my own footsteps along the forest track, which is cushioned by a layer of fallen pine needles. There are few sounds besides: conifer plantations like this one aren't rich in winter birdlife, though I can just pick out the squeaky-toy calls of a coal tit high in the Scots pines.

But then, without warning, comes an explosion of sound, an insistent clamour of 'jip-jip' calls which can only mean that the birds I've come to see – crossbills – are up there somewhere, wheeling above the tree-tops. They're frustratingly invisible above the thick canopy, but I'm able to tail the flock from below by following their excitable chorus. Soon I emerge into a clearing and there they are – at the very tops of the tallest trees.

Crossbills are large finches, nearly starling-sized. The brick-red males have glowing scarlet rumps; the females are olive-grey with lime-green rumps. I remain half hidden in the shadows of the pines and the birds begin to flutter down into the branches.

Crossbills have evolved crossed tips to their beaks to allow them to twist and lever apart the scales of woody pine cones, releasing the papery seeds that they relish. Watching them feed, I'm reminded of small parrots as they sidle along the twigs and even hang vertically to seize a ripe cone with their hooked mandibles.

When they're feeding like this, they tend to stay silent, a useful strategy. Sparrowhawks hunt through the tunnels of branches and a calling, brightly coloured crossbill could make an easy target. More than once I've only been alerted to the presence of a feeding flock by a gentle rain of pine or larch seeds spinning around me.

This dry resinous diet is thirsty work and so crossbills will often gather at puddles along forest tracks. Hide near one and wait and your reward will be a rare view of crossbills on the ground, allowing you to see their bright colours, huge bills and powerful cheek muscles.

The thrill of seeing crossbills is heightened by their unpredictability. Ian Newton, the renowned ornithologist, describes them as 'the most elusive and exasperating of the European finches to study'. Their lives are intimately tied to conifer crops, which can vary greatly from year to year. In a poor year, large numbers of birds leave their breeding area in what's known as an irruption and wander widely in search of food. Some of these irrupting birds may breed in new areas, which means that any mature stand of conifers could host the birds at sometime. Because they feed their young on masticated conifer seeds, rather than on insects like most finches, they can breed at any time of year, even midwinter. If the crop fails again, they simply move on.

As more of the commercial conifers planted in the British Isles since the 1940s have matured, crossbills have been able to find breeding places in larger forests across the whole of the UK. That means a greater chance of seeing these chippy and charismatic birds among the winter pines.

NEW YEAR'S EVE
31 December

However much we hate it – and many people do – the last day of the year is one we cannot ignore. The symbolism weighs heavy, even though it is a purely arbitrary date, especially when it comes to nature.

The shortest day took place over a week ago, but although from now on each day will get gradually longer, as the mornings and evenings become lighter minute by minute at a time, the average temperatures will continue to drop for the next month or more. So for our wildlife, there is little or no respite from the perils of winter.

As twilight approaches each New Year's Eve, I take part in a small, but for me significant, ritual. I go out into our Somerset garden and sit on the garden seat that belonged to my late mother, with whom I shared so many happy times watching birds.

It's a time of sadness, but also of hope: for each year, as the dusk falls, I am filled with anticipation for the next morning. Tomorrow is another year, when the world seems reborn, and wildlife watchers up and down the country engage in that strange ritual of wiping the slate clean and beginning another year's sightings.

Just before darkness finally engulfs the scene around me, a gaggle of rooks and jackdaws flies overhead towards their night-time roost. As their ragged black shapes pass overhead, etched against the inky sky, I hear their calls – a sound that marks the end of the year. In the morning, as they return to the fields just as dawn breaks, those same sounds will mark the start of a new one, with all the hope another year brings.

S.M.

Beating the bounds of my local patch has become a New Year's Eve ritual. It's partly a challenge to add to the annual total at the quietest time of year, and partly a reaffirmation of an acquaintance that stretches back over forty years.

Much has changed in that time. My first visits in the late 1970s and early 1980s were when sewage was spread over large areas of farmland, raising the nutrient levels and soil temperatures as it fermented. In harsh winters, pools of sludge remained unfrozen, attracting snipe that beetled between the grass tussocks and wheeling flocks of curlew whose rasping alarm calls seemed incongruous in this tame Midlands farmland.

Later in the 1990s, when sewage distribution had stopped, the fertile fields sprouted jungles of nettles – perfect hunting grounds for song thrushes. There were sentinel stonechats here too, which perched on thistle-tops, flitting on ahead as I pushed through the dead vegetation.

Now the nettles are gone and the fields have reverted to cereal growing. As light wanes, I sit at a convenient viewpoint and scan the ragged thorn hedges. If I'm lucky there will be a distant merlin alert on a topmost twig, waiting to snatch a passing pipit or skylark. Sometimes the raptors come to me. One New Year's Eve, hunkered down in the lee of a hedge, I felt a swish of air across my ear, announcing the passage of a female sparrowhawk as she sped through the scrub, intent on flushing roosting birds.

I love the intimacy of these crepuscular encounters in the gloom of the dying year. As far from a road as I can get, but with the knowledge that later I'll be celebrating with friends, I wallow in the moment while the light thickens and I wait for the star turn.

If I'm lucky, it will appear in the gloaming, no more than a will-o'-the-wisp dancing over the darkening field. For me this spectral dot, wavering at the very edge of visibility, is the true essence of the barn owl, ungraspable, diffuse and utterly at home on its own local patch. A photographer in search of the perfect picture would be disappointed, but as I reluctantly stand and turn to crunch my way home across frost-stiffened grass in the pitch-darkness, I'm already anticipating another wonderful year.

B.W.

ACKNOWLEDGEMENTS

Thanks, as always, go to the amazing team at John Murray: managing editor Caroline Westmore, illustrator Josie Shenoy, art director Sara Marafini, publicity manager Ruby Mitchell, production manager Amanda Jones, Jess Kim in marketing, sales director Ben Gutcher, consumer director Lucy Hale, and managing director Nick Davies. It has, as always, been a delight to work with such a great team. Special thanks go to our editors, Kate Craigie and Georgina Laycock, who have so expertly guided us from start to finish.

Huge thanks, too, to Rob Collis, our former colleague at the BBC Natural History Unit, who read through the whole text and provided many helpful suggestions based on his incomparable knowledge of British wildlife.

Although some of the entries in this book are based on very recent events, others go back many years – even decades. So, finally, we'd like to thank all the many naturalists – named and unnamed – who appear in these pages, and who have so generously given their time, effort and expertise to help us find out more about Britain's wildlife. Nature watching can be – and often is – a solitary pursuit, but we both enjoy it more when we share its delights and wonders with others.

Brett Westwood & Stephen Moss
January 2017

FURTHER READING

DIARIES AND LANDSCAPE

Birdwatcher's Year, A, Leo Batten, Jim Flegg, Jeremy Sorensen, Mike J. Wareing, Donald Watson and Malcolm Wright (Poyser, 1973)

Britain's Habitats: A Guide to the Wildlife Habitats of Britain and Ireland, Sophie Lake, Durwyn Liley, Robert Still and Andy Swash (Princeton University Press, 2015)

Claxton: Field Notes from a Small Planet, Mark Cocker (Jonathan Cape, 2014)

Natural History of Selborne, The, Gilbert White (1789, new edn Thames & Hudson, 1981)

Peregrine: The Hill of Summer and Diaries, The, J.A. Baker (new edn HarperCollins 2010)

Unofficial Countryside, The, Richard Mabey (1973, new edn Little Toller Books, 2010)

Wild Hares and Hummingbirds: The Natural History of an English Village, Stephen Moss (Square Peg, 2011)

IDENTIFICATION GUIDES

Britain's Birds: An Identification Guide to the Birds of Britain and Ireland, Rob Hume, Robert Still, Andy Swash, Hugh Harrop and David Tipling (Princeton University Press, 2016)

Butterflies of Britain and Ireland, The, Jeremy Thomas and Richard Lewington (2010, 3rd edn Bloomsbury, 2014)

Collins Wild Flower Guide, David Streeter (HarperCollins, 2016)

Comprehensive Guide to Insects of Britain and Ireland, A, Paul D. Brock (Pisces Publications, 2014)

Field Guide to the Bees of Great Britain and Ireland, Steven Falk (British Wildlife Publishing, 2015)

Field Guide to the Dragonflies and Damselflies of Great Britain and Ireland, Steve Brooks and Steve Cham (revised edn British Wildlife Publishing, 2014)

Field Guide to the Moths of Great Britain and Ireland, Paul Waring, Martin Townsend and Richard Lewington (3rd edn British Wildlife Publishing, 2017)

Guide to Garden Wildlife, A, Richard Lewington and Ken Thompson (British Wildlife Publishing, 2008)

Tracks and Signs of the Birds of Britain and Europe, Roy Brown, John Ferguson, Michael Lawrence and David Lees (1987, new edn Christopher Helm, 2003)

INDEX